AF394636

THE BATTLE OF CHERBOURG
FIRST ALLIED VICTORY IN NORMANDY
THEN AND NOW

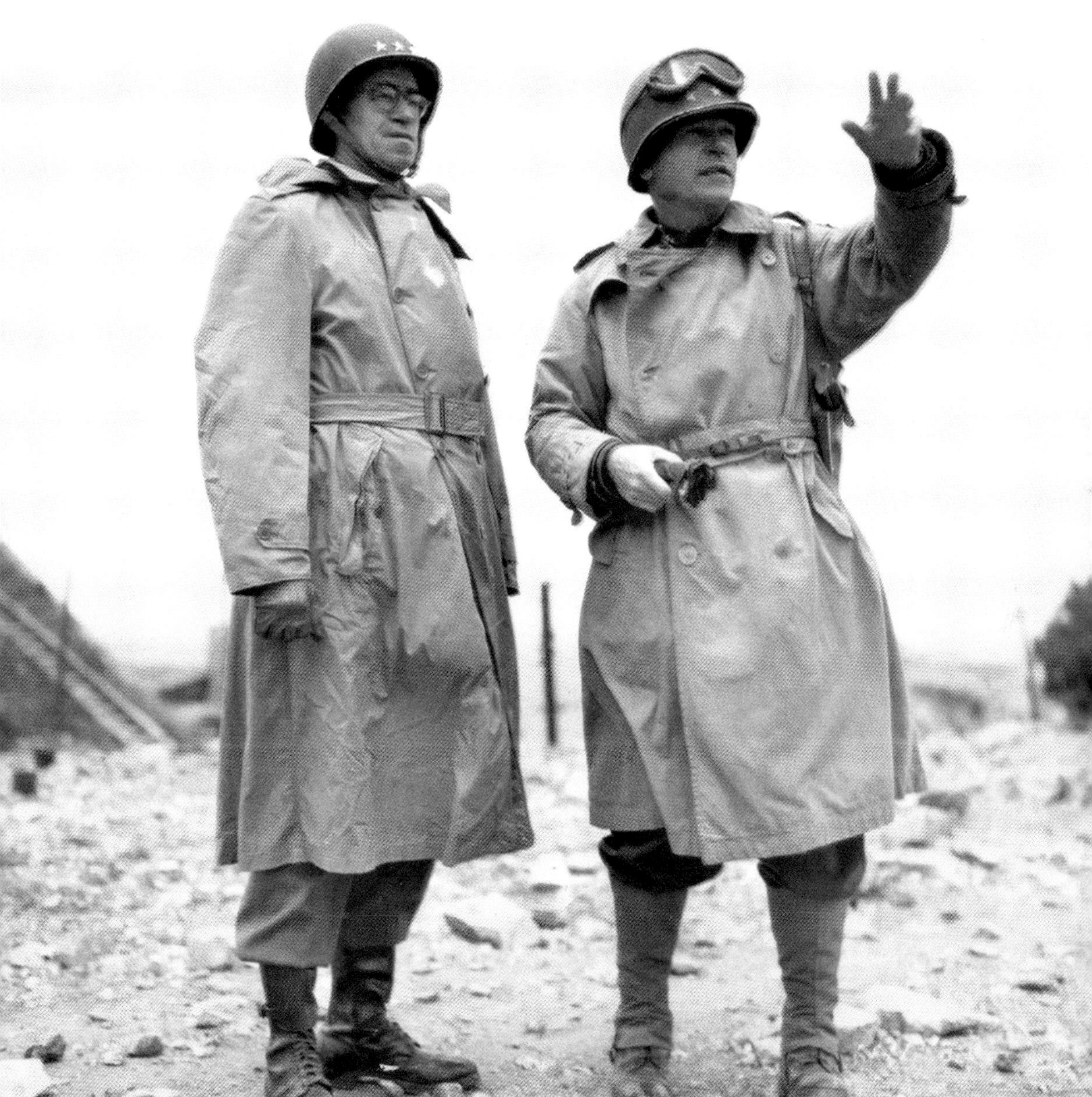

THE BATTLE OF CHERBOURG
FIRST ALLIED VICTORY IN NORMANDY

THEN AND NOW

by Jean Paul Pallud

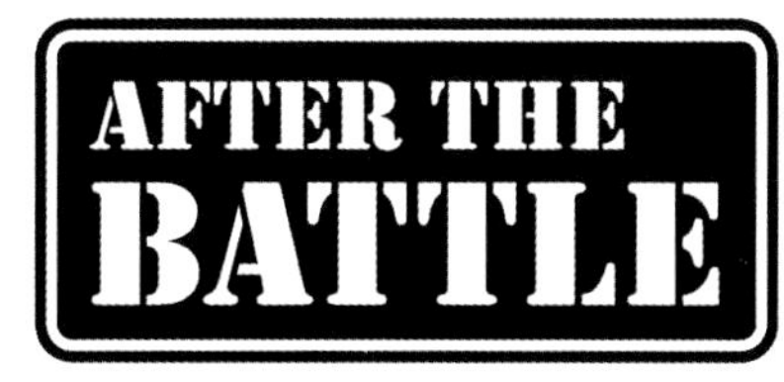

An Imprint of Pen & Sword Books Ltd

The Battle of Cherbourg
First Allied Victory in Normandy – Then and Now
Copyright © *After the Battle* and Jean Paul Pallud, 2025

Published by After the Battle
An imprint of Pen & Sword Books Ltd
Yorkshire – Philadelphia
Website: **www.afterthebattle.com**
          www.pen-and-sword.co.uk

ISBN: 9781036196813

Commissioning Editor: Rob Green
Editor: Jean Paul Pallud
Design: Paul Wilkinson, Cover design: Jon Wilkinson

The Publisher's authorised representative in the EU for product safety is Authorised Rep Compliance Ltd., Ground Floor, 71 Lower Baggot Street, Dublin D02 P593, Ireland. **www.arccompliance.com**

Credits:
Parts of this book were originally published as articles in *After the Battle* magazine: 'Cherbourg Naval Base 1940-44' in issue 146; 'The Battle for Cherbourg in issue 147; and 'The Rehabilitation of the Channel Ports' in issue 178. These have been adapted and enhanced to produce this book and additional photos are included.

Acknowledgements:
The Publisher would like to acknowledge the work of Gordon A. Harrison, author of the official US Army history volume *Cross-Channel Attack* (Washington, 1951), and Roland G. Rupperthal, author of the official US Army history volume *Logistical Support of the Armies* (Washington, 1959) and thank them for the parts from their books that we have used. The Publisher would especially like to thank the French Marine Nationale, particularly Amiral Philippe Périssé, Préfet Maritime at Cherbourg, and the Direction des Constructions Navales (DCNS) for allowing the author to visit their installations. The Publisher would also like to thank La Cité de la Mer, the Berton family who accompanied the author to the battlefield, as well as Count and Countess Arnaud de Pontac who allowed the author access to the historic room where the German commander of Cherbourg signed the surrender of the fortress. The Publisher extends his appreciation to Wikimedia Commons contributors for the remarkable photos they make available to all.

Photo Credit Abbreviations:
BA – Bundesarchiv; ECPAD – Médiathèque de la Défense, Fort d'Ivry; SETO – Society for the Study of the ETO; USNA – US National Archives. Parts of these photos, credited as ATB/USNA, are from negatives obtained in the 1970s by ATB from the collection of seized enemy documents. Unless specified otherwise, all illustrations are from the *After the Battle* archive.

Front Cover: Pushing forward in the early morning of June 26, the leading troops of the 313th Infantry Regiment, 79th Infantry Division, reached the beach in their sector by 8 a.m. but the 314th was delayed by enemy fire from the left and they only reached the sea in mid-afternoon. Signal Corps photographer Franklin pictured a GI of the 314th making a dash forward while another soldier covered his advance. Avenue de Paris Then and Now, at the junction with Avenue Étienne Lecarpentier. The Divette river, which was the boundary line between the 79th and 9th Divisions, is just across the road, off to the left. (USNA and ATB) ♥ 49.631524, -1.617595

Back Cover:
Helping along their wounded comrades, the last German prisoners are being marched away three abreast along a rubble-strewn street on June 27. The curved wall visible in the left background is the one at the foot of the hill along the tracks in the railway station, and identifies this spot as being on the Avenue de Paris. (USNA and ATB) ♥ 49.630799, -1.617748

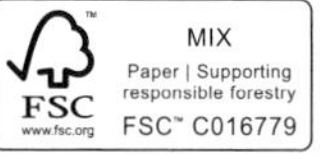

CONTENTS

Following the sidelining of the 90th Division due to its slow progress, the attack westwards to seal off the base of the Cotentin peninsula was taken up by the 9th Division on the right wing, and the 82nd Airborne Division on the left. The attack of the 82nd Airborne Division made rapid progress on June 16, and before noon both the 325th Glider Infantry and the 505th Parachute Infantry reached the line of the Douve opposite Saint-Sauveur-le Vicomte. Observing the Germans withdrawing, the division pressed on and quickly occupied the town (this photo). Early on the 18th, the leaders of the 9th Division entered Barneville and cut the coastal road, thus closing off the Cotentin peninsula. (USNA)

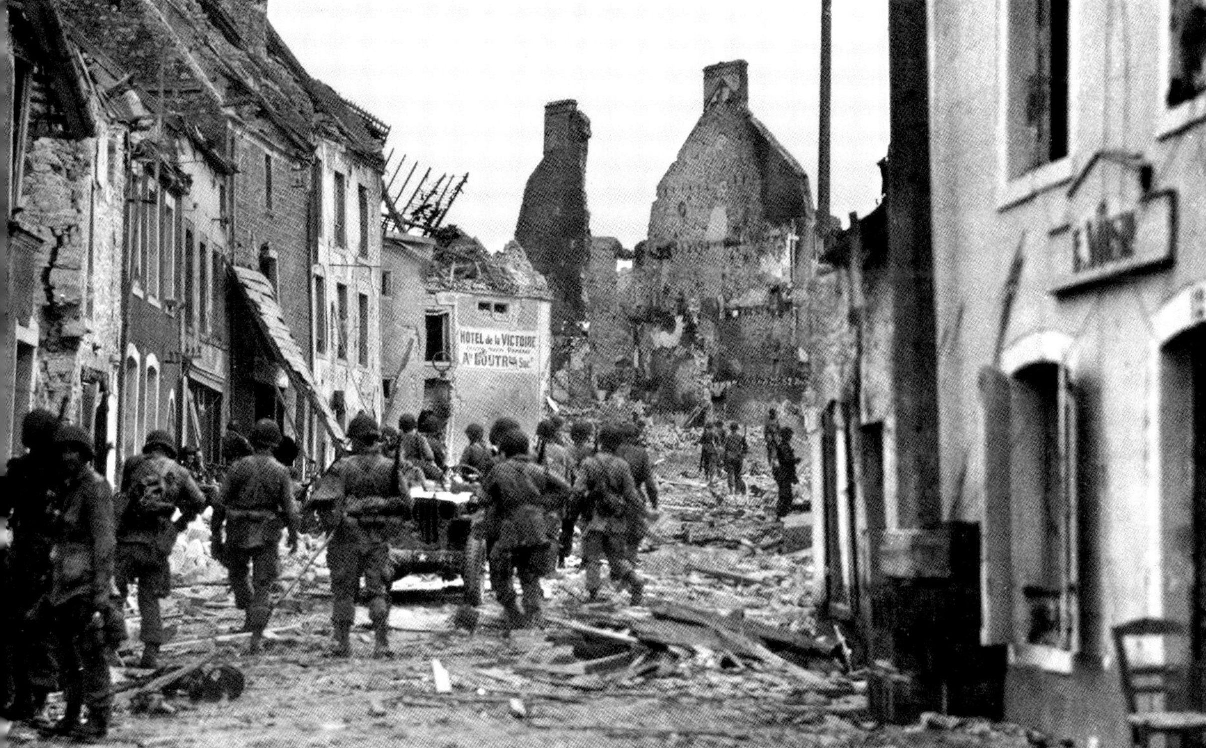

INTRODUCTION

IN DEVELOPING PLANS for the Allied invasion of France, from the very beginning, SHAEF planners considered the vital need to secure deep-water ports to bring in the supplies needed to support an army of hundreds of thousands of troops. Cherbourg, at the tip of the Cotentin Peninsula, was the closest to the landing beaches chosen for Operation 'Overlord'.

At first, worried that a landing on the eastern coast of the peninsula would be separated from the main beachheads in Normandy by the Douve River valley, which the Germans had flooded as a defensive measure, the planners did not plan to land directly on the Cotentin Peninsula. In January 1944 however, they decided to land forces at the base on the peninsula, in order to widen the beachhead and be in a position to quickly attack Cherbourg. In the plans for Operation 'Overlord', the First US Army was tasked with clearing the Cotentin Peninsula and capturing Cherbourg as quickly as possible.

In the early hours of June 6, paratroopers from the 82nd and 101st Airborne Divisions landed inland from Utah Beach to capture the beach exits, and secure the crossings over the Douve River. On June 10, the 101st Airborne Division captured Carentan, thus liaising with the Omaha beachhead and ensuring the Allies a continuous front

Though the initial lodgement gained during the first week was smaller than the Allies had planned, they had grounds for optimism in that their casualties had been unexpectedly light and the anticipated German counterattack had failed to materialise. By mid June, as German armoured elements arrived to face the Second British Army on the left wing, emphasis was placed on pulling the Germans there while on the right wing the First US Army pushed toward Cherbourg.

The VII Corps then advanced westward to isolate the Cotentin Peninsula and on the 18th, the 9th Infantry Division reached the west coast of the peninsula. Within 24 hours, the 4th, 9th, and 79th Infantry Divisions advanced northward.

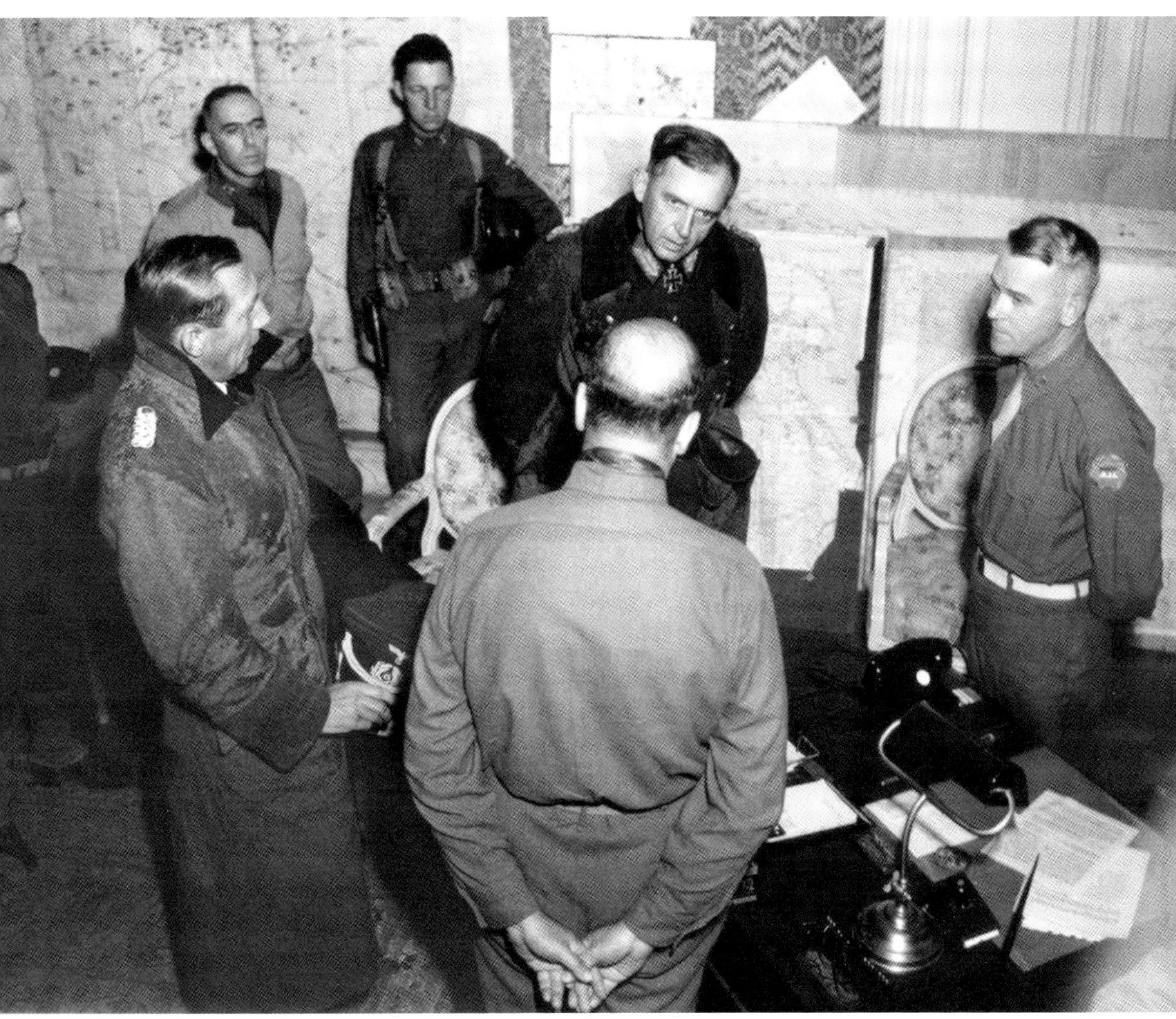

Generalleutnant von Schlieben, the Festung Commander, surrendered to General Collins at his command post at the Château de Servigny at Yvetot-Bocage. The talks and the signing of the formal surrender were held in a room on the first floor. Today known as the 'Salon de la Reddition' (surrender room), the room is now decorated with exhibits of that historic day in June 1944, including a copy of the surrender document. (USNA)

WATCHTOWER OF THE CHANNEL

CHERBOURG LIES AT the northern extremity of the Cotentin peninsula and has been a strategic possession since earliest times. The peninsula was first conquered by the Roman Quintus Titurius Sabinus in 56 BC, and Cherbourg is believed to occupy the site of the Roman camp of Coriallum which they later built on the western bank of the River Divette, the name 'Cherbourg' being regarded as a corruption of Caesaris Burgus (Caesar's Borough).

Having suffered from raids by Saxons and Danes, in 933 Cherbourg was attached, as was the whole of the Cotentin peninsula, to the Duchy of Normandy. The town was taken in 1204 by King Philippe Auguste of France and suffered further raids in the latter part of the 13th century, though the castle was never taken. During the Hundred Years' War (1337-1453), Cherbourg was lost and recovered six times. Captured by the English in 1418 after a four months' siege, the town was finally recovered by Charles VII of France in 1450.

In the late 17th century, a start was made under Louis XIV to construct a military harbour at Cherbourg but the real creation of the port dates from 1738 when two jetties, a lock and a wet basin were built for both naval and commercial purposes. Shortly afterwards however, in 1758, these works were destroyed when an English expedition ravaged the town and burnt the shipping. Reconstruction was not completed until 1789 and King Louis XVI then decided to make Cherbourg the strategic military port for the defence of the Channel coast. The plan was to build a harbour for 80 warships. Work came to a halt at the end of the 18th century but was resumed by Napoléon I only to be stopped again between 1813 and 1832. It was left to Louis Philippe, and particularly to Napoléon III, to complete the construction.

The huge breakwater – the Digue Centrale nearly four kilometres long – was finally completed in 1853, a magnificent feat of engineering given the resources of the time. In 1858 the successful realisation of the Cherbourg military port was celebrated in the presence of Queen Victoria. The first Atlantic liner entered the new harbour in 1869.

Three forts were built on the central mole and the roadstead was completed by the construction of two breakwaters running out from the mainland at Querqueville in the west and Tourlaville in the east, these being completed by 1895. The huge works were finally completed by the addition of the Petite Rade (inner harbour) with two inner breakwaters running out from the mainland, the Jetée du Homet (1914) and the Jetée des Flamands (1922).

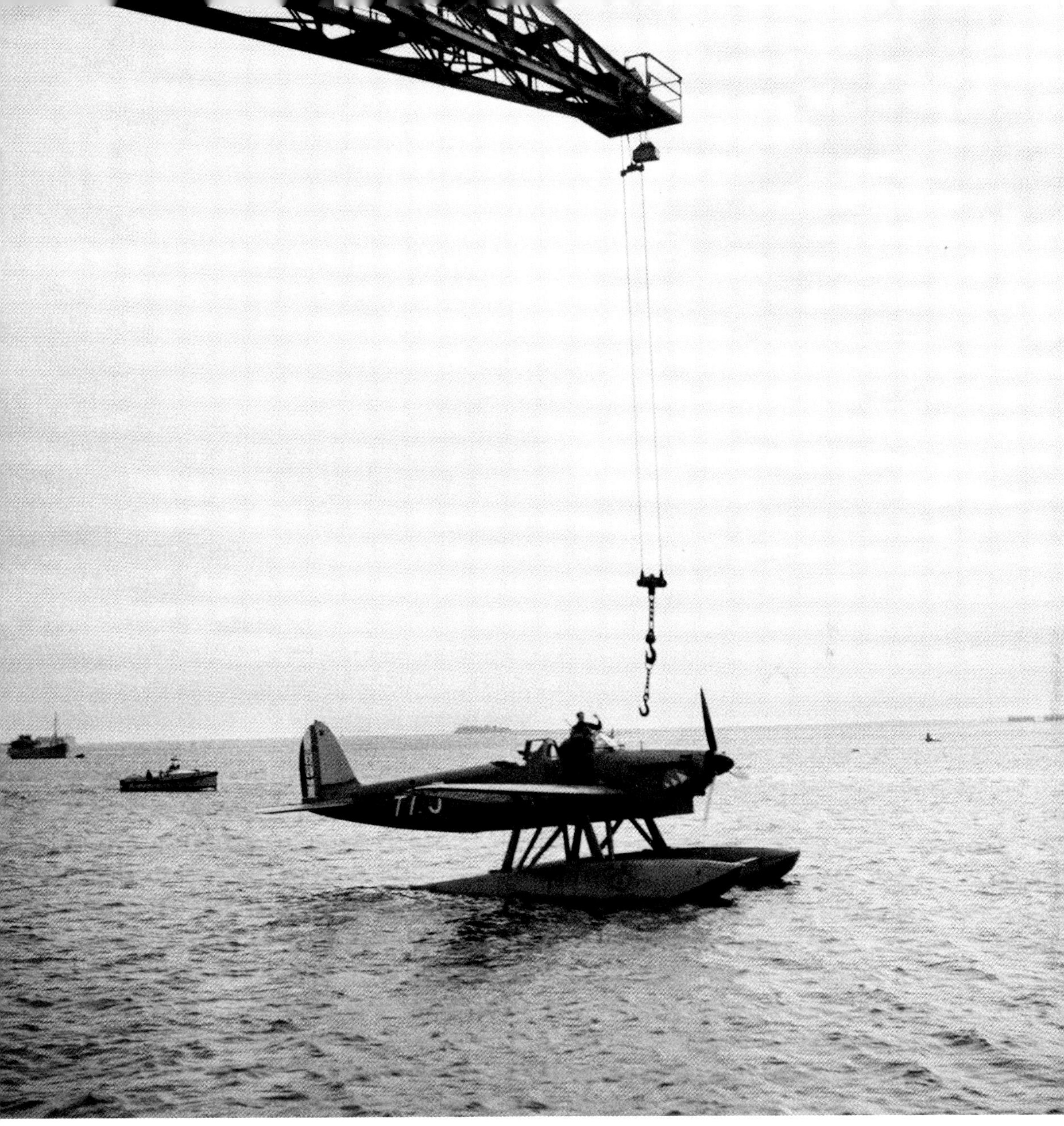

Offering important repair facilities and large armament warehouses, Cherbourg was the major support harbour of the French Navy in the Channel sector. It was also the base of several squadrons of the Navy air arm. Latécoère 298 torpedo bombers being put to sea at the Chantereyne Naval Air Base in March 1940. (ECPAD)

During the First World War, Cherbourg was an important port for both the British and American forces. After the war a liner mole was built beside a deep-water basin, the Darse Transatlantique, and Cherbourg soon became the main transatlantic passenger port of France. Travellers to and from Europe and America passing through Cherbourg neared 200,000 in 1927 although numbers declined during the years of depression to 80,000 in 1936.

The Gare Maritime (port railway station) on the mole was completed in 1933, and by 1937 the Quai de France was able to berth the world's largest liners.

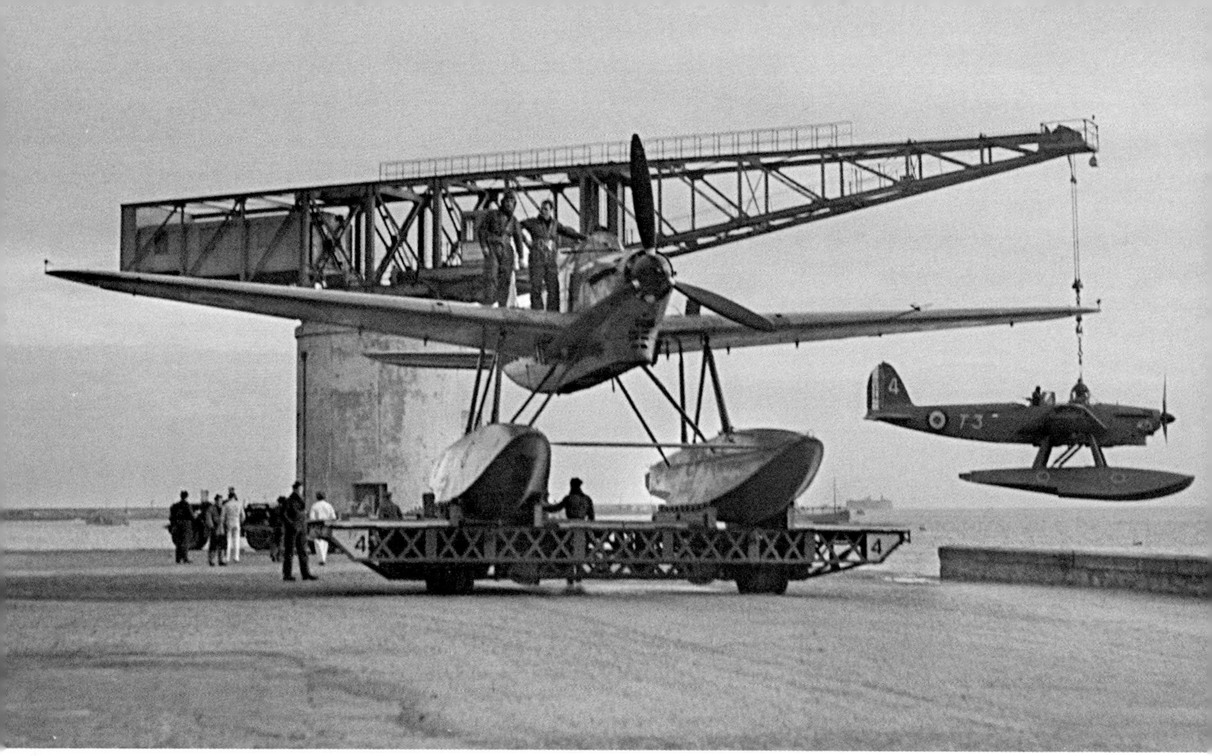

The large crane used to put seaplanes to water was blown up by the Germans as they wrecked the dock installations in June 1944. However, the base of the apparatus still remains. This section of the harbour is still fenced off, although it is no longer strictly speaking a military zone. (ECPAD and ATB)

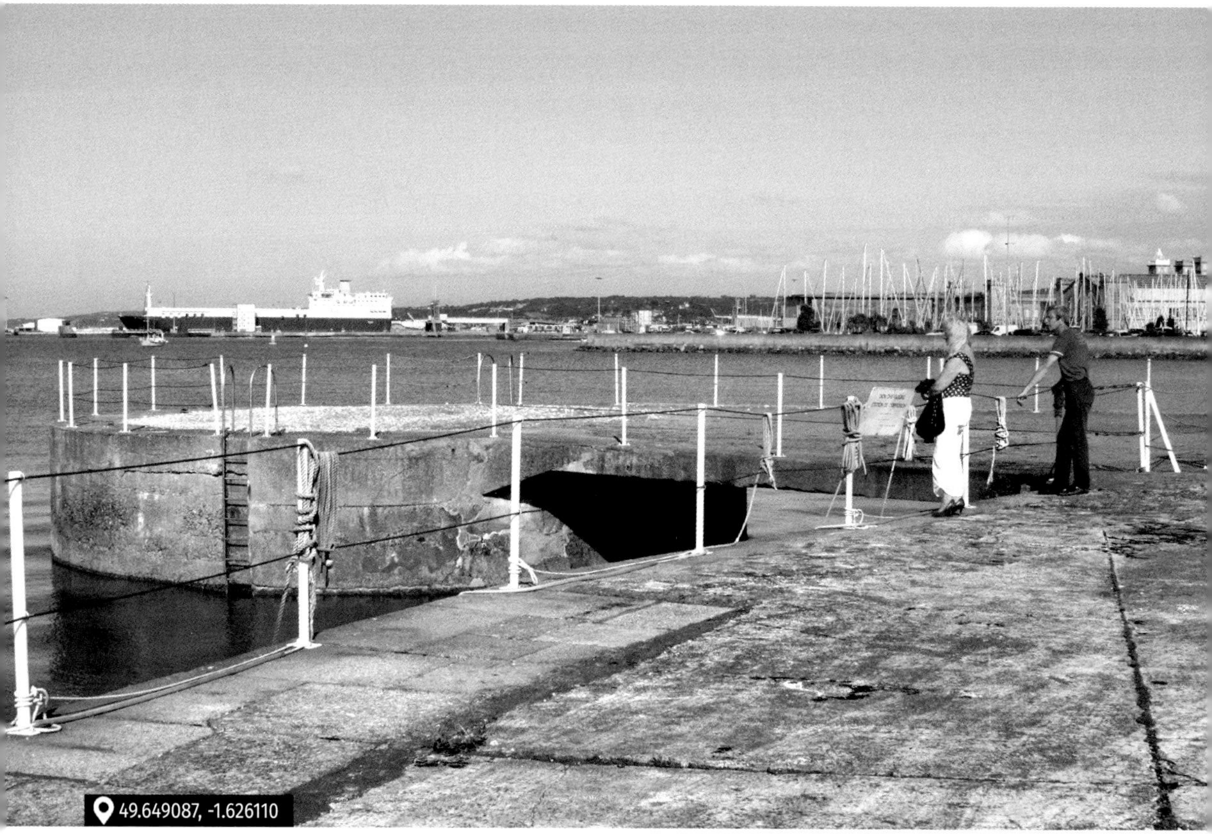

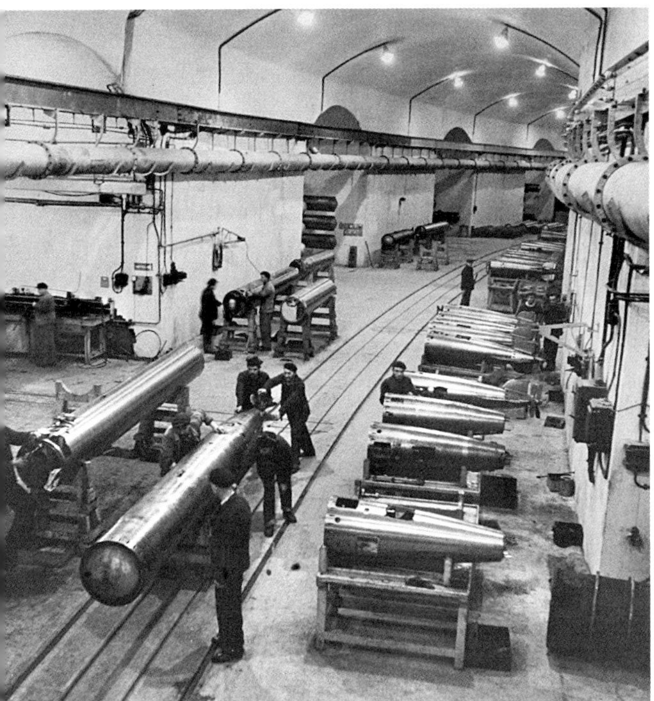

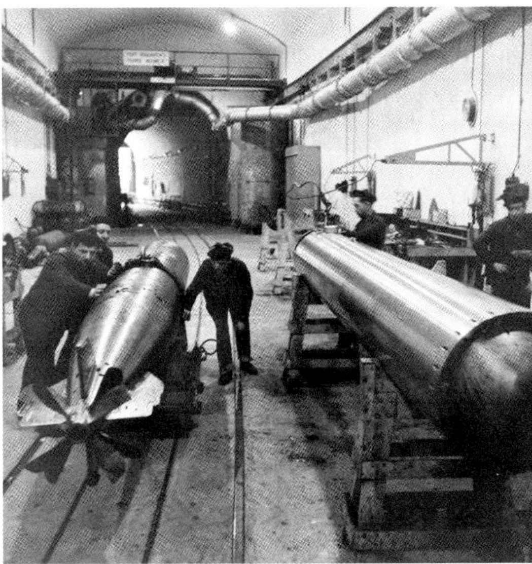

Dug out deep under the Roule mountain a large underground complex served as workshops and storage for torpedoes. It comprised eight galleries, four on each side of the main tunnel. These photos were taken in November 1939. The Marine Nationale (French Navy) very agreeably allowed the author into its installations, including this tunnel which today houses transmission equipment. (ECPAD and ATB)

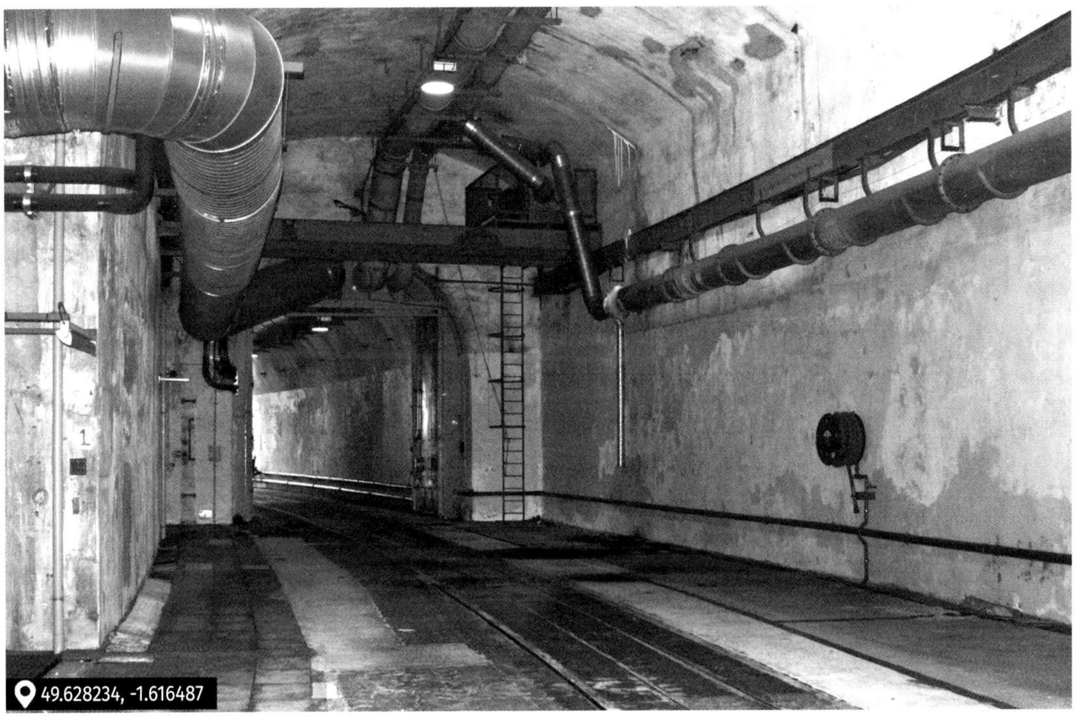

THE KRIEGSMARINE TAKES OVER

FOLLOWING THE OUTSTANDING success of the German offensive in the West, with the Netherlands and Belgium conquered, three French armies defeated, and the British Expeditionary Force forced to evacuate, abandoning all its equipment, German troops entered Paris on June 14. Three days later, Generalmajor Erwin Rommel's 7. Panzer-Division was approaching Cherbourg. During the night of June 17/18, Admiral François Darlan, the Commander-in-Chief of the French Navy, ordered a general evacuation of Cherbourg and all other harbours on the Atlantic coast. Of the ships in Cherbourg harbour, the two old battleships, the *Courbet* and *Paris*, departed for Portsmouth on the 19th. Even though four of the ten destroyers in the port were under repair, all managed to set sail as did the four submarines being refitted. Four other submarines in various stages of construction in the Arsenal had to be scuttled.

About midday on June 19, as his artillery was firing 'on anything moving' in the naval dockyard, Rommel sent civilian representatives back into the town to make urgent representations. The formal surrender took place in the evening at the Préfecture Maritime.

In August 1940, the Marinegruppenkommando West (Kriegsmarine High Command in the West) transferred its headquarters from Wilhelmshaven to Paris. The command divided its new fief into three sectors: to the north-west, the Befehlshaber Kanalküste (Commander Channel Coast) covered the zone between Blankenberge and Saint-Malo; to the west, the Befehlshaber Atlantikküste (Commander Atlantic Coast) spread from Saint-Malo (excluded) down to Spain, while the Befehlshaber Südküste (Commander South Coast) controlled the Mediterranean zone between Italy and Spain.

The Kanalküste sector was then further sub-divided into four Seekommandanten (Seeko): Seeko Pas de Calais covering Belgium down to the River Somme; Seeko Seine-Somme from the Somme to the Seine; Seeko Normandie from Le Havre to Saint-Malo (HQ at Cherbourg) and Seeko Kanalinseln covering the Channel Islands.

From July, S-Boats (small and fast motor torpedo boats with a displacement of about 100 tons) started to operate out of Cherbourg. They were joined in September by ten T-Boats (large torpedo boats with a displacement of 1,000 to 1,500 tons), and by five destroyers.

The RAF bombed the harbour on the night of September 17, sinking the transport *Johann Blumenthal* and damaging torpedo boat *T-11* and minelayer

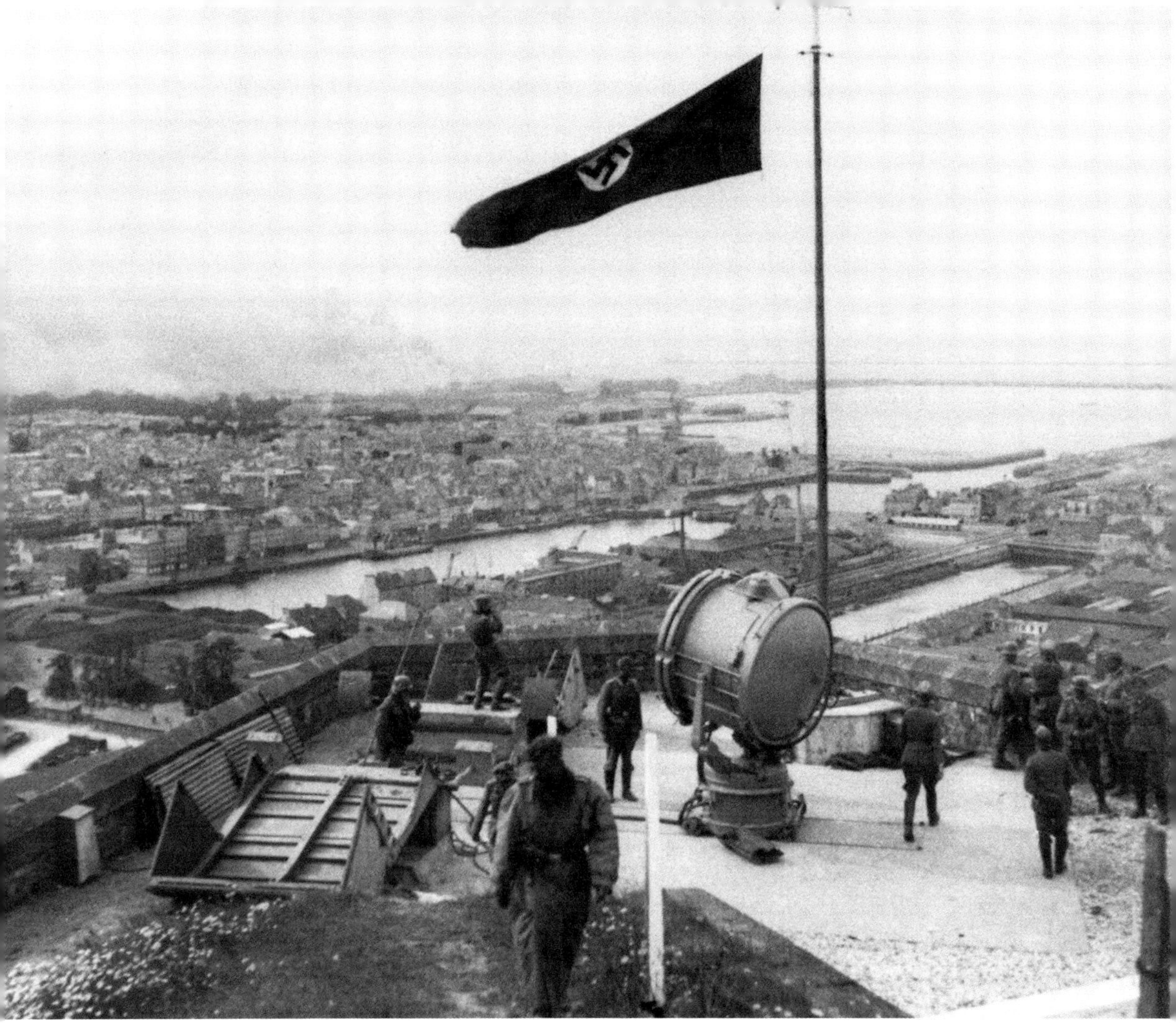

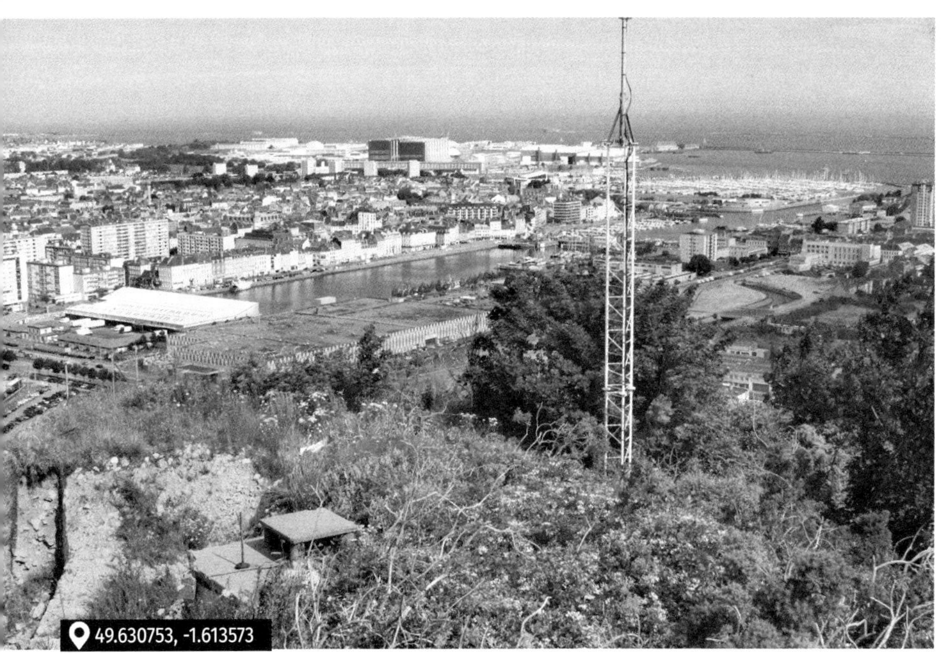

Generalmajor Erwin Rommel's 7. Panzer-Division captured Cherbourg on June 19, 1940. From the top of the Fort du Roule, which stands on a hill commanding the city and its harbour, Rommel contemplates his victory. The French Navy allowed the author access to the same hilltop, today fenced-off and crowned by numerous antennas.

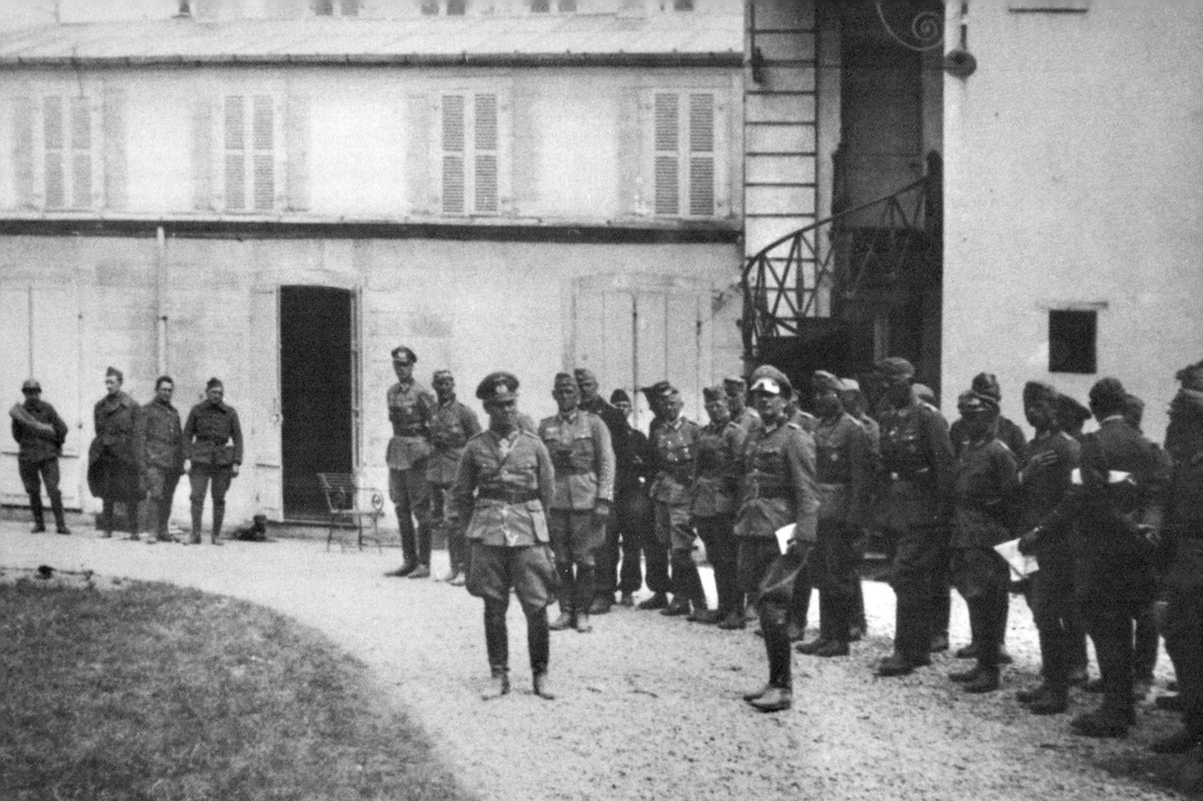

At the Préfecture Maritime (Naval Headquarters), Rommel addressed French officers: 'I take note of the fact that the fortress has surrendered and wish to express my pleasure that the surrender has taken place without bloodshed among the civilian population.' The building is now the private residence of the Préfet Maritime.

Schiff 23. On October 10, the battleship HMS *Revenge* sailed from Plymouth with seven destroyers to shell the port in the early hours of October 11. German torpedo boats sailed from Cherbourg and briefly attacked the minesweeping force but without result.

Detailing the operations of the Kriegsmarine from Cherbourg is not within the scope of this work, but, as examples, it is interesting to report a few specific events. On September 19, five destroyers departed Cherbourg for a strike in the area between the Lizard and Start Point, but the sweep was soon cancelled due to bad weather. During the night of September 30 to October 1, four torpedo boats laid minefield 'Werner' off Dover. Six sailed to operate off the Isle of Wight during the night of October 8 to 9, and five during the night of the 11 to 12. This night, they engaged the Royal Navy's 17th Anti-Submarine Group off the Isle of Wight, sinking one armed trawler, one anti-submarine trawler, and three submarine chasers.

Early on October 17, six torpedo boats sailed from Cherbourg to act as a support force to four destroyers sailing from Brest to raid British shipping at the western exit of the Bristol Channel. The light cruisers HMS *Newcastle* and *Emerald* sailed from Plymouth to counter the German intruders and contact was made about 4 p.m. but the two forces were never closer than 12 miles and no damage was caused to either side.

With the attack on the Soviet Union, most of the German ships in the West were transferred to the Baltic and the number of S-Boats operating

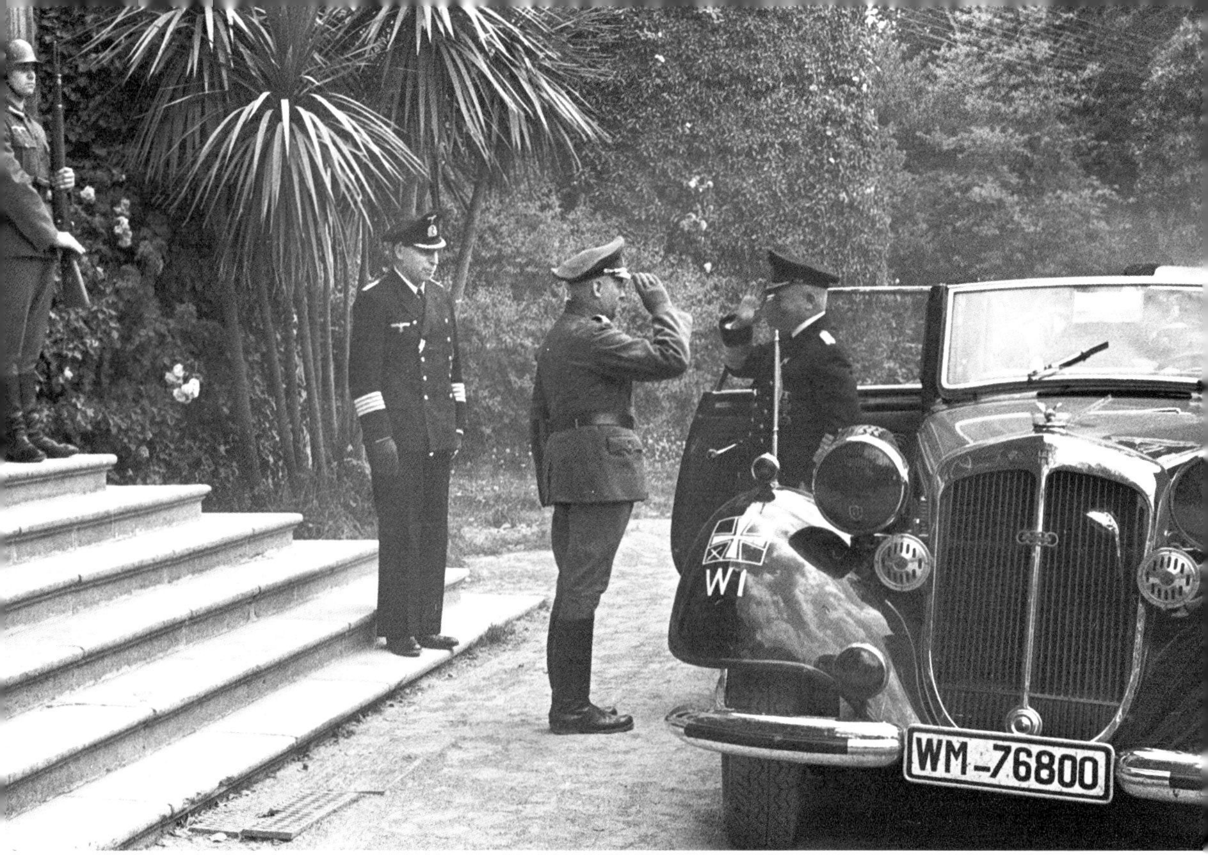

In August 1940 Marinegruppenkommando West installed its headquarters in Paris, with Admiral Alfred Saalwächter at its head. Here Saalwächter is greeted at the Château of Tourlaville by Kapitän zur See Max Fink, Seekommandant Normandie, and Fregattenkapitän Wilhelm Vogel, commanding Marine-Artillerie-Abteilung 260, during a visit at Cherbourg in August 1941. (ECPAD)

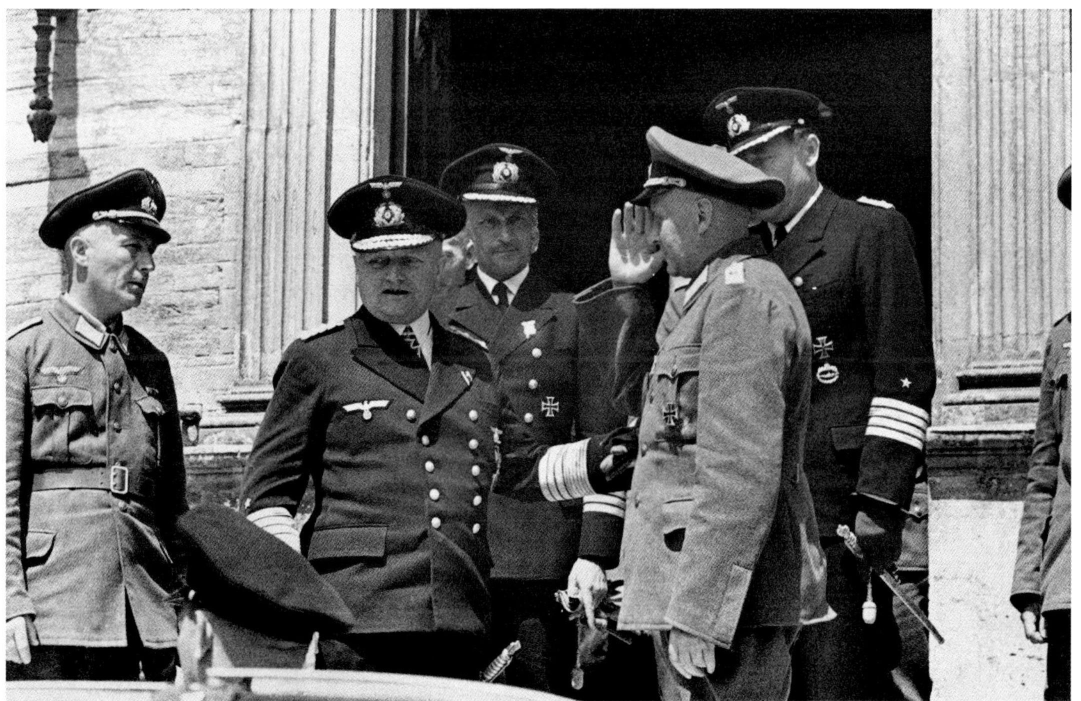

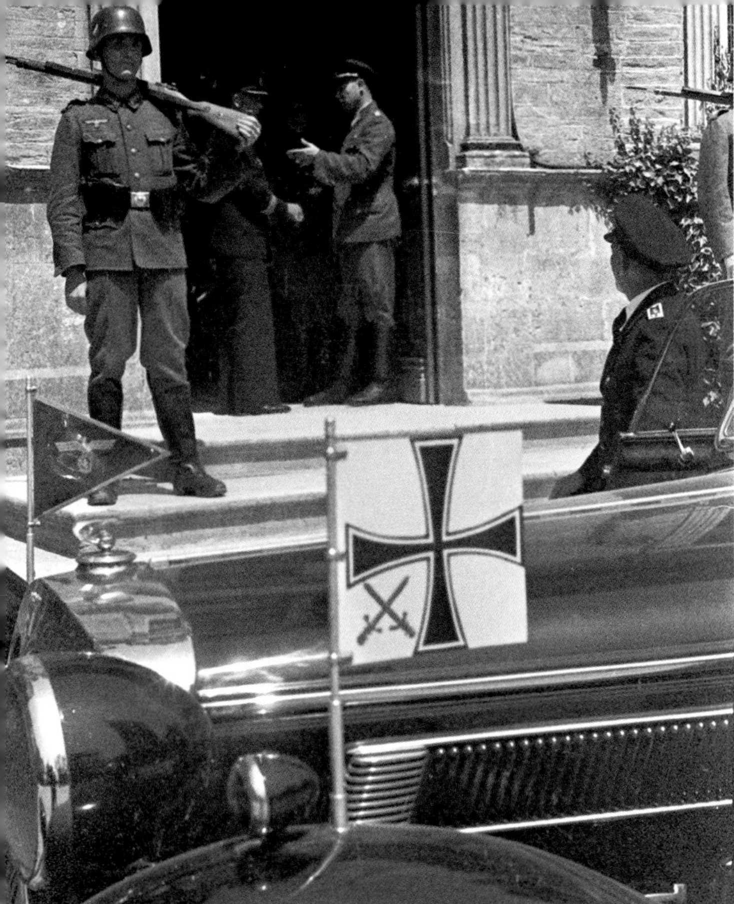

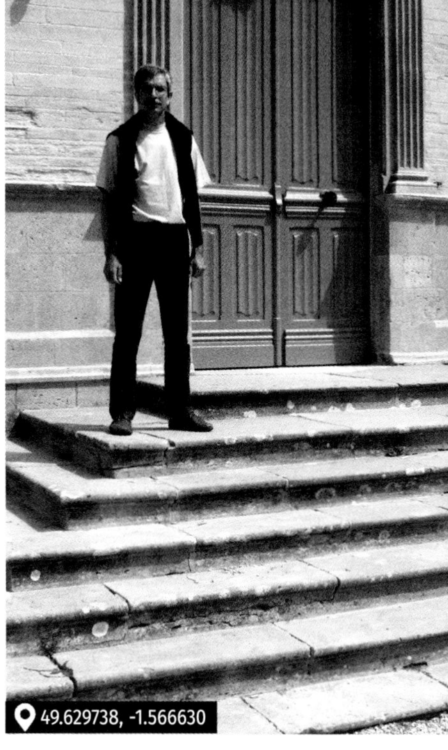

49.629738, -1.566630

Saalwächter taking leave after the meeting. Today, in the 21st century, little has changed at the château, except for the German sentry who has faded into the pages of history. (ECPAD and ATB)

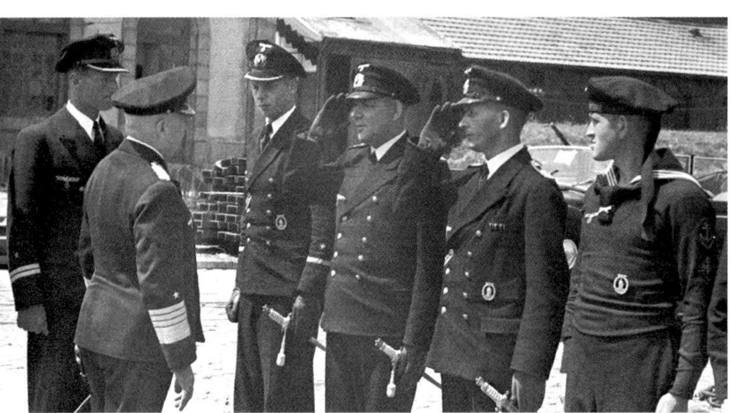

Saalwächter addresses a selected party of Kriegsmarine officers and men on a quay in the military harbour. Then and Now on the Quai Duquesne in the Avant-Port. (ECPAD and ATB)

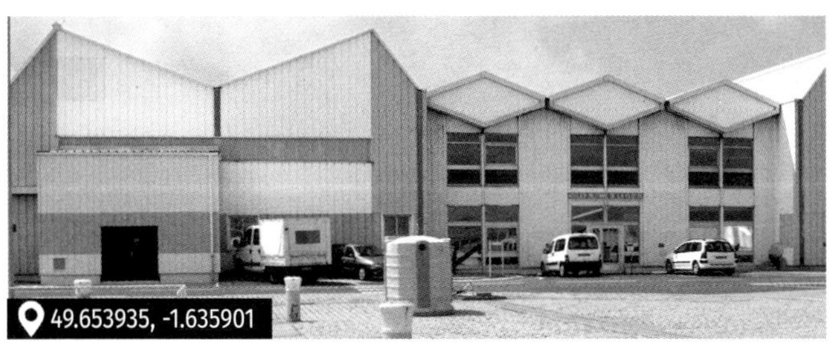

49.653935, -1.635901

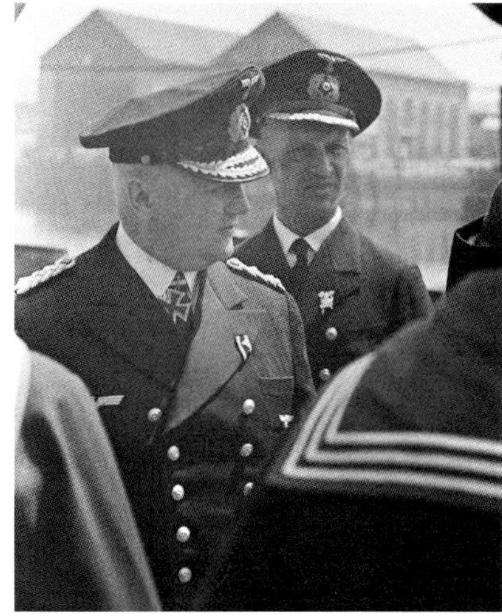

Replaced by Admiral Wilhelm Marschall in September 1942, Saalwächter resigned from active service. Arrested by the Soviets in June 1945, he was convicted for alleged war crimes by a Soviet military tribunal and executed by a firing-squad the following December. After the demise of the Soviet Union, he was exonerated by a Russian court in 1994. (ECPAD)

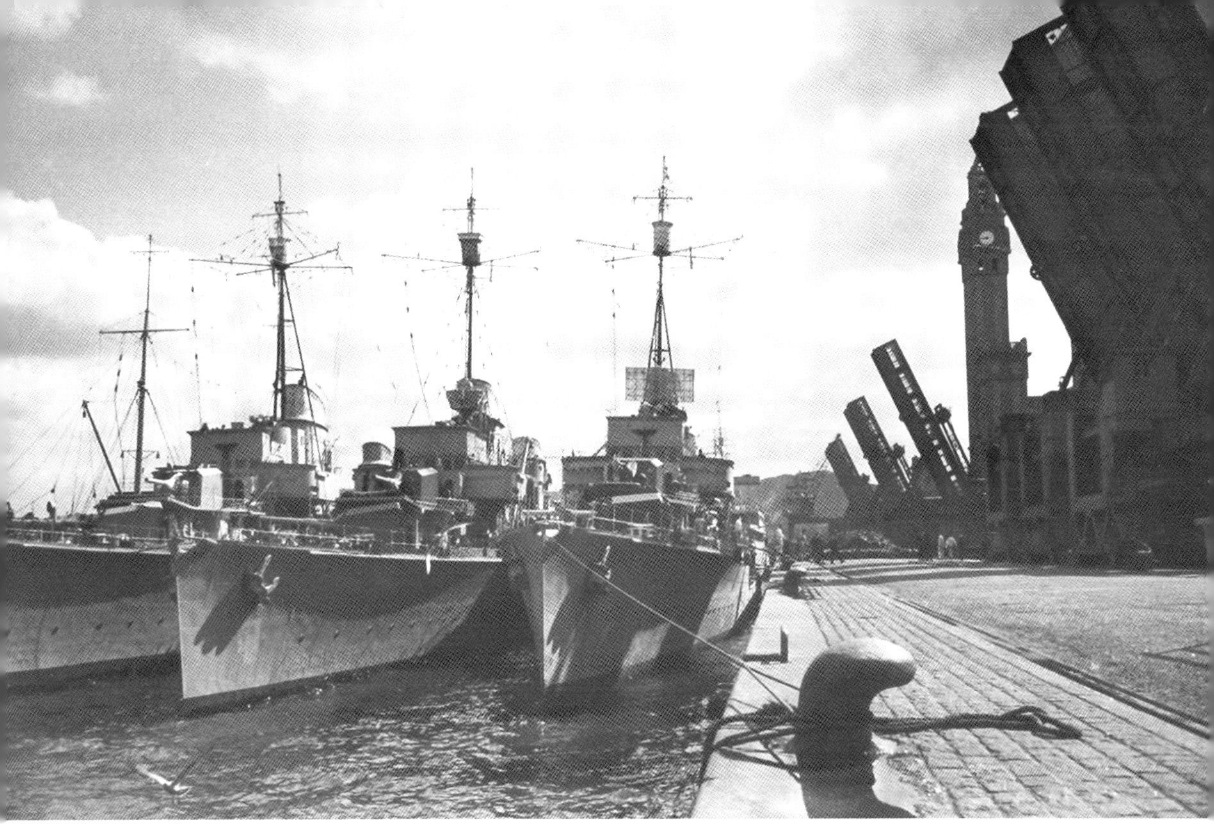

Coming from Wilhelmshaven, five destroyers arrived at Cherbourg on September 11, 1940. Here three of them, Z10 *Hans Lody, Z14 Friedrich Ihn* and *Z6 Theodor Riegel*, moored along the Quai de France, the western side of the Darse Transatlantique. Of Type 1934, they had a full-load displacement of about 3,100 tons and were armed with five 127mm guns, four 37mm and six 20mm Flak guns, and eight torpedo tubes. On the right appears the Gare Maritime (port railway station) with mobile ship-to-train access galleries which allowed passengers to directly access the station. This quay was destroyed in June 1944 when the trapped German garrison carried out the methodical demolition of the port installations. Fortunately, some of the Gare Maritime's movable galleries survived destruction and are still in use today when large cruise ships make a call to Cherbourg. (ECPAD and ATB)

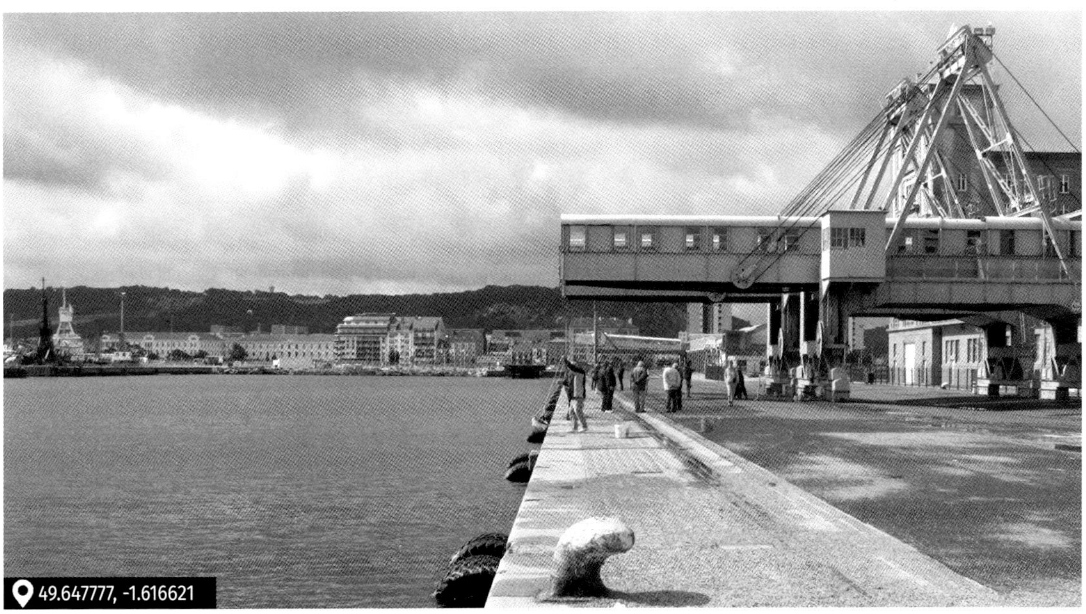

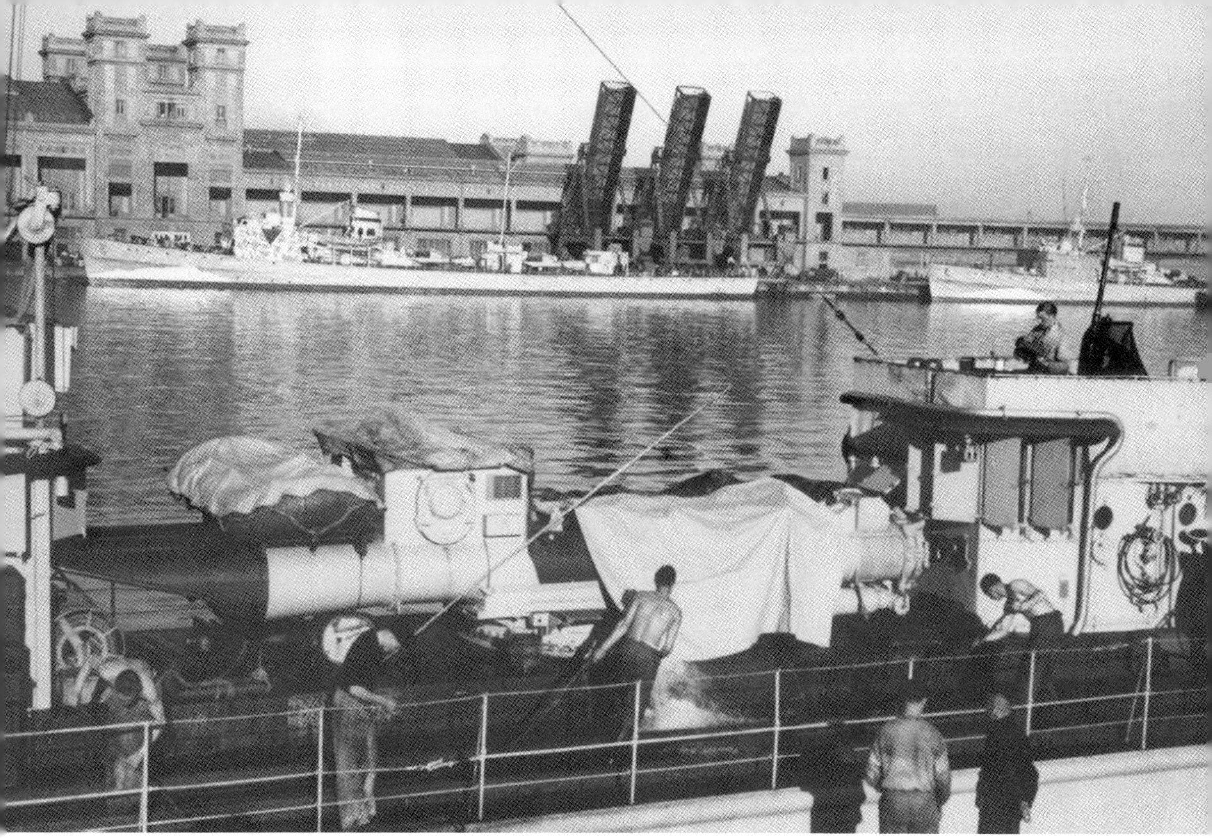

Across the Darse Transatlantique, T-Boats were moored along the Quai de Normandie. In the background, the Gare Maritime. Built by Deschimag at Bremen and launched in 1939, the T-Boats of this series had a full-load displacement of about 1,090 tons and were armed with one 105mm gun, eight 20mm Flak guns and six torpedo tubes. They were also fitted for minelaying and could carry up to 30 mines. (ECPAD)

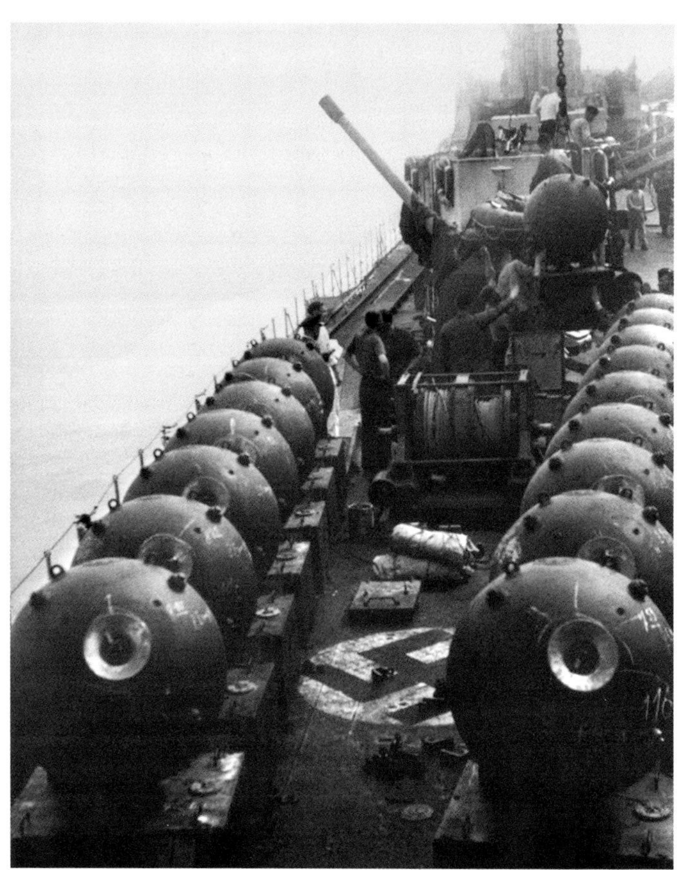

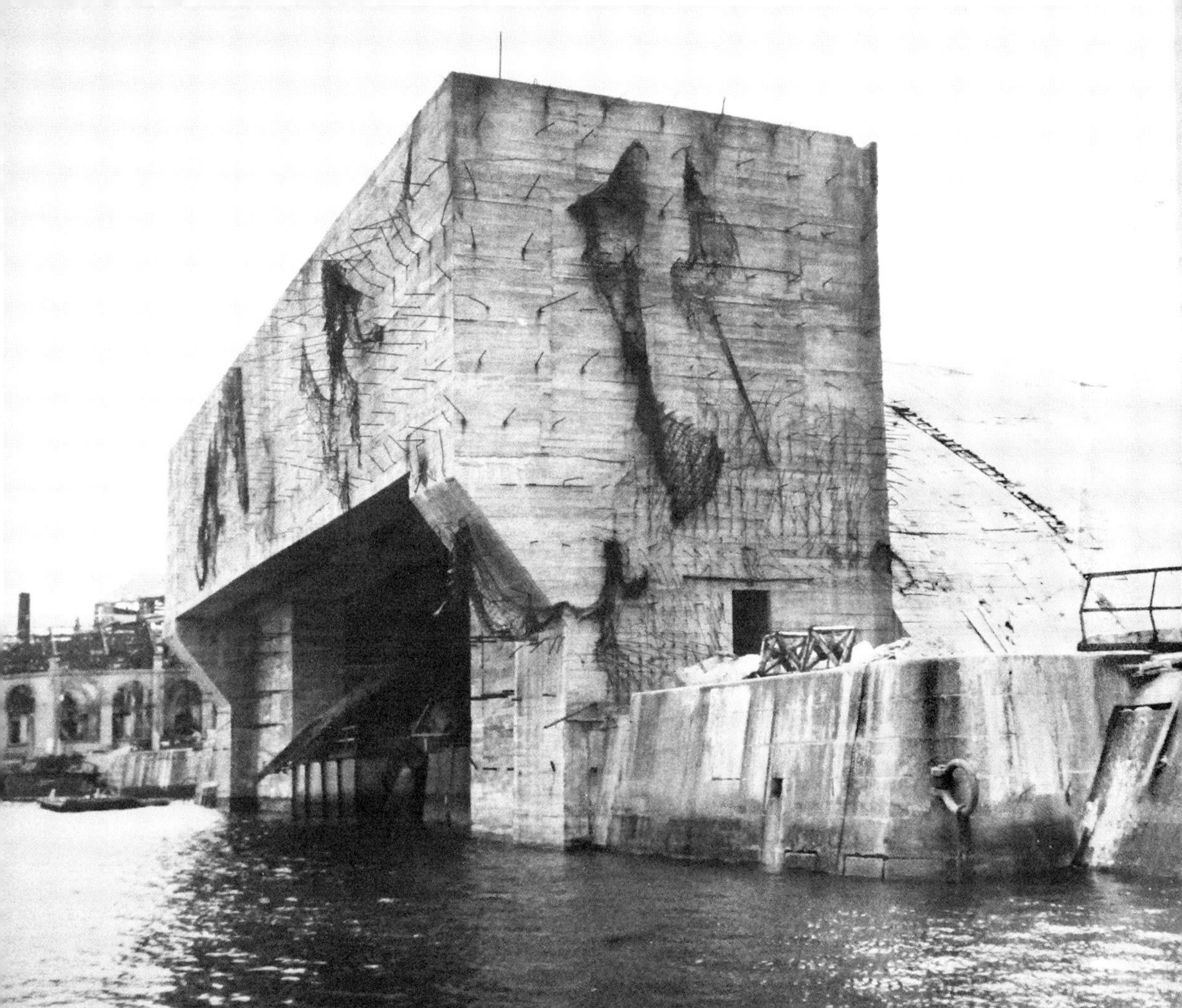

The Germans soon began building a semi-circular concrete roof over two existing quays. One of them, the Forme Cachin, was located on the south side of the Avant-Port. This photo was taken by a US Signal Corps photographer after the port was captured in June 1944. The Forme Cachin was demolished in the late 1980s, as was the German concrete cover, when the DCNS built its new shipyard. (USNA)

off the east and south coasts of England remained small throughout 1941. The number of S-Boats operating in the Channel increased again in the first half of 1942, with the 2. and 4. S-Boots-Flottillen moving to Cherbourg in June. In August, the former moved to IJmuiden and the latter to Boulogne, their place at Cherbourg being taken by the 5. S-Boots-Flottille. By October, with four flotillas in operation, the S-Boat strength in the West was 40 boats conducting minelaying operations and attacks against convoys. During 1942 they accounted for two destroyers, HMS *Vortigern* and HMS *Penylan*, one motor launch, one tug, four trawlers and 24 merchant vessels.

With the Royal Navy improving its defences, by 1943 it was becoming increasingly difficult for the S-Boats operating in the Channel. During the year they managed to sink the Norwegian destroyer *Eskdale*, one LCT, nine trawlers and ten merchant ships. Early in 1944, there were five S-Boats flotillas operating in the Channel: two from IJmuiden, one from Rotterdam and two from Cherbourg. The latter, the 5. and 9. S-Boots-Flottillen had

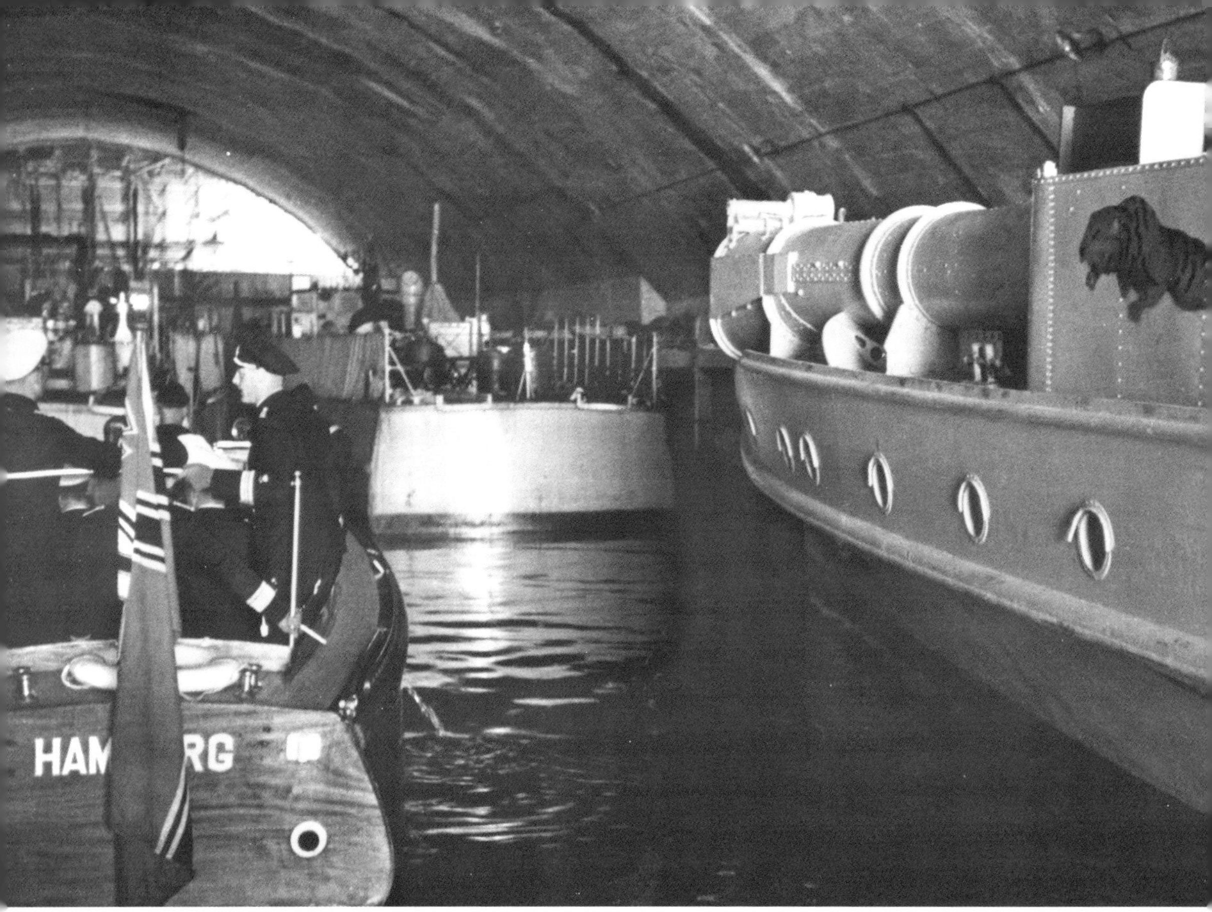

Located on the western side of the Bassin Napoléon III, the second shelter built by the Germans still survives to this day. This dock is about 100 metres long and 20 metres wide. The boat moored with the Tiger coat of arm was *S19*. The French Navy kindly agreed to let the author photograph it, now with a floating quay running along its whole length.

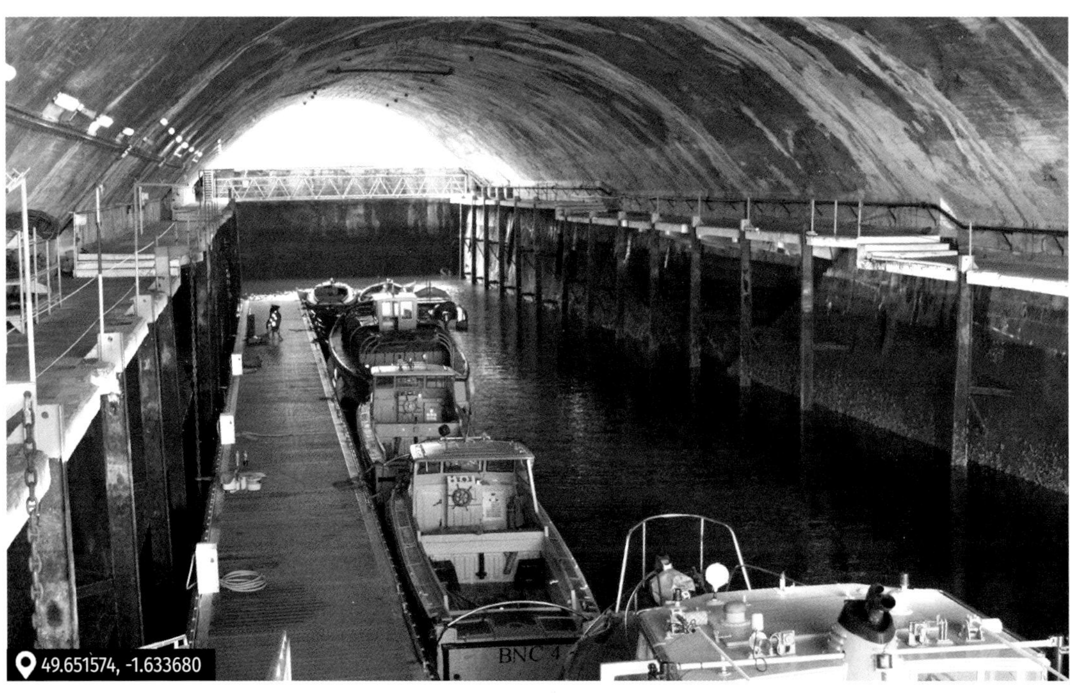

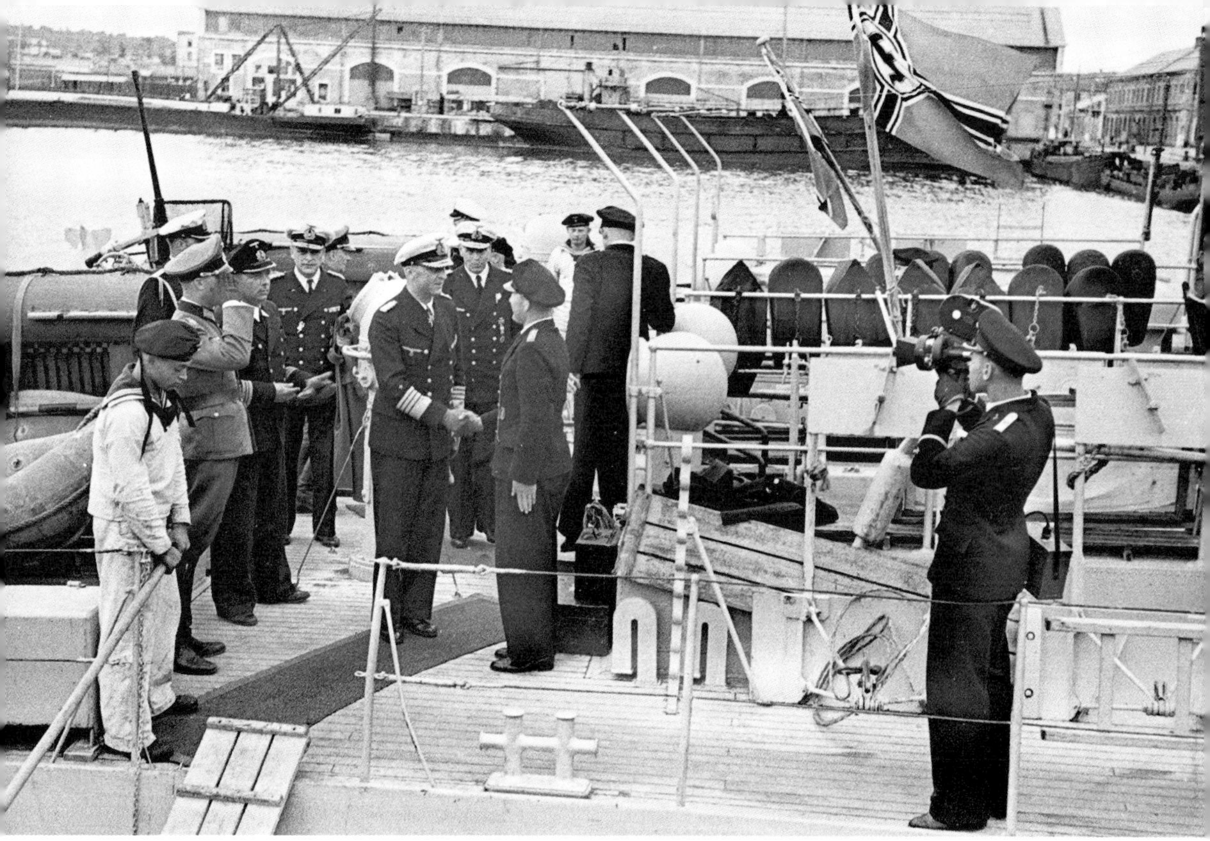

Returning from an inspection to the Channel Islands in July 1941 Admiral Otto Schultze, the Admiral Frankreich (Commanding Admiral France) returned to Cherbourg. The building in the background enabled the author to identify the quay at the north-eastern corner of the Bassin Charles X. Visible in the foreground is the prow of one of the six ships of the first generation of French SSBNs (nuclear-powered ballistic missile submarine) taken out of service between 1991 and 2008. The first, *Le Redoutable*, is now on display at La Cité de la Mer in the Gare Maritime.

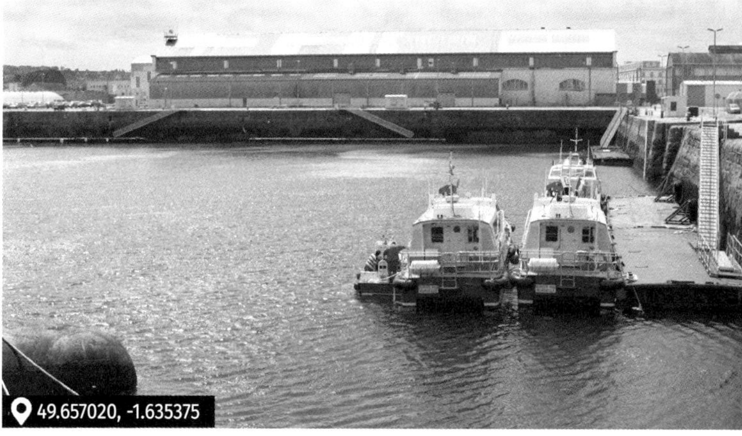

about 16 operational boats between them. They conducted several attacks against Allied shipping off the southern coast of England including, on April 22, a successful attack on motor gun boats in Lyme Bay.

On the morning of April 27, an Allied convoy left Plymouth for Lyme Bay as a preliminary to Operation 'Tiger', a rehearsal for the forthcoming D-Day landings on Utah Beach. The German radars monitored the convoy progress and about 9 p.m., as soon as it was completely dark, nine S-Boats slipped out of Cherbourg. They evaded the small covering force of Allied MTBs off Cherbourg and, steaming at 36 knots under radio silence, quickly covered the 90-odd nautical miles to the north-west. Approaching Lyme Bay, the S-Boats advanced slowly and quietly in order to retain surprise. Identification of

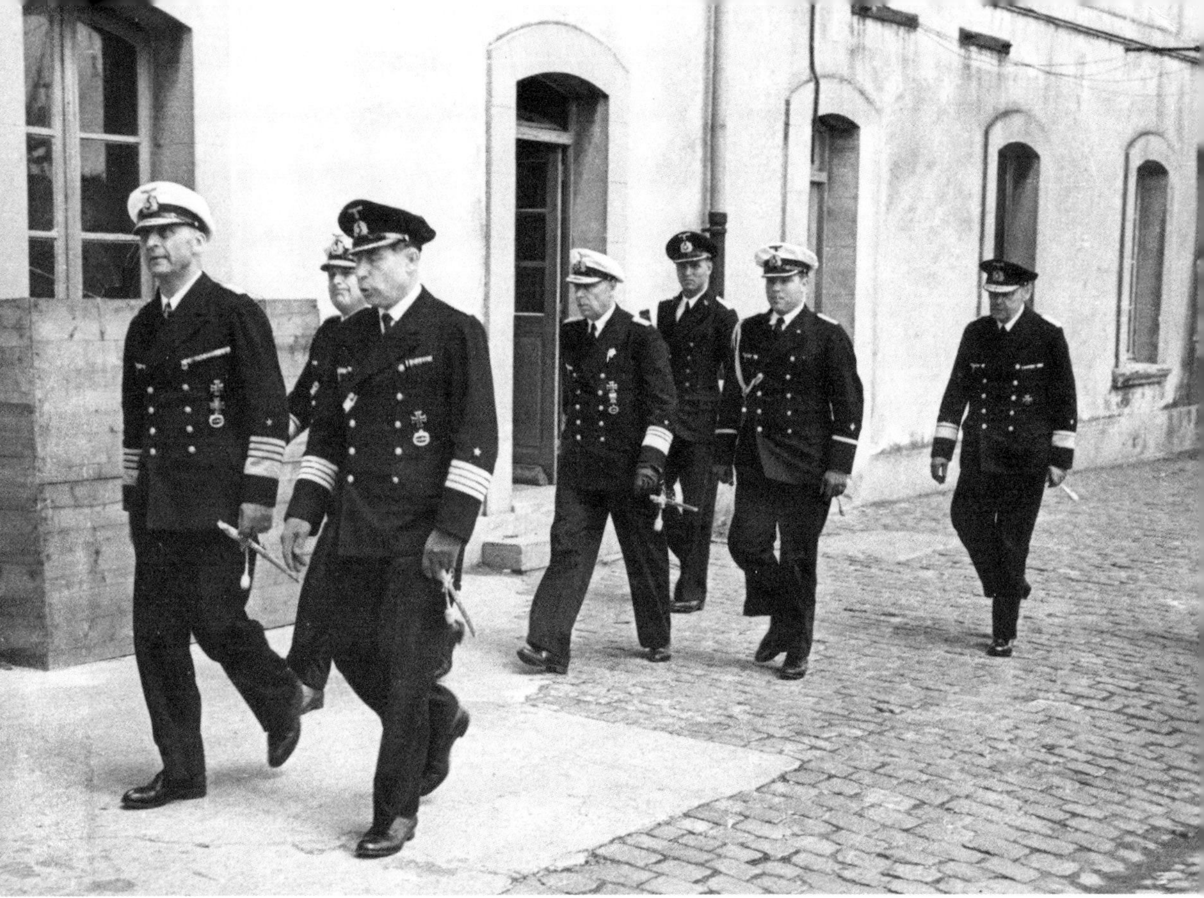

The party swiftly walked its way through the harbour, Admiral Schultze and Kapitän zur See Fink leading, followed by Konteradmiral Joachim Lietzmann, Schultze's Chief-of-Staff, Vizeadmiral Hermann von Fischel, Admiral Kanalküste (Commanding Admiral Channel Coast), and Konteradmiral Friedrich Hilbig, chief of the Marine-Ausrüstungs- und Reparatur-Betrieb Cherbourg (Naval Equipment and Repair Service Cherbourg).

targets was difficult in darkness but at about 1.30 a.m. *S-136* and *S-138* spotted two ships at a range of 2,000 metres and they then closed at speed, firing torpedoes. *S-140* and *S-142* had also identified targets at about the same time and opened fire too. *LST 507* and *LST 531* were sunk and *LST 289* and *LST 511* damaged. A total of 639 Americans were killed and missing, some ten times the actual losses suffered on Utah Beach on D-Day. The commander of the S-Boats in the West, Kapitän zur See Rudolf Petersen, and Korvettenkapitän von Mirbach, the commander of the 9. S-Boots-Flottille, were both awarded the Oakleaves for this remarkably successful operation.

Two weeks later, the tables were turned however when on May 12 around ten S-Boats patrolling south of the Isle of Wight were surprised by Allied destroyers. During the ensuing engagement, the Free French ship *La Combattante* succeeded in sinking *S-141*. Among the 18 crew who died was Oberleutnant zur See Klaus Dönitz, the son of Grossadmiral Karl Dönitz, Commander-in-Chief of the Kriegsmarine.

GERMAN DEFENCES IN THE COTENTIN

WITH THE BUILDING of the 'Atlantikwall' gaining speed in the spring of 1942, Oberbauleitung Cherbourg (Chief Construction Section) of the Organisation Todt was created with its headquarters in the town's Hôtel Atlantique. Its workforce consisted of 20,000 men split into eight Bauleitungen (Construction Sections), five in the Cherbourg sector, one at Caen, one at Granville and one at Alderney.

By June 1944, the Kriegsmarine had nine coastal batteries in the Cherbourg area and along the Cotentin's eastern coast. Batterie 'Brommy' near Bretteville, just east of Cherbourg, was manned by the Marine-Artillerie-Abteilung 260 and comprised four 150mm SK C/28 guns in Type M271 casemates. An aerial photograph taken after the fighting ended from a Piper L-4H observation plane. (USNA)

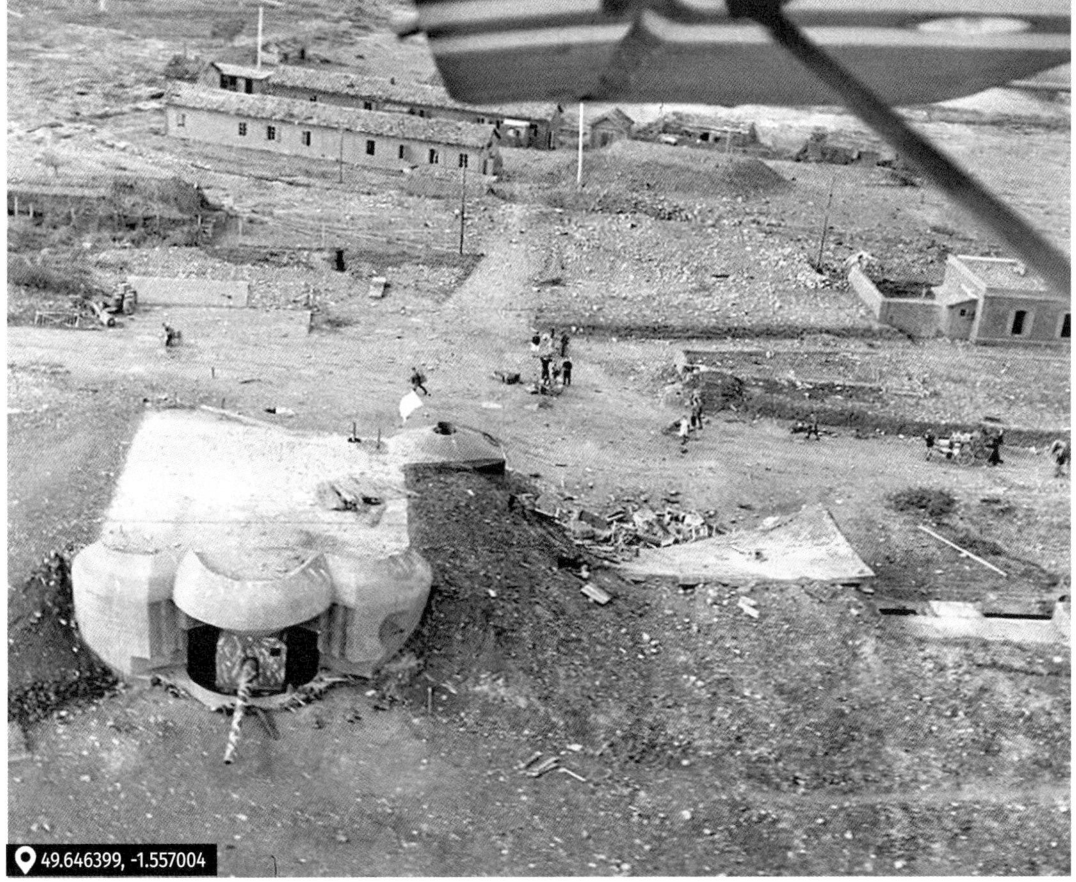

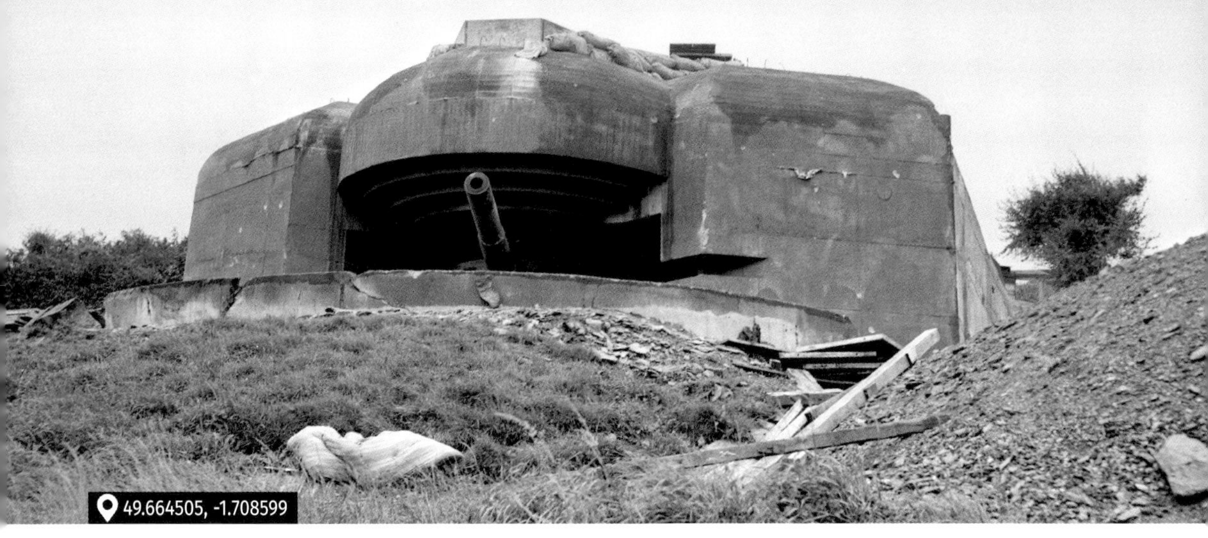

Batterie 'York' near Amfreville, a few kilometres west of Cherbourg, was manned by the 8. Batterie of Marine-Artillerie-Abteilung 260 and comprised four 170mm SK L/40 guns in Type M271 casemates. They had a maximum range of 27,000 metres. (USNA)

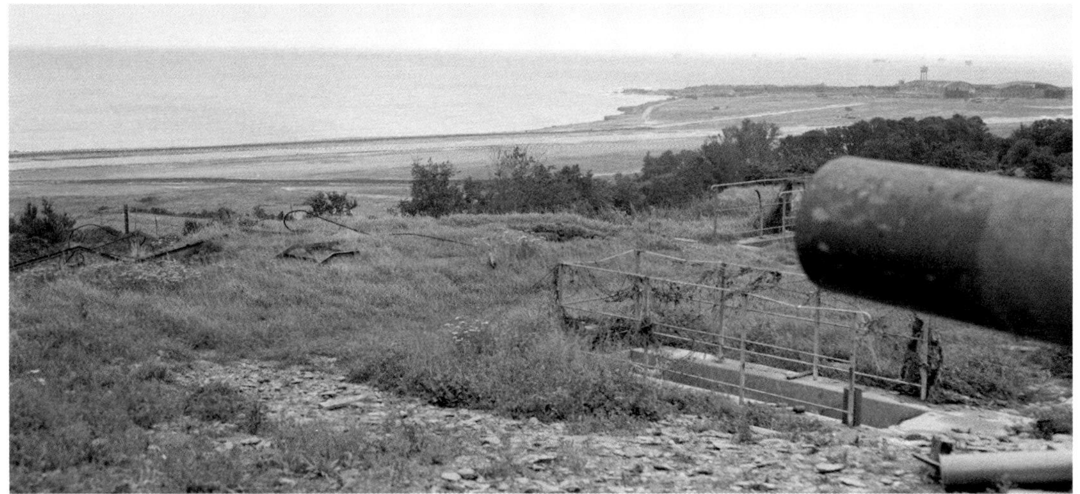

An American Signal Corps photographer pictured Battery 'York' in September 1944, apparently to show the field of fire of its 170mm guns, with Hameau de la Mer in mid-distance and the moles off Cherbourg in the far background. Comparison taken from in front of the second casemate from the west. (USNA and ATB)

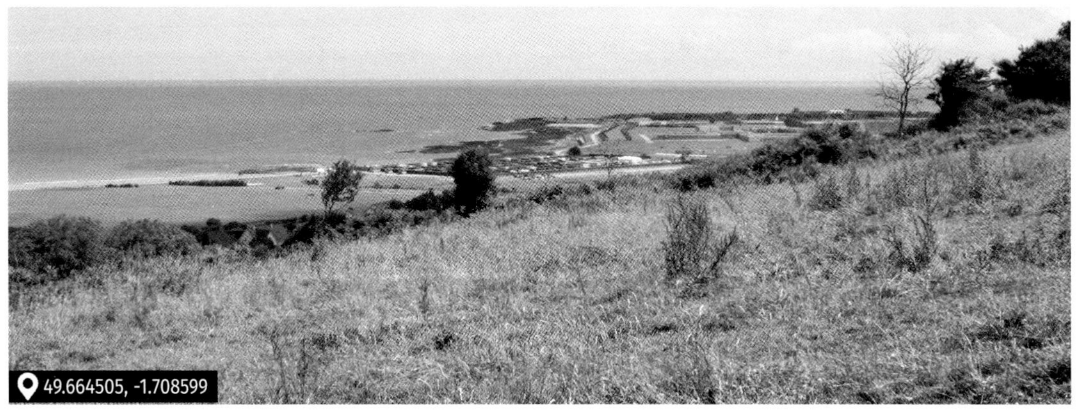

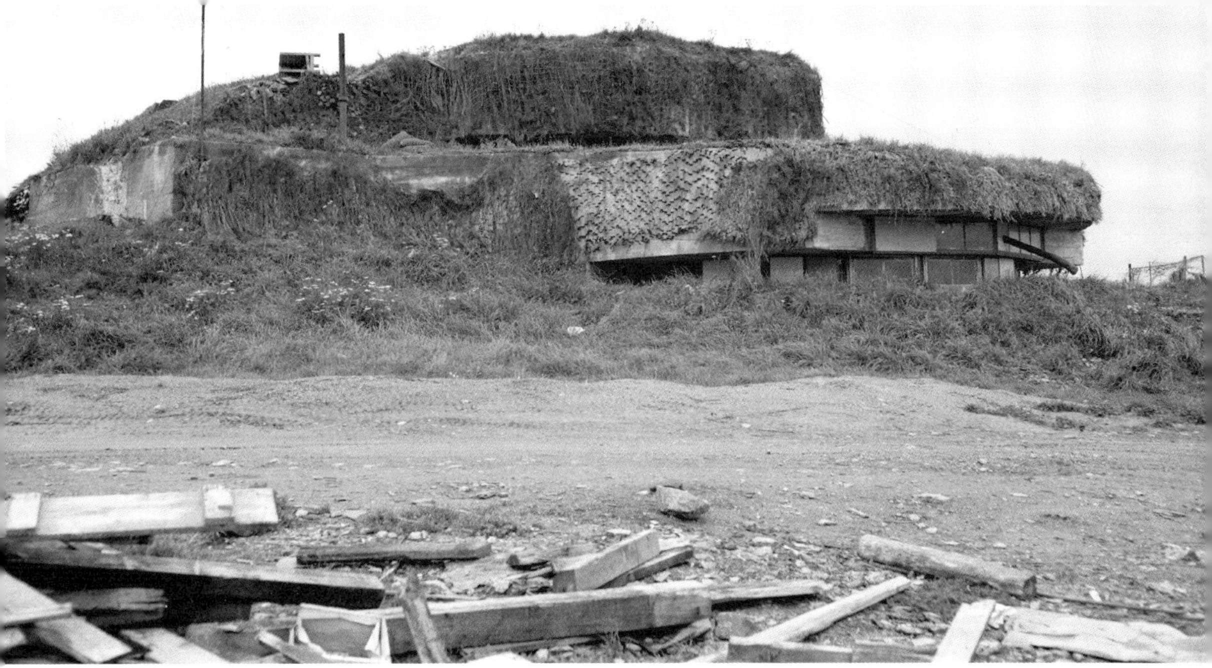

The fire-control bunker stands a little higher up the hill, approximately behind the third casemate from the west. Though built in a line, each of the four casemates faced in a slightly different direction. Thick undergrowth makes it difficult to take an exact comparison and a post-war French addition to the bunker's roof has altered its shape. (USNA and ATB)

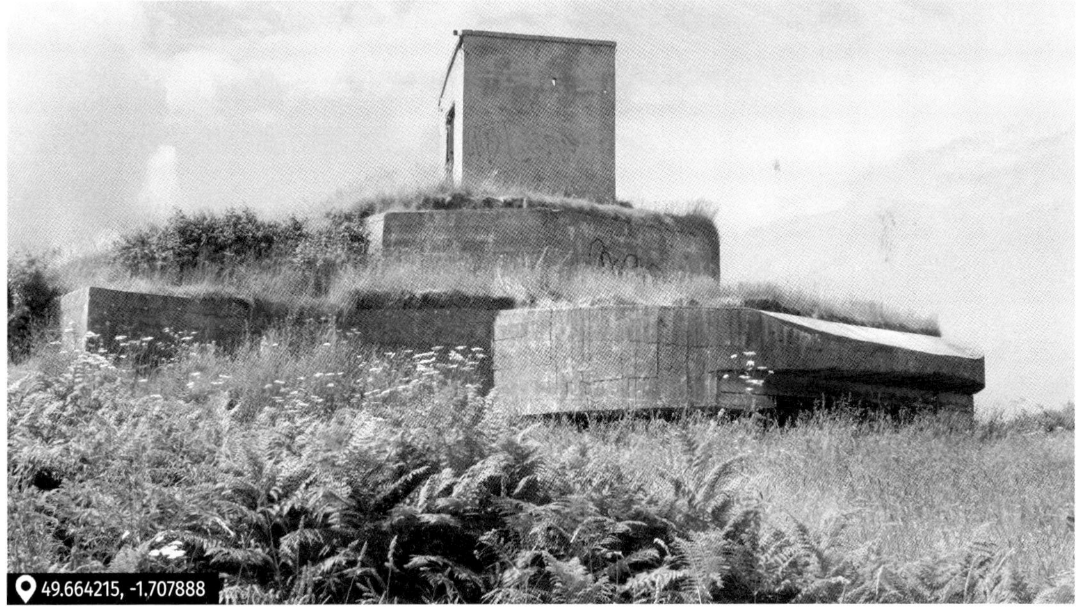

The German command expecting the Allied invasion to take place at the shortest crossing point, i.e. the Pas de Calais, priority in the apportionment of labour and concrete was given to this sector. In consequence, fewer bunkers and gun positions were built in Normandy than elsewhere: over 1,350 bunkers were built by Oberbauleitung Belgien (Belgium) and about 800 by Oberbauleitung Nordwest (the Pas de Calais area), but only 540 were built by Oberbauleitung Cherbourg in Normandy and the Channel Islands.

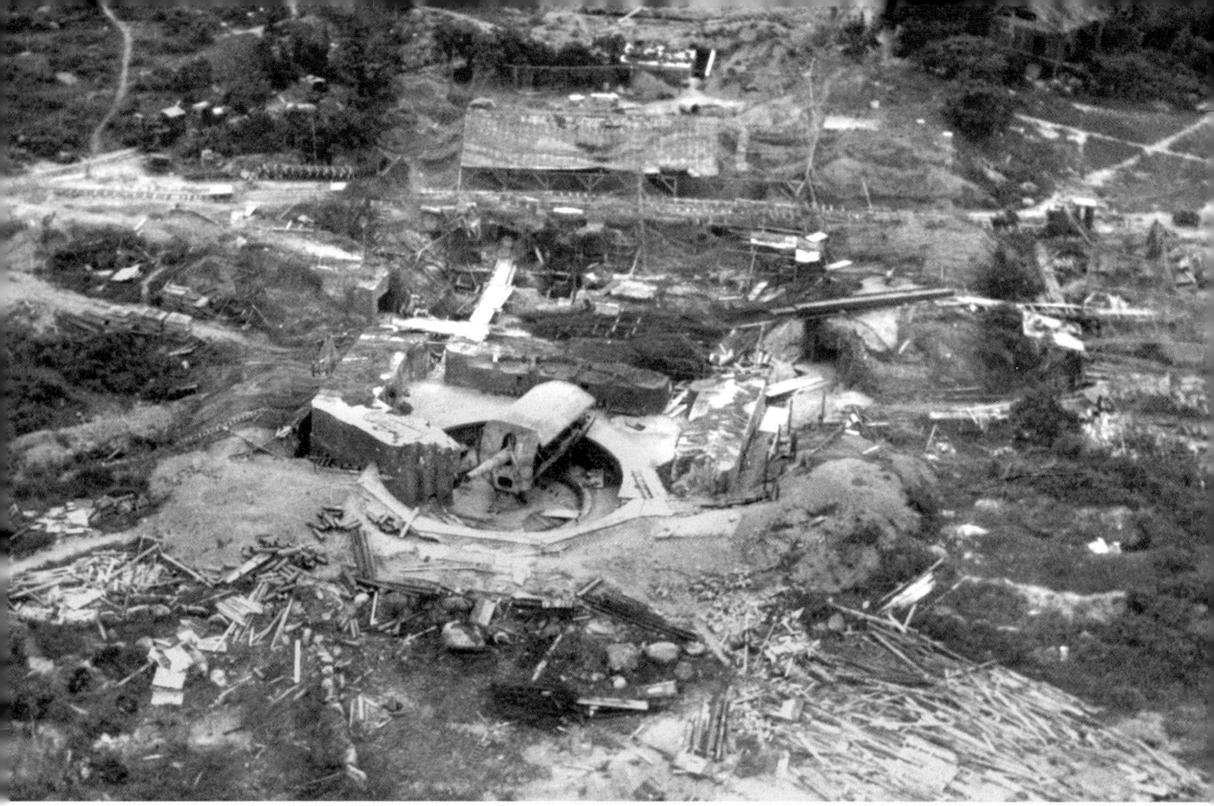

Batterie 'Hamburg' near Fermanville, 12 kilometres east of Cherbourg, was another batterie manned by Marine-Artillerie-Abteilung 260. It consisted of four 240mm SK L/40 guns, another type of pre-First World War naval gun adapted for coastal defence. Mounted in revolving armoured turrets, these guns had a range of 27,000 metres. They were planned to be protected by casemates but only the walls had been finished by June 1944 and the concrete roofs were all lacking. (USNA)

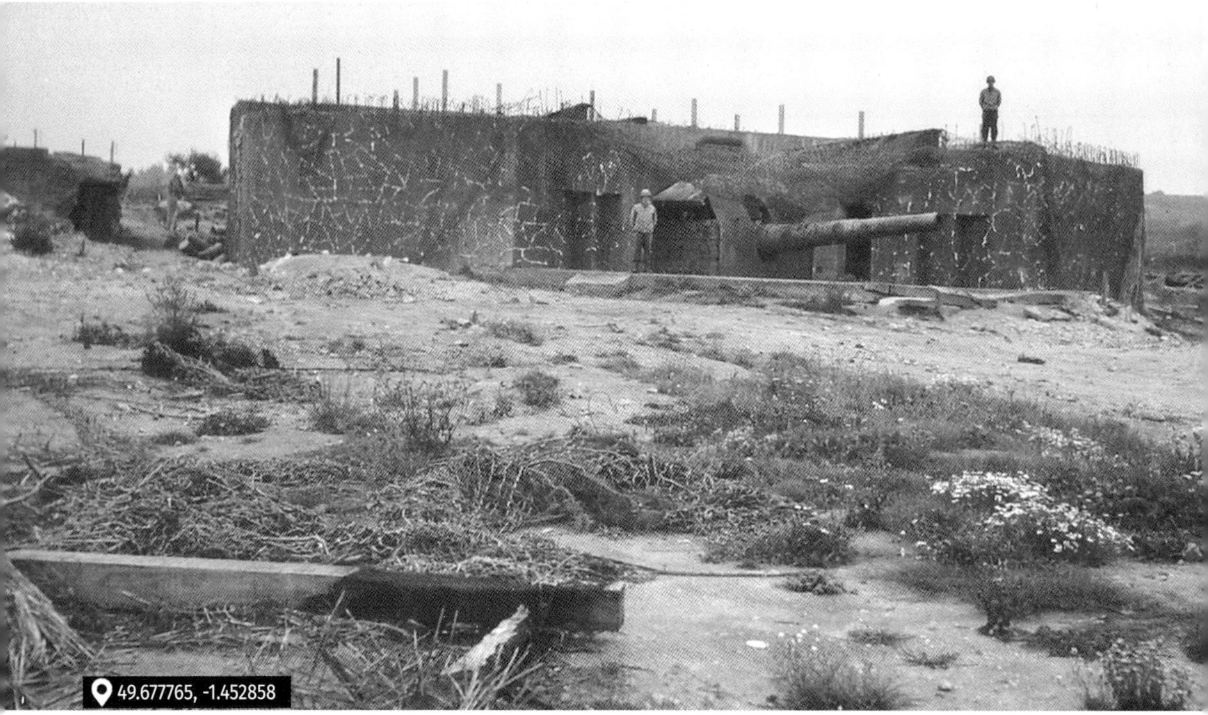

49.677765, -1.452858

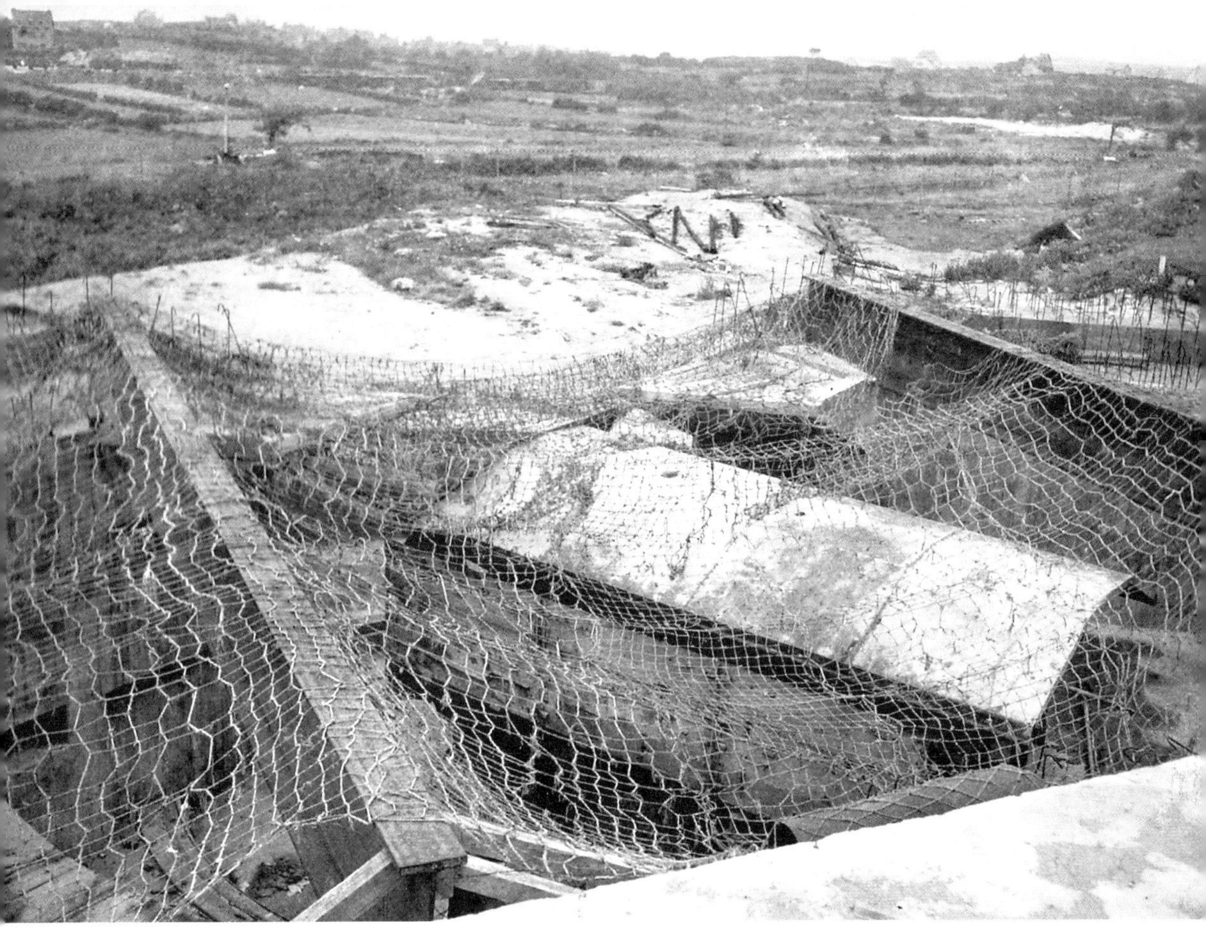

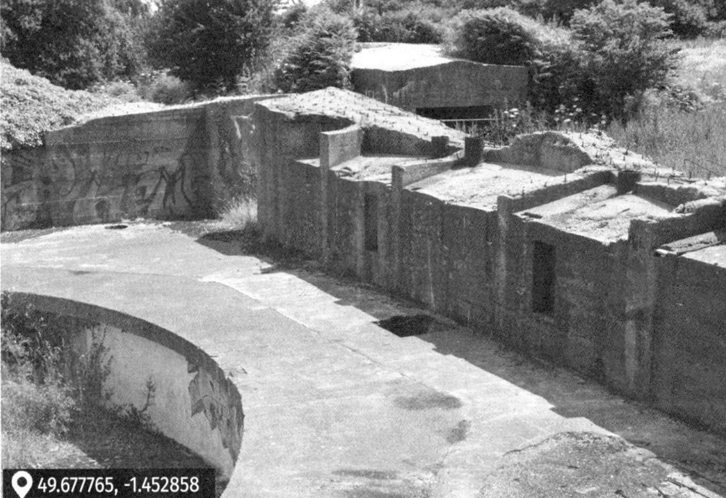

During the fighting in June, Oberleutnant Rudi Gelbhaar, the commander of the 9. Batterie manning Batterie 'Hamburg', ordered that the left side wall of one casemate be blown up to enable its gun being trained south-westwards at approaching American troops.
(USNA and ATB)

On the eve of D-Day, the LXXXIV. Armeekorps had two divisions deployed along the coast from the sector east of Caen to Carentan, three divisions in the Cotentin peninsula, plus one holding the Channel Islands. The defence of the peninsula was as follows: the 709. Infanterie-Division was along the eastern coast and in the Cherbourg area; the 243. Infanterie-Division along the western coast; and the 91. Infanterie-Division, which had arrived in May, was stationed in between.

In addition, subordinated to the 91. Infanterie-Division, Fallschirmjäger-Regiment 6 was in reserve in the Lessay – Périers area. MG-Bataillon 17, an

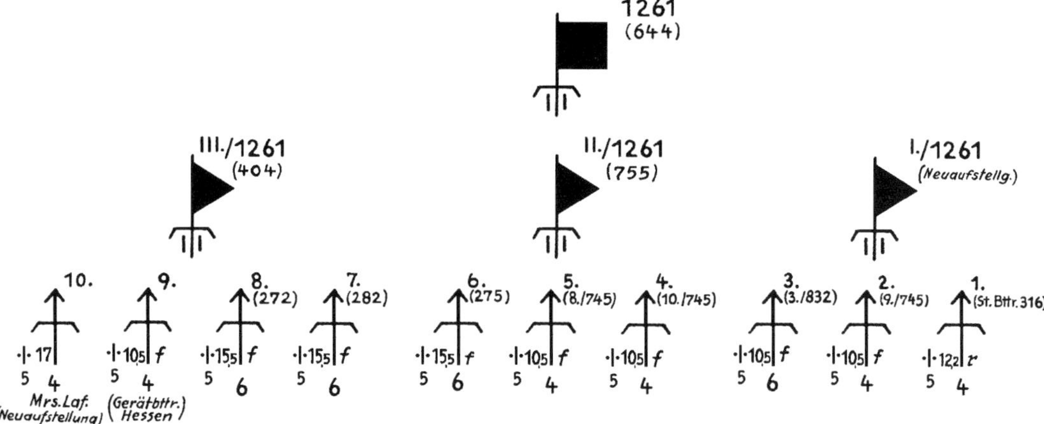

The Army deployed two coastal artillery regiments in the Cotentin, Heeres-Küsten-Artillerie-Regiment 1261 and Heeres-Küsten-Artillerie-Regiment 1262. The former controlled ten batteries along the peninsula's eastern coast and in the Cherbourg area, the latter eight batteries along the western coast. This original German document of early 1944 detailed the composition of Heeres-Küsten-Artillerie-Regiment 1261. When formed in December 1943, the regiment integrated odd existing artillery elements (see figures between brackets); only the staff of the I. Abteilung and the 10. Batterie were new units. The 'arrow' signs identify coastal guns and the letter just right of it tells the origin of the guns: most were from French origin here, but for the 1. Batterie had ex-Russian guns and the 10. Batterie that had German guns. The figures, 4 or 6, under the arrows indicate the number of guns available with the battery.

This document indicates that the 8. Batterie had six 155mm guns captured from the French, 155mm K 420(f) in German nomenclature. Building of eight open circular concrete gun platforms started in the summer of 1942 at Equeurdreville, near the old French fort Les Couplets. The construction of four H679 type casemates began late in 1943, as well as a H636 type fire control bunker. The third casemate from the west can be seen in this aerial taken in July 1944, with a gun on the platform just behind (the fourth platform from the west) and the fire-control post in the background. (USNA)

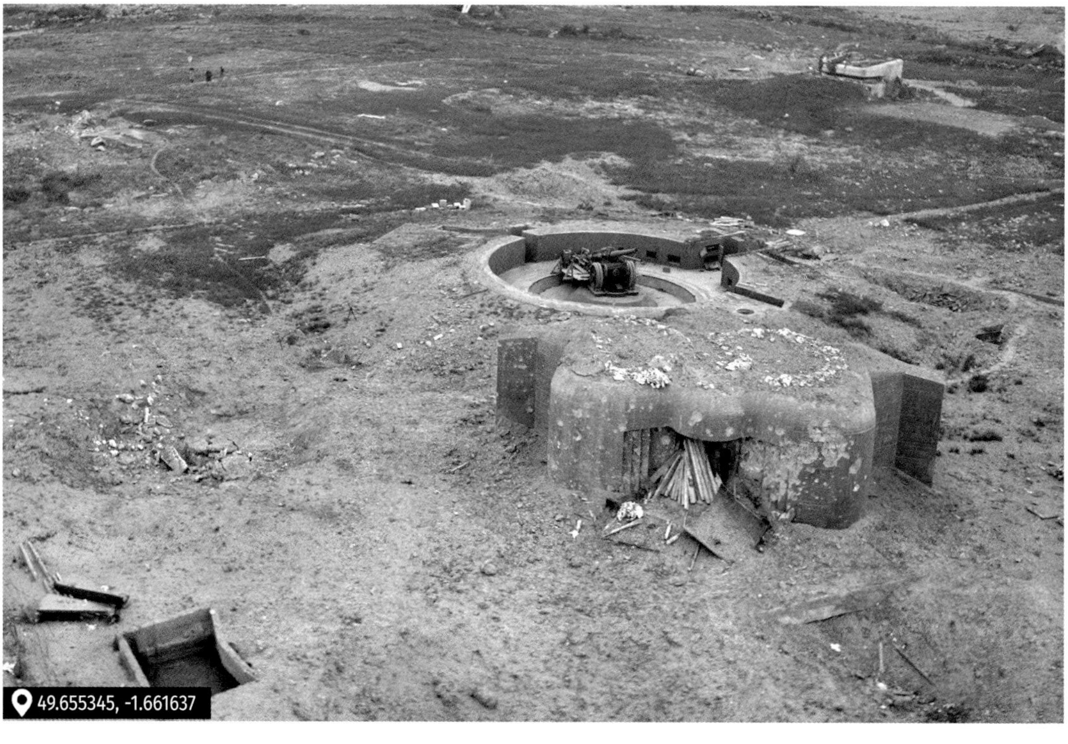

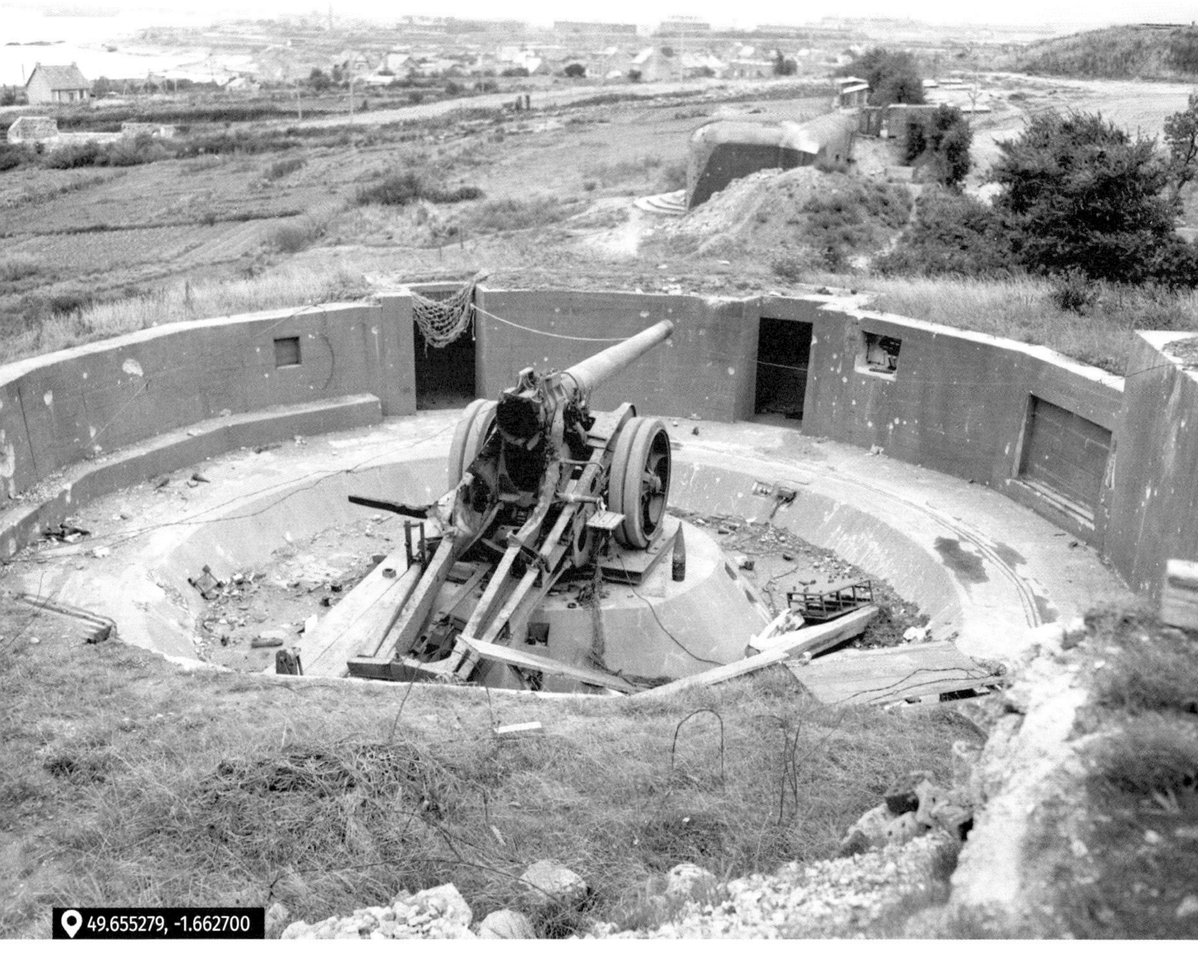

The battery's ex-French 155mm guns had a maximum range of 21,000 metres, with shells weighing 43 kilos. This second aerial view shows a gun on the third platform from the west, with the third casemate in the centre, and the fourth gun platform in the background on the right. Today, the batterie stands within a park area and the casemates can be seen up close, although they are all sealed up and it is impossible to enter to see inside. The open gun positions have been buried under mounds of earth, but parts of several of them still emerge from the grass. (USNA)

independent army heavy machine-gun unit, and Ost-Bataillon 561, a unit of Russian soldiers captured on the Eastern front, were in the Cap de la Hague area, west of Cherbourg, both subordinated to the 709. Infanterie-Division. Also in the same area was Panzer-Abteilung 206, equipped with some 45 obsolete French light tanks of miscellaneous types. In the Cherbourg area were the I. Bataillon of Festungs-Stammtruppen LXXXIV, an ad-hoc fortress battalion formed in 1943, comprising four companies and totalling about 1,350 men, and the II. Bataillon of Sicherungs-Regiment 195, a battalion of security troops, also with four companies and just moved in from the Caen area. Further south, stationed near Carentan, was Panzer-Ersatz-Abteilung 100, another unit equipped with some 30 ex-French tanks of slight combat value.

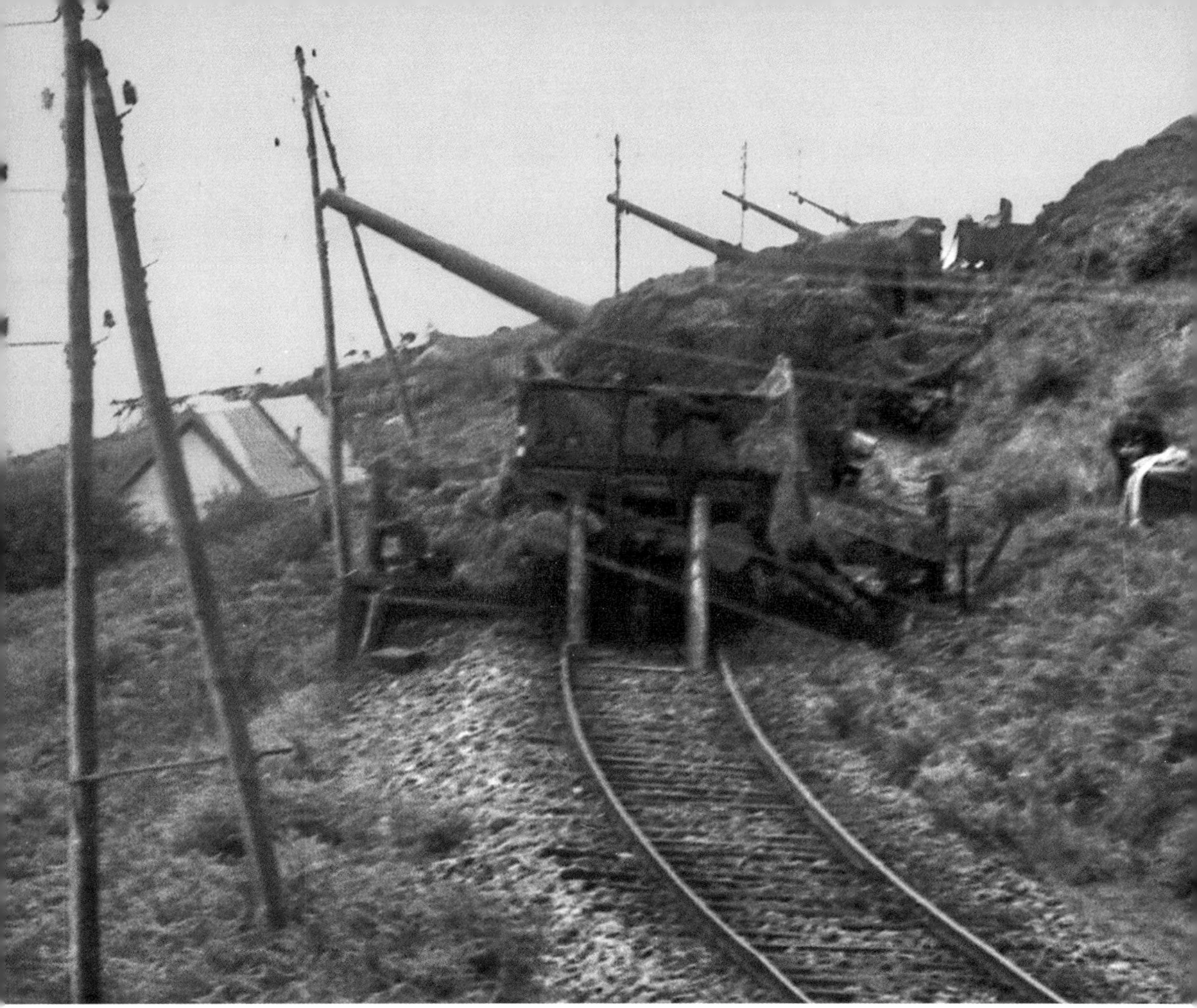

While they built concrete casemates to shelter coastal guns, the Germans moved railway gun batteries close to the coast. In the summer of 1942, Eisenbahn-Artillerie-Batterie 'Gneisenau' emplaced its four 150mm Kanone (E) SK L/40 guns in the Anse du Brick, some ten kilometres east of Cherbourg. These four guns were the only ones of their type, as production was quickly stopped because the punch of the old 150mm pieces was too small to justify the use of a costly railway mounting. The battery stayed only a short time in the Cherbourg area, being transferred to the Mediterranean coastline at the end of the year. The railway then linking Cherbourg to Barfleur has been completely lifted and a road now runs along the coast in its place.

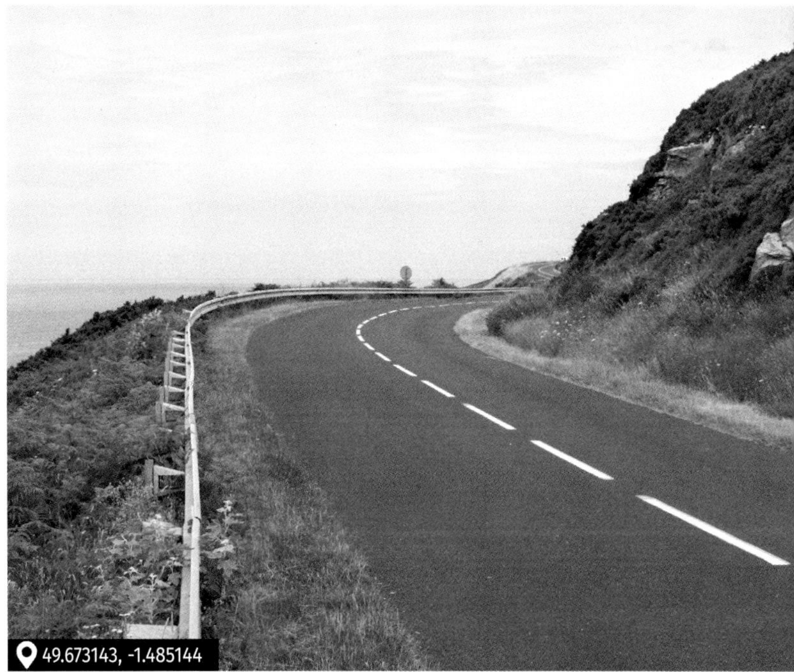

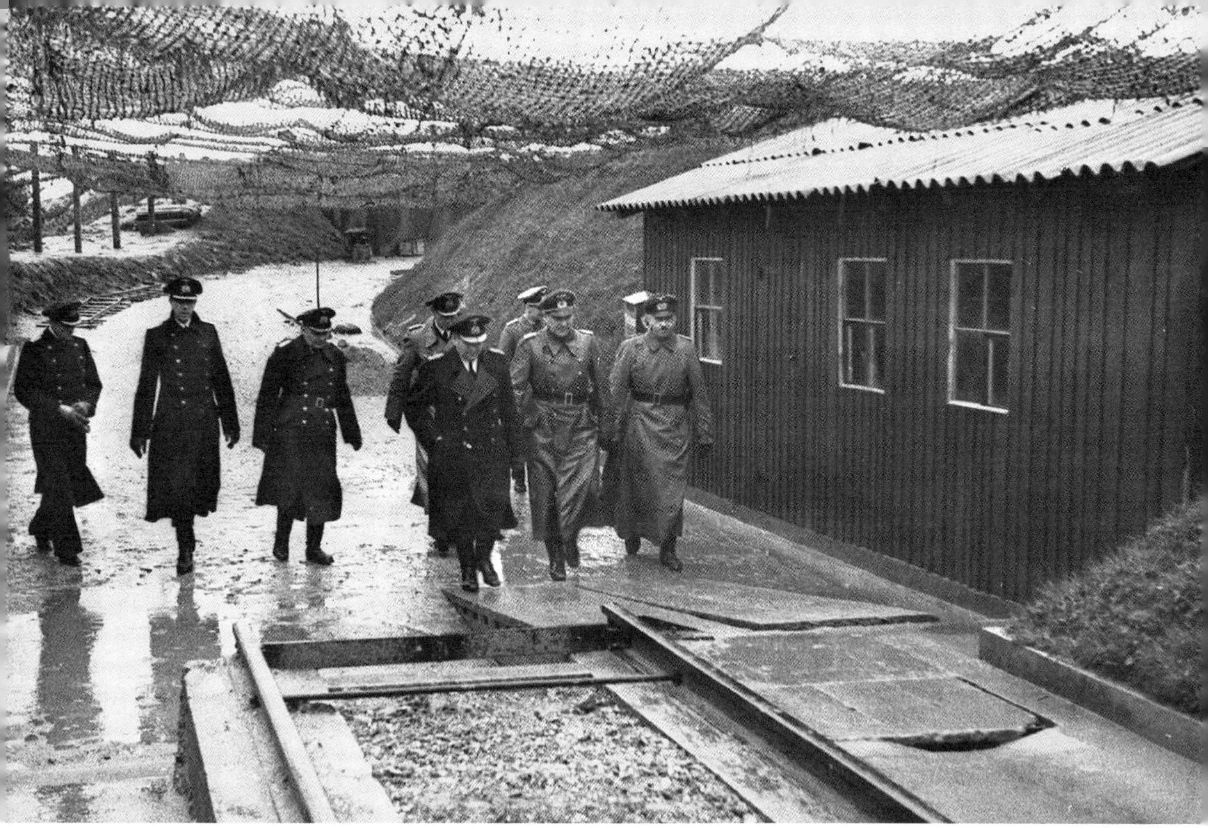

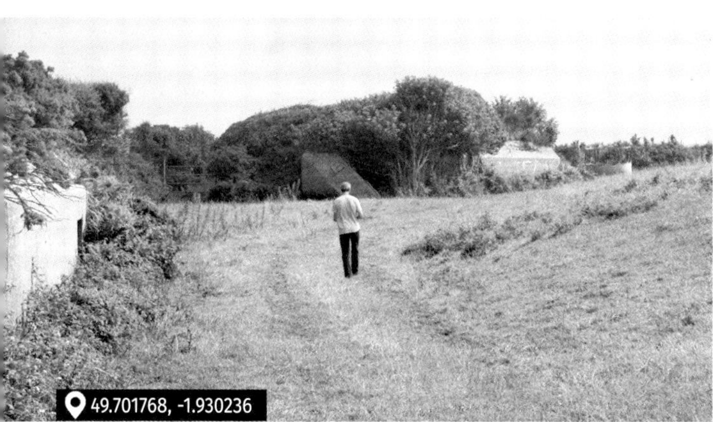

Another unit of railway guns moved to the Cherbourg area was Eisenbahn-Artillerie-Batterie 685 pictured here by PK photographer Kietzmann. Integrated into Heeres-Küsten-Artillerie-Regiment 1262 when this unit was formed in December 1943, it then lost its initial designation and was renumbered as the regiment's 3. Batterie. The unit built two circular platforms at Auderville-Laye, in Cap de la Hague, the western tip of the Cotentin peninsula, for its two guns. This is the entrance to the battery with an H622 personnel shelter on the left and an H134 ammunition bunker in the background. (BA and ATB)

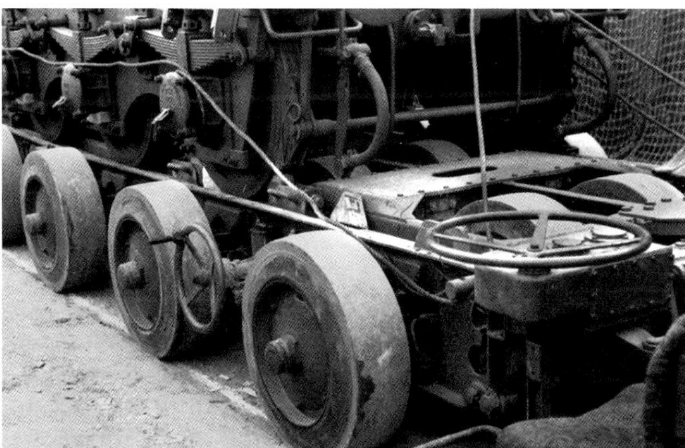

The battery was equipped with two 203mm Kanone (E) SK C/34. Redundant naval guns intended for the 'Admiral Hipper' class of heavy cruisers these guns had a maximum range of 36,500 metres with shells weighing 122 kilos. As there was no railway line nearby, the 85-ton guns were transported to the site on road carriages, quite an enterprise for the local roads were all narrow, steep, and winding. (BA)

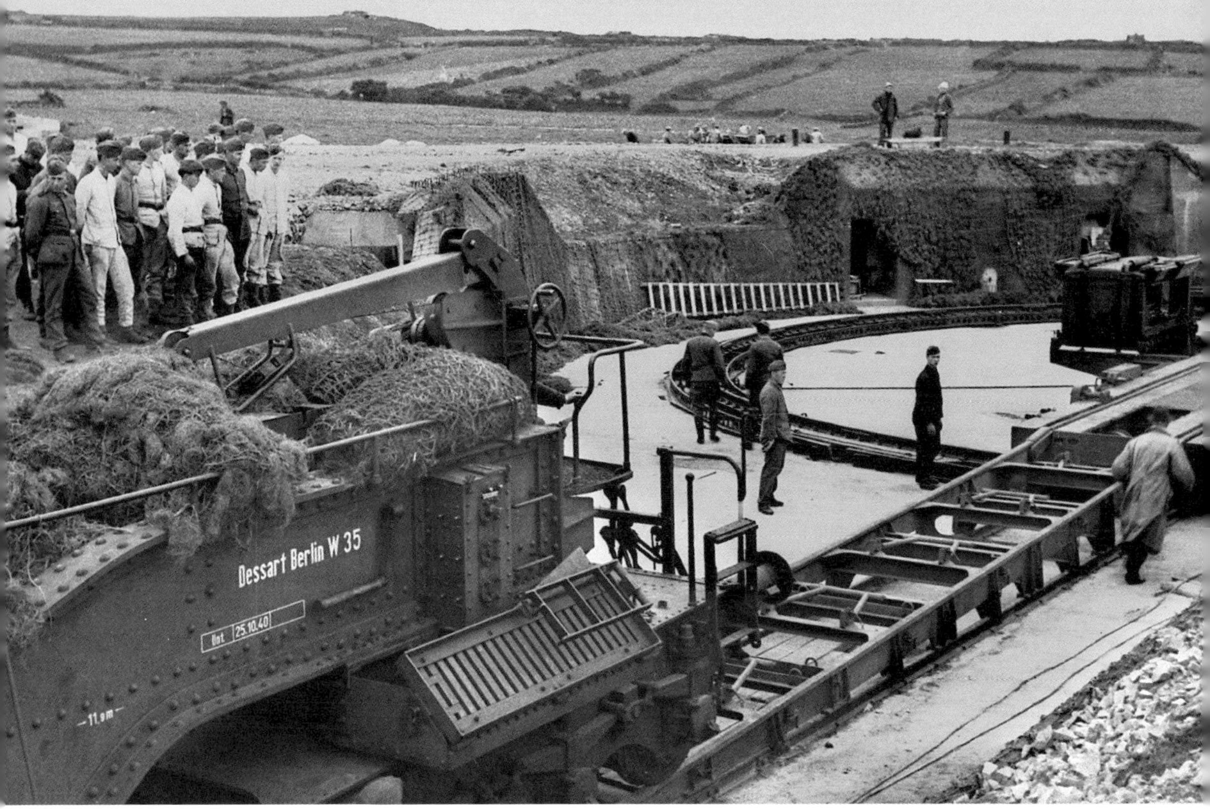

A traverse of 360 degrees was obtained by means of a turntable composed of a circular track set over the main track, with a power unit attached to the turntable. The internal diameter of the circular platform was about 12 metres. The author had to work his way through thorny bushes to reach the spot where photographer Gefreiter Zwirner had stood: Then and Now from the top of the roof of a concrete ammunition shelter built on the edge of the platform. (BA and ATB)

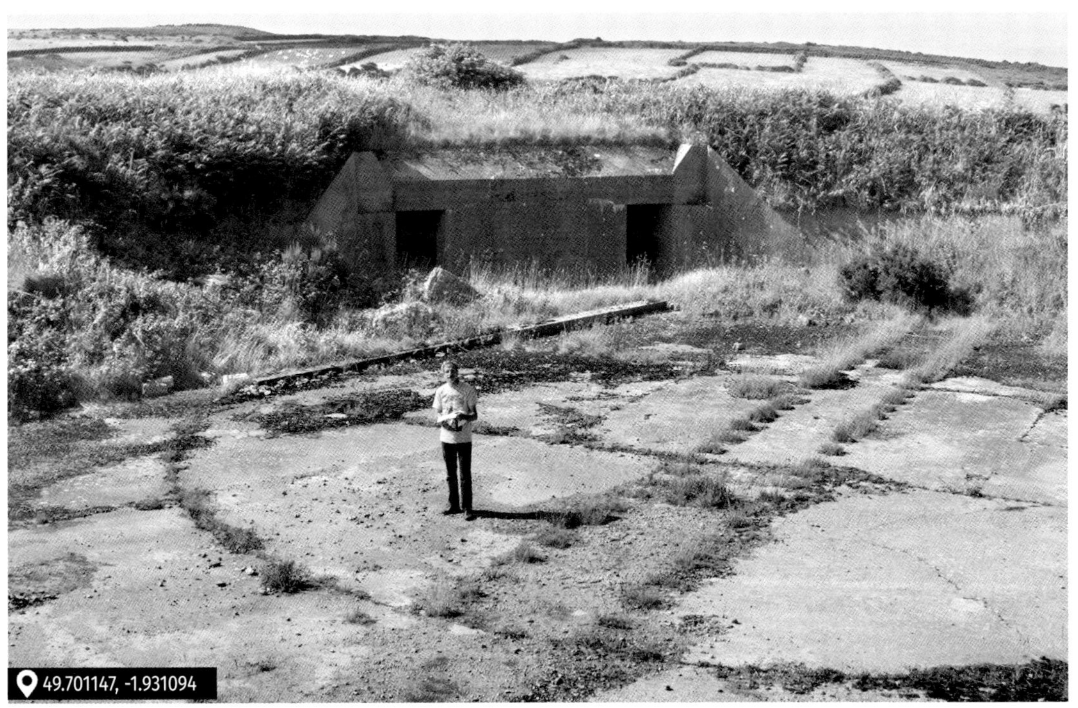

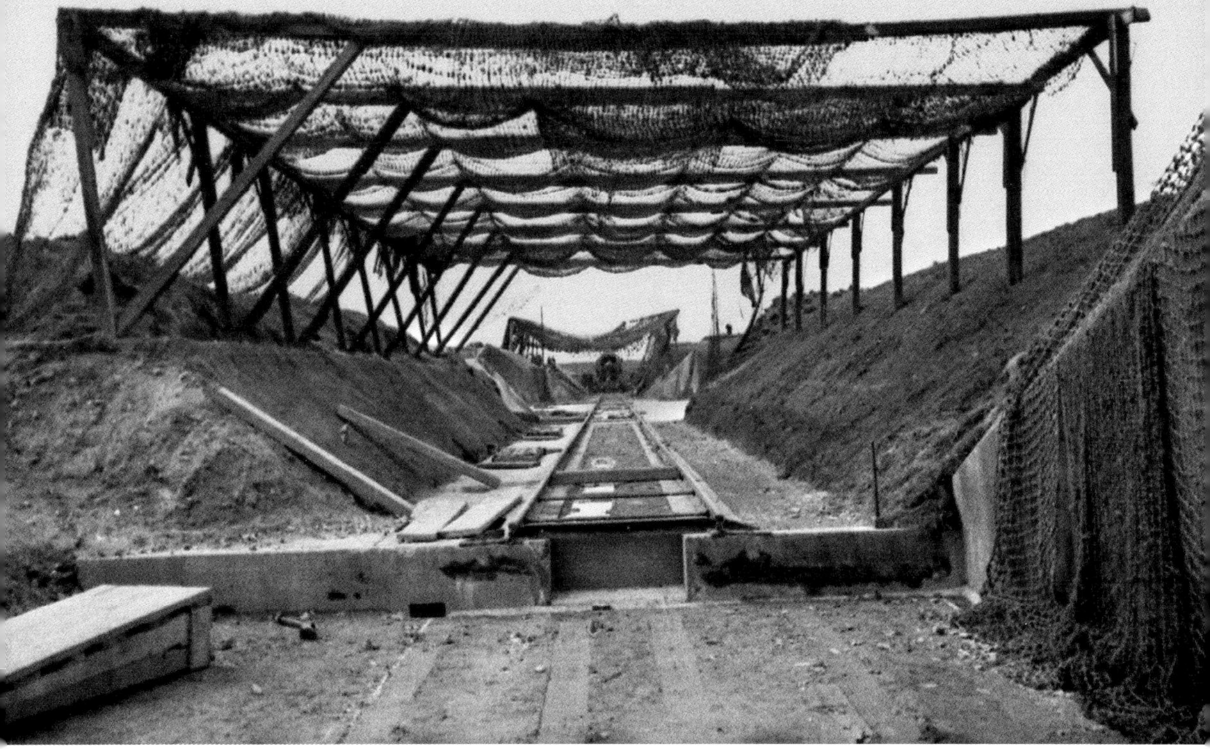

A railway line about 150 metres long was built to serve the two platforms, the two sections outside the platforms being hidden under an overhead camouflage 'tunnel', pictured here by PK photographer Zwirner. The railway line has disappeared but the straight line of its trace remains, seen here from close to the first platform. (BA and ATB)

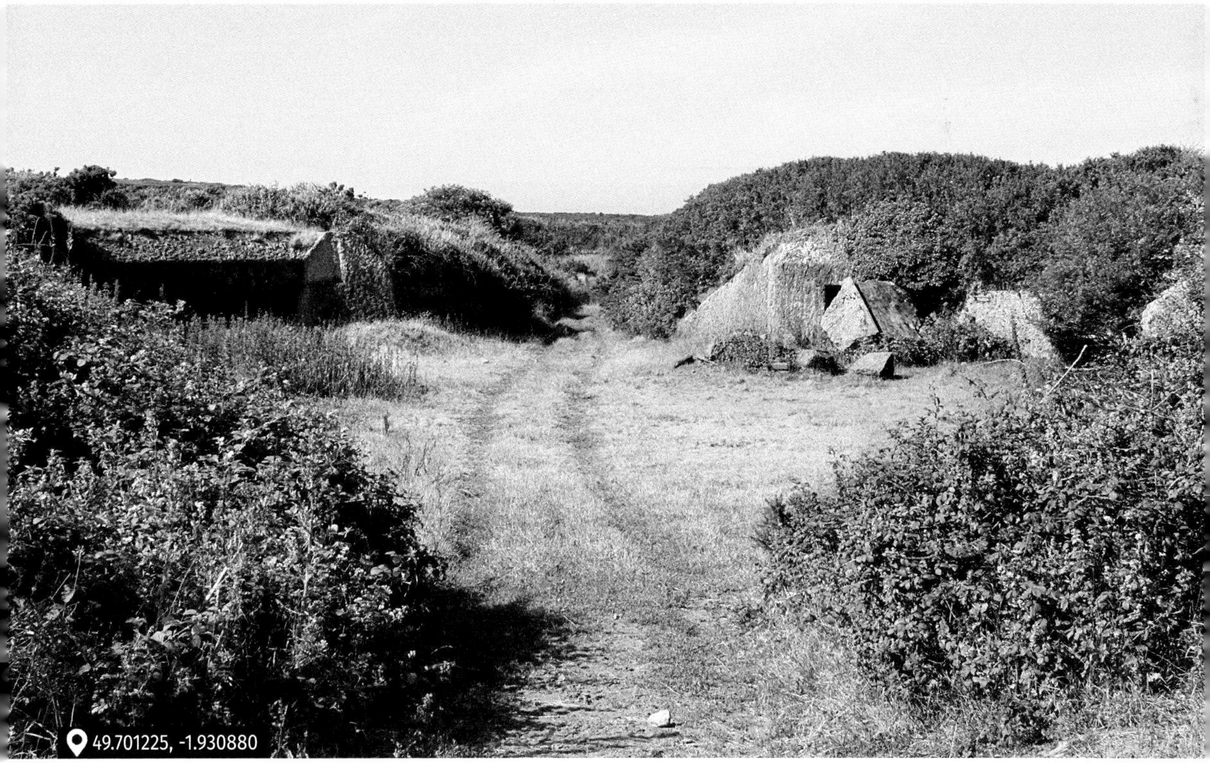

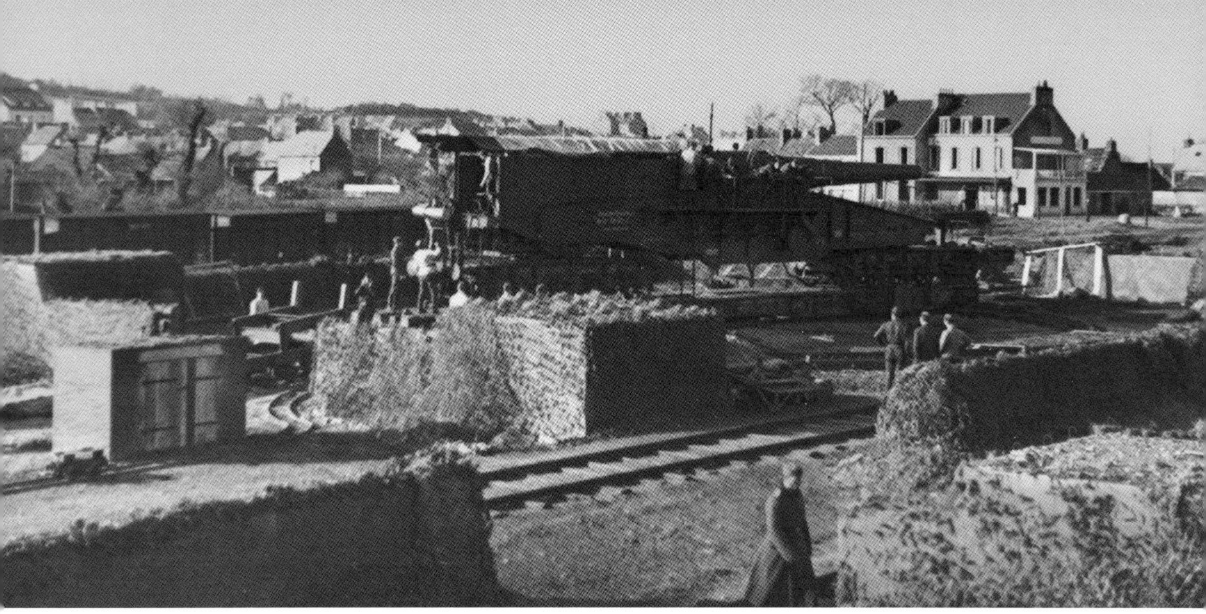

Yet another battery of railway guns, Eisenbahn-Artillerie-Batterie 722, had just reached the Cherbourg sector when these pictures were taken by PK photographer Kietzmann in 1941. The battery comprised four 240mm Theodor Bruno Kanone (E). Six of these were produced between 1937 and 1939 with pre-First World War guns originally built for the 'Wittelsbach' class of battleships mounted on a specially designed railway mounting. Test-firing out to sea from the railway complex near the Arsenal in the western part of Cherbourg. The 240mm guns had a maximum range of 20,200 metres, its shells weighing a hefty 150 kilos. (BA)

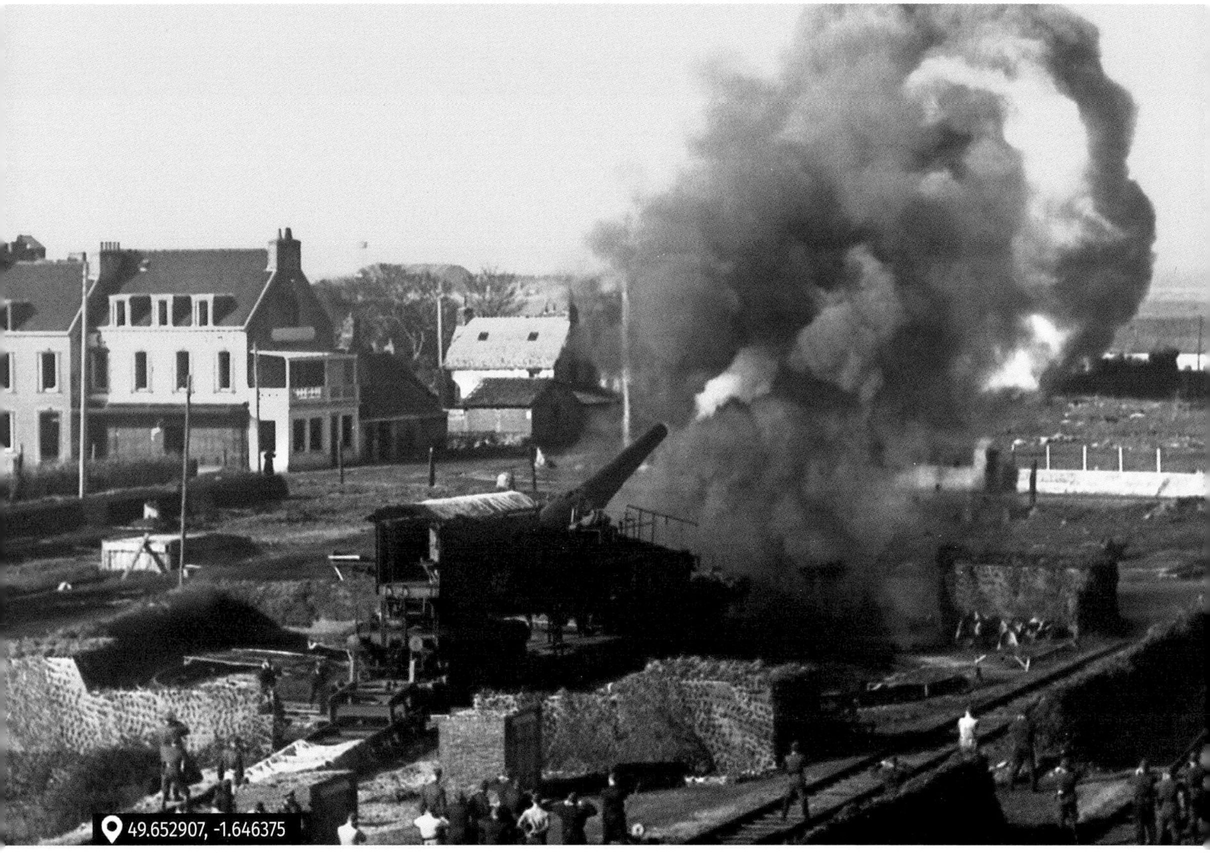

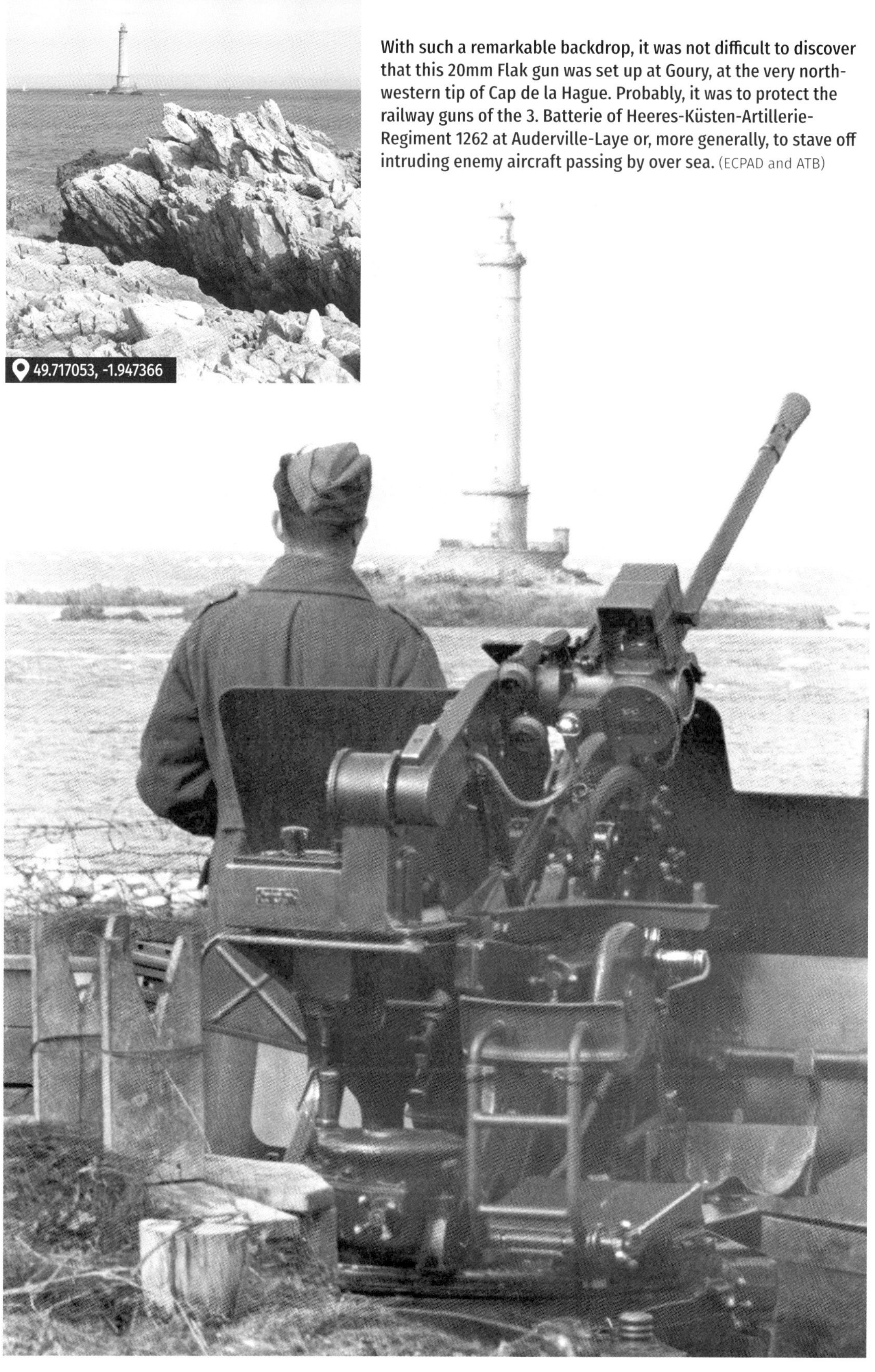

With such a remarkable backdrop, it was not difficult to discover that this 20mm Flak gun was set up at Goury, at the very north-western tip of Cap de la Hague. Probably, it was to protect the railway guns of the 3. Batterie of Heeres-Küsten-Artillerie-Regiment 1262 at Auderville-Laye or, more generally, to stave off intruding enemy aircraft passing by over sea. (ECPAD and ATB)

D-DAY AND SEALING OFF THE BASE OF THE PENINSULA

ON THE EVE of D-Day, the Kriegsmarine fleet in the West was desperately small, and Marinegruppe West was down to six torpedo boats, five at Cherbourg and one, *T-24*, at Brest. The five S-Boat flotillas distributed from Cherbourg to IJmuiden in Holland consisted of 31 operational boats. At Cherbourg, the 5. and 9. S-Boots-Flottillen had 13 operational boats with two under repair.

The only intervention by the Kriegsmarine on D-Day was that of three torpedo boats – *Jaguar*, *Möwe* and *T-28* – which sailed from Le Havre at 4.30 a.m. They made good use of the smokescreen laid by Allied aircraft to protect the assault fleet and at 5.35 a.m. they suddenly emerged within range of the Allied fleet. They quickly fired 15 torpedoes and retreated into the smoke cover. One torpedo sank the Norwegian destroyer *Svenner* and HMS *Largs*, the headquarters ship of Force 'S', just managed to avoid another.

S-Boats also sailed from Cherbourg in the early hours of June 6 but they were all forced to return to port before dawn due to the heavy sea. They again sailed on the night of June 6/7 but without success and two of them were lost to mines.

More S-Boats were transferred to Le Havre from ports further east, and those at Cherbourg were also progressively transferred to Le Havre. They finally claimed two LSTs, two LCTs, two tugs towing components for the 'Mulberry' artificial harbour, one motor torpedo boat and three small freighters, but in the same period six S-Boats were sunk and ten others damaged.

When plans were drawn up for the Allied invasion of France, one important consideration was that it would be necessary to secure a deep-water port to allow reinforcements to be brought in directly from the United States. Cherbourg, at the tip of the Cotentin peninsula in Normandy, was closest to the landing beaches and the planners consequently decided that the US First Army's main task should be 'to capture Cherbourg as quickly as possible'.

The US 82nd and 101st Airborne Divisions spearheaded Operation 'Overlord' in the west, landing at the base of the peninsula. Their landings were scattered but they nevertheless secured most of the routes by which the

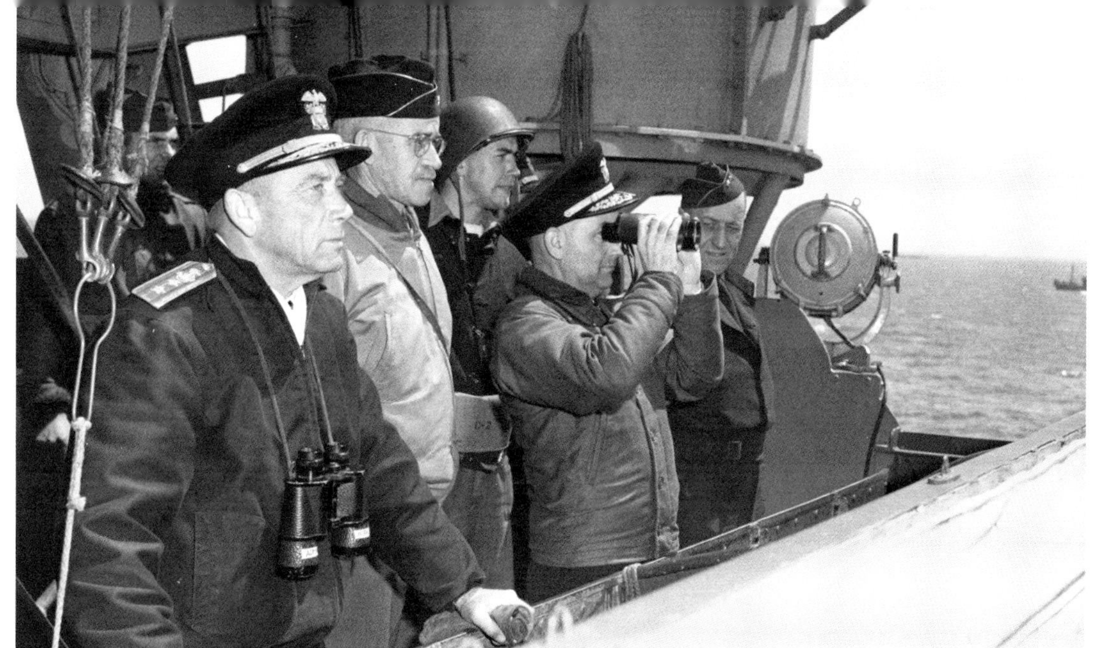

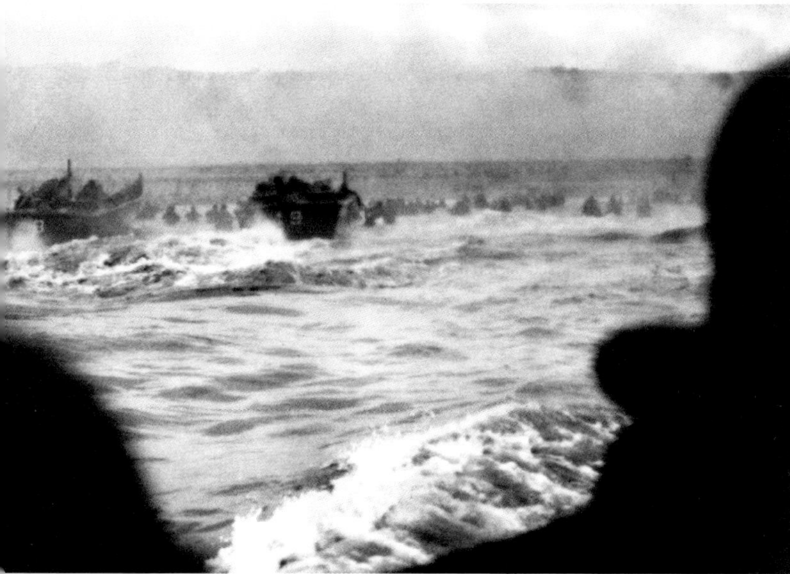

Off Omaha Beach, LCVPs from the USS *Anne Arundel* advance toward Easy Red. In the background, the cruiser USS *Augusta*, the naval flagship, with Admiral Alan G. Kirk, commander of the Western Task Force, and General Omar N. Bradley, commander of the First US Army, on board. After establishing the beachhead, the major objectives of the Allied forces were to seize Caen and Saint-Lô, two road centres of great importance to both sides, and to take Cherbourg, the major Channel port on the Cotentin peninsula considered vital for supplying American forces. (USNA)

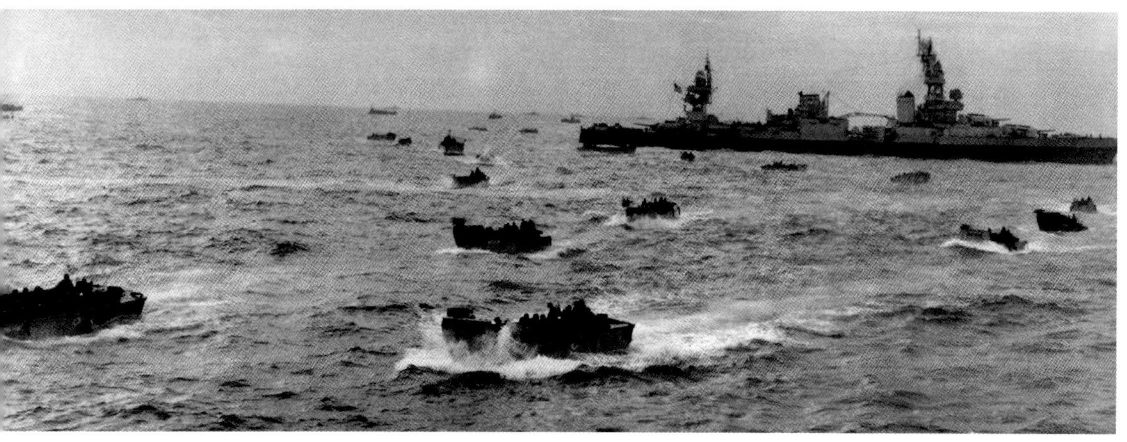

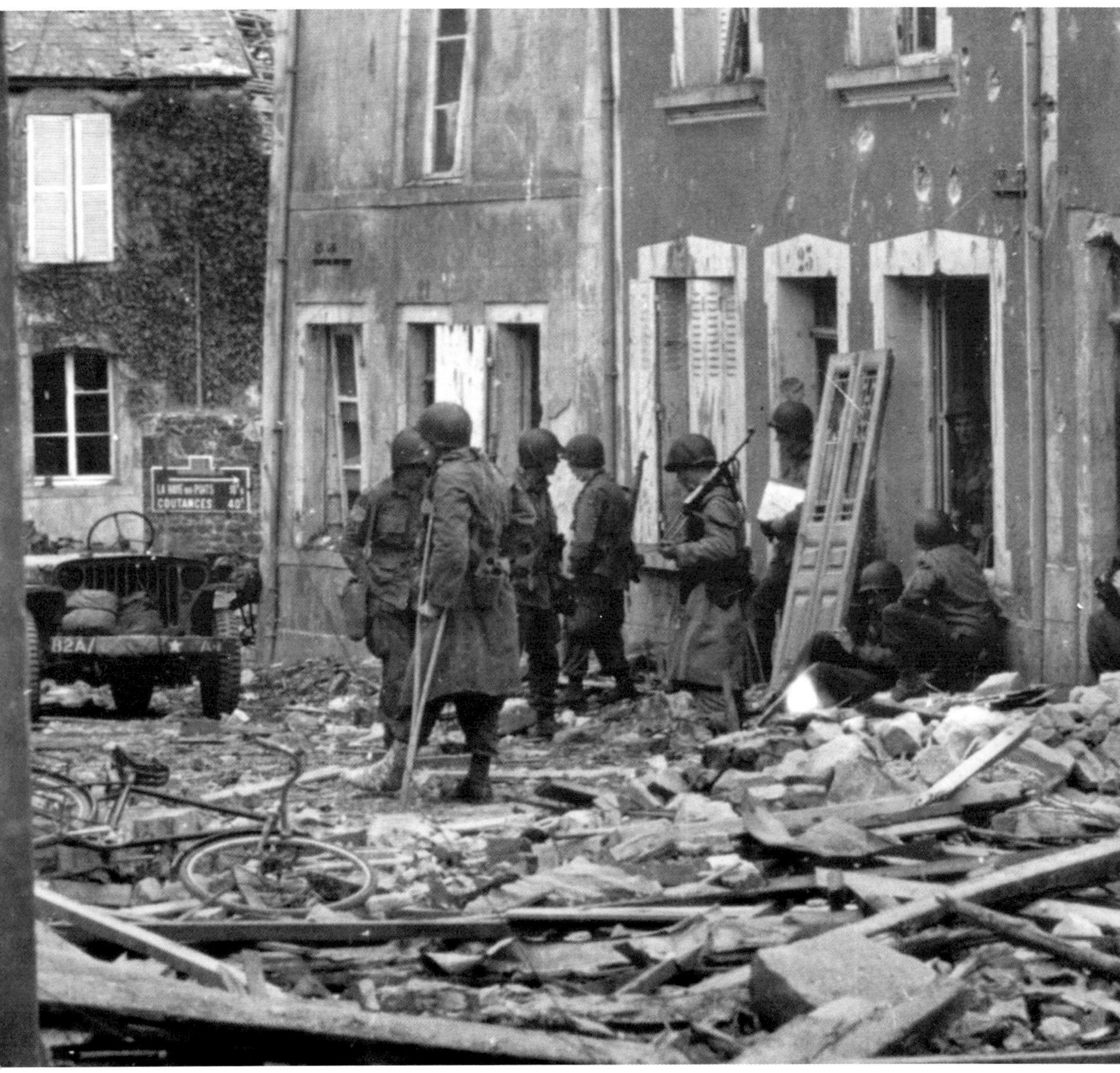

Taken on June 17, just after the 82nd Airborne Division captured Saint-Sauveur-le-Vicomte, this remarkable photo shows Lieutenant Colonel Benjamin H. Vandervoort, commander of the 2nd Battalion, 505th Parachute Infantry Regiment, who fractured his ankle when he parachuted near Sainte-Mère-Église in the early hours of D-Day. He refused to be evacuated and continued to lead his unit after his leg was temporarily splinted. (He was portrayed by John Wayne in the 1962 war film *The Longest Day*). On the right, we also see the famous photographer Robert Capa changing the film on his Rolleiflex 6x6 camera. He took several photos in the ruined town that day. (USNA)

American forces landing at Utah Beach would advance. The US 4th Infantry Division landed on Utah Beach shortly after dawn with few casualties. For the first days, the priority was to link up with the main Allied landings further east. The flooded Douve valley was crossed on June 9 and Carentan captured the next day, giving the Allies a continuous front at which point US VII Corps began to drive westwards to cut off the peninsula at its base.

On June 9, concerned over the threat of an enemy breakthrough to Cherbourg, the German 7. Armee ordered the 77. Infanterie-Division, then coming up from Brittany, to proceed up the peninsula to Valognes. Two days later, Generalfeldmarschall Gerd von Rundstedt, the German Commander-in-Chief in the West, and Generalfeldmarschall Erwin Rommel, the commander of Heeresgruppe B, met to discuss the serious situation and agreed to report independently to Hitler. Both reports gave the same appreciation of the German situation in Normandy and of the Allies' intentions. Von Rundstedt explained that 'the formations of Heeresgruppe B fighting in Normandy are forced on to the defensive between the Orne and the Vire. Offensive operations cannot as yet be conducted in this broad sector for lack of forces and because the panzer divisions had to be used for defence.' In order to prevent a breakthrough to Cherbourg, which was obviously the immediate American objective, they proposed to counter-attack in the Cotentin. Pointing out that the purpose of this strike would be 'to annihilate the enemy there', Rommel stressed that 'only when this has been accomplished can the enemy between the Orne and the Vire be attacked'.

Refusing the field-marshals' demand that a counter-attack in the Cotentin was an urgent need, Hitler's reaction on June 12 was to insist that 'the enemy bridgehead between the Orne and Vire must be attacked and destroyed piece by piece'.

By June 14, it was clear that the Americans were close to cutting the peninsula in half so Rommel decided that two divisions (the 243. and 709. Infanterie-Divisions) would be sufficient for the defence of Cherbourg and that the 77. Infanterie-Division should be moved south to oppose the American push to the south. Accordingly, the 7. Armee issued orders to divide the forces in the Cotentin into two groups. Gruppe von Schlieben (under Generalleutnant Karl-Wilhelm von Schlieben, the commander of the 709. Infanterie-Division), consisting of his own division and all the troops deployed on the Montebourg line (save the 77. Infanterie-Division), was charged with the defence of Cherbourg. Meanwhile, Gruppe Hellmich (under Generalleutnant Hans Hellmich, the commander of the 243. Infanterie-Division), with the 77. Infanterie-Division and all those troops south and west of the Merderet river, received the task of building a defensive line near the base of the Cotentin, between the marshlands west of Carentan and the peninsula's west coast near Portbail.

However, the following day an order from Hitler arrived which stipulated that the present line must be 'held at all cost'. Rommel, who was at the LXXXIV. Armeekorps headquarters near Saint-Lô when the Führer decree reached him, tried to make the best of an impossible situation. He decided that the 77. Infanterie-Division should send some elements southwards while ostensibly holding its ground. However, the 7. Armee soon forbade any move and orders given to the 77. Infanterie-Division were countermanded. As a consequence, nothing was accomplished during the night of June 16/17, squandering the last chance of rescuing the 77. Infanterie-Division from the closing trap.

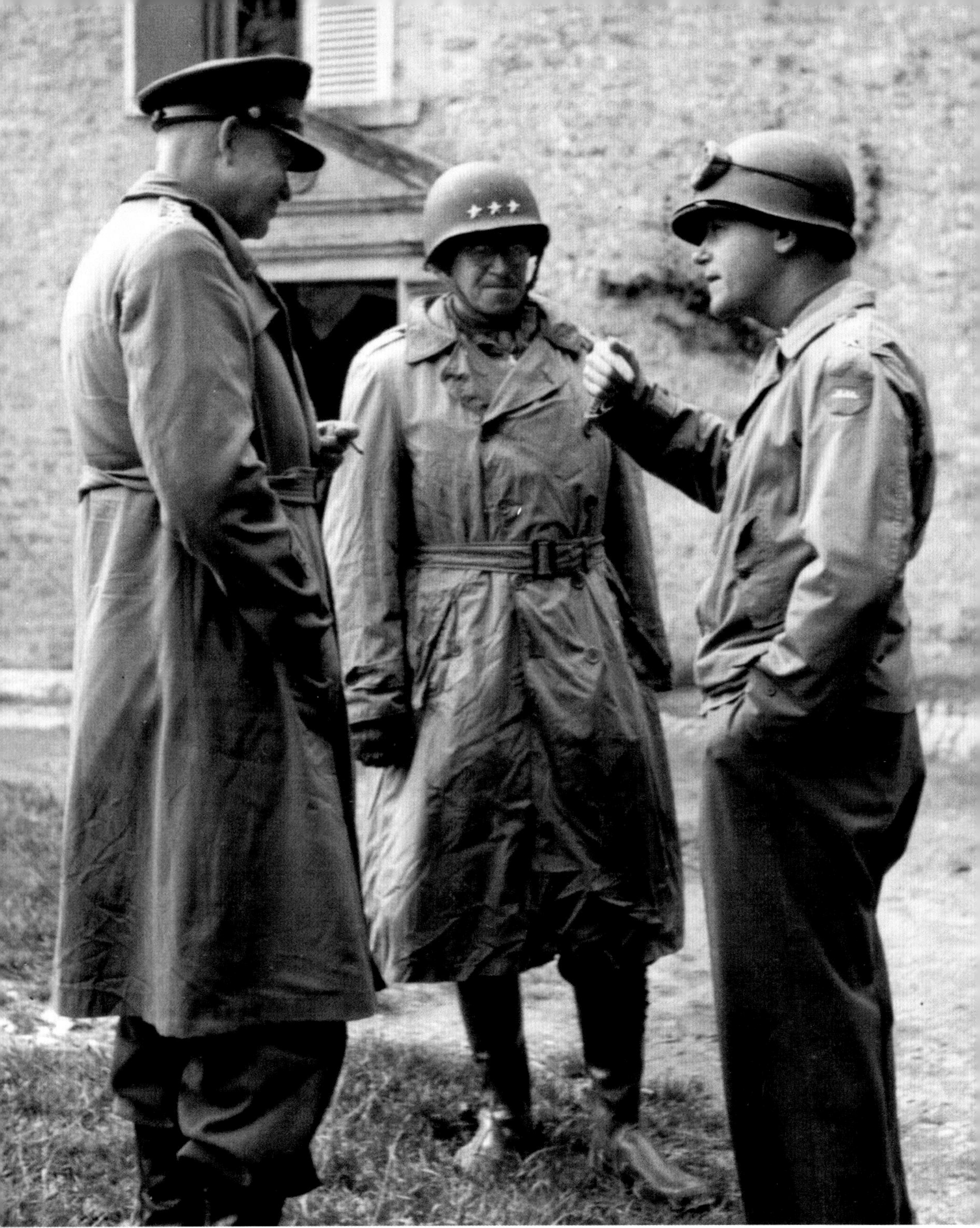

The initial plan for the drive on Cherbourg called for a two-division attack, by the 4th and 90th Divisions, while the 9th Division took up a blocking position on the west coast. However, on June 18, after consultation with General Bradley, Major General J. Lawton Collins, commander of VII Corps, changed his plans in favour of a stronger attack with three divisions – the 9th, 79th, and 4th – driving northwards abreast while the 90th Division would take up a blocking position along the west coast. This photo of Collins with Bradley and Eisenhower, the Supreme Commander, was taken on July 3, just after the capture of Cherbourg. (USNA)

Following a demand from von Rundstedt on June 15 that someone from the Oberkommando der Wehrmacht (OKW, German Armed Forces High Command) must come to France to discuss the situation, Hitler decided to come personally. A conference was arranged at the Führerhauptquartier 'Wolfsschlucht 2' at Margival, north-east of Soissons, on the morning of the 17th. Finding fault with the local commanders, Hitler expressed his dissatisfaction with their attempts to counter the Allied landings. Von Rundstedt and Rommel sought to obtain freedom of action, including permission to draw at will on reserves from coastal areas not immediately threatened by invasion. They also recommended certain withdrawals in order to shorten their lines and concentrate their forces but Hitler refused all of this. Instead, he ordered that fortress Cherbourg must be held at any cost as long as possible.

Originally, VII Corps planned a two-division drive on Cherbourg with the 90th Division on the right and the 4th Division on the left. However, the 90th had demonstrated too many signs of unreadiness in the recent fighting, and on June 13 its commander, Brigadier General Jay W. MacKelvie was relieved and replaced by Major General Eugene M. Landrum. (Two regimental commanders, Colonel Philip H. Ginder of the 357th Infantry and Colonel James W. Thompson of the 358th Infantry, were relieved at the same time.) As a fresh division – the 79th Infantry Division – was available, the VII Corps commander, Major General J. Lawton Collins, asked for and received it as a replacement for the 90th.

The division was left in the line, but Collins reorganised his attack, the 9th Division was assigned the northern part of the 90th Division's original attack zone, and the main attack to cut the peninsula. The 82nd Airborne Division was assigned the southern part.

The attack made rapid progress and on June 16, the 82nd Airborne took Saint-Sauveur-le-Vicomte. Early on the 18th, troops of the 60th Infantry, 9th Division, entered Barneville, cutting the coast road and thus practically sealing off the base of the Cotentin. During the night and the following morning columns of Gruppe Hellmich tried to force their way southwards. On the 19th, elements of Grenadier-Regiment 1050 (of the 77. Infanterie-Division) succeeded in taking a bridge over the Ollande river, capturing more than 100 Americans, and permitting some 1,400 men to slip through to the south. This was one of the few German successes. Many other columns were caught on the road and destroyed, among them the remainder of the divisional artillery. Delay in making vital decisions resulted in a disastrous confusion that sacrificed the bulk of the 77. Infanterie-Division for no gain. Among those who failed to escape were Generalleutnant Hellmich, killed on June 17, and Generalmajor Rudolf Stegmann, the commander of the 77. Infanterie-Division, fatally wounded near Bricquebec during a fighter-bomber attack the following afternoon.

ADVANCE TO THE CHERBOURG FRONT

ON JUNE 18, A new plan of attack was developed by General Collins in consultation with Lieutenant General Omar N. Bradley, the commander of the US First Army, and some of the division commanders. The drive on Cherbourg would now be carried out by three divisions abreast: the 4th on the right, the 79th in the centre and the 9th on the left. The 4th Division was to bypass the coastal defences in order to advance as rapidly as possible with its right flank protected by the 24th Cavalry Squadron. The 4th Cavalry Squadron was to be used to attack between the 9th and 79th Divisions while the 90th Division was to take over the role initially envisioned for the 9th Division of blocking the west coast.

Through capture by the 9th Division of field orders of the LXXXIV. Armeekorps and the 77. Infanterie-Division, VII Corps had a pretty accurate picture of the state of German defences in the peninsula. General Collins knew of the splitting of German forces and of the order to General von Schlieben to withdraw on the fortress Cherbourg. The last-minute attempt of the 77. Infanterie-Division to pull south of the 9th Division lines had been cut off, and it could be assumed that disorganisation existed in the western half of the German lines. By attacking fast and hard VII Corps might exploit the disorganisation as well as push General von Schlieben's planned withdrawal into a rout. VII Corps Intelligence estimated that the enemy would fight delaying actions and would stand for a defence of Cherbourg on the line of hills ringing it to a depth of about five miles. Fixed defences in this position had been reconnoitred and plotted accurately long before D-Day. Although the exact number of German troops at von Schlieben's disposal for the defence of Cherbourg could only be guessed at, it was known that all his major combat units (the 709., 243., 91. and 77. Infanterie-Divisions) existed only in fragments. The total enemy force locked in the peninsula was variously estimated at between 25,000 and 40,000 including Flak and naval personnel and Organisation Todt workers.

The VII Corps attacked early on June 19. On the left, the 9th Division (Major General Manton S. Eddy) encountered no opposition and easily reached its designated objectives. In the centre, the 79th Division (Major General Ira T. Wyche) did the same on its left wing although it experienced some difficulties on its right south-west of Valognes. Only the 4th Division (Major General Raymond O. Barton) on the right wing came up against organised resistance when the 8th and 12th Infantry Regiments attacked side by side

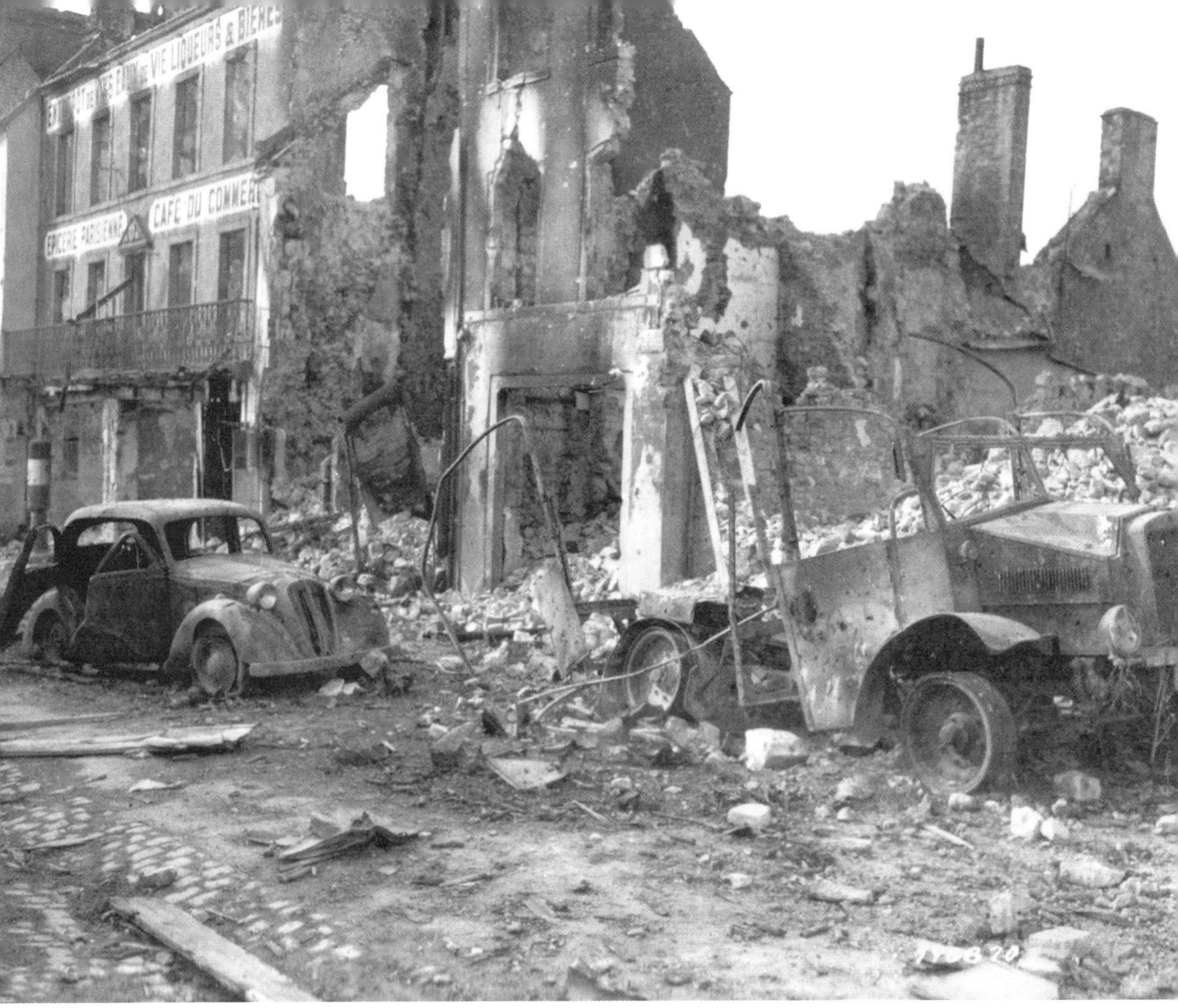

'Whoever owns Montebourg owns Cherbourg'. This saying was born during the Hundred Years' War, when the village changed hands several times from 1346, when English troops burned it, until 1450 and the final capitulation of the English garrison of Cherbourg. On the afternoon of June 8, an Allied plane strafed a German convoy as it passed through Montebourg, en route to Valognes. (USNA)

on a north-west axis on either side of Montebourg. However, tank support got the attack moving and both regiments soon broke the German line. By nightfall the 8th Infantry was just south and east of Valognes with the 12th Infantry on its right. The 22nd Infantry entered Montebourg at 6 p.m. and found the town deserted.

The resistance in front of the 4th Division on June 19 was little more than a gesture by General von Schlieben at carrying out his orders to fight his way slowly back to fortress Cherbourg. The orders could scarcely have been carried out. On his west flank, von Schlieben had no positions to hold and only disorganised troops who would have been needlessly sacrificed if they had attempted a stand. The plunge forward of the 9th and 79th Divisions during June 19 rendered defence of the sector opposite the 4th Division useless and dangerous. During the night, therefore, von Schlieben ordered a general disengagement on this front and drew all his force back to the fortress ring immediately defending Cherbourg.

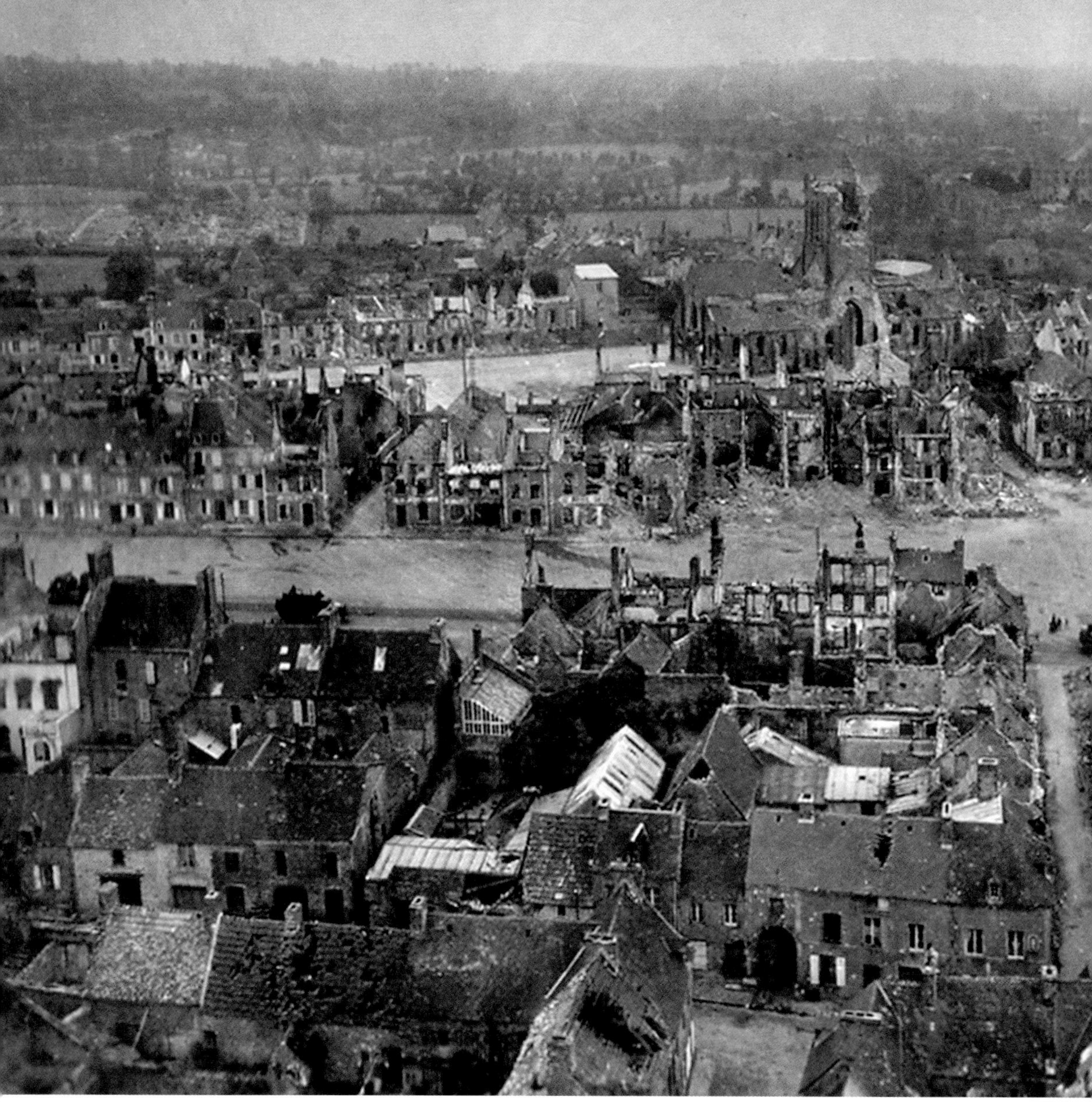

The battle for Montebourg lasted ten days until June 18 when, with the 9th Division's advance on the west side of the peninsula threatening to outflank his positions, the German commander, Generalleutnant Karl-Wilhelm von Schlieben, ordered all his troops back to the fortress ring defending Cherbourg. Montebourg was abandoned that night and the 22nd Infantry entered the deserted town without difficulty the next day. Of the town's 487 buildings, 393 were totally destroyed, and the streets were lined with ruins and filled with rubble. To the right in this aerial view is Rue Paul Lecacheux, the city's main artery, which can be seen in several photos. (USNA)

When the 4th Division resumed the attack on June 20, it found open country ahead. At first the troops advanced cautiously. They paused to investigate Valognes. The city was choked with rubble but no enemy were in sight. By noon it was clear that the enemy had broken all contact and the regiments took route march formations on the roads and walked north. In this way all arrived by nightfall on their objectives in a line from Le Theil to the Bois de Roudou. This line was just in front of the main enemy defences of Cherbourg and, as the leading companies approached, they brushed with

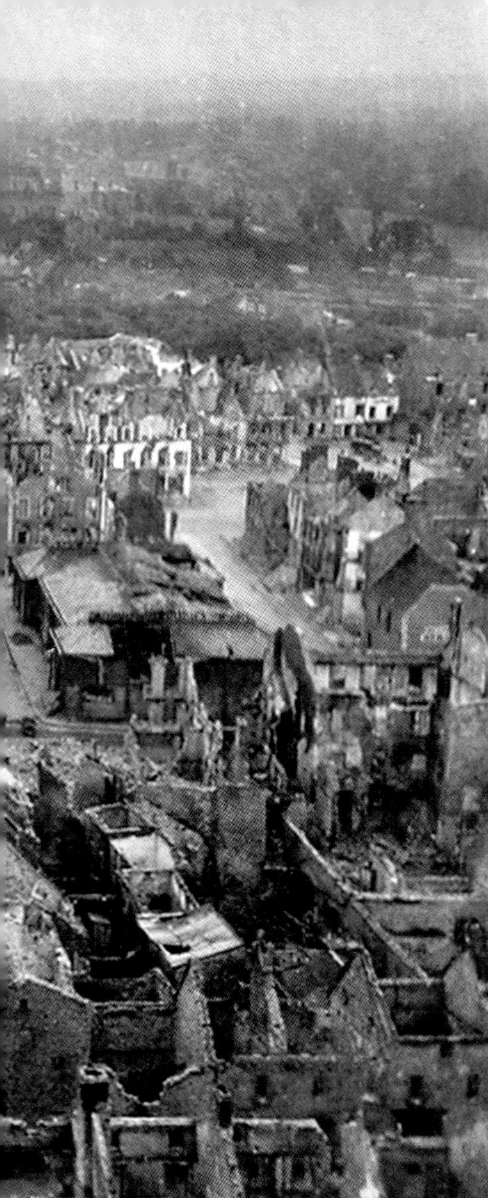

enemy outposts and in some cases came under severe hostile artillery fire.

The experience of the 79th Division on June 20 was similar. Both the 313th and 314th Infantry Regiments advanced to the road running roughly east-west between the Bois de Roudou and Saint-Martin-le-Gréard. On that line both met resistance which clearly indicated that they had hit outposts of the Cherbourg defences. Eloquent of the haste with which the Germans had withdrawn was the capture intact at one point of four light tanks and an 88mm gun and at another of eight tanks. The 315th Infantry during the day cleared stragglers from the Valognes area and then moved into reserve positions behind the lead regiments.

The 9th Division, which on June 19 had already come up against the outer veil of the main enemy defences, had quite a different experience on June 20. On wings of optimism in the course of the rapid unopposed advance of June 19, VII Corps had given General Eddy objectives deep inside fortress Cherbourg: Flottemanville, Octeville and positions athwart the Cherbourg–Cap de la Hague road.

The advance of the 60th Infantry, paralleling the main enemy defences, was rapid until about noon when it reached high ground a few hundred yards from its initial objective, Hill 170. It was slowed then by increasing enemy artillery fire. Delay here, however, was not serious, for sufficient advance had been made to permit the 47th Infantry following to come up west of its objectives and make the turn east. The 1st and 2nd Battalions attacked abreast north and south of the Bois de Nerest. Both were stopped not far from their line of departure as the enemy suddenly uncovered a stiff and carefully prepared defence. The experience of the 2nd Battalion was typical of what happened all along the front as VII Corps pressed in on the enemy's last bastion. Fired on by German outposts in houses at a crossroads south-east of Acqueville, the battalion was first checked. Then from the main enemy positions on hills

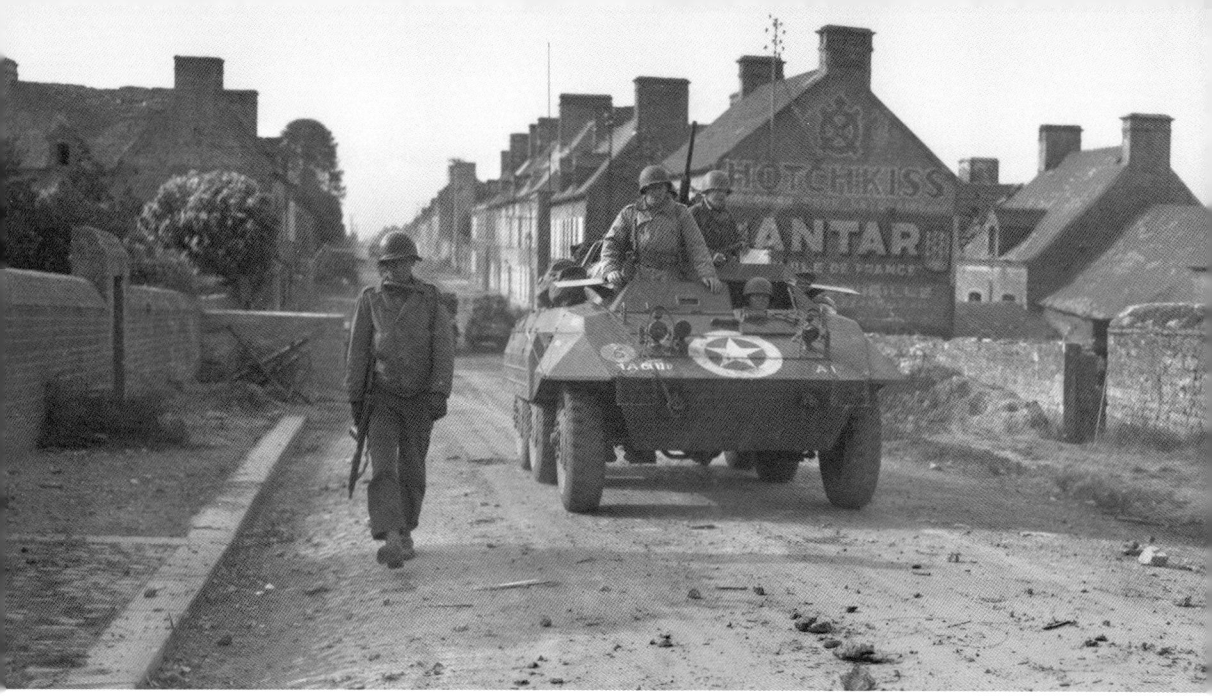

Engineers quickly cleared the streets of collapsed buildings and walls, and traffic soon headed towards Valognes, the next town on the road to Cherbourg. Signal Corps photographer Sergeant Peter J. Petrony pictured a M8 armoured car of the 801st Tank Destroyer Battalion entering Montebourg during the northward advance toward the port city. (USNA and ATB)

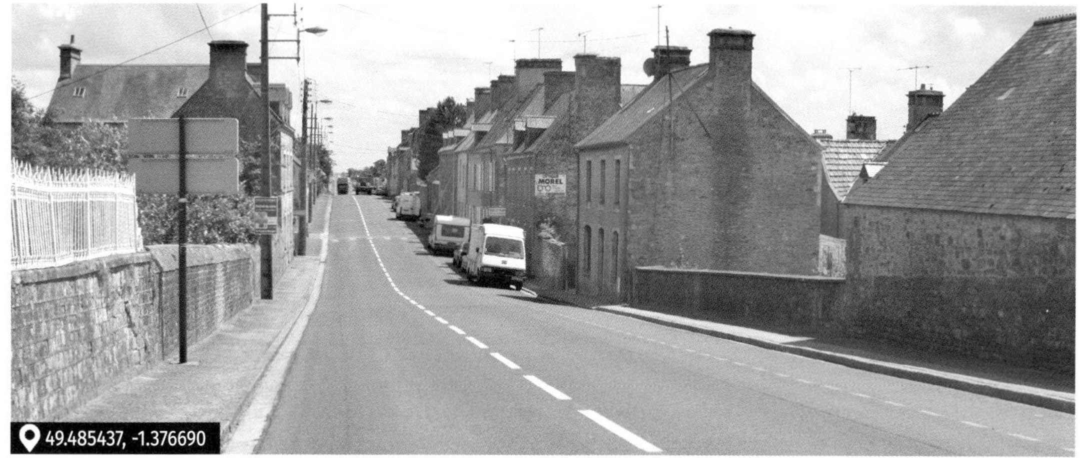

to the east came withering direct and indirect fire from 88mm, 20mm and machine guns. The command group of the battalion was hit by a shell burst, the commander, Lieutenant Colonel James D. Johnston, mortally wounded, and several of his officers injured. Unable to push forward, the battalion had to withdraw out of the area of concentrated fire.

Since, with the 47th Infantry stopped, the 39th would be unable to advance past it toward objectives to the north, General Eddy promptly altered the division plan. Objectives at Flottemanville were assigned to the 1st and 2nd Battalions of the 60th Infantry while the 3rd Battalion was directed to carry out a portion of the regiment's original blocking mission by taking positions on the crossroads formed by the junction of the Les Pieux and Cherbourg

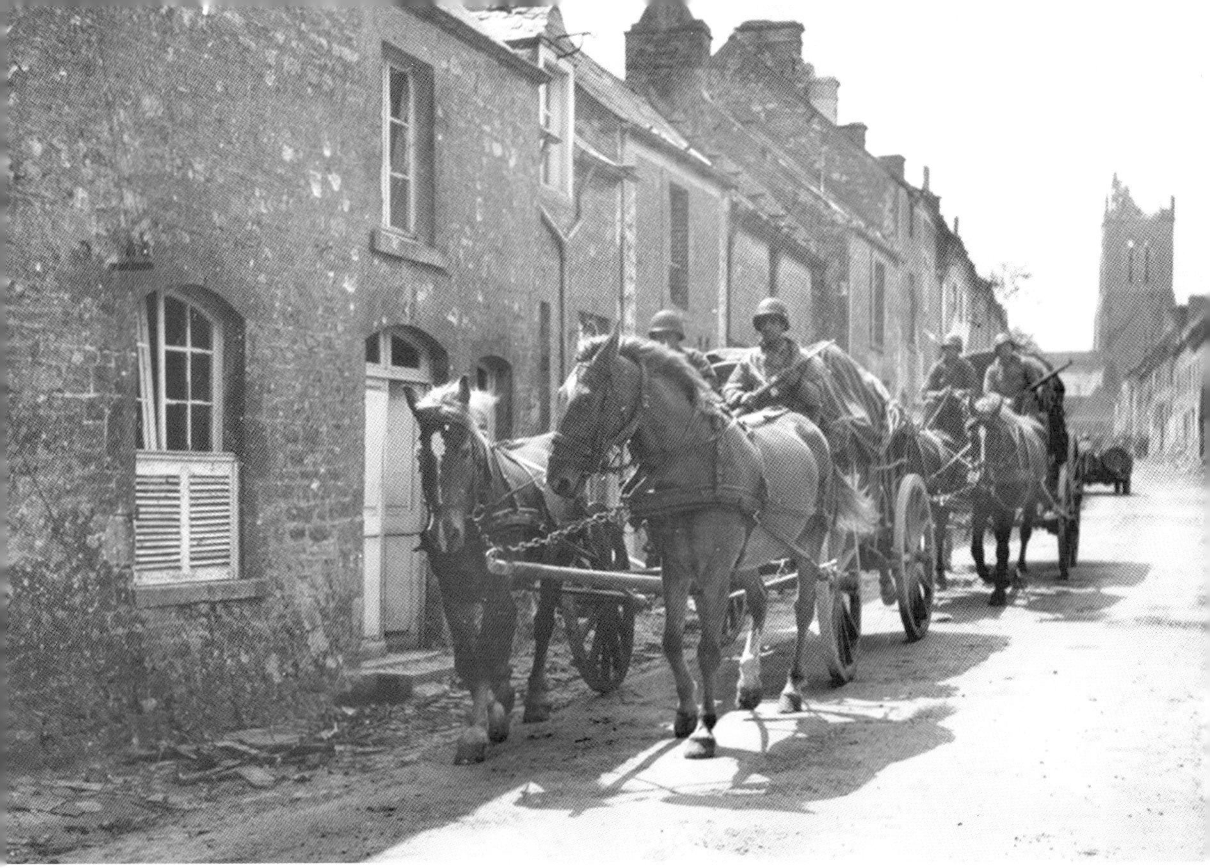

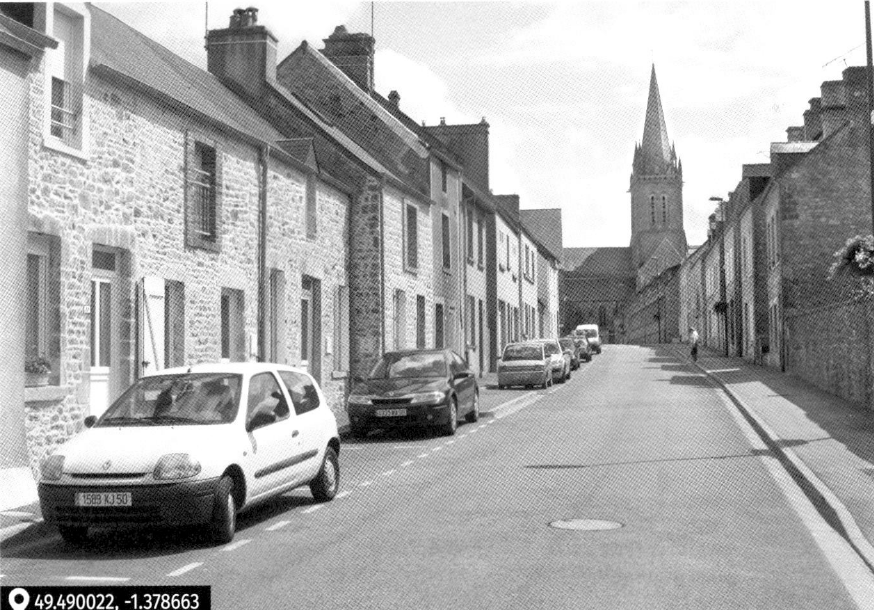

Horse drawn carriages abandoned by the Germans were recovered and put into service. In the background, the ruined Saint-Jacques church. Rue Verglais, Then and Now. (USNA and ATB)

roads into Cap de la Hague. Again, the advance north proved relatively easy and the 3rd Battalion came within 1,000 yards of its objectives. But the two battalions that attempted to turn east were stopped virtually in their tracks in front of Gourbesville. The 9th Division ground to a halt. Road marches were over; hard fighting lay ahead.

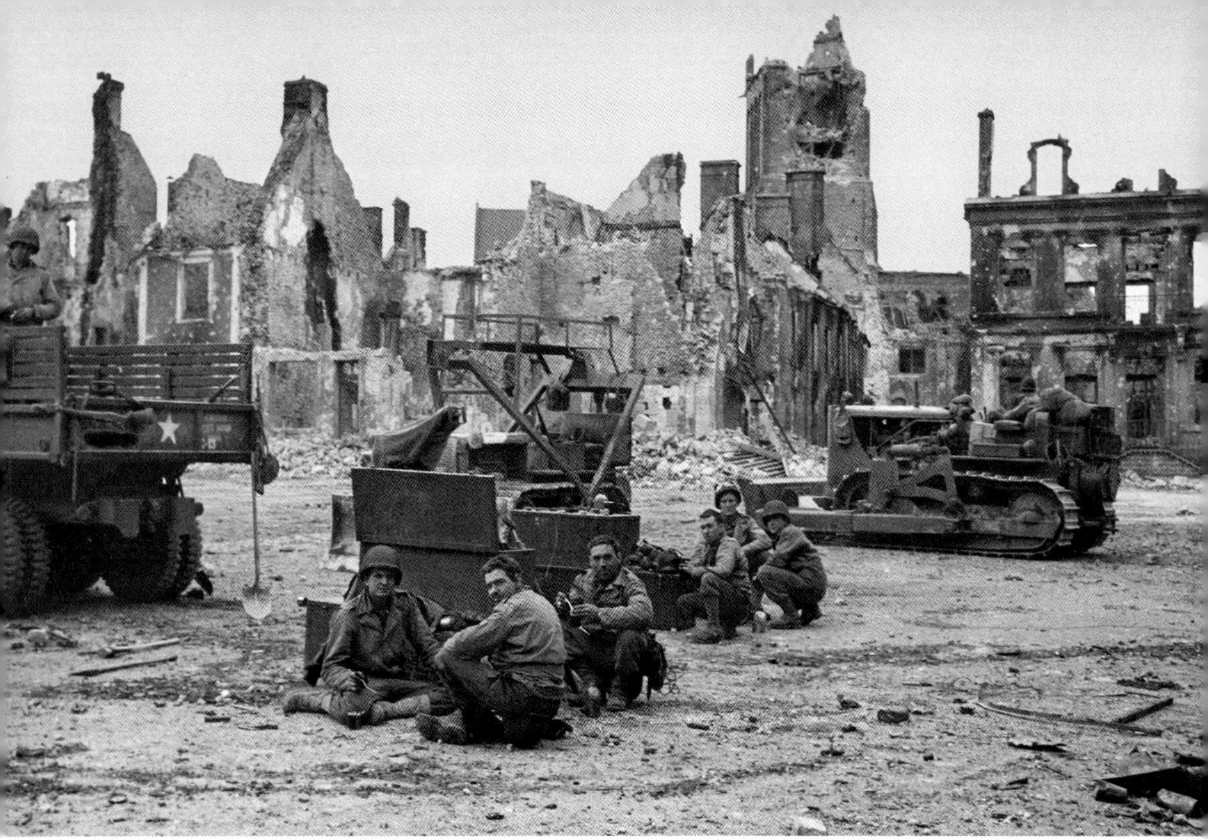

Bulldozer teams took a break on Place Jeanne d'Arc after hours of work to clear a path into devastated Montebourg. (USNA)

Valognes was repeatedly bombed from June 6 onwards, with the worst raid taking place on the 8th when the centre of the town was destroyed and over 100 civilians buried under the rubble. Jeep 'Always Ruth' belonged to the 298th Engineer Combat Battalion. This part of Valognes was so utterly devastated that it was completely rebuilt. However, the surviving parts of the Saint-Malo church were incorporated into the new church. (USNA)

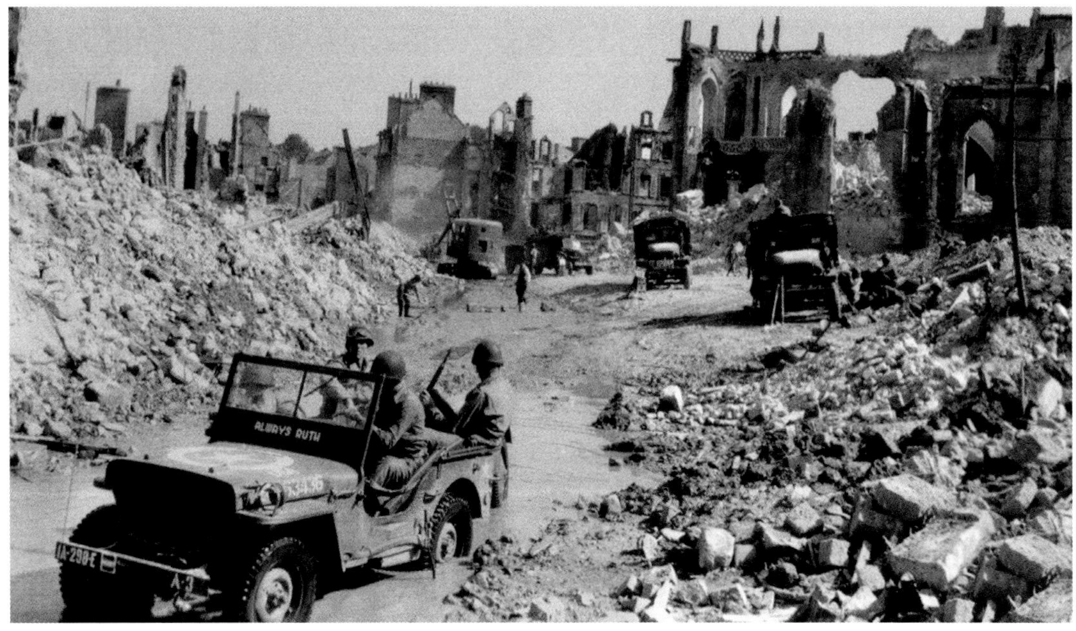

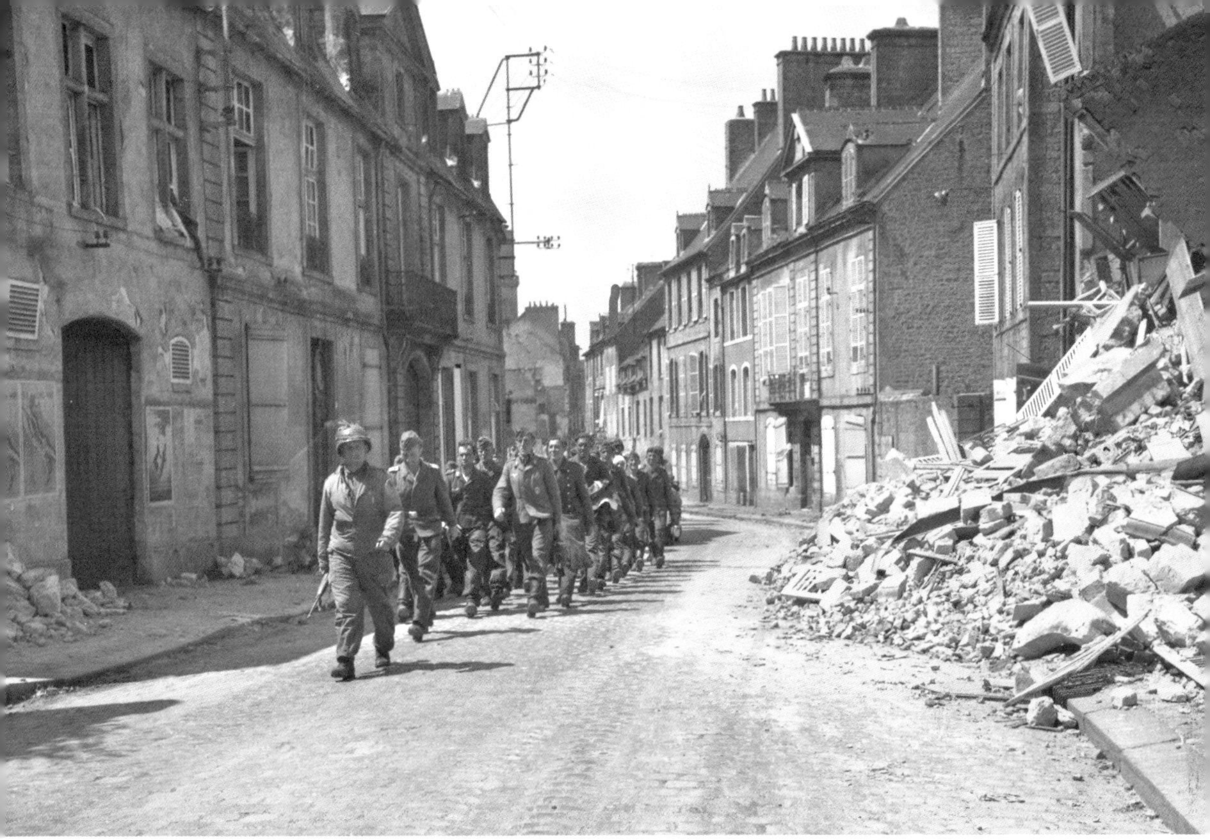

Private Malvin A. Gillespie led a group of German prisoners through a less-damaged section of Valognes on June 21. The picture was taken in Rue des Religieuses and the prisoners were being marched south-eastwards in the direction of Montebourg. (USNA and ATB)

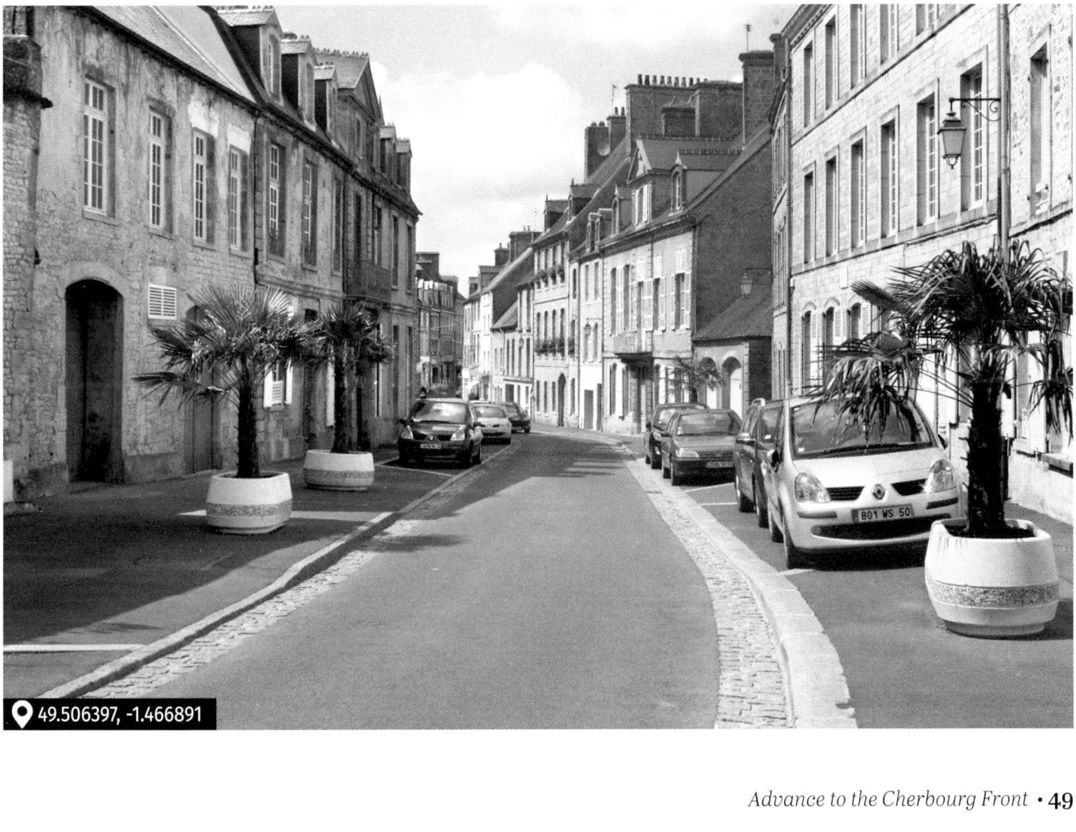

FESTUNG CHERBOURG

THE GERMAN DEFENCES facing the VII Corps consisted of a belt of field fortifications disposed in a rough semi-circle along favourable terrain from six to ten kilometres out from the harbour. However, the German command had fallen into the same trap as had the British at Singapore, namely forgetting that Cherbourg might be attacked from the rear, so that defences facing inland were only very partially built by June 1944. Only two positions on the coast – Osteck (Eastern Corner) near Carneville and

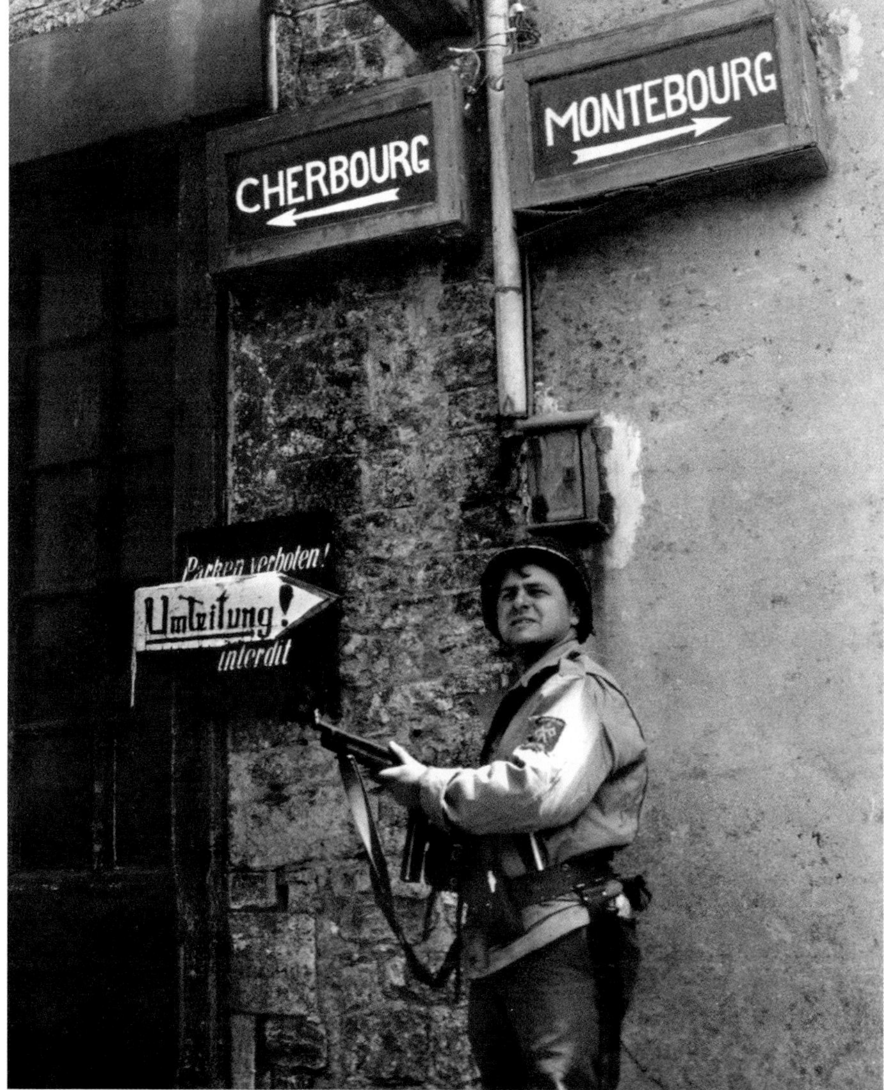

On June 21, Signal Corps photographer Corporal David Balberg, posed in front of German signs pointing to Cherbourg and Montebourg. 'Parken Verboten' means 'No Parking' and 'Umleitung' means 'Diversion'. A member of the 165th Signal Photo Company, he wore a Signal Corps patch on his jacket. (USNA)

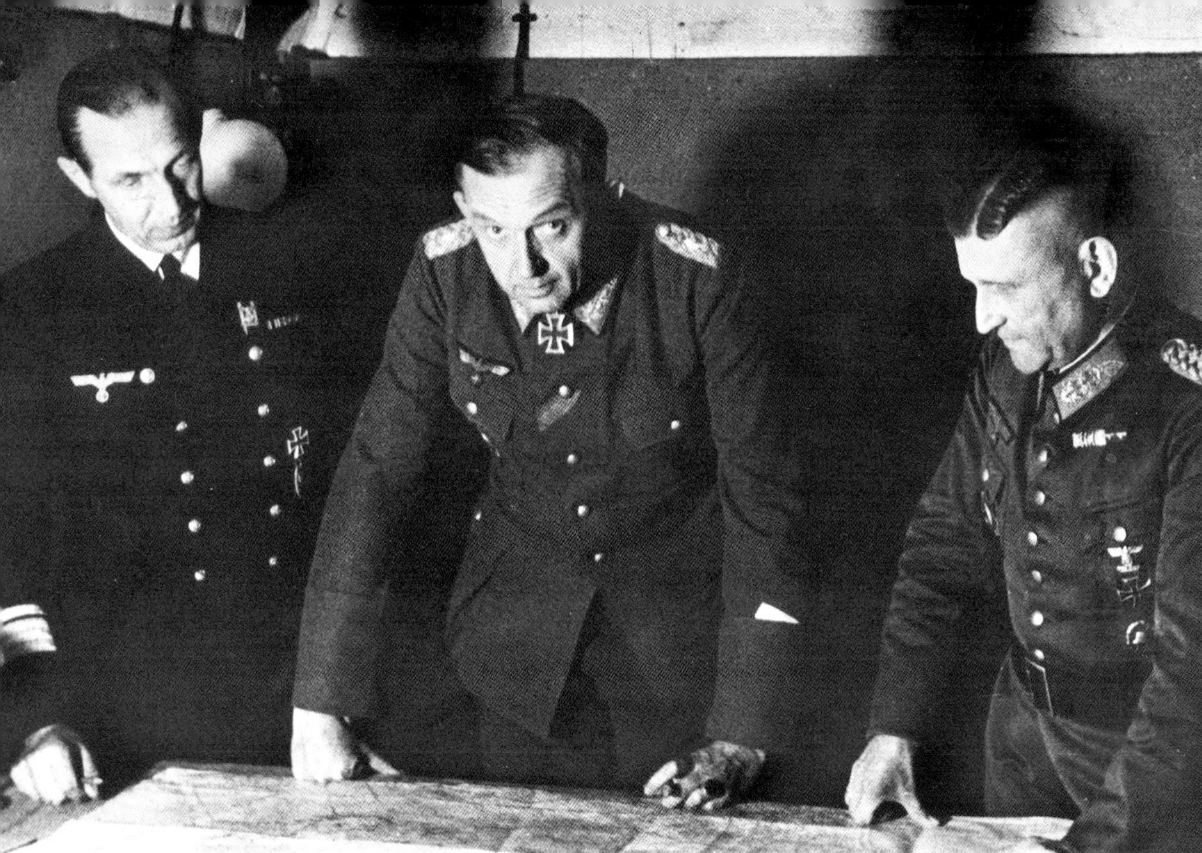

On June 23, Generalleutnant von Schlieben (centre) was appointed commander of Festung Cherbourg, relieving Generalmajor Robert Sattler (right), who became his subordinate. Here they are in their command post with Konteradmiral Walther Hennecke, Naval Commander Normandy (left). (BA)

Westeck (Western Corner) near Gréville-Hague – were well developed, as was a position named Les Chèvres controlling the N13 Valognes to Cherbourg main road. The defence line consisted mainly of trenches and foxholes, but in the best-developed sectors there were some concrete structures with machine-gun turrets and mortars. Most of these fixed defences were known to the Allies and already overprinted on the maps issued to all the American commanders. From east to west, the line ran approximately as follows: Cap Lévy – Maupertus – Le Theil – Hardinvast – Sideville – Hills 128 and 131 – Flottemanville – Sainte-Croix-Hague – Branville – Gruchy. Inside, closer to the harbour, a weak second line of defence had been built along a belt of old French fortifications.

With a total of 20,000 men, at first sight Festung Cherbourg might seem to have been strongly defended. However, this total included a motley collection of security and fortress troops, untrained Flak gunners and naval personnel, and Todt workers. In addition, most of the regular soldiers were over-age and a sizeable part of the force, about one-fifth, were Osttruppen – volunteers from the East, generally Russian ex-prisoners of war. The combat efficiency of these troops was extremely low and General von Schlieben had already reported his worries about this to the 7. Armee. Ammunition was generally sufficient for immediate needs and, except for a shortage of machine-gun cartridges,

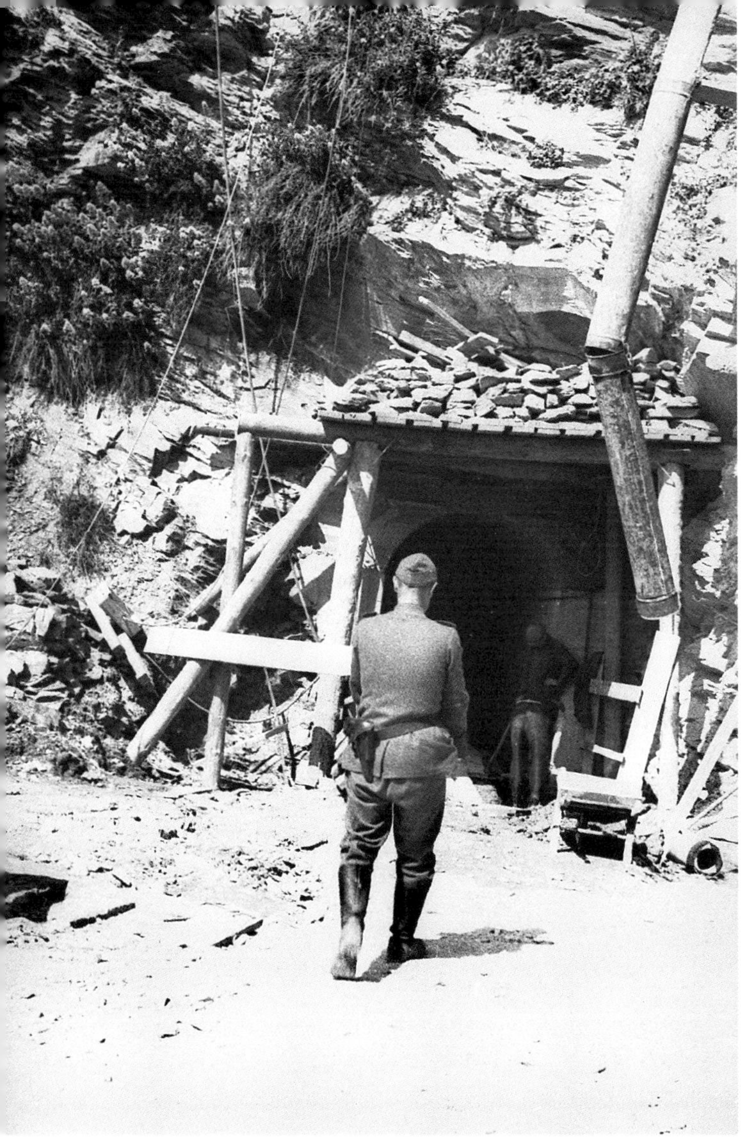

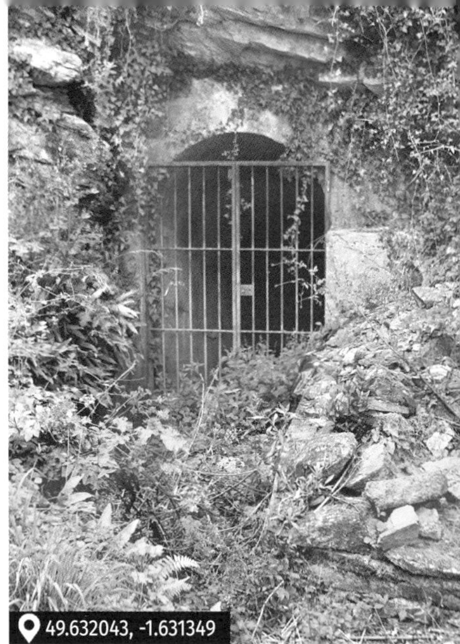

As American troops rapidly invested the fortress, von Schlieben moved his command post into an underground shelter in a quarry at the suburb of Saint-Sauveur, on the south-west outskirts of Cherbourg. Located about 20 metres below the surface, the complex comprised four parallel tunnels, each 4.5 metres wide and about 85 metres long, with two entrances in the quarry at the north-east end and one entrance at the south-west end. A German photographer pictured the main entrance sometime in mid-June, although the exact date is unknown. The main entrance disappeared decades ago when a part of the quarry front subsided but the second entrance still exists, now closed by a strong iron gate. (BA and ATB)

stocks were maintained at adequate levels during the siege by U-Boat and S-Boat deliveries and air drops. (Between June 20 and 30, 107 transport planes dropped 188 tons of supplies to the Cherbourg garrison.)

On June 20, after the retreat from the Montebourg line, von Schlieben reorganised the defences in order to put, as far as possible, regimental commanders with their units in sectors familiar to them. Four regimental Kampfgruppen were formed. On the west was a group under Oberstleutnant Franz Müller, commander of Infanterie-Regiment 922, mainly comprising the remnants of the 243. Infanterie-Division and holding the line from Vauville on the peninsula's west coast to Sainte-Croix-Hague. From there to the Bricquebec – Cherbourg road the line was held by a Kampfgruppe consisting of Infanterie-Regiment 919 and MG-Bataillon 17 (a heavy machine gun battalion) under Oberstleutnant Günther Keil. From there eastward to a point south of Le Mesnil-au-Val was Oberst Walter Köhn with Infanterie-Regiment 739, and on the east was Oberst Helmuth Rohrbach with his Infanterie-Regiment 729.

THE BATTLE OF CHERBOURG

TO THE ALLIES, the capture of Cherbourg was given dramatic urgency by a four-day storm which struck without warning on June 19. When winds began to moderate on June 22, the artificial port at Omaha Beach was a total loss, the beach being littered with wreckage leaving few free areas where new landings could take place. Utah Beach suffered less both in craft losses and beach wreckage since landings could be extended northward and unloading was resumed at full scale on the 23rd. Before the storm had ended, General Collins had issued orders for the resumption of the attack on Cherbourg, stressing that the attack was now to be 'the major effort of the American army'.

The 9th and 79th Divisions devoted the 21st to patrolling and reorganisation while the 4th Division, still a little short of the enemy's ring of prepared defences, continued its advance to the main line of German resistance. By evening, all three divisions of VII Corps were drawn up tight against the Cherbourg fortress, ready for the final assault.

Collins requested air pulverisation of some 20 square miles before the jump-off, more to demoralise the Germans and force surrender than as direct preparation for the ground advance. The air strike would employ the entire US IX Bomber Command (medium bombers) as well as large numbers of US and British fighter-bombers. The plan was developed under great difficulties not only because time was short but also because all the units of the US Ninth Air Force participating in the attack were based in England.

All air preparation was to be concentrated in the zones of the 79th and 9th Divisions south and south-west of Cherbourg. Starting 80 minutes before H-Hour, four squadrons of Typhoon fighter-bombers of the British Second Tactical Air Force were to attack with rockets throughout the northern portion of the attack zone concentrating on enemy anti-aircraft positions. Following them, six squadrons of Mustangs also belonging to the British tactical air forces would strafe throughout the area. From H minus 60 minutes, 12 groups of Ninth Air Force fighter-bombers would bomb and strafe enemy strong points in front of the American lines, attacking in waves at five-minute intervals. As ground troops moved out, all 11 groups of the US IX Bomber Command were to bomb 11 defended localities in a pattern bombing designed to constitute a kind of rolling barrage in front of the ground attack. Despite the large number of aircraft involved, the bombs to be dropped amounted to only about 1,100 tons over a wide area. The attack was not intended as a carpet bombing of the type later used at Caen and in the Saint-Lô break-out. The idea was to achieve the maximum demoralisation of an enemy who, because he was already in a state of hopeless siege, might be expected to have an already weakened morale.

The hopelessness of the German position was pointed out to the Cherbourg garrison in a multilingual broadcast (German, Russian, Polish, and French) on the night of June 21/22 when General Collins demanded the immediate surrender of Cherbourg. General von Schlieben was given until 0900 hours the following morning to capitulate. But the ultimatum expired without answer from von Schlieben. Preparations were therefore completed for the assault.

Attack into Cherbourg itself was to be made by the 9th and 79th Divisions while the 4th Division sealed off the city from the east. The 9th Division, making its main effort on its right, would seize Octeville while the 79th Division captured the nose of high ground which terminated in the Fort du Roule overlooking Cherbourg from the south. This would bring both divisions up on the high ground immediately ringing the port. The 4th Division on the right was to capture Tourlaville and send patrols from there to the sea. H-Hour was set for 1400 hours.

The large bombing operation began according to plan at 1240, June 22. For 20 minutes hundreds of fighters dived, strafed and skip-bombed from altitudes as low as 300 feet. Twenty-five were lost to the Flak. The end of the nerve-wrecking attack signalled only the beginning of an hour of relentless bombing – wave after wave (375 bombers in all) B-26s and A-20s dropped their bombs on or near the six principal targets, forming a 55-minute aerial barrage moving north in advance of the ground forces: Flottemanville, Martinvast, Les Chèvres, La Mare-à-Canards, Fort du Roule, and a defended locality just west of Octeville. (In the 9th Division zone, the white phosphorous and yellow smoke markers laid by the division artillery were unfortunately moved back by the wind and the 47th and 60th Infantry were bombed and strafed by their own aircraft, causing many casualties.) At the same time, artillery shelled enemy anti-aircraft batteries, with particular effectiveness in the 9th Division zone, and then, after troops began to move, fired on enemy defences.

All three divisions made slow advances during the afternoon. The 9th Division attacked with the 60th Infantry on the left and the 47th Infantry (backed by the 39th Infantry) on the right. The axis of advance remained the same: the 60th pointed toward Flottemanville, the 47th toward the Bois du Mont du Roc. The 39th Infantry was assembled near Helleville. The 60th Infantry, attacking with battalions echeloned to the left to guard its open flank, at first moved rapidly and captured Acqueville within half an hour of the jump-off. The 47th similarly moved past Crossroads 114 where it had been held up on June 21 and pushed one battalion beyond Beaudienville. But the latter advance was made by bypassing the enemy at the crossroads and it had to be halted in the early evening to permit mopping up. At the end of June 22, forward battalions were dug in on the slopes of Hill 171 just west of the Bois du Mont du Roc. The 60th Infantry pressed the attack to the edge of enemy fortifications at Flottemanville but could not penetrate the position before dark.

The 79th Division, attacking with three regiments abreast, came up against similarly stubborn enemy resistance. The 313th Infantry, making the division's main effort along the Valognes – Cherbourg highway, was first stopped by the Les Chèvres strong point which straddled the road. The German line was broken by the 3rd Battalion on the left and rolled up, while the 1st Battalion attacked frontally. After reorganisation, the regiment pushed on against lighter resistance to reach a point just south of its next major obstacle – the fortified anti-aircraft position at La Mare-à-Canards. The 315th Infantry meanwhile spent the day fighting to clear the Hardinvast area. The 314th Infantry fought in the draws east of Tollevast until after dark, when one battalion slipped around the enemy positions and made contact with the 313th Infantry west of Crossroads 177. At this point the 314th was only a few hundred yards from a German communications bunker which contained the switchboard for the entire Cherbourg sector. The bunker was not discovered and remained to function for a day or so behind the American lines, reporting to von Schlieben some details of American movements.

The three regiments of the 4th Division experienced hard, confused fighting on June 22 which netted only small gains. The main effort was made by the 12th Infantry attacking north-west from the northern tip of the Bois du Coudray with the mission of seizing Tourlaville. But in confused fighting, during which the enemy continually filtered to the rear of the forward battalions, the regiment was able to advance only a few hundred yards. On its right the 22nd Infantry, which was to have attacked from positions near Gonneville to take Digosville and so support the effort of the 12th Infantry, found itself surrounded by the enemy and spent the whole day trying to clear its own rear areas to keep its supply routes open. The 8th Infantry on the division left flank had the mission of capturing high ground east of La Glacerie in the triangle between the Trottebec river and its principal tributary, where it would be pinched out by the north-west advance of the 12th Infantry on Tourlaville. Attacking from the north edge of the Bois de Roudou, the regiment made little progress. One of its battalions, attempting to envelop the enemy line, was caught by delayed enemy fire from prepared hedgerow positions and by tree-burst artillery fire; it lost 31 killed and 92 wounded.

On June 22 General von Schlieben received from Hitler full authority for the defence of the port: 'Even if worst comes to worst, it is your duty to defend the last bunker and leave to the enemy not a harbour but a field of ruins... The German people and the whole world are watching your fight; on it depends the conduct and result of operations to smash the beach-heads, and the honour of the German Army and of your own name.'

Von Schlieben knew well that the final stand would not last long. He told Rommel that his own troops were exhausted in body and spirit; that the port garrison was over-age, untrained and suffering from 'bunker paralysis' (verbunkert), and that the leaderless remnants of the 243. and 77. Infanterie-Divisions were more of a burden than a support. 'Reinforcement', he concluded, 'is absolutely necessary'.

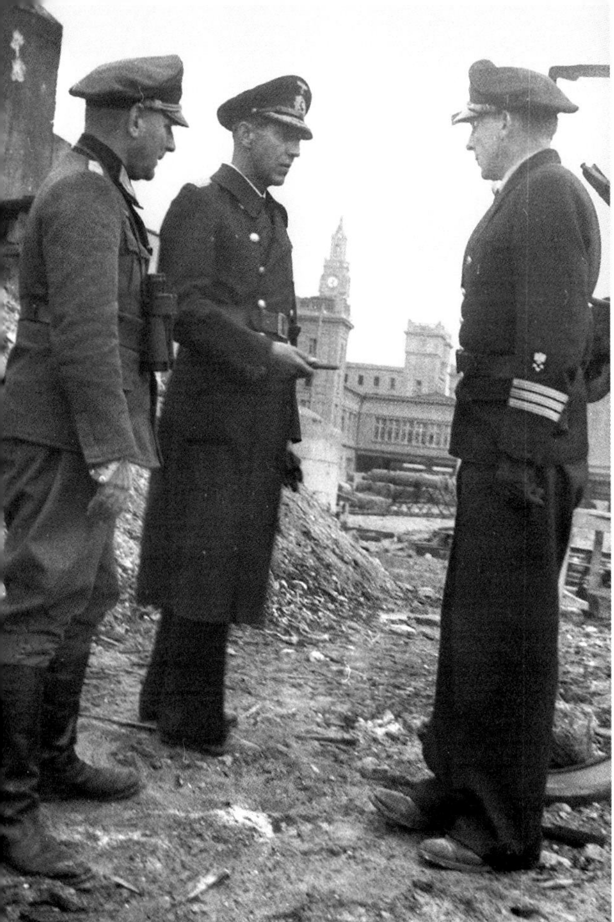
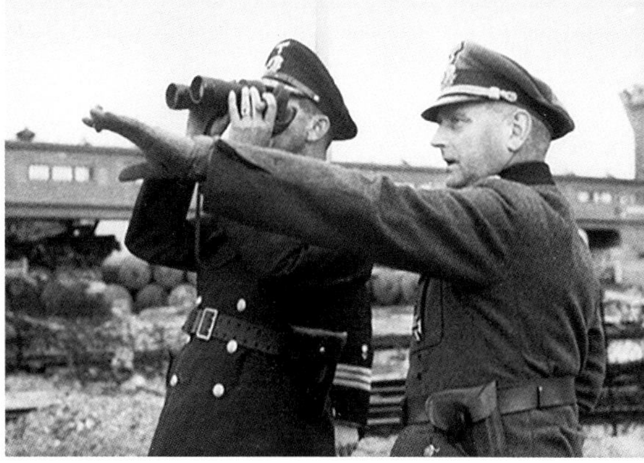
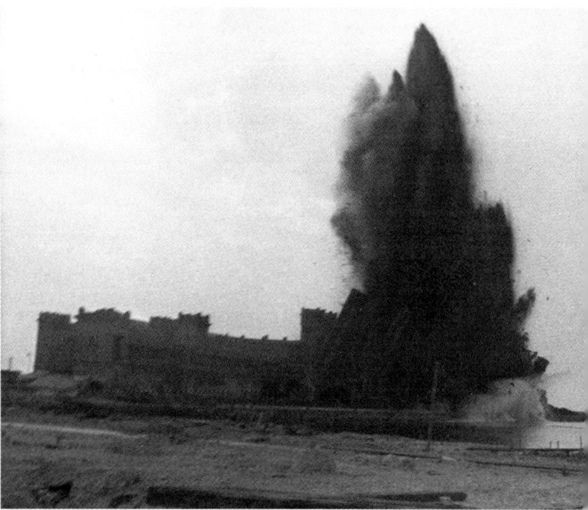

Methodically carried out by Kriegsmarine personnel, the destruction of port installations began on June 7 and continued until the final capitulation. In company with an unidentified Korvettenkapitän (right), Fregattenkapitän Hermann Witt (left), harbour commander, and Konteradmiral Hennecke (centre) completed their plans to destroy the Gare Maritime. The 70-metre-high Campanile was still standing when a PK photographer took this photo sometime in June 1944 but it was soon to be blown down. (BA)

Reinforcement was briefly contemplated the next day, Fallschirmjäger-Regiment 15 in Brittany being alerted for movement by sea to Cherbourg. However, a few hours later, reports of the complete destruction and closing of the Cherbourg harbour (by German engineer troops) caused the move to be cancelled. Dropping of parachute troops was considered but no aircraft were available.

JUNE 23

Fighting on June 23 was still heavy, but all three American divisions made significant penetrations into the main German defences. In the 9th Division zone, the 39th Infantry cleared fortified positions north-west of Beaudienville, which had been bypassed. The 47th Infantry completed the reduction of enemy defences on Hill 171, capturing 400 prisoners during the day's fighting. The two regiments thus established themselves firmly astride the ridge leading to Cherbourg inside the outer ring of enemy defences. The 60th Infantry, after a long-delayed air bombardment and artillery concentrations on the Flottemanville area, moved in to occupy its objective with comparative ease in the evening.

The 79th Division was troubled at first by enemy infiltrations behind the forward regiments. While these were cleared up, the 314th Infantry attacked the enemy positions at La Mare-à-Canards. The attack failed to achieve its objective, but one company worked around to the north-west and was able to hold there while the remainder of the regiment was withdrawn a little to await air bombardment.

The 4th Division, though unable to reach its principal objective, Tourlaville, made good progress on June 23 as the attack of the 12th Infantry with tank support began to gather momentum. Two tanks attached to each of the forward companies of the lead battalion moved generally along the roads, firing in support of the infantry and, on occasion, turning into the fields to steamroller enemy riflemen. In the evening, behind a rolling artillery barrage laid close to their front, the troops marched up a hill that commanded the approaches to Cherbourg and dug in for the night, ready for the final assault on Tourlaville. The 22nd Infantry again on June 23 was occupied mainly with clearing enemy from its own sector. One battalion, eventually released for attack north-west, was stopped at once by heavy German fire. The 8th Infantry, while scoring only minor advances during the day, had one notable success when the 3rd Battalion launched an attack at the very moment when the enemy was forming for counter-attack. Finding the Germans lying head to heel along some hedgerows, the battalion opened rifle and tank fire and routed them with heavy losses.

With the penetrations into the outer ring of the Cherbourg fortress, the battle for the port entered its final phase. General von Schlieben reported on the morning of the 24th that he had no reserves left. The fall of Cherbourg, he said, is inevitable. 'The only question is whether it is possible to postpone it for a few days'.

JUNE 24

On June 24 VII Corps closed in on the city. The 9th Division overran three defended Luftwaffe installations as the 47th and 39th Infantry Regiments attacked along the ridge north-east into Octeville while the 60th Infantry held and cleared the north flank. Enemy fire was often heavy but, when the American infantry closed in, the defence crumbled. The 39th Infantry in the evening halted and established positions in front of Octeville under corps orders not to become involved in the city that day. The 47th Infantry, after assisting the 39th in the capture of an anti-aircraft emplacement, turned north toward the old French fort of Equeurdreville, the German coastal battery north of it, and the Redoute des Fourches. With the coming of darkness, however, attack on these positions was postponed.

In the 79th Division zone the 314th Infantry, supported by dive-bombing P-47s of the Ninth Air Force, cleared La Mare-à-Canards and pushed on to within sight of the Fort du Roule. Three attempts to break through to the fort were frustrated by fire from the direction of Octeville on the division's dangling left flank. The 315th Infantry on the left was far behind, still engaged at Hardinvast. The 313th Infantry, on the other flank, kept pace, veering slightly eastward to reduce resistance west of La Glacerie and at Gringor. At the latter position 320 prisoners and several artillery pieces were taken.

The whole Cherbourg defence was collapsing and nowhere more completely than on the east. But the collapse was preceded by some bitter last stands that exacted heavy toll of some of the attacking units. The 8th Infantry making its last attack before being pinched out between the 12th Infantry and 79th Division, hit determined resistance east of La Glacerie. The Germans here, defending with light artillery, anti-aircraft guns, mortars, and machine guns, threw back the first American attack. The second attempt made with tank support got around to the east of the enemy position and the Germans pulled out. The cost of the day's fighting to the 8th Infantry was 37 killed, including Lieutenant Colonel Conrad Simmons, the 1st Battalion commander.

The 12th Infantry, again making the main divisional effort, now with one battalion of the 22nd Infantry attached, by evening had occupied the last high ground before Tourlaville, from which the city of Cherbourg was visible. In the attack Lieutenant Colonel John W. Merrill, who had taken command of the 1st Battalion the day before, was killed. One of the hardest fights in the area was fought at Digosville where the enemy stood to defend an artillery position. The position was overrun by one company with tank support, after a dive-bombing attack by 12 P-47s. Tourlaville was occupied that night without a fight. In the day's advance the 12th Infantry took 800 prisoners.

That evening General von Schlieben reported: 'Concentrated enemy fire and bombing attacks have split the front. Numerous batteries have been put out of action or have worn out. Combat efficiency has fallen off considerably. The troops squeezed into a small area will hardly be able to withstand an attack on the 25th.'

JUNE 25

To coincide with the final ground assault, General Bradley arranged a strong naval bombardment of the batteries and shore defences guarding the approaches to the city. Commanded by American Rear-Admiral Morton L. Deyo, Task Force 129 comprised three battleships (USS *Arkansas*, *Nevada*, and *Texas*), four cruisers (USS *Quincy* and *Tuscaloosa* and HMS *Enterprise* and *Glasgow*), three American and six British destroyers to provide additional firepower and anti-submarine protection, and the British 9th and 159th Minesweeping Flotillas and US 7th Minesweeping Squadron to clear lanes.

The long-range bombardment initially planned was cancelled shortly before the start of the operation when First Army expressed worries that

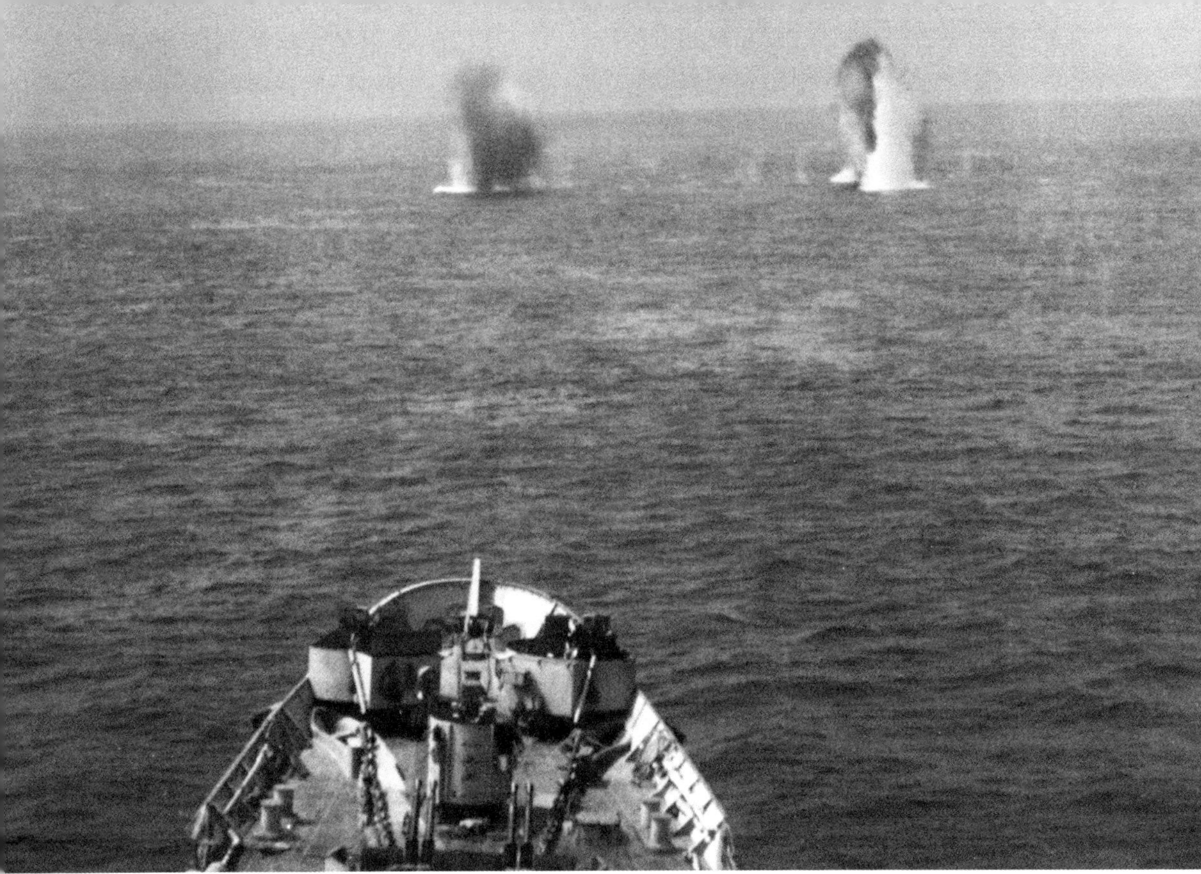

Shortly after noon on June 25, a strong Allied naval force – three battleships, four cruisers, and nine destroyers – manoeuvred off Cherbourg to bombard the German defences. The coastal batteries opened up. The destroyers quickly made smoke, the minesweepers were withdrawn, and the Allied fleet opened up. Seen from the bridge of USS *Quincy*, two shells fell short off the bow. (NHHC)

the leading ground forces might already have entered the firing zones. Therefore, the bombarding ships were brought closer in, to a position about 14,000 metres north of Cherbourg, before opening fire. A congested situation developed at the southern end of the approach channel, where the *Nevada*, *Quincy*, *Tuscaloosa*, *Glasgow*, and *Enterprise* were forced to reduce speed to keep clear of the minesweepers when the whole force was turning from the approach channel into the firing area.

While the ships were in this awkward position, turning at slow speed, German shore batteries – particularly Batterie 'Hamburg' near Fermanville, Batterie 'Brommy' near Le Béquet and Batterie 'York' near Amfreville – opened fire with accuracy. Destroyers made smoke, the bombarding ships increased speed, and within minutes all had opened up on their designated targets, fire soon being shifted to the batteries that were shelling the ships. The *Texas* received a direct hit on her conning tower which wrecked the navigational bridge and facilities. *Glasgow* and destroyers *O'Brien*, *Laffey* and *Barton* also sustained hits and damage to various degrees. The *Nevada* had several near misses that covered her decks with water and splinters but she was not hit. The naval force withdrew at 1530 hours, having fired about 3,000 shells, own casualties being given as 13 killed and 86 wounded.

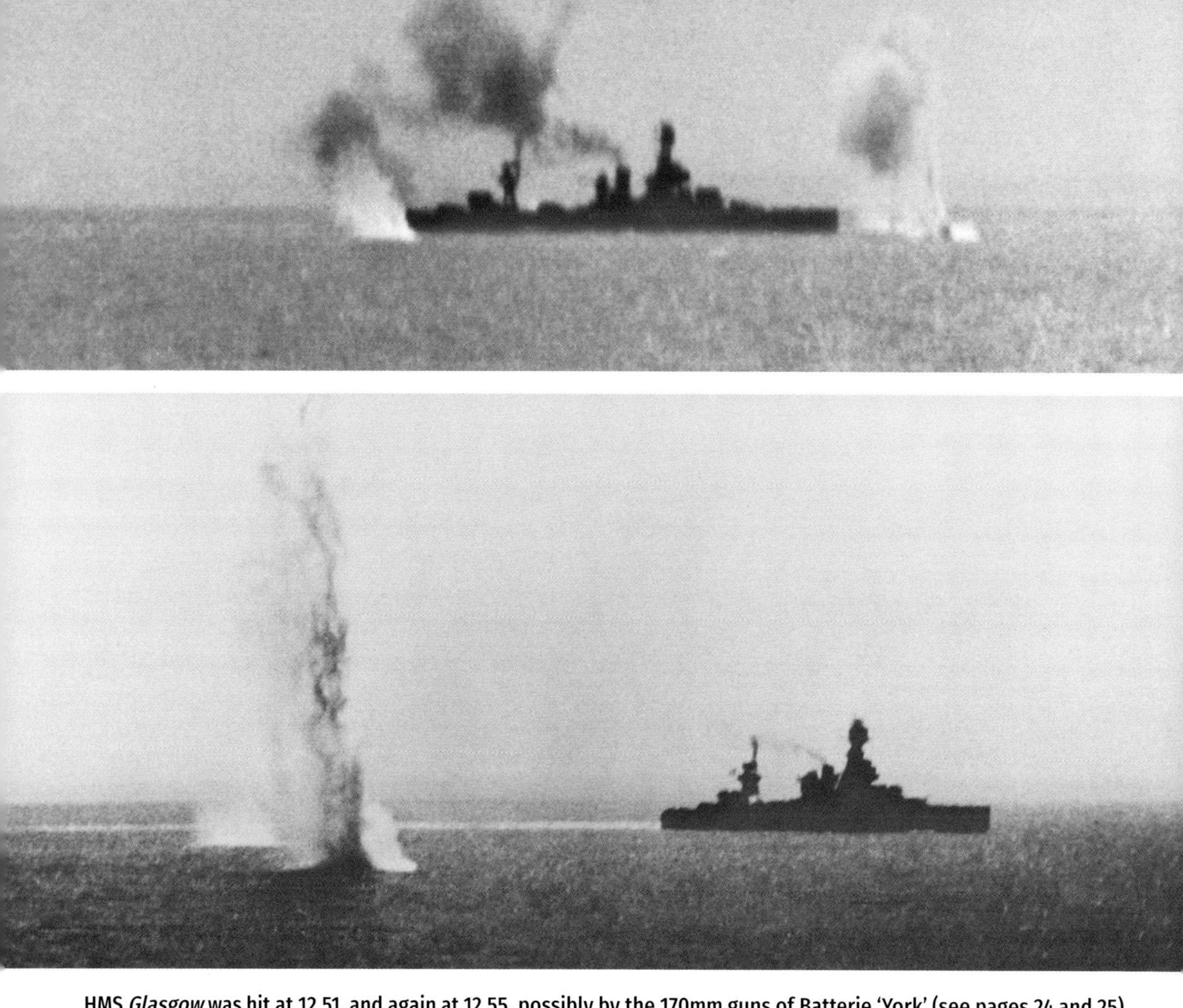

HMS *Glasgow* was hit at 12.51, and again at 12.55, possibly by the 170mm guns of Batterie 'York' (see pages 24 and 25). German shells straddled the USS *Texas* as she bombarded her designated targets. (NHHC)

Early that afternoon von Schlieben reported: 'In addition to superiority in materiel and artillery, air force and tanks, heavy fire from the sea has started, directed by spotter planes'. . . 'I must state in the line of duty', he concluded, 'that further sacrifices cannot alter anything'. To this Rommel replied by radio: 'You will continue to fight until the last cartridge in accordance with the order from the Führer.'

Meanwhile VII Corps was closing in. On the right, the 12th Infantry scarcely paused on reaching its objective of June 24. Continuing the attack through the night and into the day of the 25th, Colonel James S. Luckett pushed hard to accelerate the enemy collapse. The 1st Battalion had a sharp fight to capture Batterie 'Brommy', the coastal battery of four 155mm guns near Le Béquet north of Tourlaville, but in early afternoon the enemy garrison of 400 finally surrendered. The other two battalions patrolled to the coast. In position blocking the eastern approaches to Cherbourg, the regiment and the division had completed their original mission. Early in the afternoon of June 25, however, General Collins altered the division boundary so that the

4th Division could share in the capture of the city. All three battalions of the 12th Infantry entered Cherbourg during the evening. Two battalions cleared the city streets in the eastern portion as far as the limit of the division's zone, hampered only by scattered fire and mines. The 1st Battalion fought all night to reduce pillboxes of beach fortifications east of the Fort des Flamands, but it was not until early the next morning when tanks were brought up that 350 Germans finally decided to surrender. Then at last the 4th Division's part in the capture of Cherbourg was complete.

On the opposite side of the city, the 47th Infantry of the 9th Division was fighting in the suburbs during June 25. After pushing down the ridge toward Octeville with the 39th Infantry, the 47th had turned north in the evening of June 24 to attack Equeurdreville and had pushed one battalion to within 500 yards of the German-held fort of 'Les Couplets' there. The fort was a formidable-appearing position on top of a hill surrounded by a dry moat like a medieval fortress. It was used, however, only as an observation post for the 'Les Couplets' coastal battery on the reverse slope (which had four 155mm guns on open platforms) and was not well defended from the south. In the morning of June 25 the fort was shelled and one company of the 2nd Battalion attacked after a mortar barrage. In 15 minutes the German garrison surrendered. Two companies then pushed rapidly into Equeurdreville and a platoon got to the beach, but it was withdrawn for the night. At the

A shell falls between USS *Texas*, in the background, and USS *Arkansas*, a photograph taken from the *Arkansas*. (USNA)

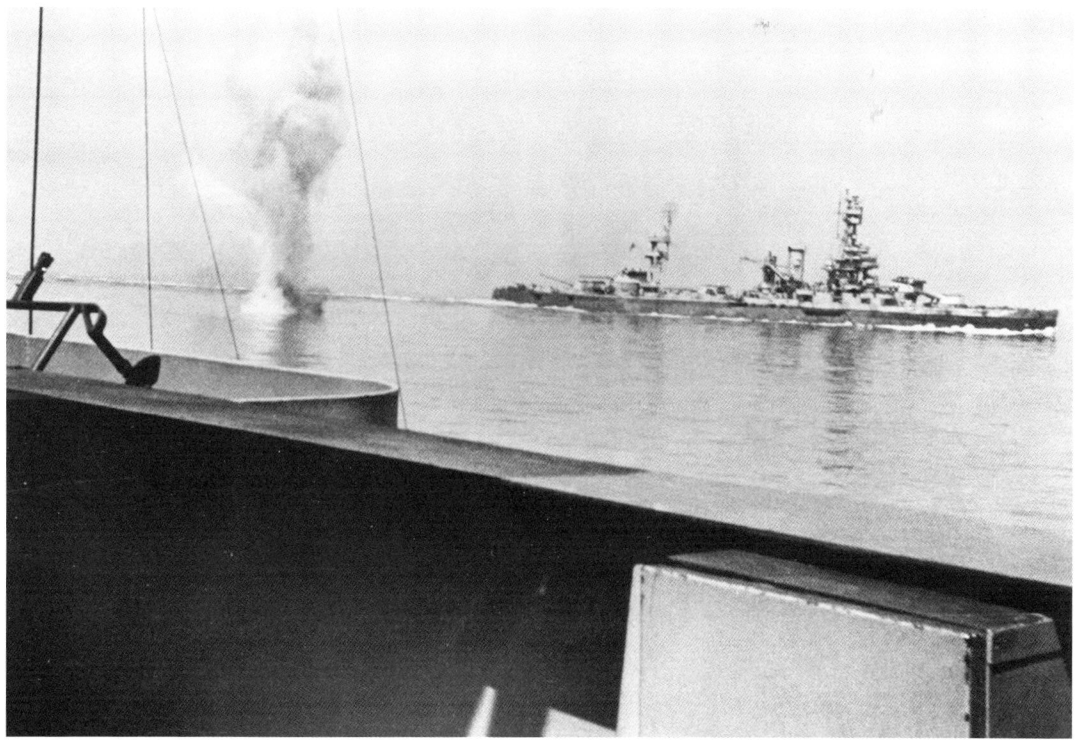

same time the 3rd Battalion reduced the Redoute des Fourches with heavy artillery support. The enemy's right had now collapsed as thoroughly as his left on the day before, although a node of resistance in Octeville held up the 39th Infantry. The 9th Division took more than 1,000 prisoners in the day's fighting.

In the 79th Division zone, just such a fanatic defence was in progress where the garrison of the Fort du Roule south of Cherbourg chose to fight it out. This fort, principal objective of the 79th Division, was one of the most formidable of the Cherbourg bastions. It was built into the face of a rocky promontory above the city and housed four 105mm coastal guns commanding the entire harbour area. The guns were in lower levels under the edge of the cliff. In the upper levels were mortars and machine guns in

This photo is reminiscent of the action of Corporal John D. Kelly, 314th Infantry Regiment, crawling up the slope of Fort du Roule to blow up a machine gun pillbox with pole charges (see the three crouching men at the bottom left of the photo). However, if the date in the original caption is correct, June 28, then this is a staged photo taken after the surrender of the German fortress. (USNA)

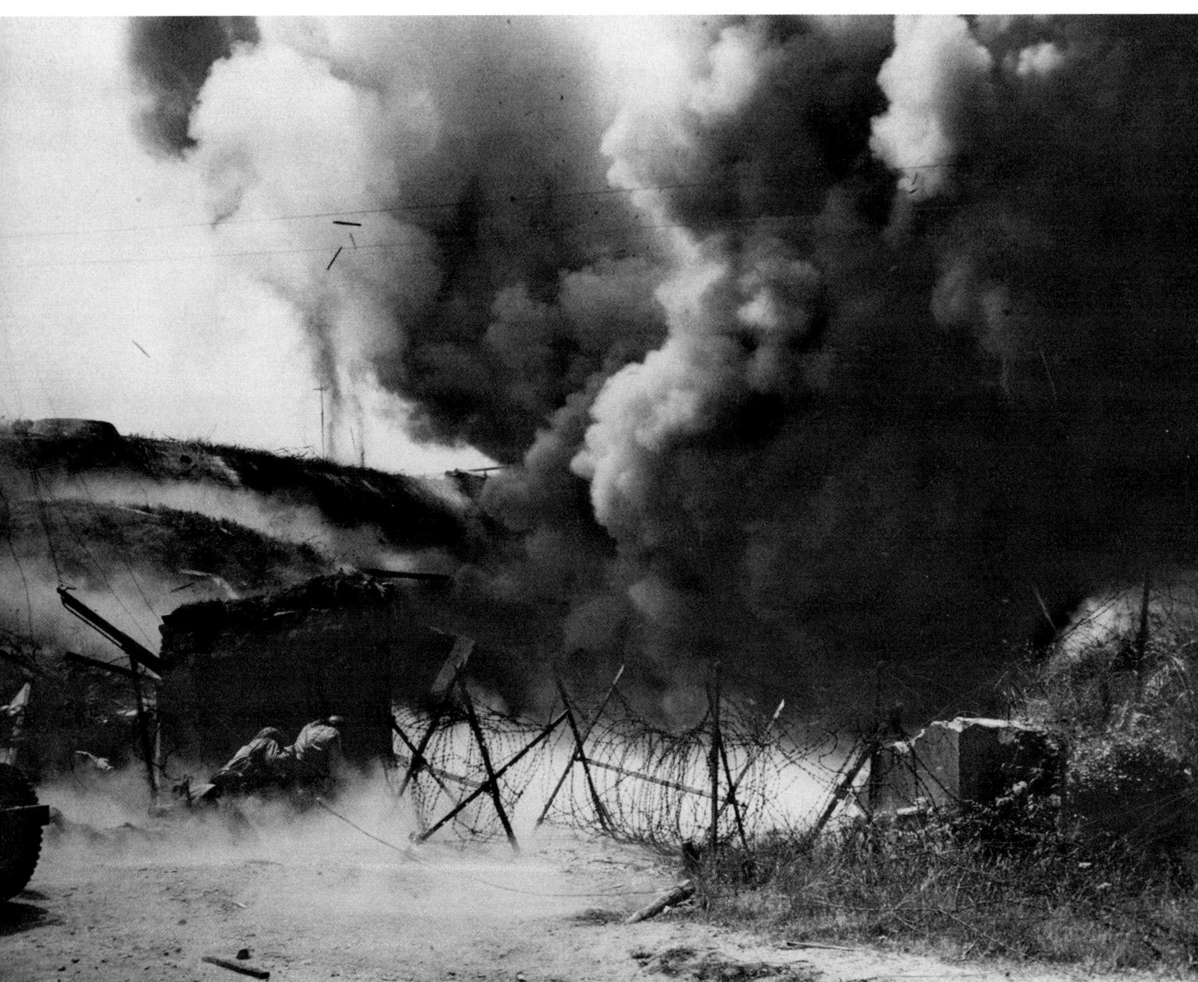

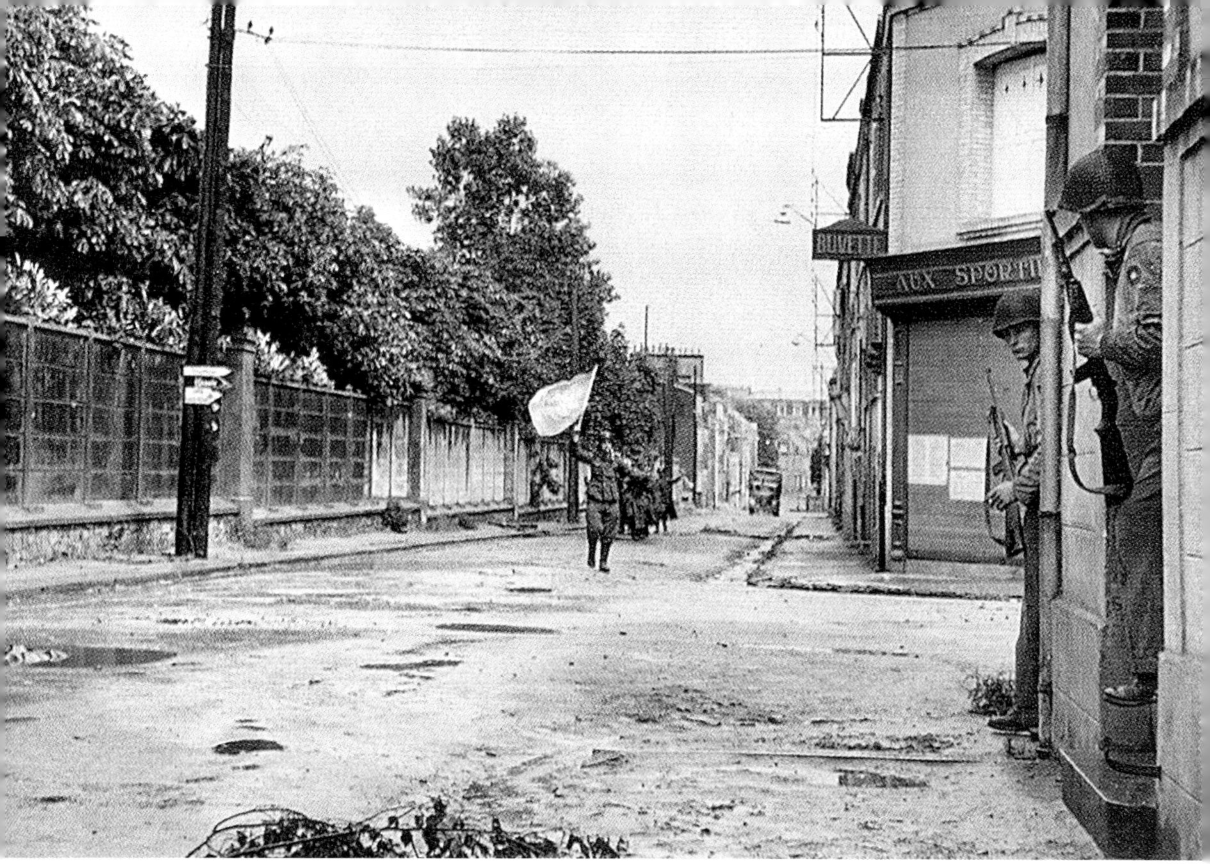

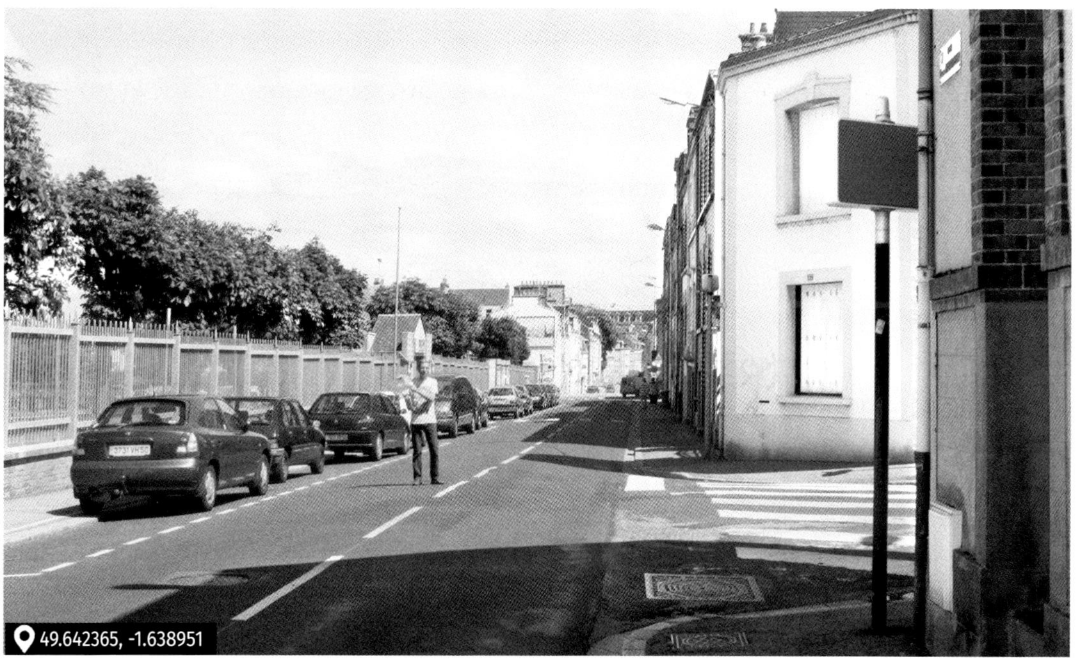

The 39th and 47th Infantry Regiments fought their way through the western half of Cherbourg on June 25. Both Company E of the 47th Infantry Regiment and the attached engineers from the 15th Engineer Combat Battalion could lay claim to having set first foot inside the city. However, the accepted version is that Pfc John T. Sarao of Company E started racing his platoon leader to see who would be first into Cherbourg, and Sarao won. Then and Now Rue Pierre de Coubertin, with Yannick Berton standing in for the surrendering Germans. (USNA and ATB)

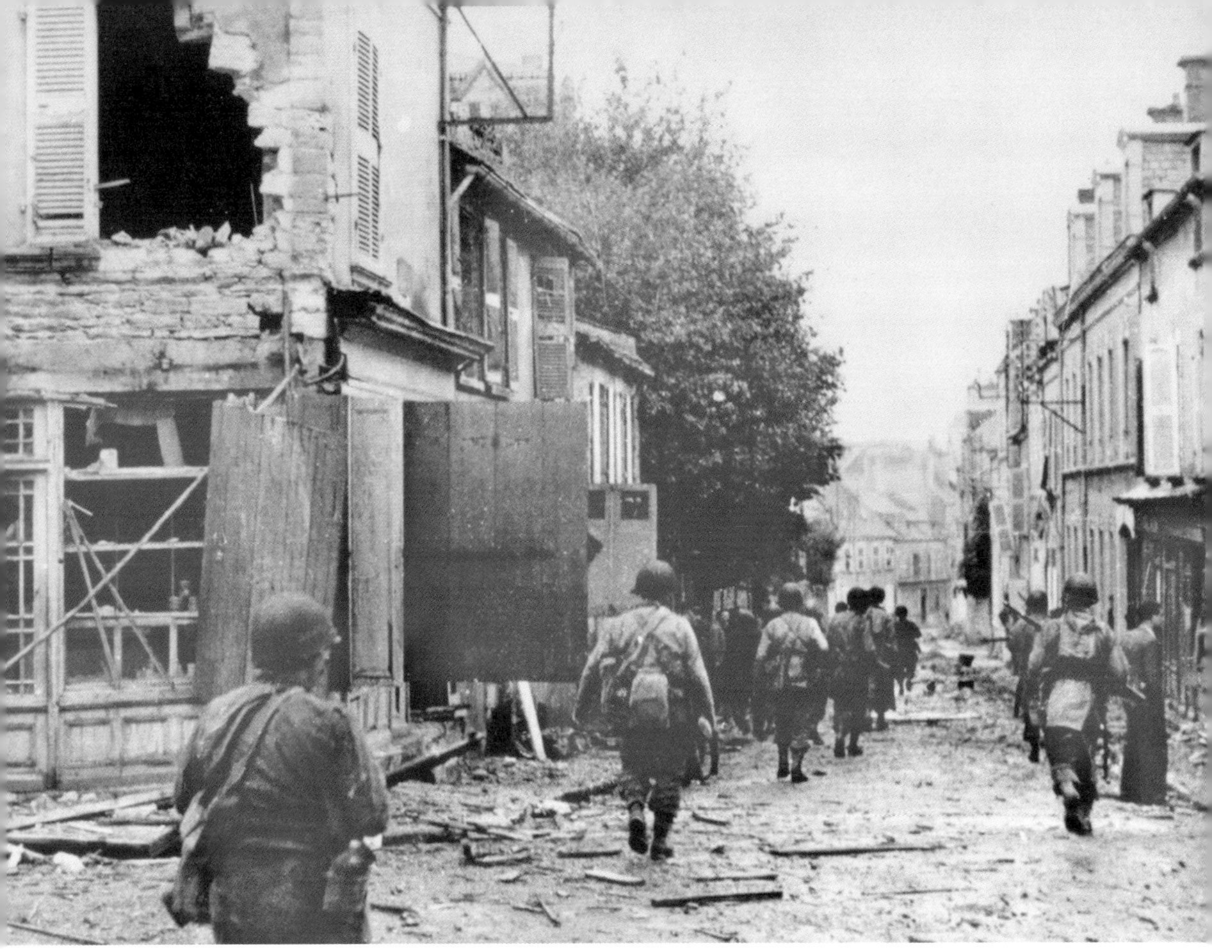

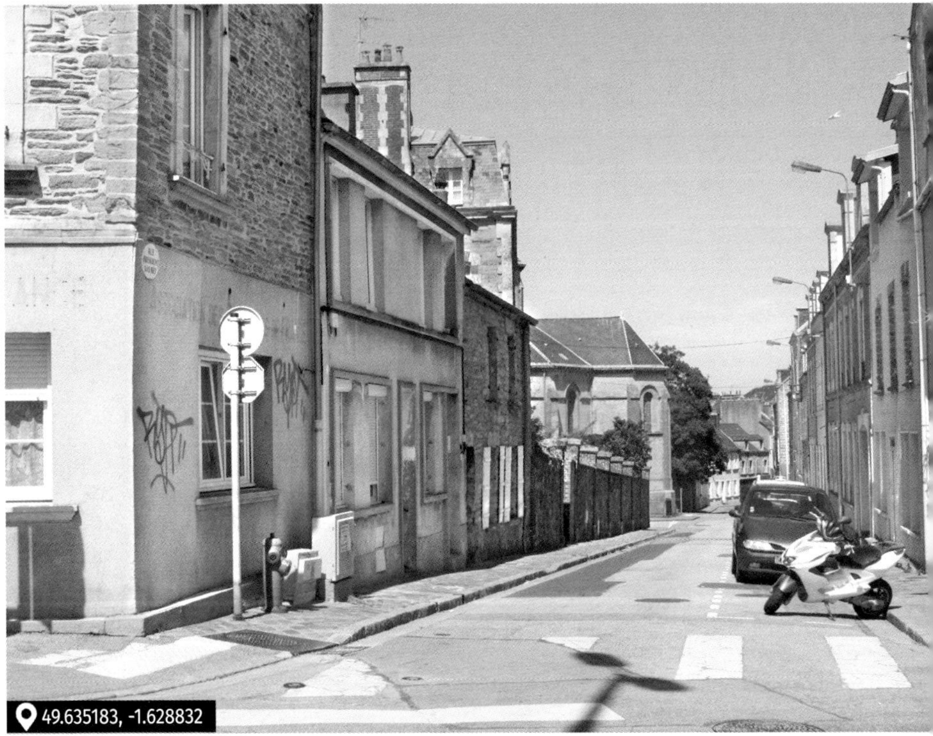

Some distance to the south, this time with men of the 39th Infantry. Looking down Rue Président Loubet with Notre Dame du Voeux church in middle distance on the left. (USNA and ATB)

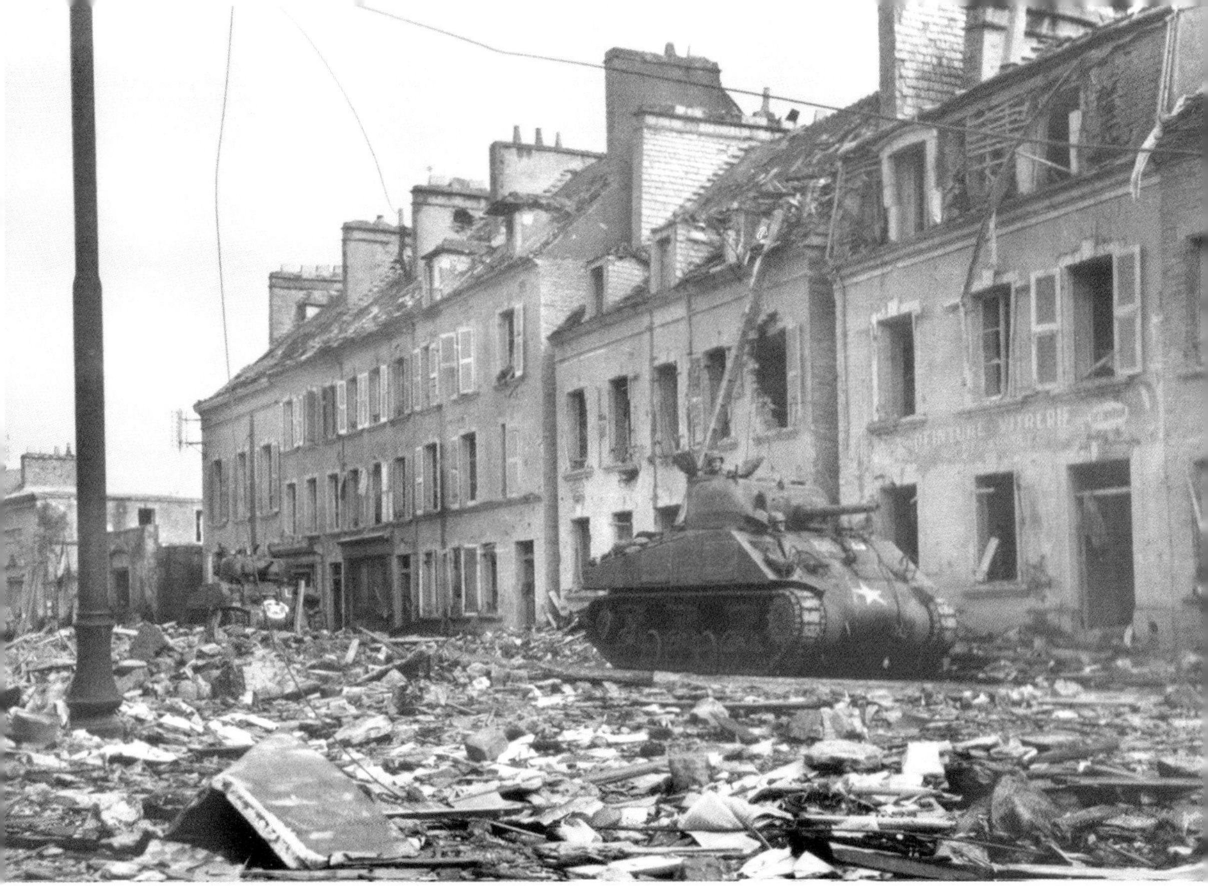

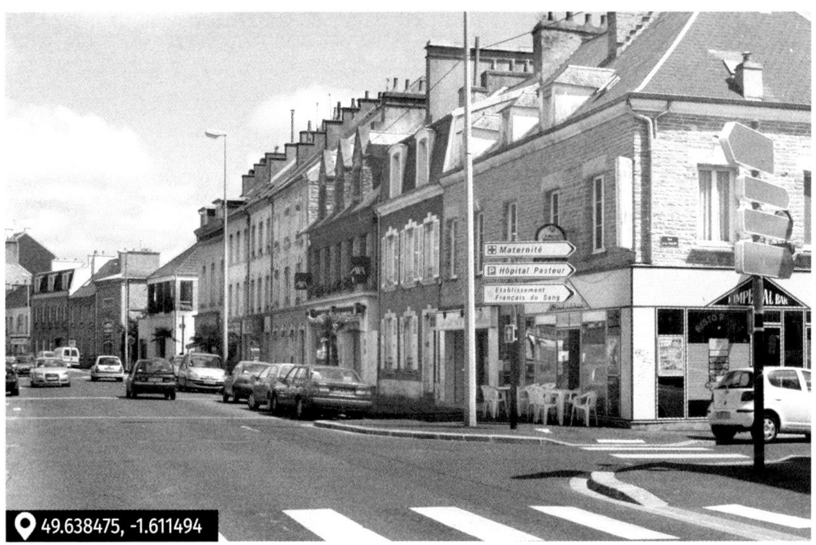

Meanwhile, in the eastern half of the city, the 79th Division advanced with the 314th Infantry on the left and the 313th on the right. Sherman tanks, most likely belonging to the 749th Tank Battalion, enter Cherbourg along Rue du Val de Saire, the main road leading to Cherbourg from the east. Then and Now, at the junction with Rue Jean Fleury. (USNA and ATB)

concrete pillboxes defending the fort from landward attack. On the southeast was an anti-tank ditch.

The Fort du Roule was attacked on the morning of June 25 by the 2nd and 3rd Battalions of the 314th Infantry, after a bombardment by a squadron of P-47s which largely missed its mark and did no appreciable damage. While the guns of the 311th Field Artillery Battalion laid fire on the fort, the 3rd Battalion led off the attack, but was halted at a draw 700 yards from the fort.

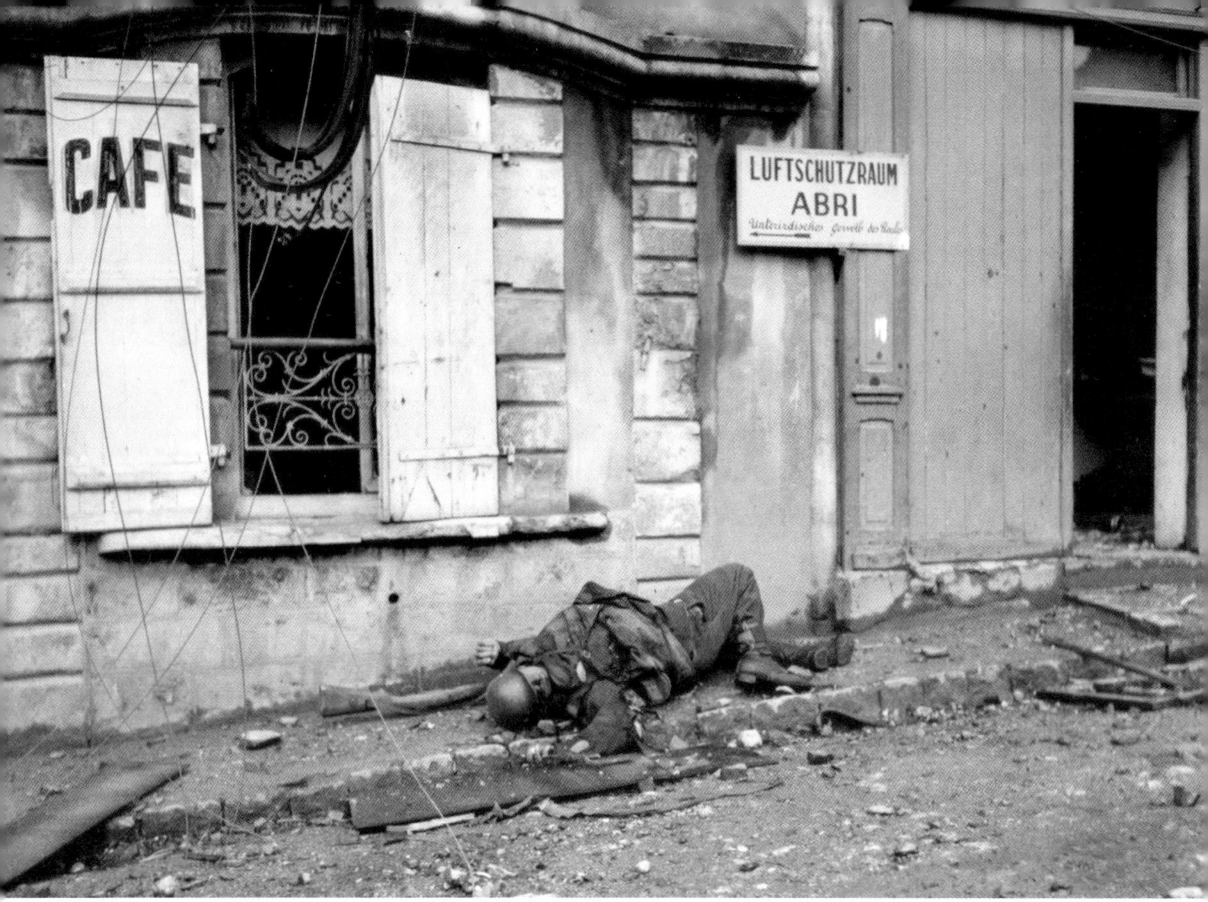

A Signal Corps photographer with the 314th Infantry photographed a dead German soldier, still clutching a hand grenade, in Rue Armand Levéel. The Café Etasse has closed but the house remains unchanged. This is the beginning of Rue Armand Levéel, just as it branches off from Avenue de Paris. (USNA and ATB)

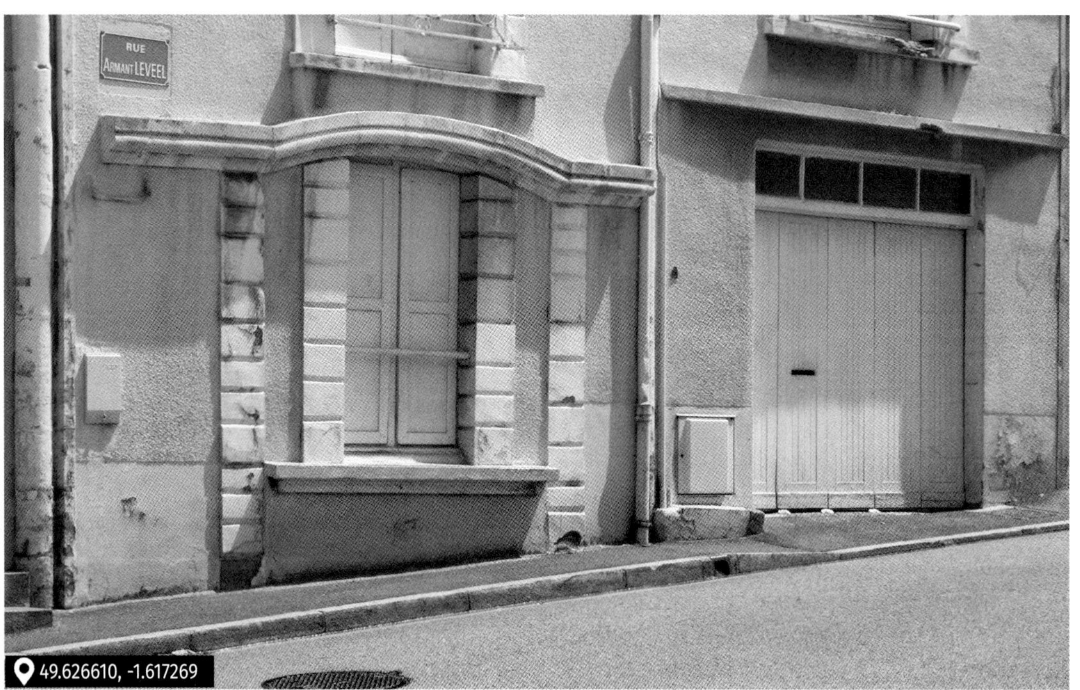

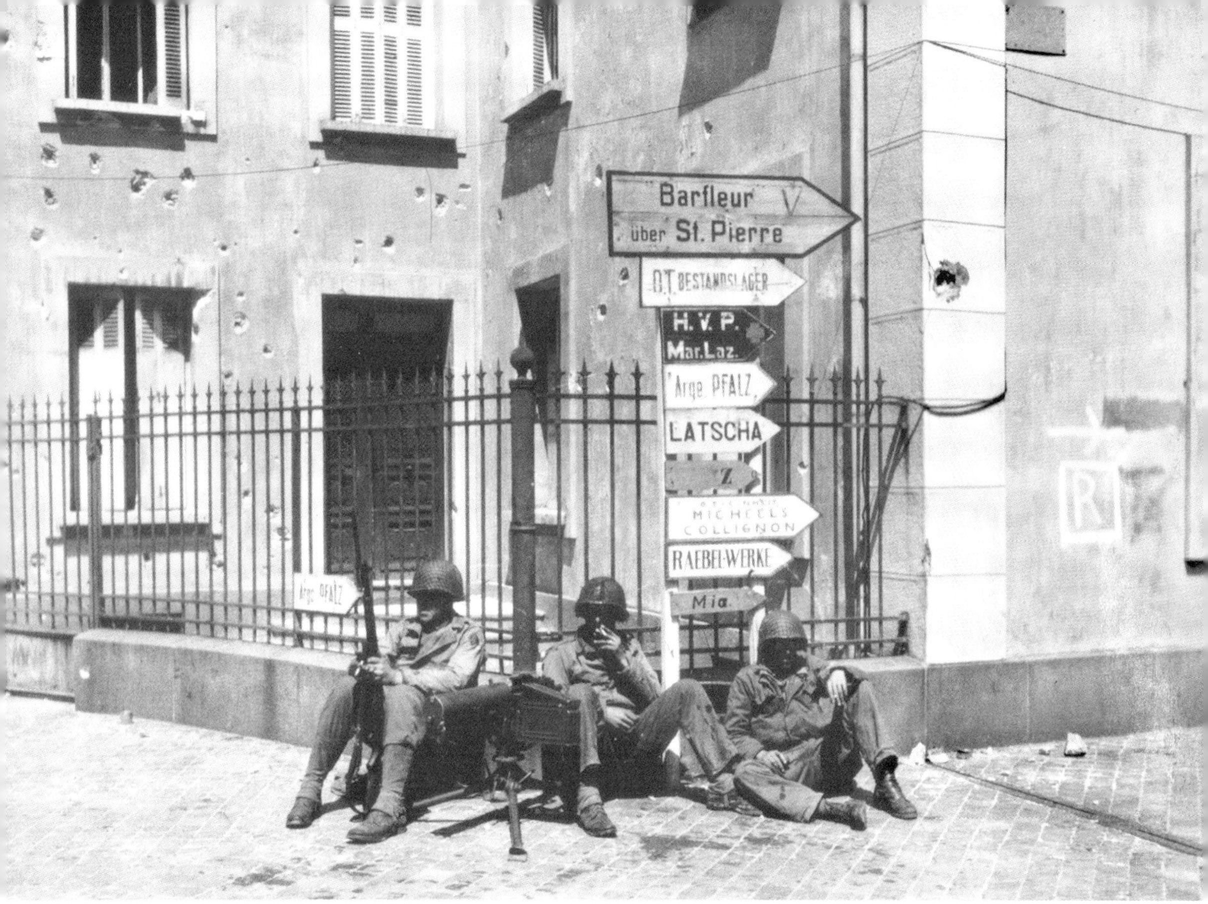

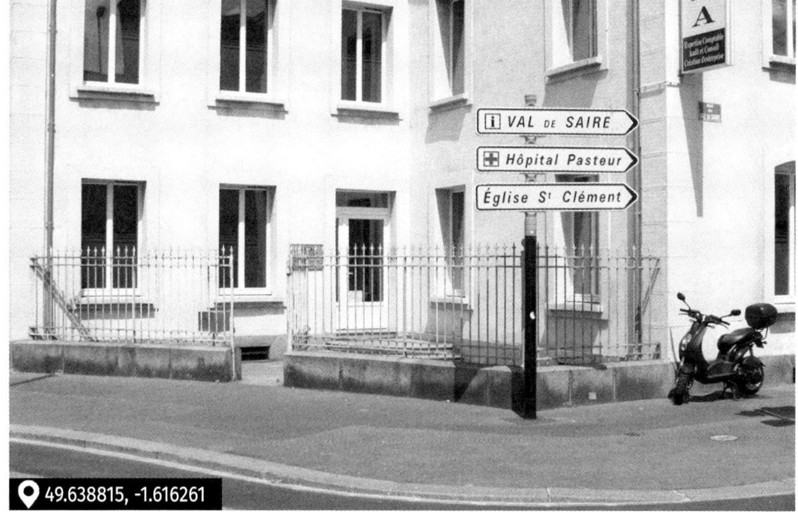

GIs with a Browning .30 water-cooled machine gun guarding the junction of Rue du Val de Saire (off to the right) and Avenue Aristide Briant (left). Bullet marks on the wall behind are evidence of the heavy fighting that has taken place around here.
(USNA and ATB)

Here it was greeted with a hail of small-arms fire from enemy dug in on the forward slope. Lacking artillery (which was fully engaged in neutralising the Fort du Roule) the 3rd and 2nd Battalions massed their machine-gun fire on the German line. Most of the defenders were killed and the few survivors retreated to the fort. The 2nd Battalion then took over the attack under the covering fire of the 3rd Battalion. The attackers came under heavy machine-gun fire from pillboxes as well as shelling from the direction of Octeville.

Reduction of the positions now became a matter largely of the courage and initiative of individuals and small groups. Corporal John D. Kelly's platoon of Company E was hugging the ground immobilised by German machine-gun fire from a pillbox. Kelly took a ten-foot pole charge, crawled up the slope through enemy fire, and fixed the charge, but the explosion was ineffective. He returned with another charge and this time blew off the ends of the German machine guns. A third time Kelly climbed the slope, blew open the rear door of the pillbox, and hurled hand-grenades inside until the enemy survivors came out and surrendered. In the 3rd Battalion zone, Company K was stopped by 88mm and machine-gun fire. Here 1st Lieutenant Carlos C. Ogden, who had just taken over the company from its wounded commander, armed himself with rifle- and hand-grenades and advanced alone under fire toward the enemy emplacements. Despite a head wound, Ogden continued up the slope until from a place of vantage he fired a rifle-grenade that destroyed the 88mm gun. With hand-grenades he then knocked out the machine guns, receiving a second wound but enabling his company to resume the advance. Through these acts and others, portions of the German garrison began to surrender. By midnight the 314th Infantry was in possession of the upper defences of the fort. (For these actions, Lieutenant Ogden and Corporal Kelly were awarded the Medal of Honor. Kelly would die of wounds sustained in another action in November 1944 so his award was made posthumously in January 1945.)

The 313th Infantry in the meantime attacked from Gringor into the flats south-east of Cherbourg. Troops entered the outskirts of the city but could not penetrate in strength because they came under fire from guns in the lower levels of the Fort du Roule, still uncaptured.

During the day, fighting had taken place in the vicinity of von Schlieben's command post in an underground shelter at Saint-Sauveur. He radioed: 'Loss of the city shortly is unavoidable . . . 2,000 wounded without a possibility of being moved. Is the destruction of the remaining troops necessary as part of the general picture in view of the failure of effective counter-attacks? Directive urgently requested.'

JUNE 26

The lower levels of the Fort du Roule were finally reduced on the 26th by lowering demolition charges from the top levels; by anti-tank fire from guns in the city, and by the assault of a demolition team under Staff Sergeant Paul A. Hurst around the precipitous west side of the cliff. In the meantime, both the 313th and 314th Infantry cleared their zones in the city.

Driven underground by American artillery fire, von Schlieben was now isolated and helpless in his underground shelter and at 1506 hours he sent a final radio message to the 7. Armee: 'Documents burned, codes destroyed.' After that, communications were broken off.

Having learnt from a prisoner that von Schlieben's command post was in a

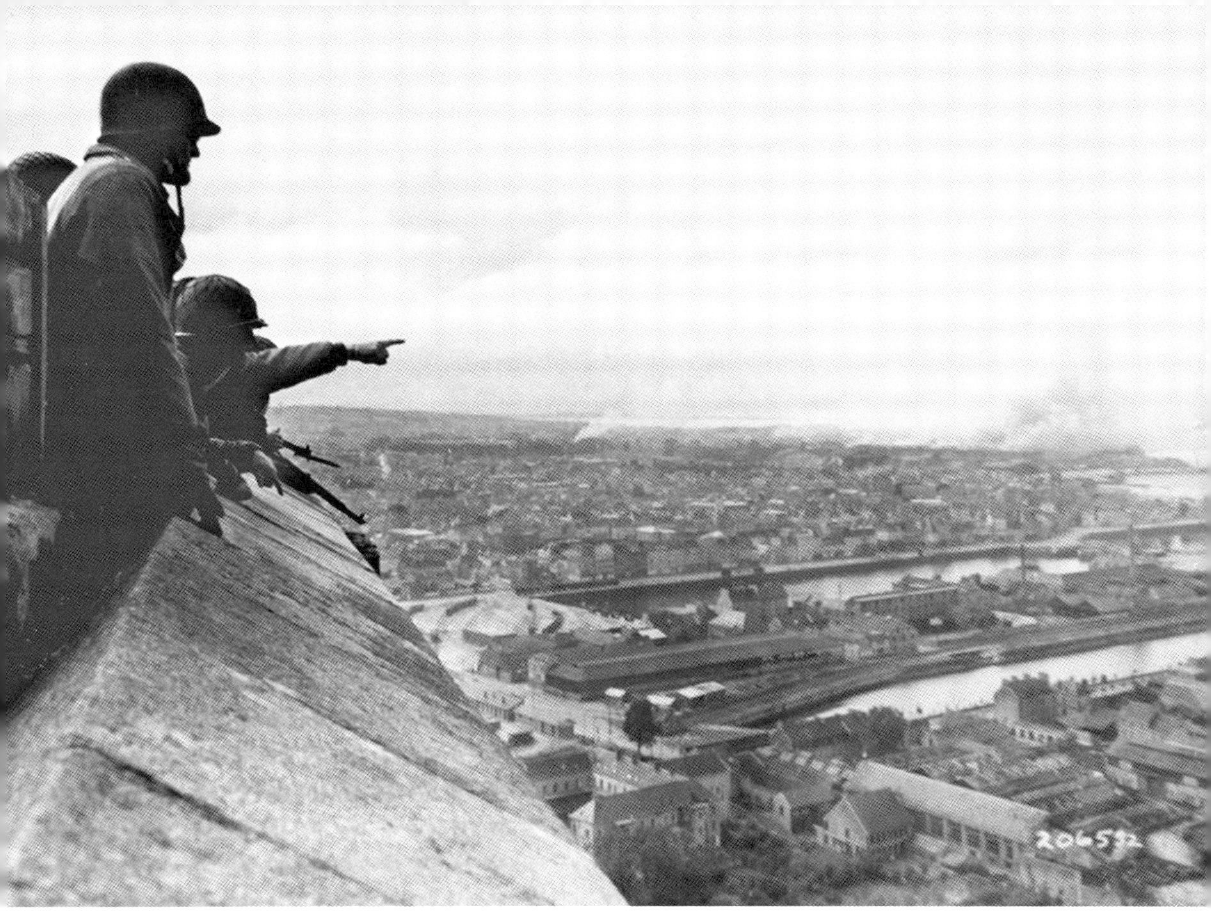

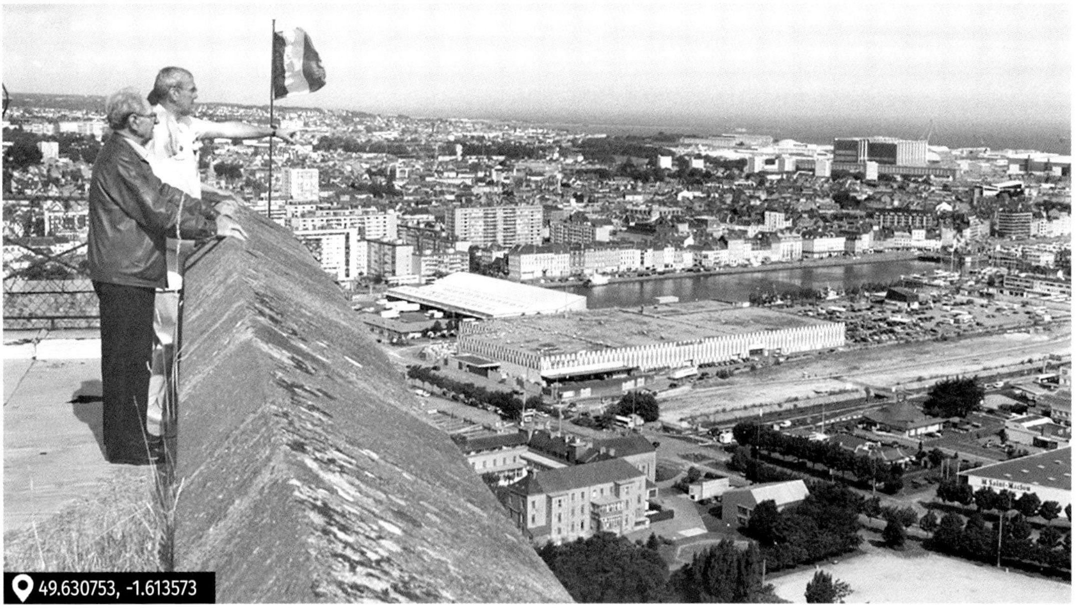

On June 26, even before the last German stronghold in the town had fallen General Collins came to the Fort du Roule to observe his conquest. Just as Generalmajor Rommel had done in June 1940, after his capture of Cherbourg (see page 13). Collins soon had to hurry off when an urgent radio message reached him that the German commanders, General von Schlieben and Admiral Hennecke, had just surrendered and been sent to his command post at the Château de Servigny near Valognes. (USNA and ATB)

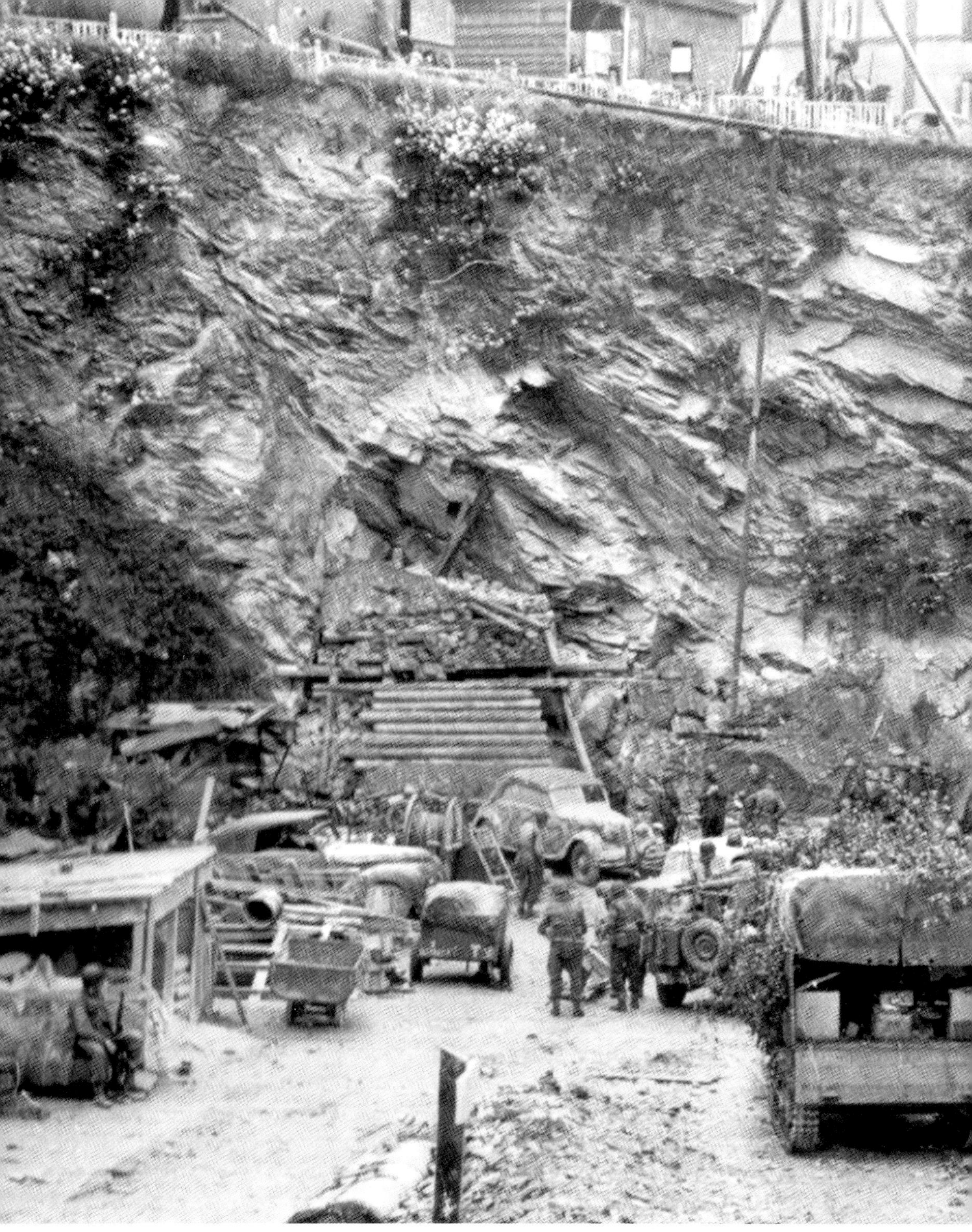

The most dramatic incident of June 26 was the capture of General von Schlieben at his underground shelter at Saint-Sauveur. In the morning Captain Preston O. Gordon, the commander of Company E of the 39th Infantry, sent a prisoner into the tunnel to demand surrender. He received no answer whereupon M-10 tank destroyers were brought forward to fire into the entrances. This photo was taken some time after the capitulation by Signal Corps photographer Sergeant William Spangle. As it happened, Spangle chose the same vantage point as his German counterpart a few days earlier (see page 52). (USNA and ATB)

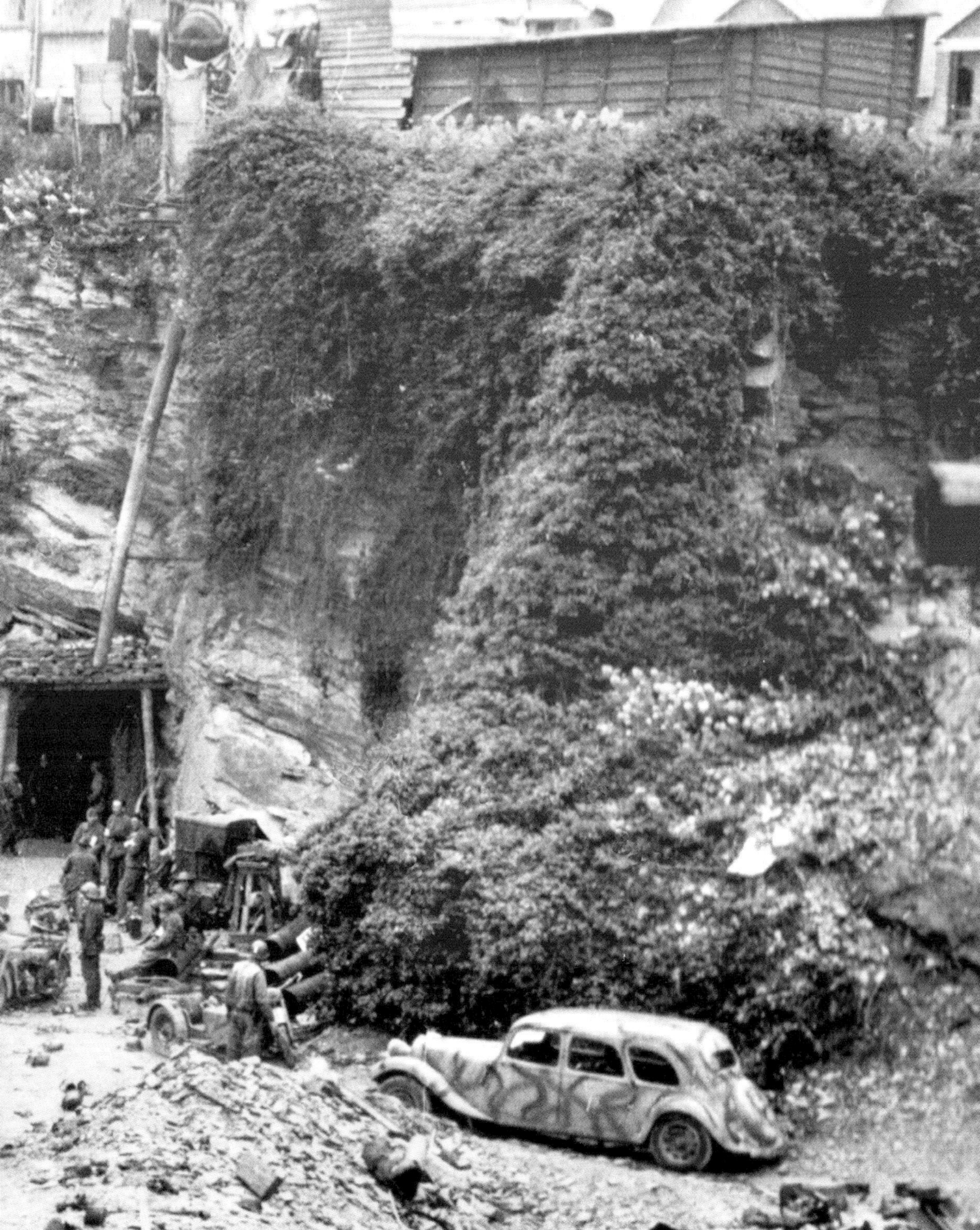

subterranean shelter at Saint-Sauveur, the 39th Infantry sent two companies from Octeville to capture him. Advancing through mortar and Nebelwerfer fire they reached the tunnel entrance. A prisoner was sent into the shelter to demand surrender, but the demand was refused. Tank destroyers were then brought up to fire into two of the three tunnel entrances while

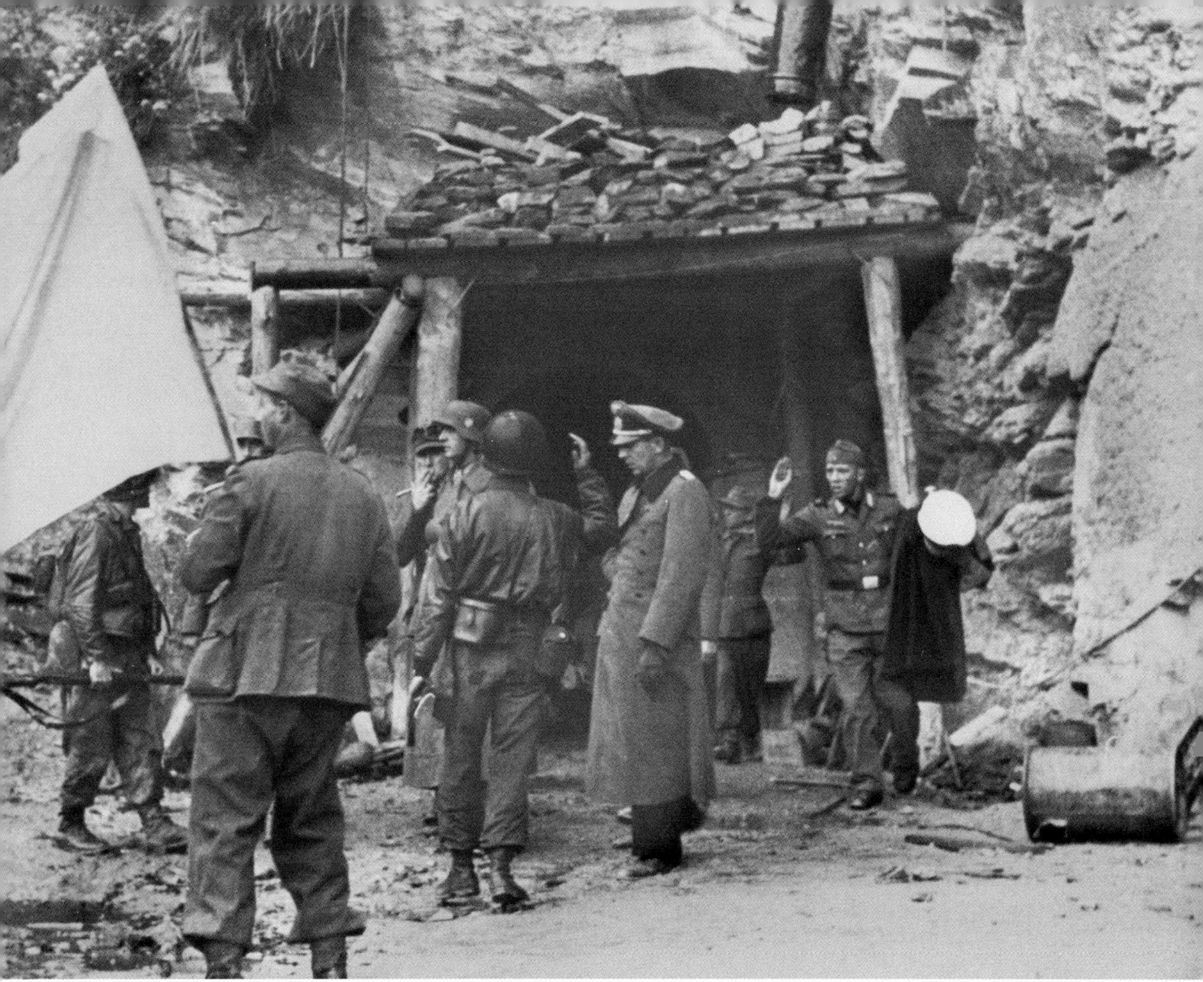

On hearing of the tunnel's discovery, Major General Manton S. Eddy, the 9th Division commander, came up to Saint-Sauveur. He later described the events in his diary: 'After a half dozen shots from the TD's three-inch gun into the rear entrances, which apparently played great havoc, a loud voice called out in German from the front entrance to cease fire. After much difficulty we were able to get all the battalion quiet. I then directed a soldier who could speak German to call and tell them that we would give them two minutes to come out. Instantly, a German with one of the largest white flags I have ever seen ran out . . . followed by a young typical German lieutenant who, I swear, all but goose-stepped . . . He informed me that the Commanding General of the 709. Infanterie-Division was in the cave and wished to surrender. He requested that I send a staff officer down with him to escort the General to me.' (USNA)

preparations were made to blow up the stronghold. Causing much dust and smoke in the tunnel, a few rounds were sufficient to bring out the enemy. Some 800 Germans in all, including both Generalleutnant von Schlieben and Konteradmiral Walter Hennecke, Seekommandant Normandie (Naval Commander Normandy), capitulated to General Eddy who just happened to be there. General von Schlieben, however, still concerned with gaining time, declined to make a general surrender of the Cherbourg fortress. The 39th Infantry therefore pushed its attack northward to the coast. In the city, Lieutenant Colonel Frank Gunn, commanding 2nd Battalion, received another surrender of about 400 troops that had barricaded themselves in the City Hall. They gave up when convinced of General von Schlieben's capture and after being promised protection from French snipers.

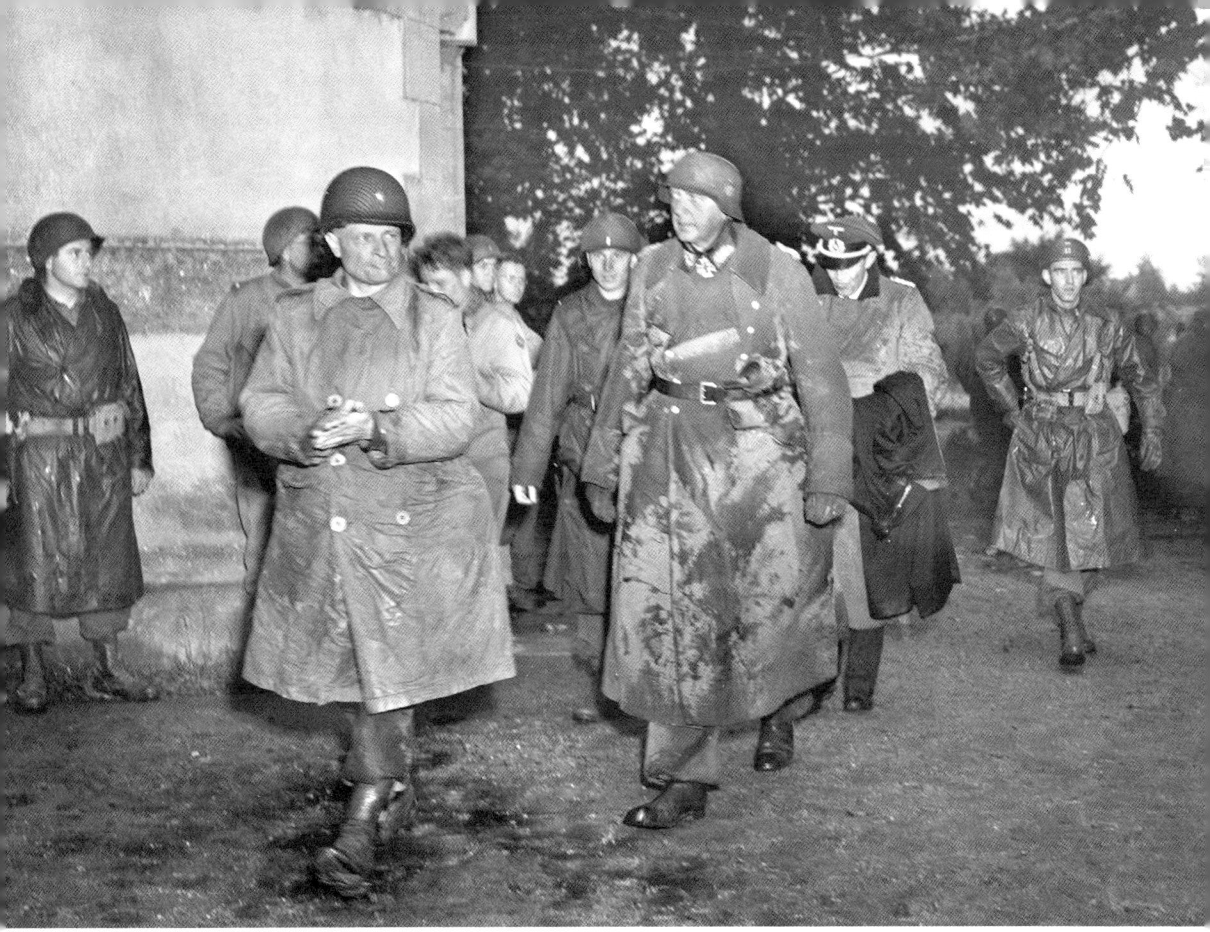

The German commanders were immediately sent to Collins' command post at the Château de Servigny, at Yvetot-Bocage, about three kilometres west of Valognes. His coat splattered with mud from the quarry tunnel, Generalleutnant von Schlieben arrives at the chateau, followed by Admiral Hennecke and some aides. (USNA)

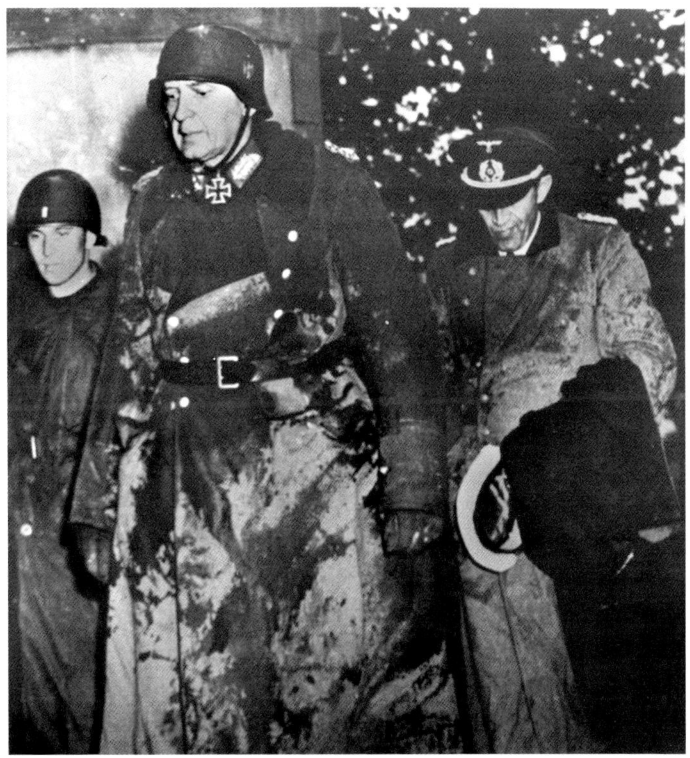

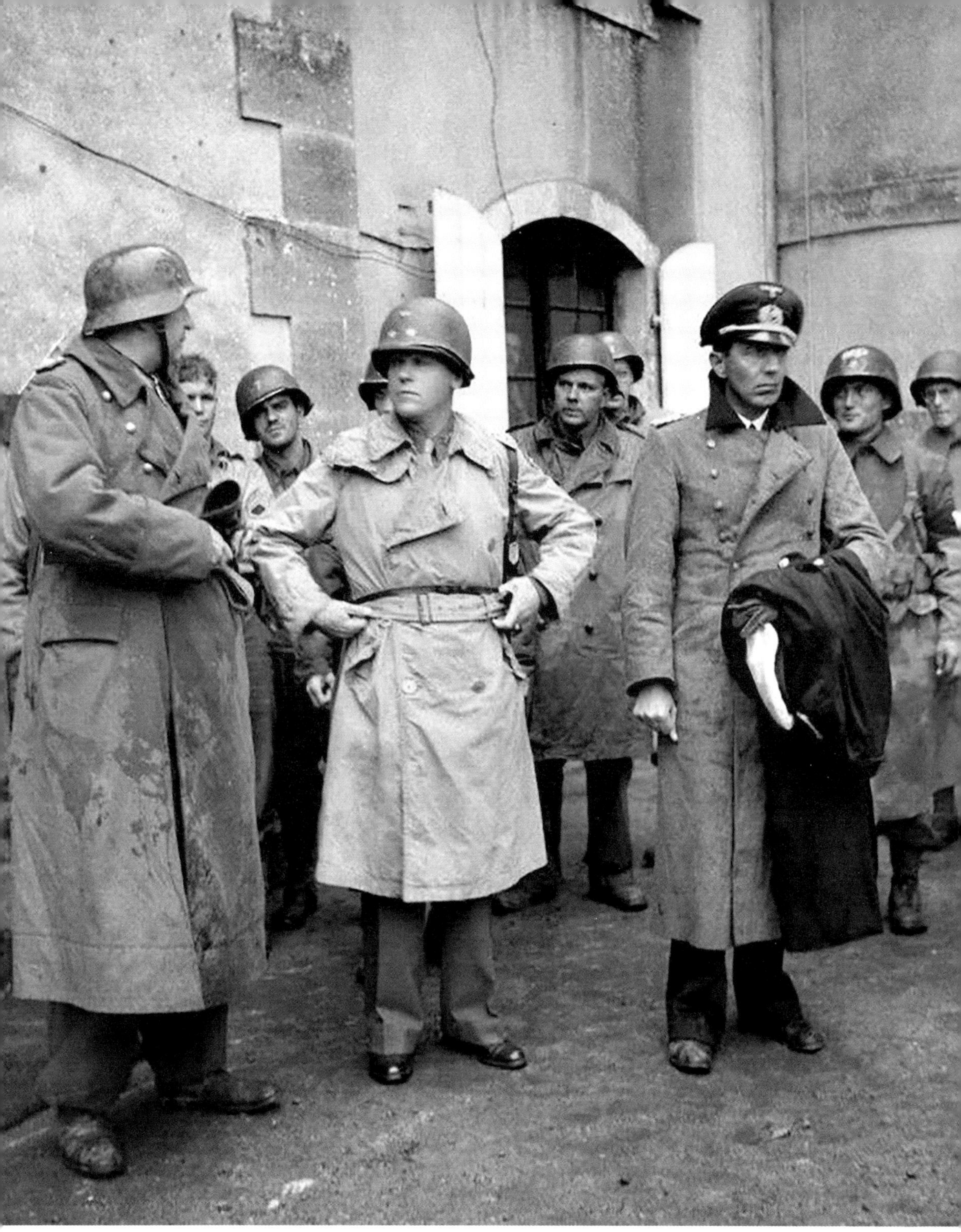

Hurrying back from the Fort du Roule (see page 69), Collins arrived at Yvetot-Bocage some time after the German party. This photo was then taken in front of the château with him in company with von Schlieben and Hennecke.
(USNA)

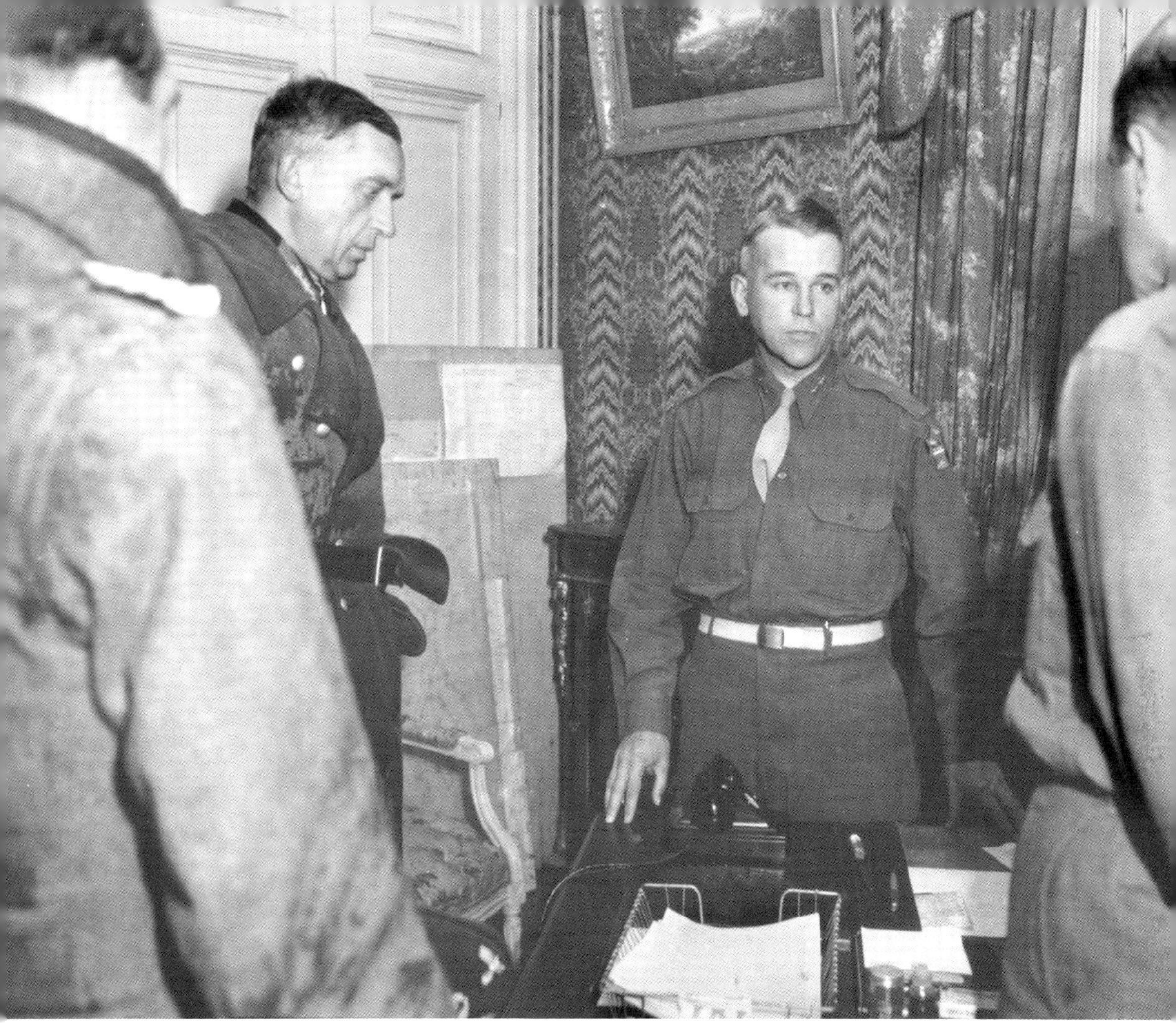

The talks and signing of the formal surrender of Cherbourg took place in a room on the first floor. In his autobiography *Lightning Joe*, published in 1979, Collins described how he demanded that the 'big, hulking' von Schlieben surrender all forces under his command. The German refused, saying that 'he had learned from the Russians that even small, scattered units could put up considerable resistance'. Today known as the 'Salon de la Reddition' (surrender room), the room is now decorated with exhibits of that historic day in June 1944, including a copy of the surrender document. The estate is privately owned and although Comte and Comtesse de Pontac very kindly allowed the author access to the historic room, no visits are possible. However, it can be booked for weekly rentals. (see **http:// chateauservigny.com**)

(USNA and ATB)

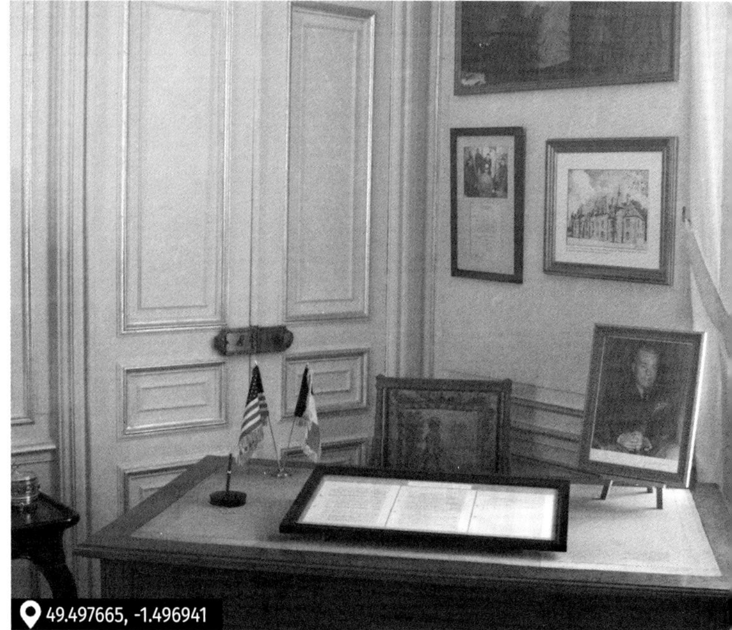

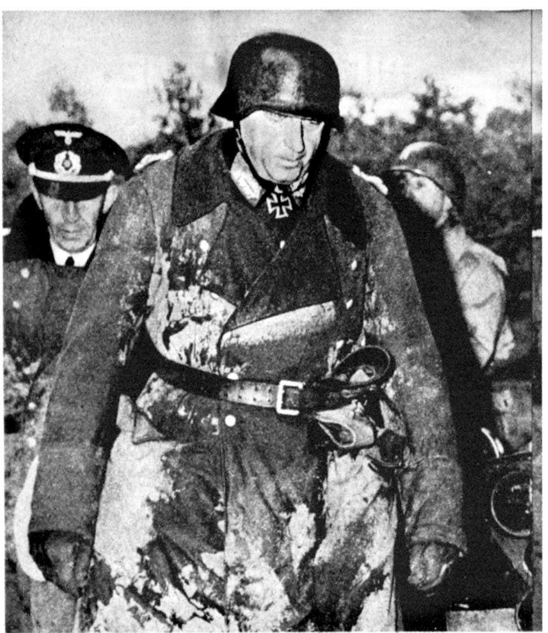

Generalleutnant von Schlieben, der Verteidiger von Cherbourg, verlässt seinen Gefechtsstand im Fort du Roule, um sich den Amerikanern zu ergeben. Die Lage war hoffnungslos. Auch Schliebens Tod hätte nichts daran ändern können. Deshalb setzte sich Generalleutnant von Schlieben, zusammen mit 18 000 anderen in der gleichen Lage, über den Führerbefehl hinweg, zu dem sie sich mit ihrer Unterschrift verpflichten mussten,

„dass sie ungeachtet der Lage ihren Platz mit Einsatz ihres Lebens bis zum letzten Mann und zur letzten Patrone zu verteidigen haben."

Generalleutnant von Schlieben und die 18 000 sind jetzt in England. Sie warten auf das Ende des Krieges und auf ein Deutschland, in dem solche erpresserischen Verpflichtungen unmöglich sind.

DIE NÜCHTERNE WAHRHEIT ÜBER KRIEGSGEFANGENSCHAFT

Deutscher Soldat: Wir versprechen Dir weder Utopien noch das Schlaraffenland, falls Du in Kriegsgefangenschaft gelangst. Aber — auf die folgenden Tatsachen kannst Du mit Bestimmtheit rechnen:

1. „FAIRE" BEHANDLUNG, wie es einem tapferen Gegner gebührt. Der Rang des Gefangenen wird anerkannt. Deine eigenen Kameraden sind Deine unmittelbaren Vorgesetzten.

2. GUTE VERPFLEGUNG. Viele Deiner Kameraden sind erstaunt, wie gut die Ernährung bei uns ist. Wir heissen mit Recht die bestgenährte Armee der Welt. (Manche Landser ziehen das deutsche Komissbrot unserem Weissbrot vor, aber über unseren Kaffee und die Zubereitung unserer Speisen hat sich noch niemand beklagt ...)

3. ERSTKLASSIGE LAZARETTPFLEGE für Verwundete und Kranke. Gemäss der Genfer Konvention erhalten Gefangene dieselbe Lazarettpflege wie unsere eigenen Truppen.

4. SCHREIBGELEGENHEIT. Du kannst im Monat drei Briefe und vier Karten nach Hause schreiben. Die Postverbindung ist schnell und zuverlässig. Du kannst Briefe und auch Pakete erhalten.

5. BESOLDUNG. Gemäss der Genfer Konvention behält der Kriegsgefangene das Anrecht auf seine Entlohnung bei. Für etwaige freiwillige Arbeitsleistungen erhältst Du aber selbstverständlich Bezahlung. Für das Geld, das Du erhältst, kannst Du verschiedentliche Marketenderwaren kaufen.

6. WEITERBILDUNG. Sollte der Krieg noch länger dauern, dann kommst Du wahrscheinlich noch dazu, Dich an den verschiedentlichen Bildungs- und Lehrkursen zu beteiligen, die von Kriegsgefangenen selbst veranstaltet werden.

Und selbstverständlich kommst Du nach Kriegsende nach Hause

ZG.20

One of the leaflets printed just after the signing and thrown into the districts of Cherbourg still held by the Germans is now exhibited at the Salon de la Reddition.

JUNE 27

In the early hours of June 27, knowing that the fall of the Arsenal was imminent, Fregattenkapitän Hermann Witt, the Hafenkommandant Cherbourg (Cherbourg Port Commander), took a party in two boats to escape to the Fort de l'Ouest on the outlying breakwater. He then took charge of the garrison of about 185 men still holding out in that fort and in another stronghold on the breakwater, the Fort du Centre.

The attempt by the 47th Infantry to clear the north-west section of the city had been checked on the 26th by the stubborn defence of the thick-walled Arsenal on whose parapets were emplaced machine guns. Artillery support was rendered difficult by the bad weather and smoke and dust from port demolitions being carried out by the Germans. Assault of the Arsenal was postponed until the morning of June 27 when an elaborately supported three-battalion attack was planned. Before it took place, however, a psychological warfare unit broadcast an ultimatum. At 0830 unarmed men were observed walking on the Arsenal wall and a few minutes later white flags appeared. Colonel George W. Smythe, the 47th Infantry commander, went forward and at 1000 hours Generalmajor Robert Sattler, deputy

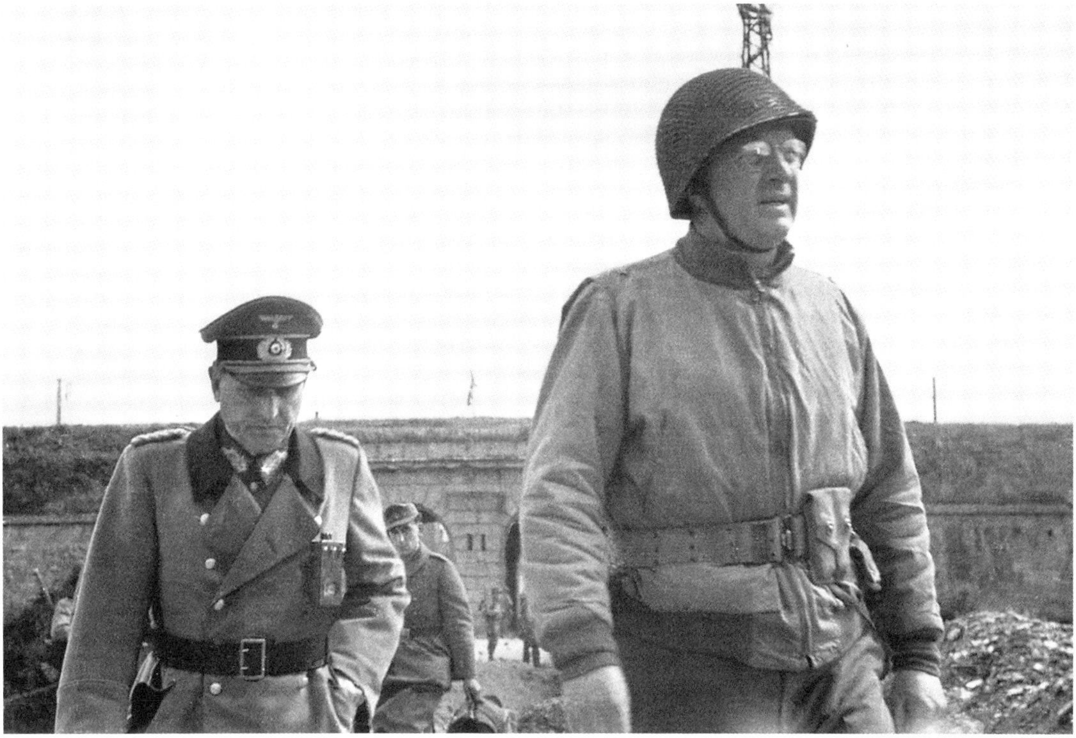

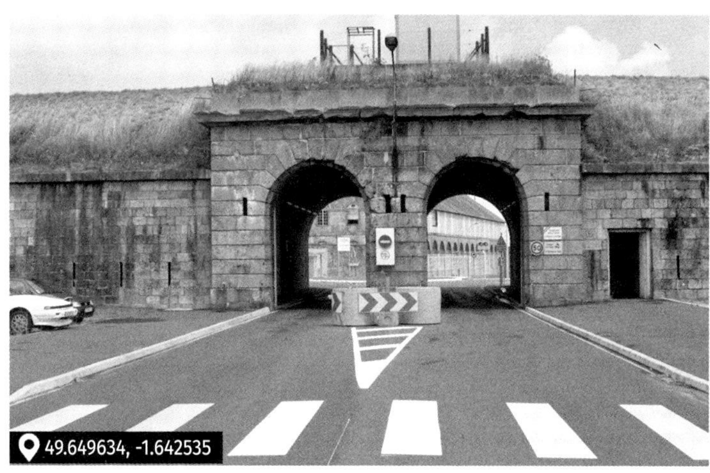

By the morning of June 27, there remained only one major German stronghold within Cherbourg itself – the rampart-surrounded naval Arsenal. Generalmajor Sattler surrendered and Colonel George W. Smythe, commander of the 47th Infantry, then came forward to receive his surrender. Here they stood in front of the Trois Hangars gate, between Bastions 5 and 6, one of the gates through the Arsenal's ancient rampart. (USNA and ATB)

commander of the Cherbourg fortress, surrendered the 400 men under his immediate control. He stated however that he had no communication with other parts of the Arsenal.

The capitulation of the Arsenal brought to an end all organised resistance in the city. In the preceding day and a half over 10,000 prisoners had been taken, including 2,600 patients and the staffs of two hospitals. However, Fregattenkapitän Witt and his small group were still holding out in the outlying forts along the breakwater. Even stronger defences held out on both sides of the port. In the east the German line ran from Cap Lévy southwards through the Maupertus airfield to Gonneville, while west of the city the main line of resistance cut the Cap de la Hague from Gruchy in the north to Vauville in the south, with advance positions from Querqueville to Vauville.

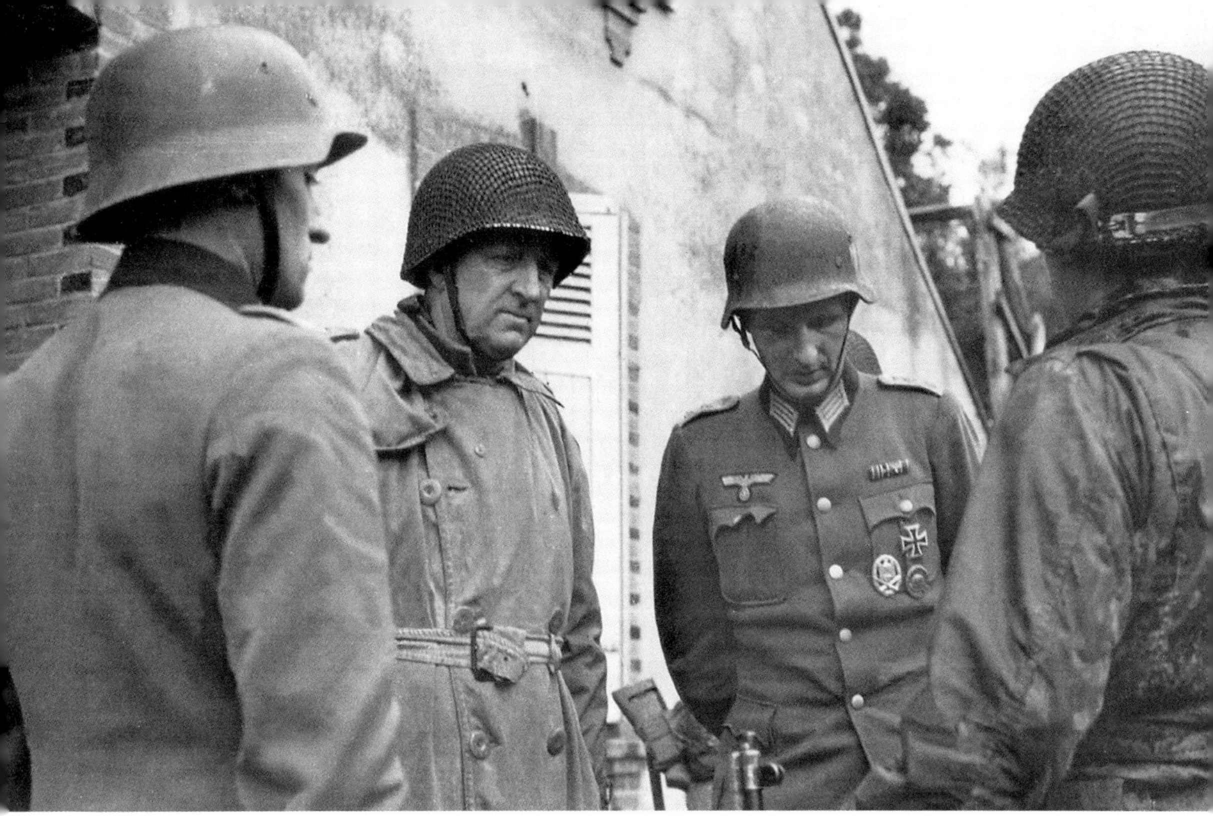

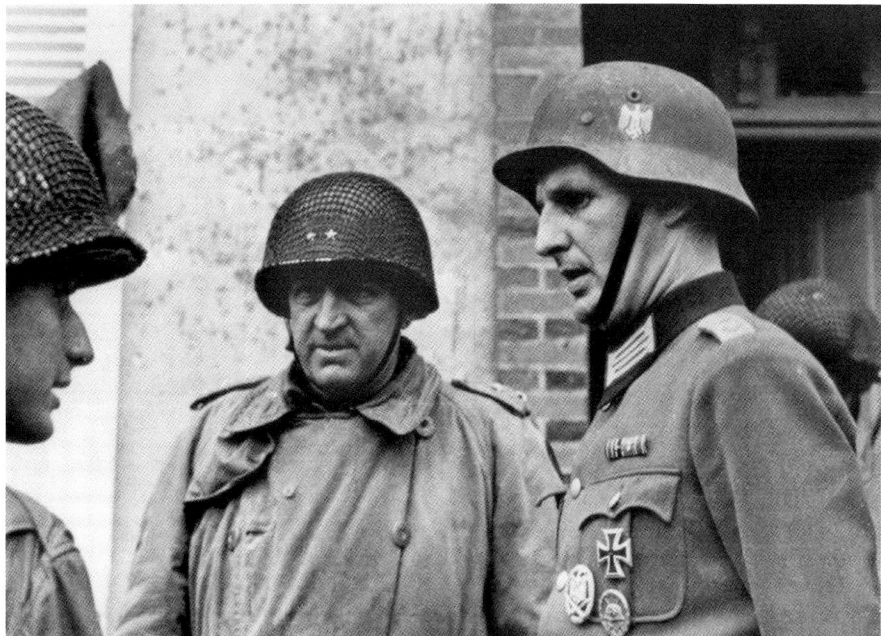

That afternoon, General Collins arrived at the City Hall, together with Major Generals Barton of the 4th Division, Eddy of the 9th Division, Wyche of the 79th Division, Matthew B. Ridgway of the 82nd Airborne Division and Maxwell D. Taylor of the 101st Airborne Division, to meet the mayor of the city, Paul Renault, and officially turn Cherbourg over to the French administration.

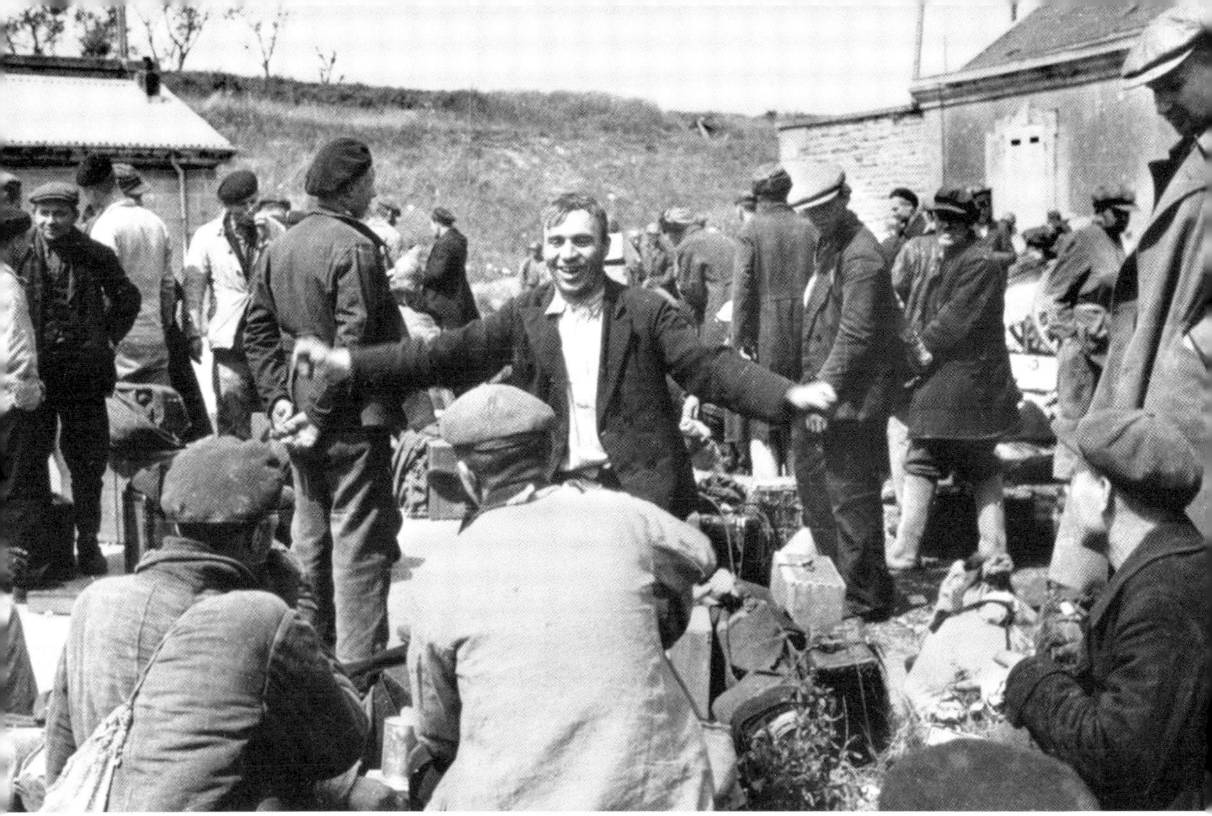

A bunch of Organisation Todt workers, mostly Russian conscripts, rejoice at the end of the fighting. Trapped in their barrack quarters inside the Arsenal, they have survived days of bombing and shelling. This photo was taken in a yard surrounded by C-shaped buildings built against the rampart close to the Trois Hangars gate. (USNA and ATB)

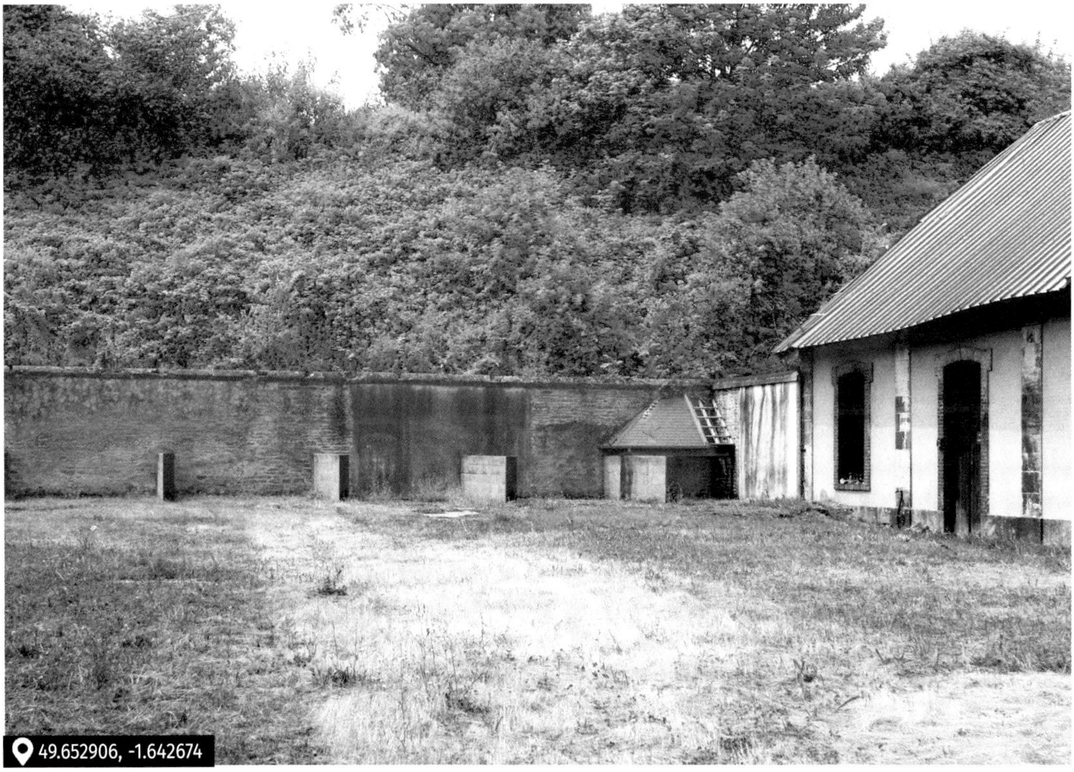

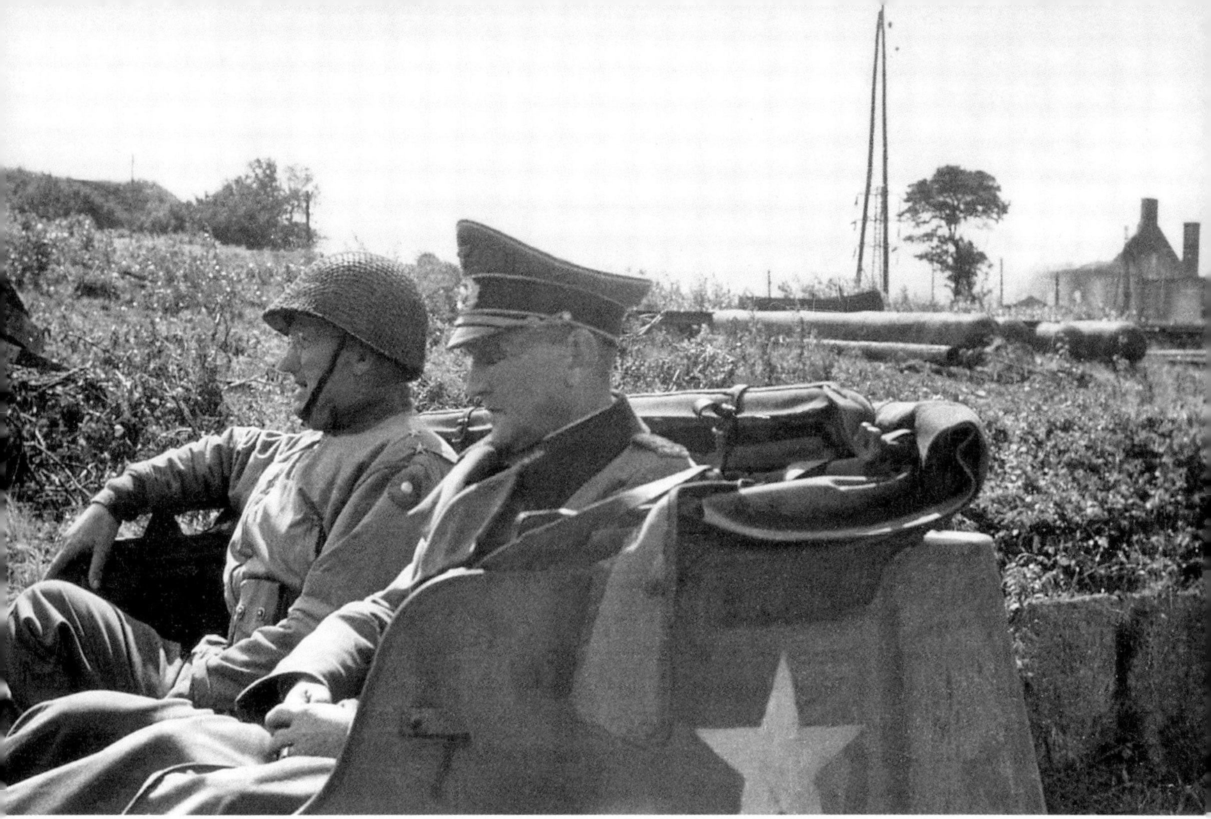

Generalmajor Sattler was then taken to Collins' headquarters at the Château de Servigny. (USNA)

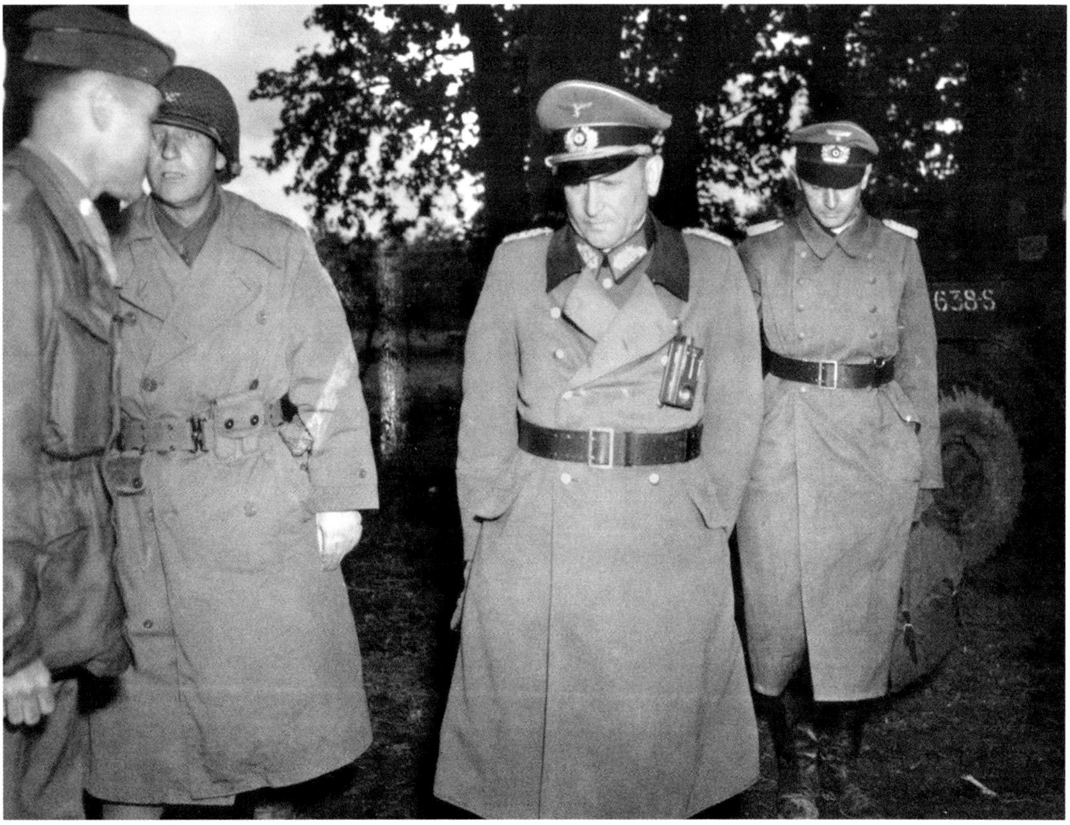

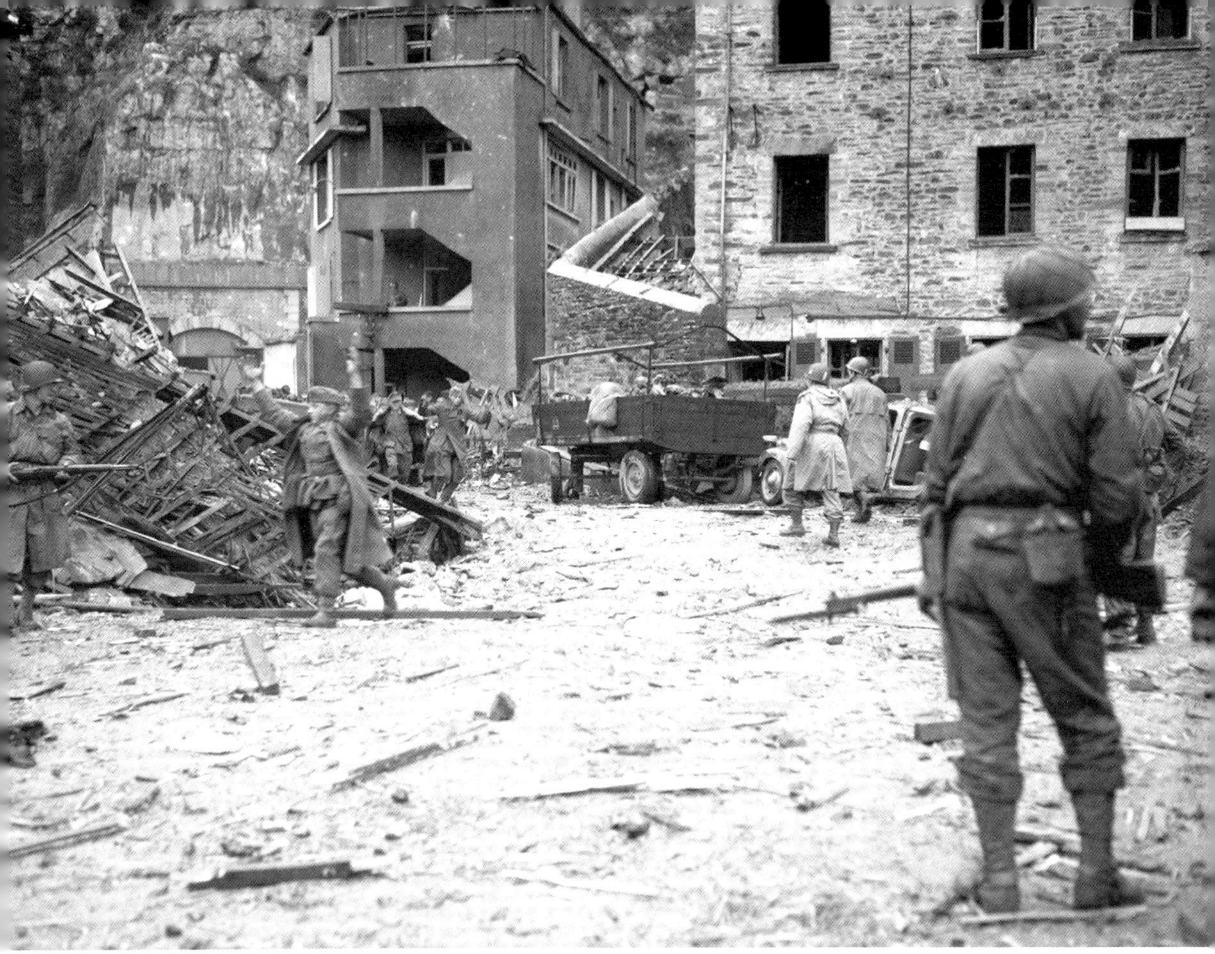

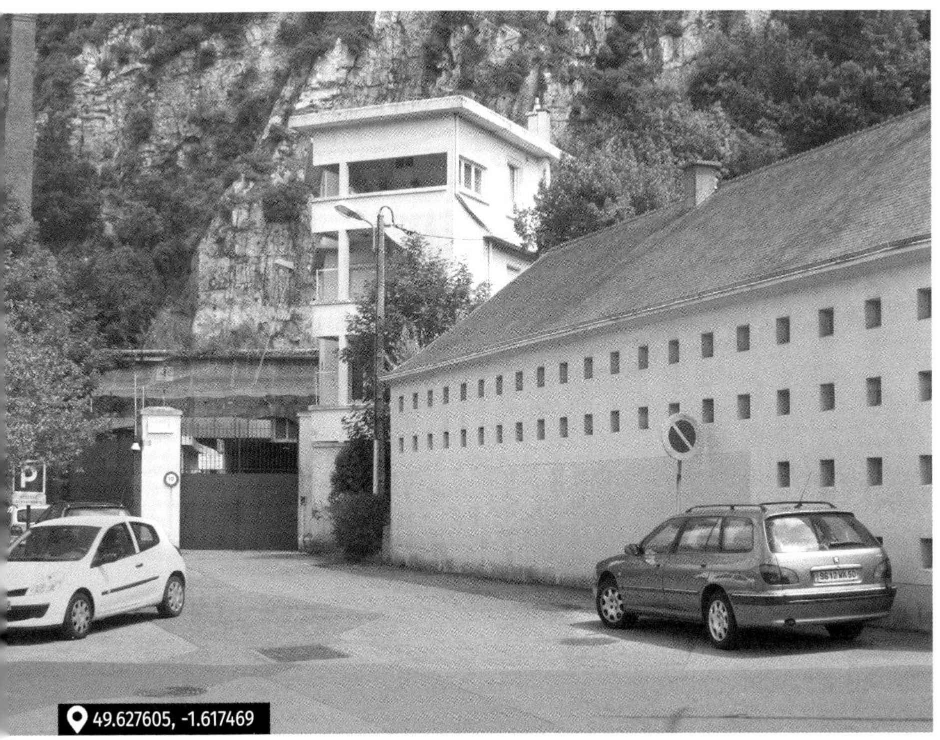

After the top of the Fort du Roule was cleared on June 25, the 314th Infantry spent the next day reducing the lower levels. All resistance at the fort was reported finished by 7 p.m. on June 26, a total of 300 prisoners having been taken. However, the subterranean complex in the mountain was seemingly not yet cleaned out and this photo was taken on the 27th when more German soldiers came out. The same entrance close to the Avenue de Paris. (USNA and ATB)

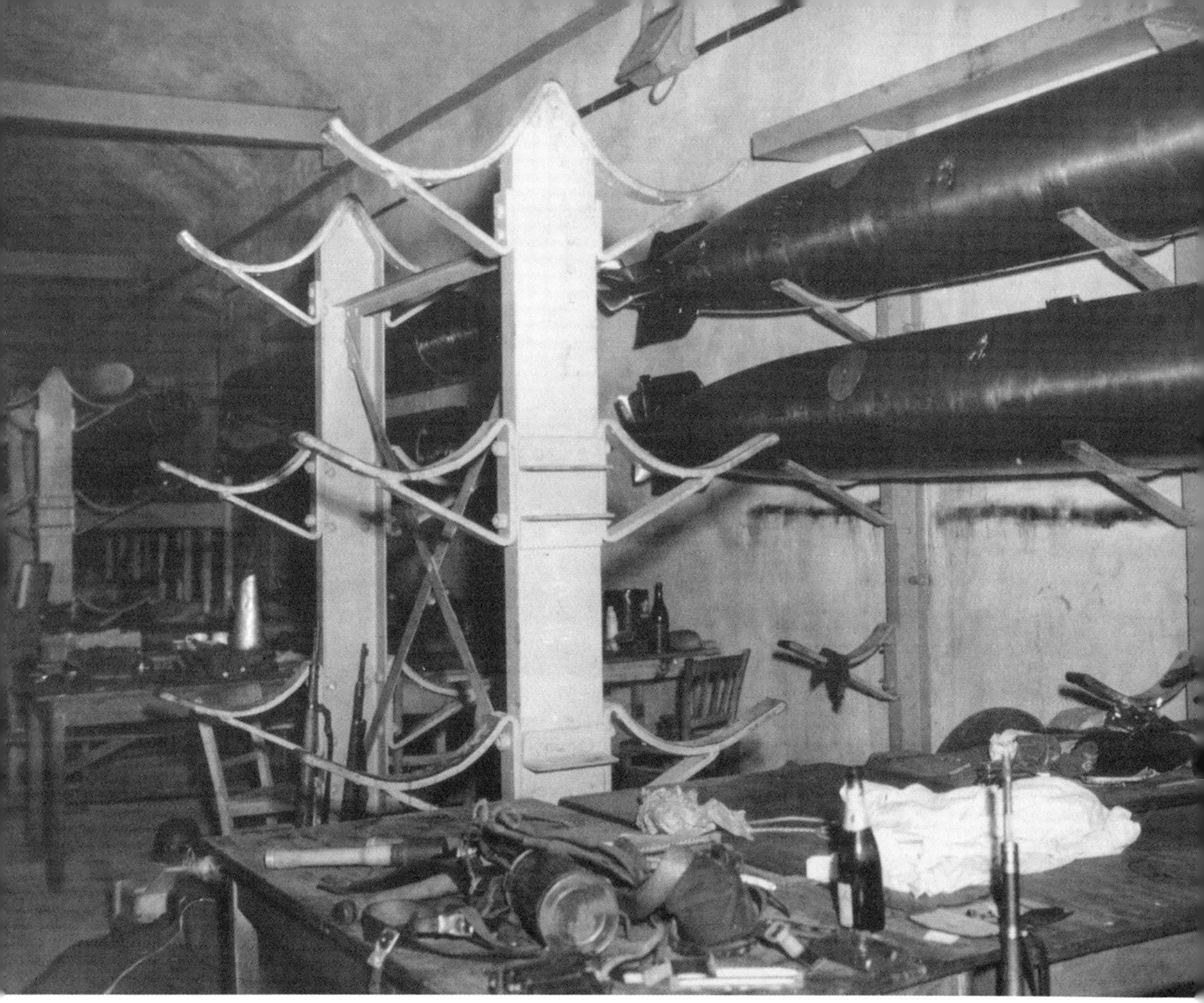

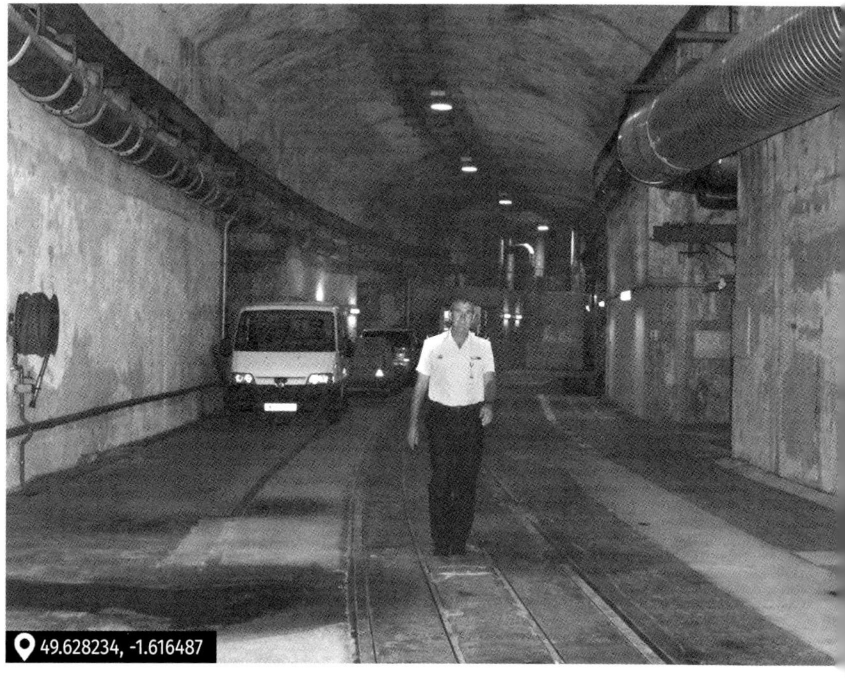

Dead Germans – 'machinists' according to the original caption– pictured by the Americans inside the underground complex on June 28. The Germans had used part of the galleries, with the existing French racks, for storing torpedoes, as evidenced by this picture. This is one of the eight side galleries to the slightly curved main gallery. The French Navy allowed the author into their Cherbourg installations and Major Christophe De Joybert showed him every corner of the complex under the Roule mountain. This is the main gallery, with the entrance to one of the side galleries on the right. (USNA and ATB)

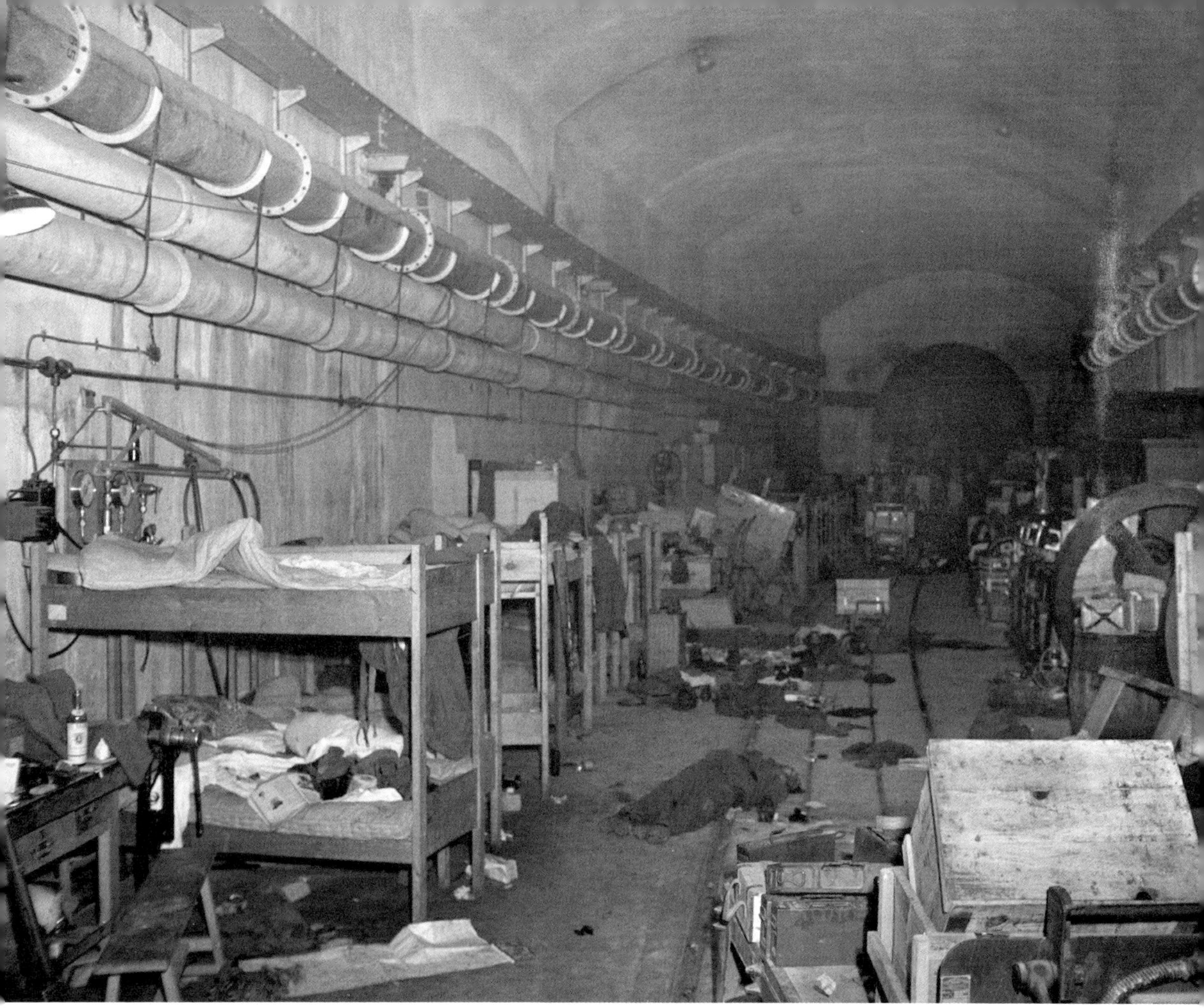

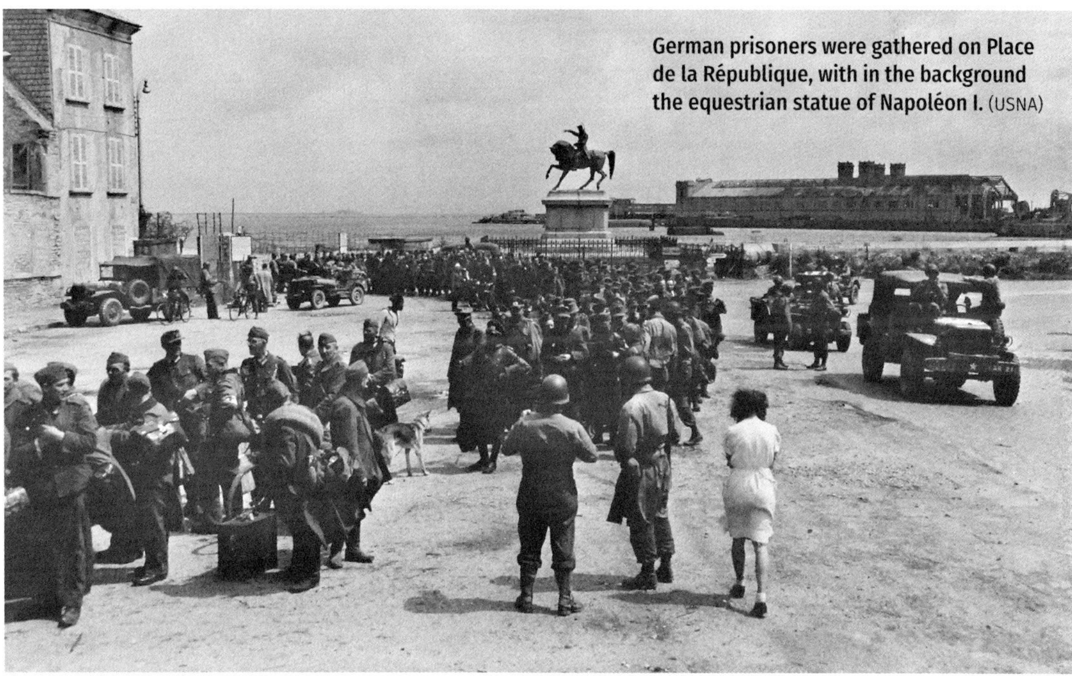

German prisoners were gathered on Place
de la République, with in the background
the equestrian statue of Napoléon I. (USNA)

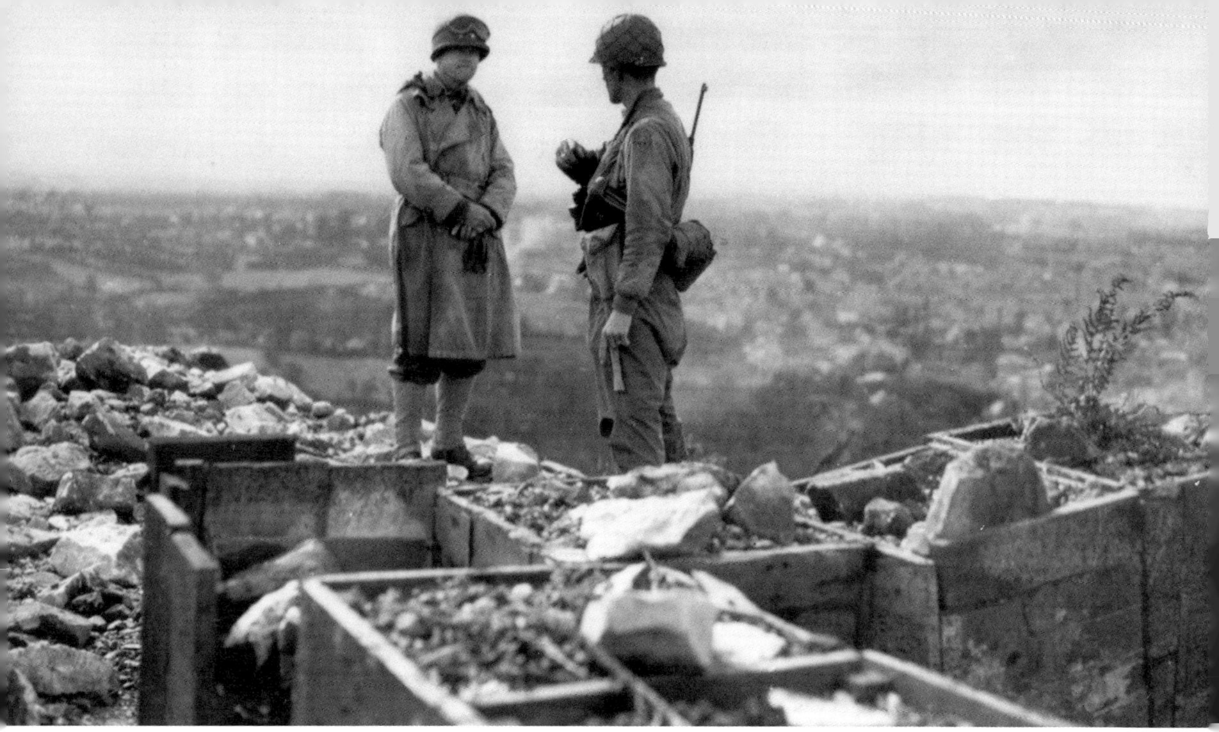

Cherbourg in his hands, Collins returned to the summit of Fort du Roule on June 27 to complete his visit. Here he listens to Captain Robert B. Kirkpatrick of the 79th Division explain his unit's part in the capture of the fort. Whether this photograph was taken during Collins's first visit to Fort du Roule, on the 26th, or his second, on the 27th, is unclear. (USNA)

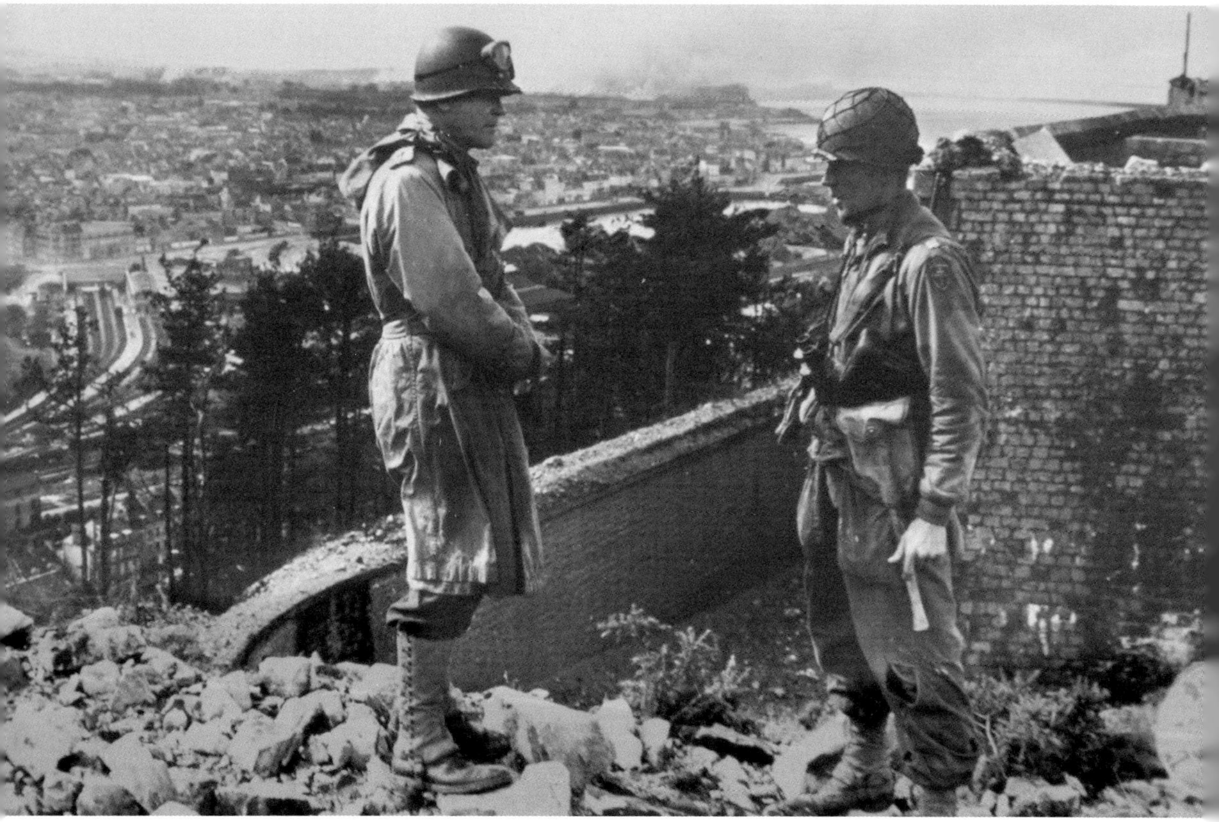

On the afternoon of June 27, in a moving ceremony in front of the city hall, General Collins formally returned Cherbourg to French civil control, presenting the tricolour to Mayor Paul Renault in the presence of the city council and the commanders of the five American divisions that, as part of his corps, had made the capture of Cherbourg possible. (USNA)

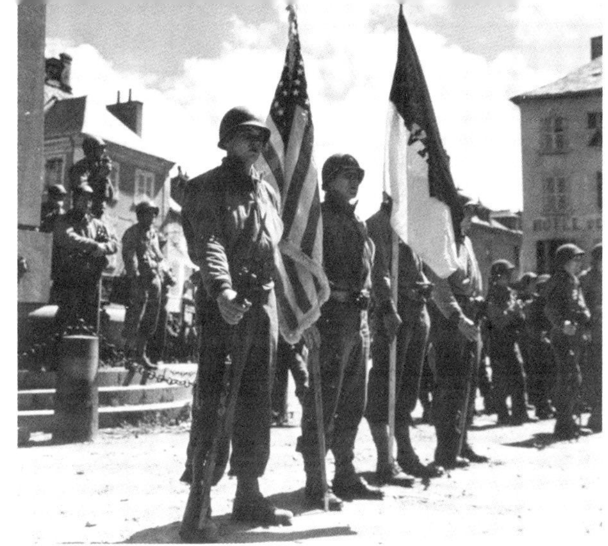

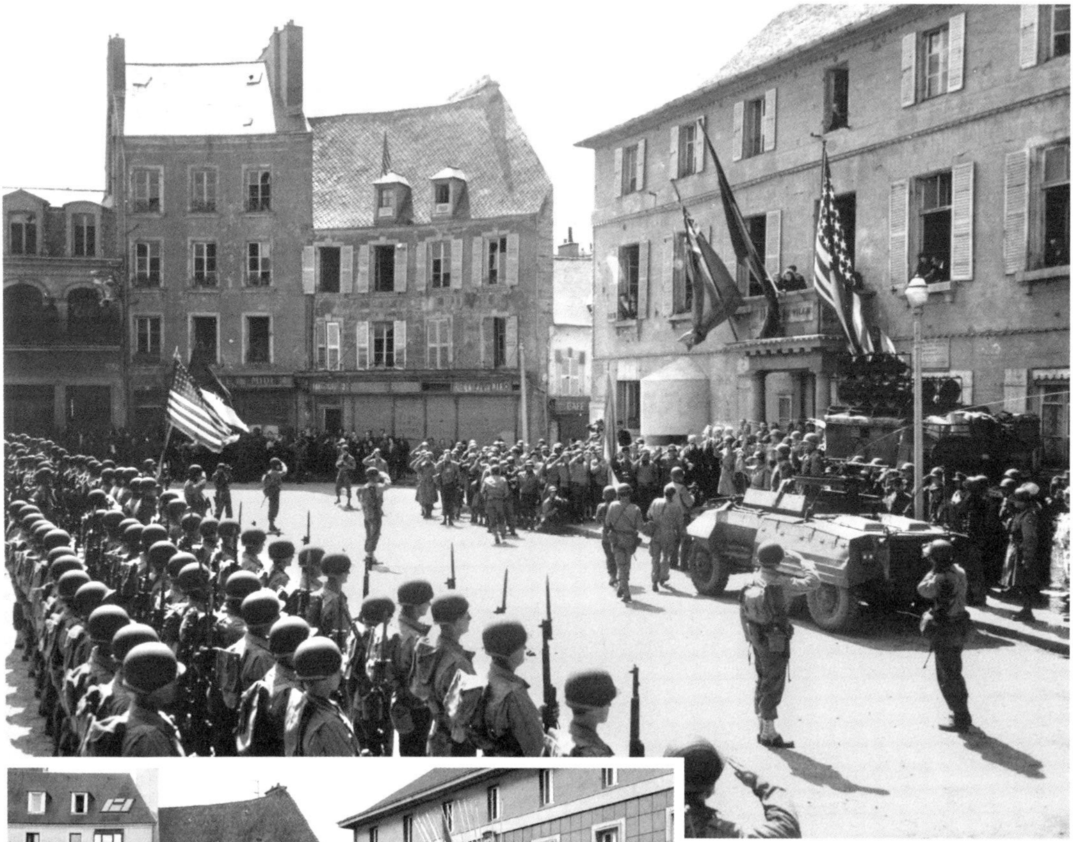

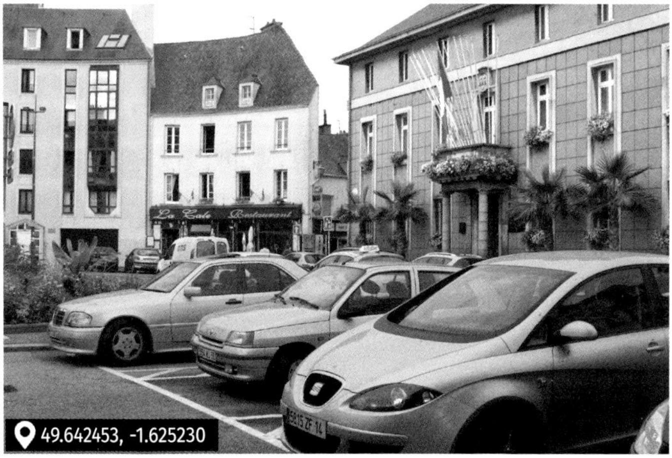

As Collins recalled in his memoirs: 'Speaking in halting French, I said simply that we Americans were proud to return to our sister republic its first city to be liberated by the Allies. Renault replied eloquently, expressing the gratitude of his townsmen at being free from Nazi control, and pledged eternal friendship of France for America.' (USNA and ATB)

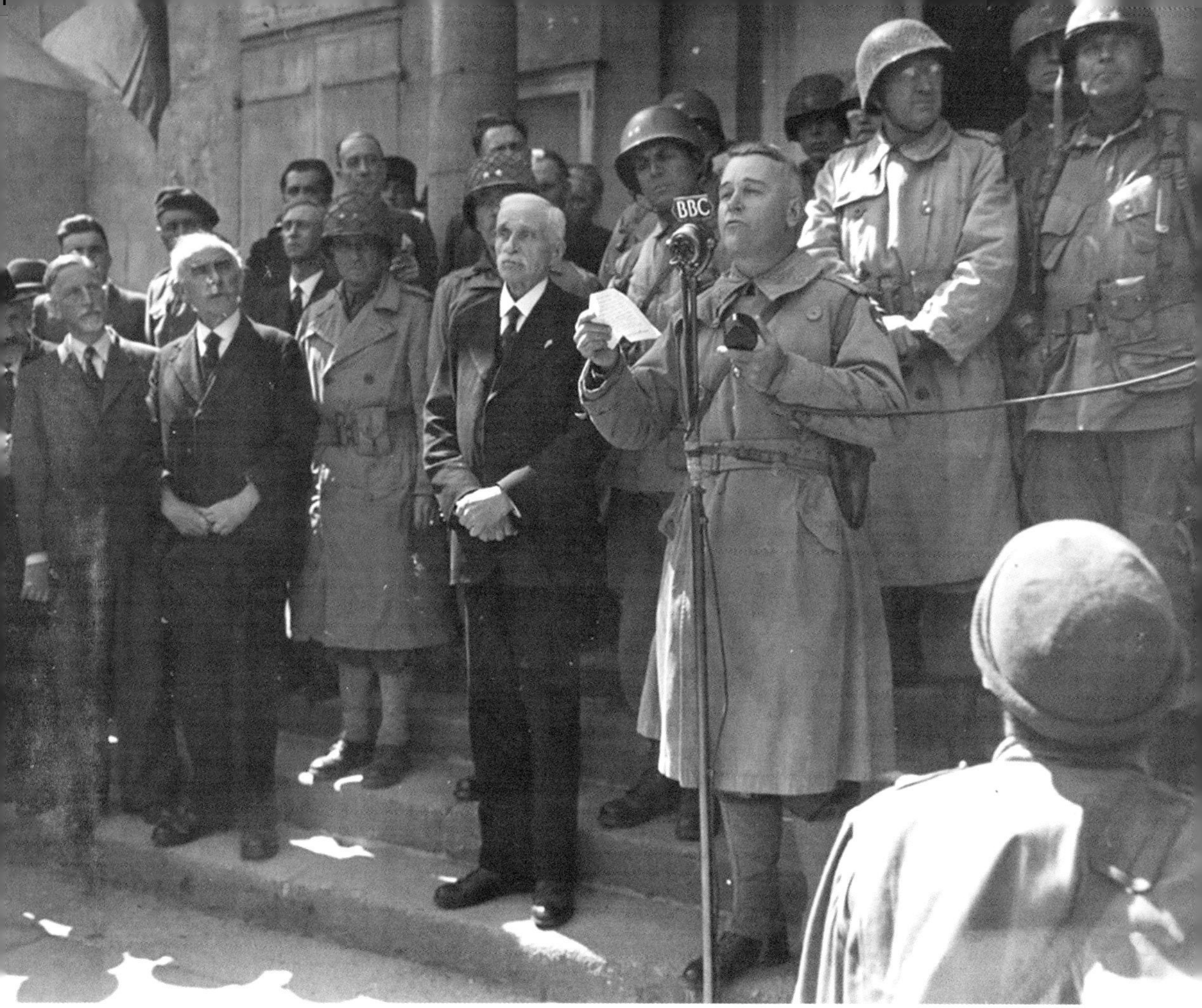

Lined up behind Renault and Collins are (L-R) Major Generals Ira T. Wyche (79th Division), Raymond O. Barton (4th Division), Matthew B. Ridgway (82nd Airborne), Manton Eddy (9th Division) and Maxwell D. Taylor (101st Airborne).

(USNA and ATB)

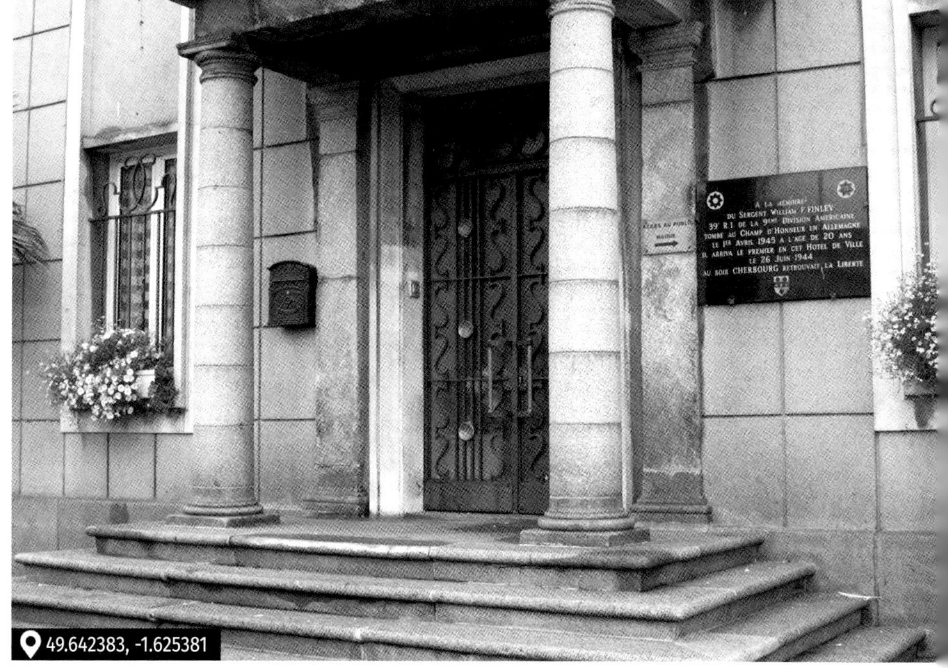

49.642383, -1.625381

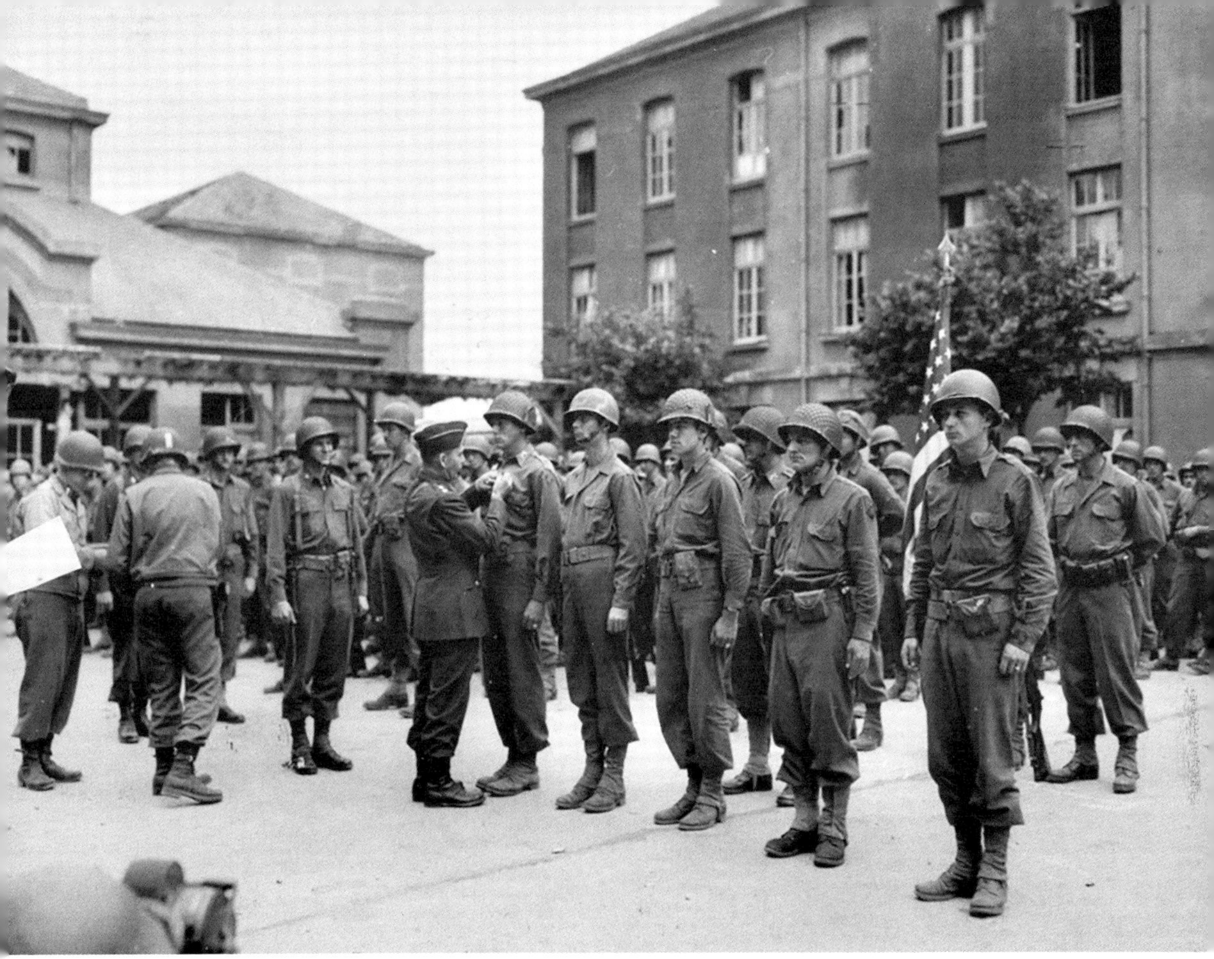

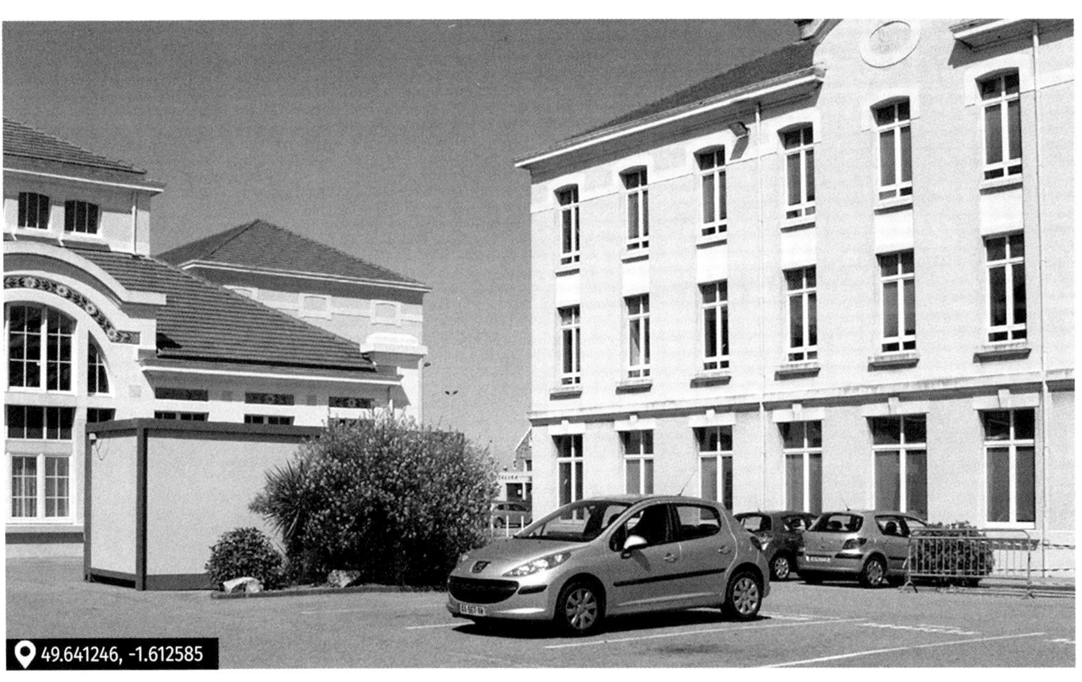

More ceremonies and parades were held in Cherbourg on July 3, when Silver Stars were awarded to men of the 4th Division. Then and Now in the yard of the Hôtel Atlantique on Rue Dom Pedro. (USNA and ATB)

REDUCING THE FINAL STRONG POINTS

On the east of Cherbourg, the 22nd Infantry fought all day on June 26 against determined resistance to clear the Maupertus airfield. The regiment did not clear the airfield until the 27th and then speedily overran the last fortified positions to the coast. Batterie 'Hamburg' surrendered 990 troops.

In the early hours of June 27, just before the surrender of the Arsenal, Fregattenkapitän Witt, the Port Commander, escaped with two boats to the Fort de l'Ouest and took command of the garrison of 185 men in that fort and in another stronghold on the breakwater, the Fort du Centre. This picture of an 88mm gun in Fort du Centre was taken on July 2, after the final surrender of Witt and his small party. Motor launch *ML 138* entered the Passe de l'Ouest, the first Allied ship to enter the Grande Rade. (USNA)

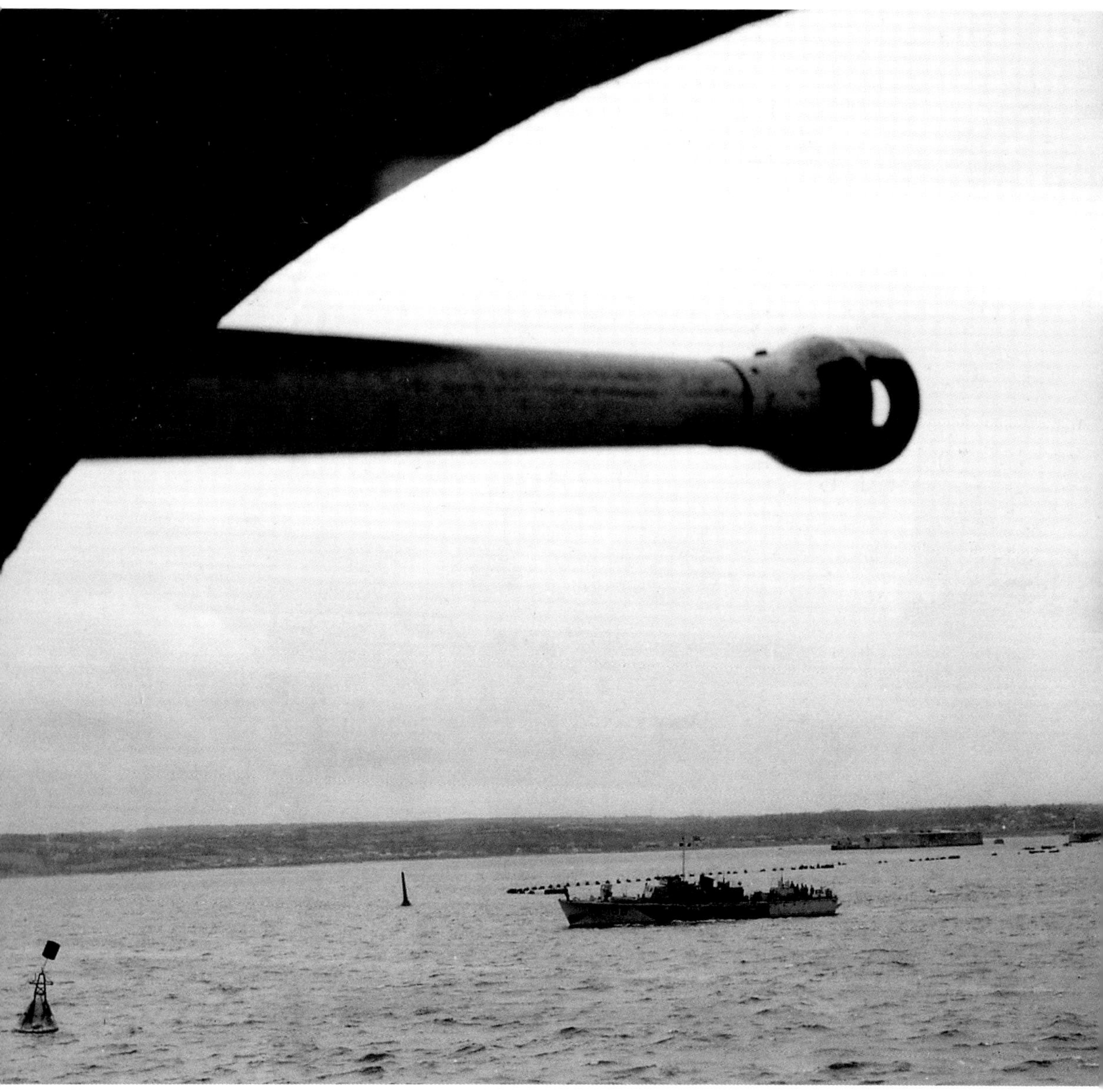

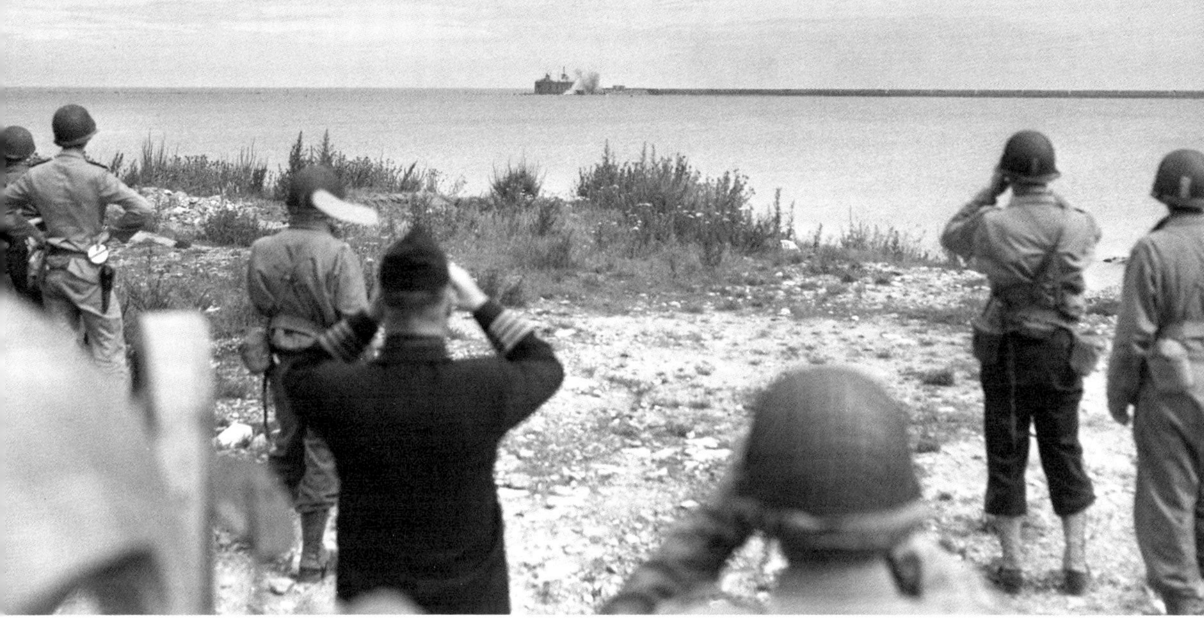

Last shots at Cherbourg. US Army and Navy officers watched P-47s delivering 'a thunderous bombardment' of the outlying forts on the breakwater. (USNA)

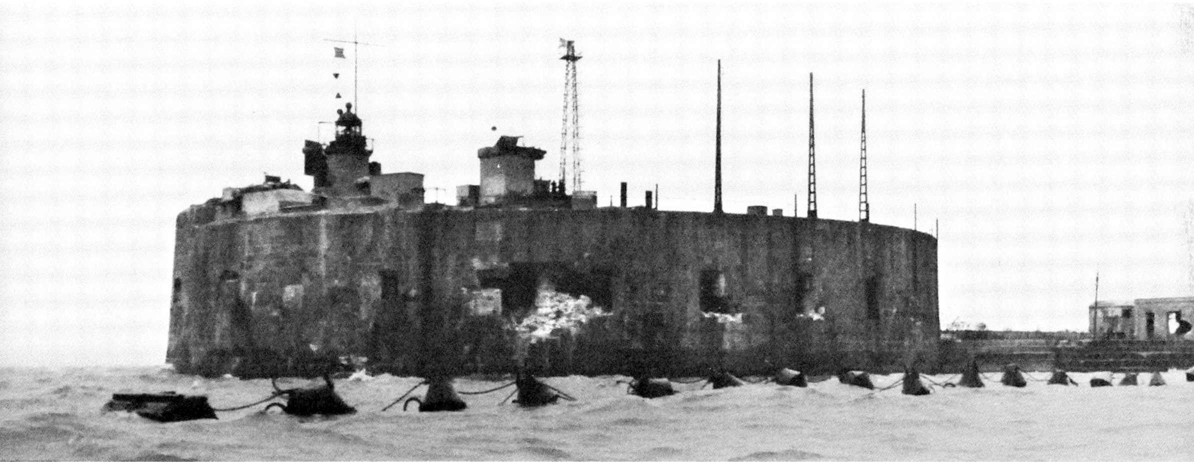

More bombing raids followed and heavier artillery fire hammered the two forts. The original caption of this photo points that 'shells from naval gun ripped into mine-control room of Fort de l'Ouest'. (USNA and Brynja Etapsdottir)

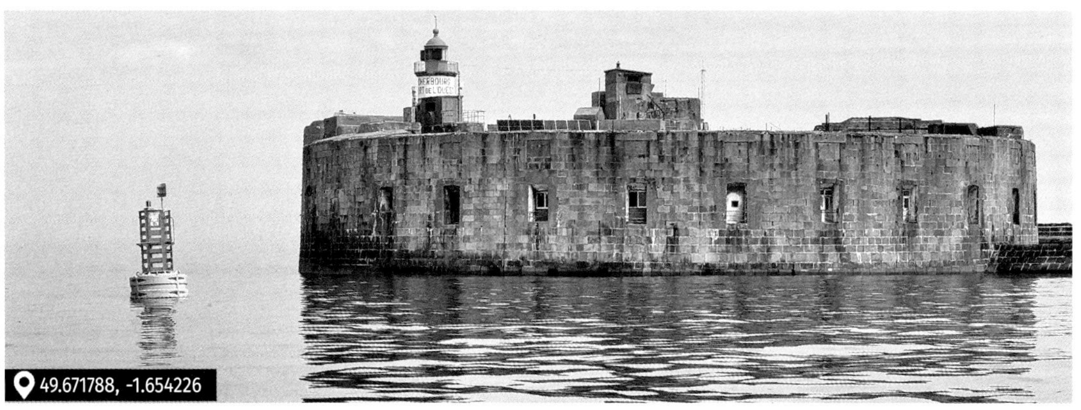

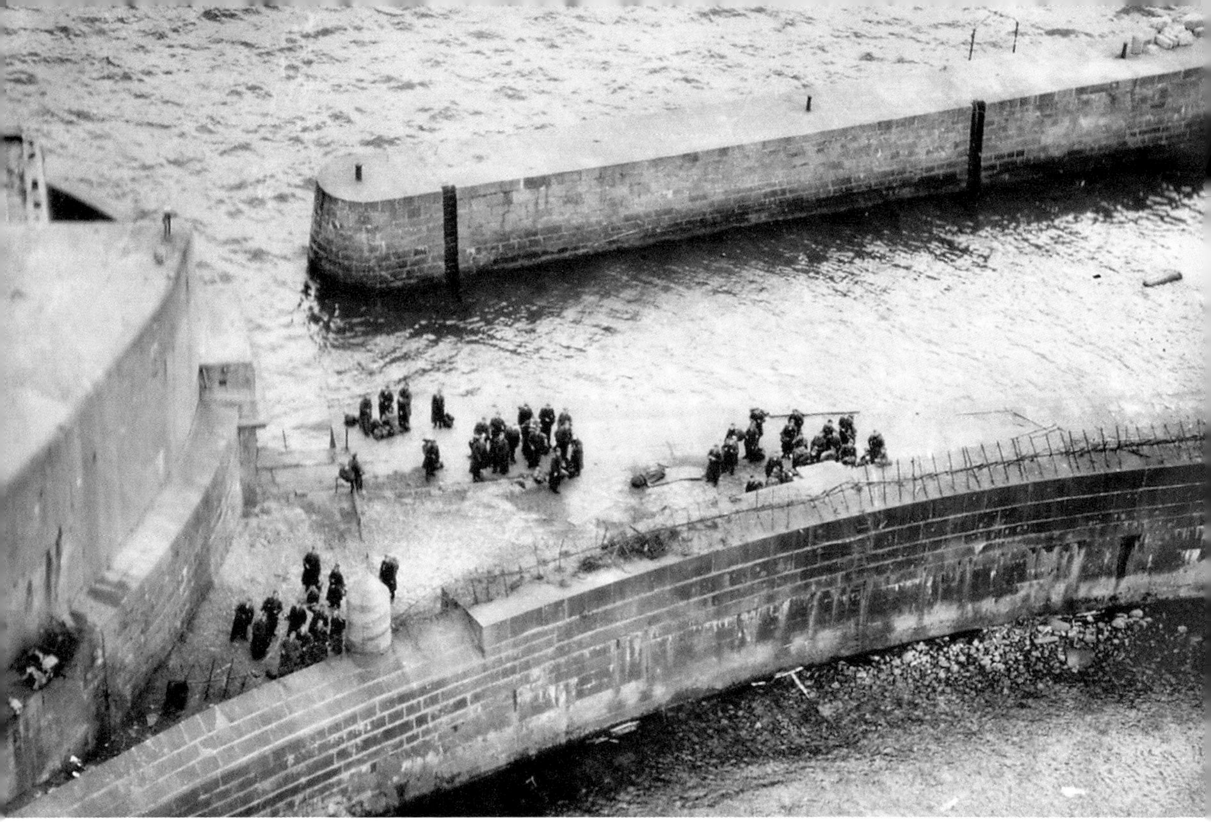

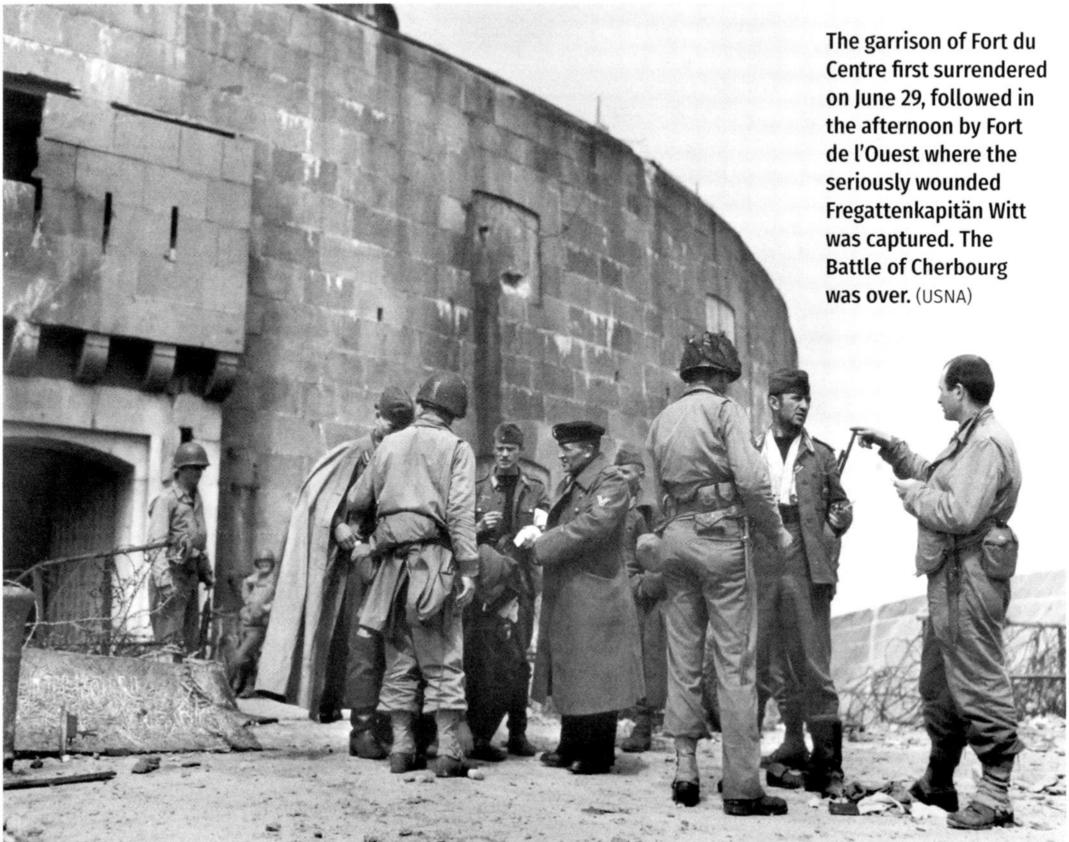

The garrison of Fort du Centre first surrendered on June 29, followed in the afternoon by Fort de l'Ouest where the seriously wounded Fregattenkapitän Witt was captured. The Battle of Cherbourg was over. (USNA)

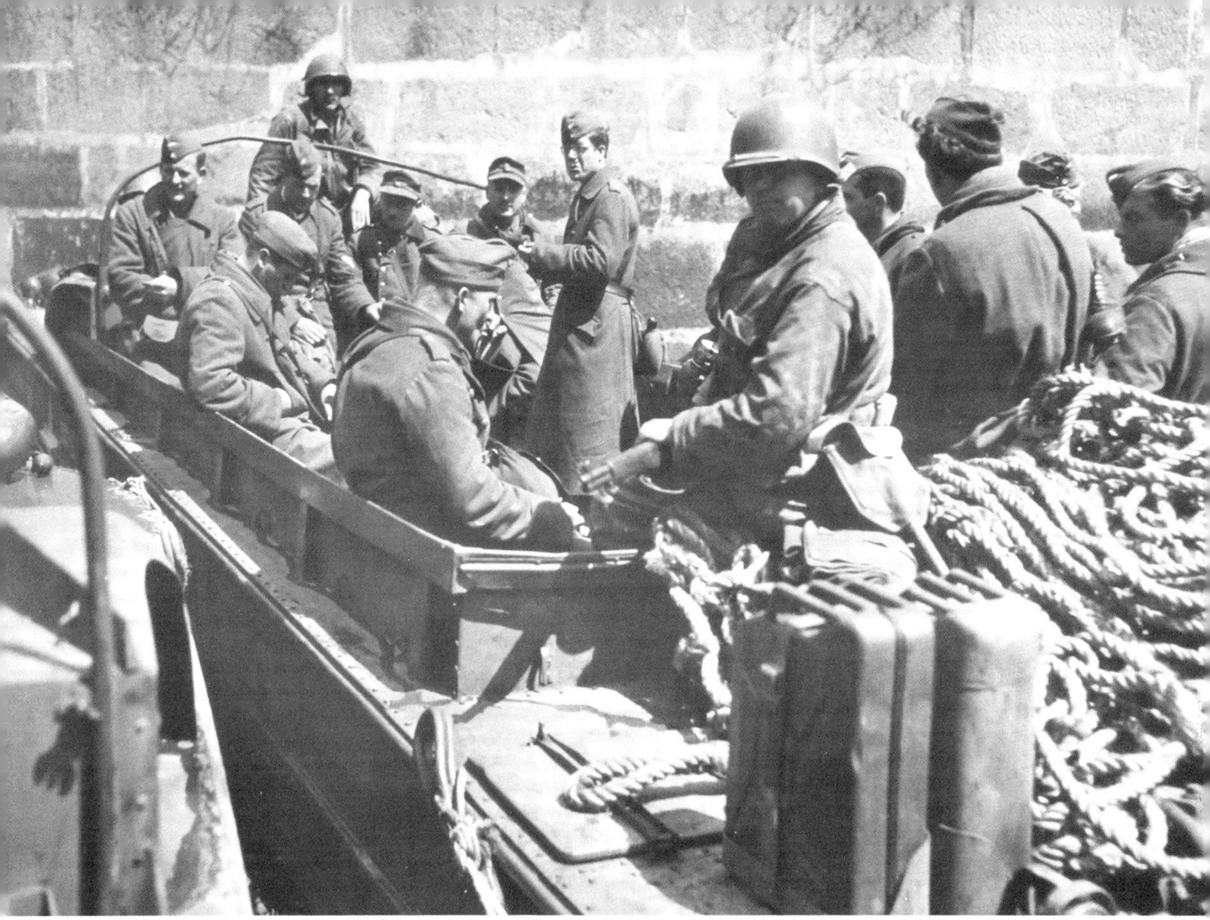

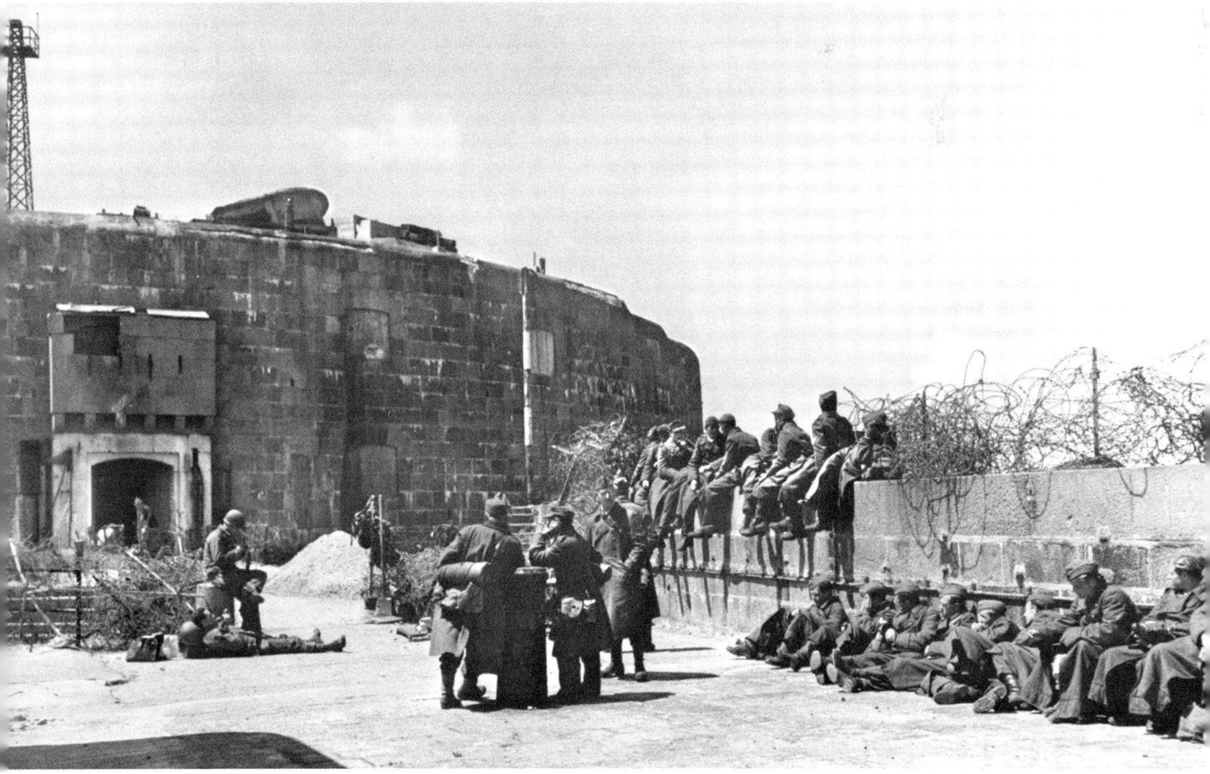

With that, organised resistance northeast of Cherbourg collapsed. Cavalry reconnoitring east to Barfleur found the area unoccupied

West of Cherbourg, the final clearing of Cap de la Hague began on June 29 when the 9th Division attacked with the 47th Infantry advancing up the north coast, the 60th Infantry in the centre, and the 4th Cavalry Group on the left. Resistance was encountered but the attackers quickly drove right up to the tip of the cape, clearing out strong points and rounding up prisoners. The senior German commander, Oberstleutnant Günther Keil, was captured about midnight on June 30 and the mop-up netted about 6,000 prisoners, or twice the number estimated to be in the cape.

In the battle for the Cotentin and Cherbourg, VII Corps had suffered a total of over 22,000 casualties, including 2,800 killed, 5,700 missing, and 13,500 wounded. The Germans had lost 39,000 men taken prisoner in addition to an undetermined number of men killed.

From the German point of view, the fall of Cherbourg had come much sooner than expected. The denial of French ports to the Allies formed a major part of German tactical planning and the German command had anticipated that, even if the Cotentin peninsula was isolated and reinforcements were prevented from reaching the Cherbourg fortress, it could still hold out for several weeks (as Brest was to do later). Hitler took the quick capitulation of Cherbourg badly, and thereafter in Nazi circles von Schlieben was held up as an example of a very poor commander.

REHABILITATION OF THE PORT

EVEN BEFORE THE last harbour forts surrendered on June 29, American engineers and naval personnel had begun detailed reconnaissance of the extent of damage to the port. What they found was not encouraging. Colonel Alvin G. Viney, who prepared the original engineer plan for port rehabilitation, wrote: 'The demolition of the port of Cherbourg is a masterful job, beyond a doubt the most-complete, intensive and best-planned demolition in history.' The harbour was strewn with a variety of different types of mines. All basins in the military and commercial port were blocked with sunken ships. The Gare Maritime, containing the electrical control system and heating plant for the port, was demolished and 20,000 cubic yards of masonry were blown into the large deep basin (Darse Transatlantique) that had been used in peacetime for docking Atlantic liners. The entrance of this basin was completely blocked by two large ships. Quay walls were severely damaged. Cranes were demolished in all areas. The left breakwater in the inner harbour (Jetée du Homet) was cratered so that the sea poured through. The whole port was as nearly a wreck as demolitions could make it. For this work of destruction, Hitler awarded the Knight's Cross to Admiral Hennecke the day after his capture by VII Corps troops, calling the job 'a feat unprecedented in the annals of coastal defence'.

Planning estimates based on experience at Naples had calculated that Cherbourg could begin operations three days after its capture. In reality it was almost three weeks before the port was opened. The minesweeping of the western portion of the harbour was not completed until July 14, and not until the end of September were all the obstructions cleared from the harbour. The work of reconstructing port facilities began before the last forts had surrendered. The advance party of the US 1056th Engineer Port Construction and Repair Group arrived in Cherbourg on June 27.

On June 28, a priority program was agreed to rehabilitate four areas of the port: (1) the Nouvelle Plage, suitable for DUKWs; (2) the Bassin à Flot or wet basin of the commercial port, for barge discharge; (3) the Reclamation area, for railway rolling stock and LSTs; and (4) the Digue du Homet, for Liberty ships and seatrains.

It was found possible to raise undamaged vessels simply by patching the breaches at low water and then floated the ship at high tide. In this way four of the sixteen vessels blocking the entrance to the Port de Commerce were

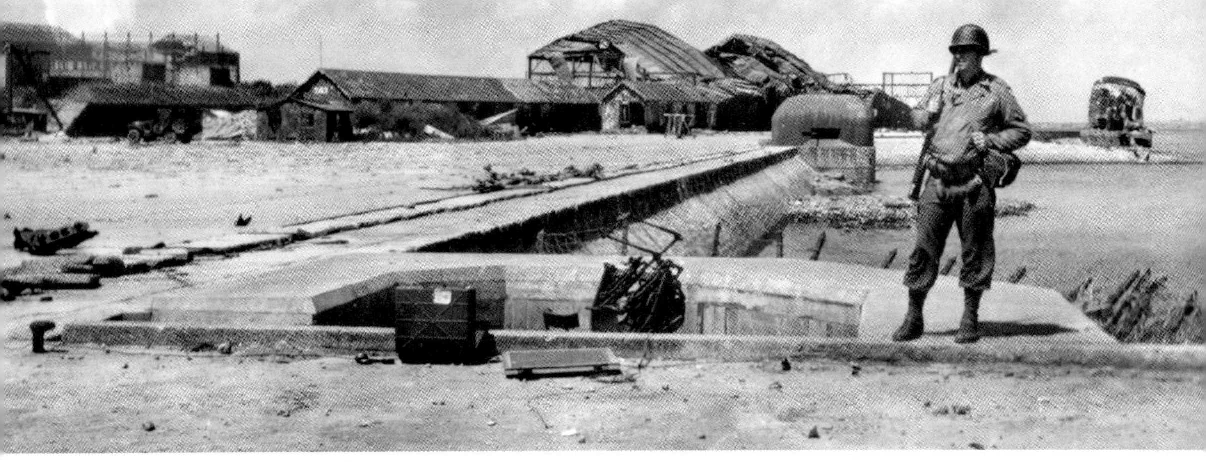

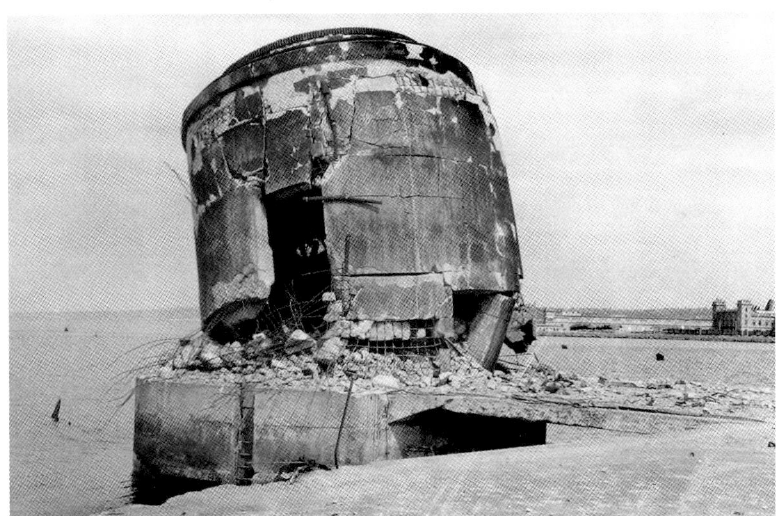

The battle over, Signal Corps photographers toured the harbour and German defences to picture ruined buildings, wrecked quays, and sunken ships. The tower (in the background of the first photograph) was not the 'ruins of a fort' as claimed by the original Signal Corps caption but the remains of the large crane used to put seaplanes to water in the French Chantereyne naval air base (see page 10). (USNA)

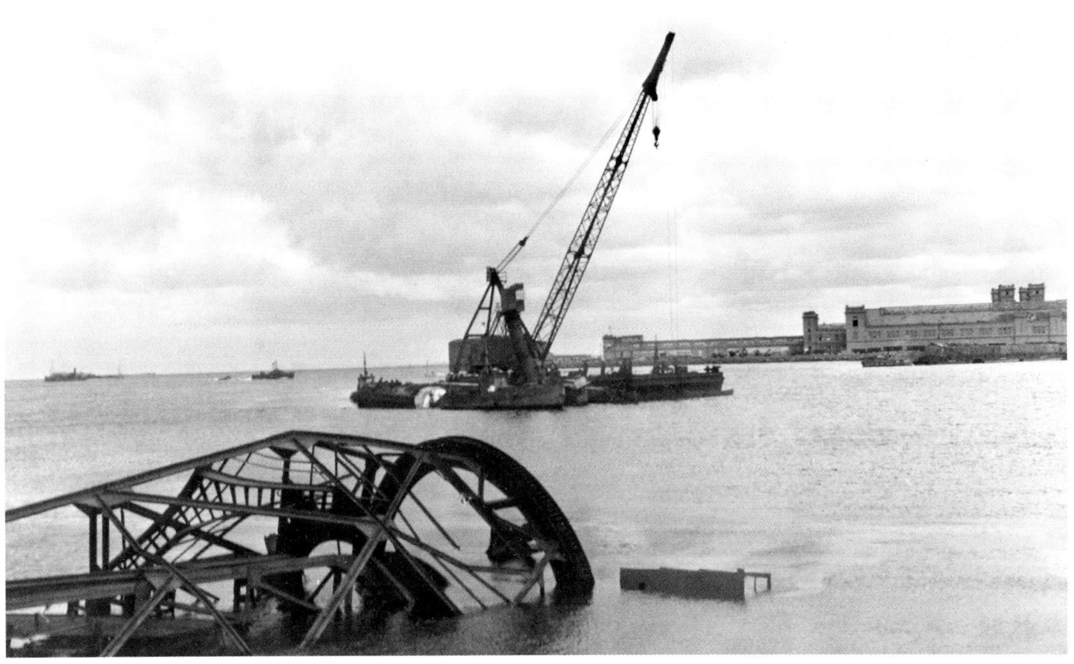

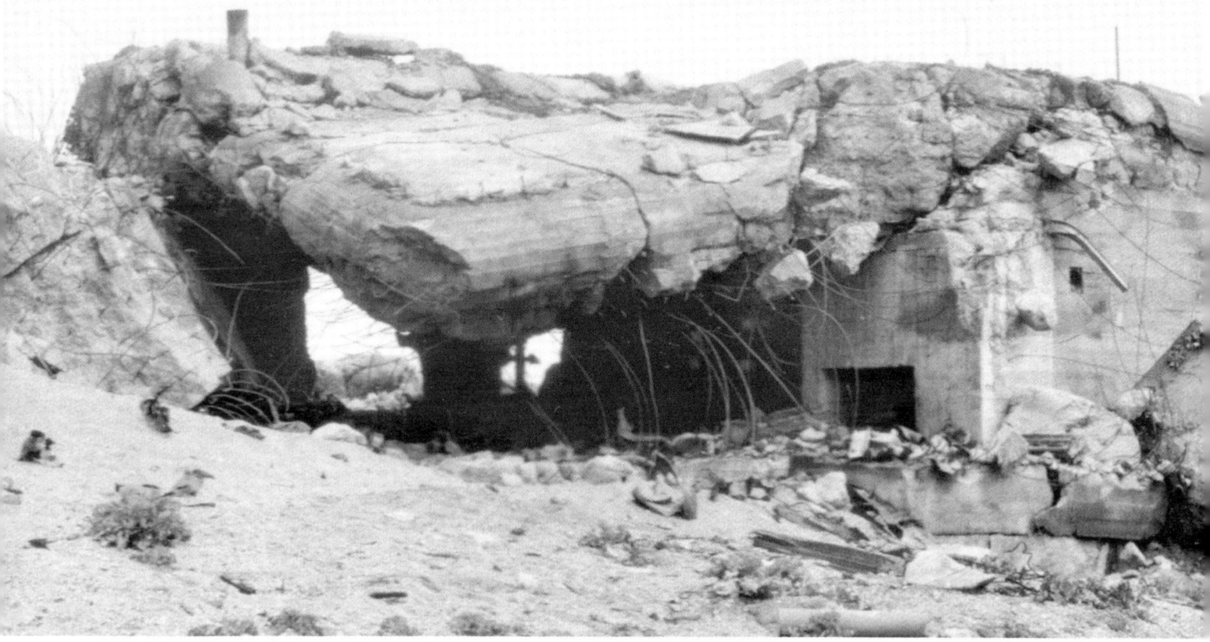

The remains of the Type M272 casemate of Batterie 'Blankenese' in the dunes near Néville, 25 kilometres east of Cherbourg. The battery was destroyed on the orders by its crew on June 18 before withdrawing into the ring of defences. This photo shows the rear of the pillbox, and the impressive damage is the result of destruction tests conducted by American engineers after the battle. (USNA and ATB)

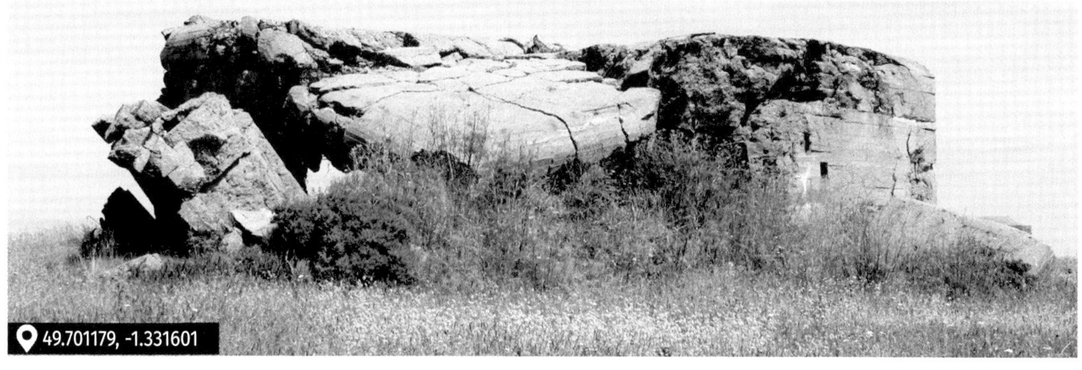

West of Cherbourg, at Auderville-Laye, Signal Corps photographers photographed the two 203mm guns of the 3. Batterie, Heeres-Küsten-Artillerie-Regiment 1262, abandoned in poor condition in their circular platforms (see pages 31 to 33). (USNA)

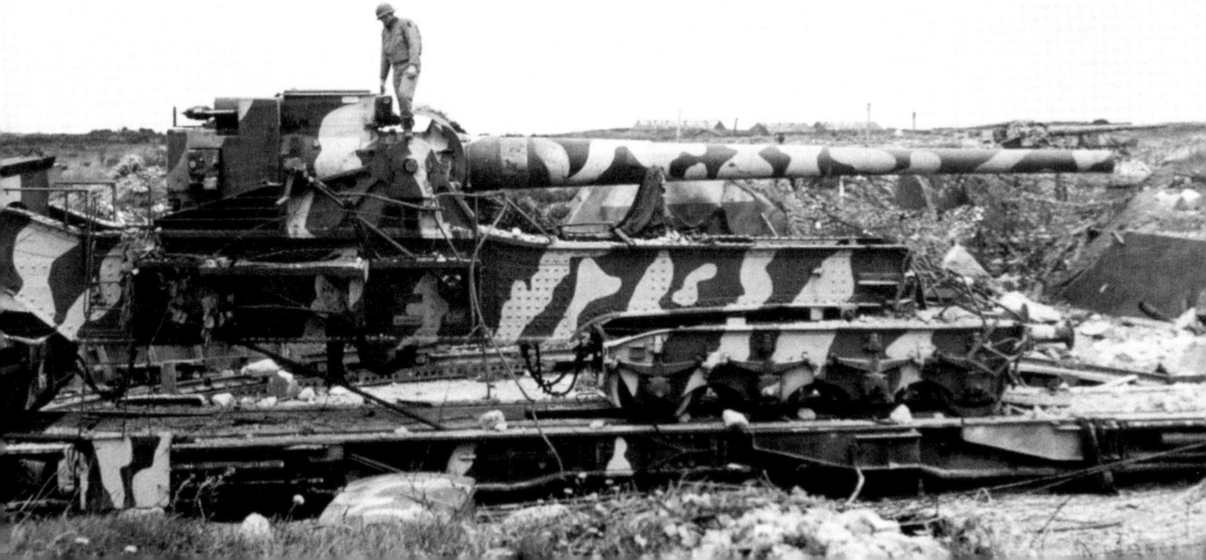

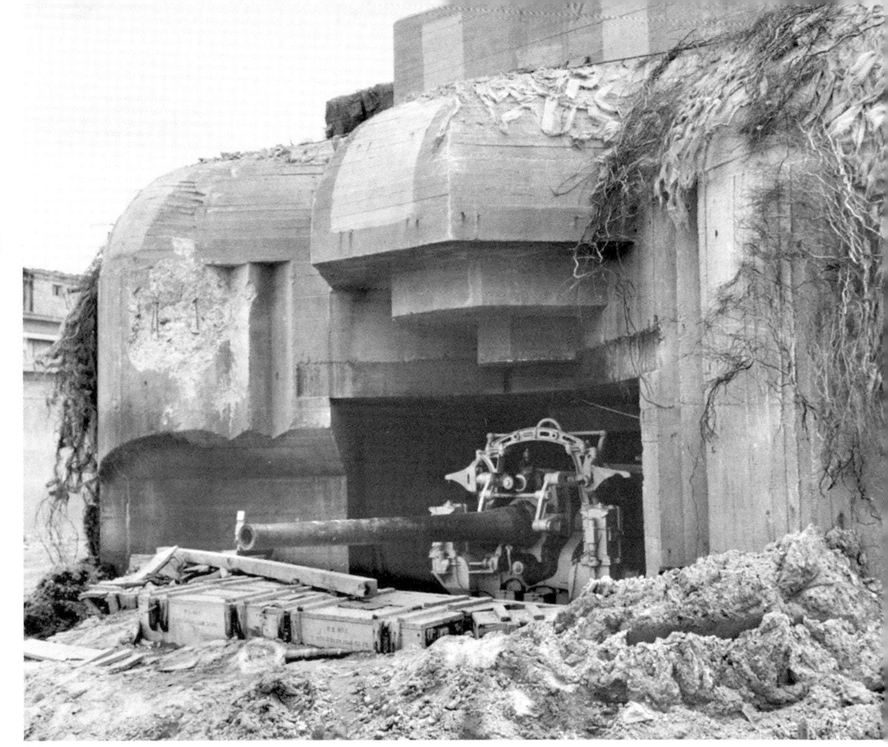

In front of the mole of the Gare Maritime, two casemates were armed with 75mm guns captured from the French, known in German service as the 7.5 cm Flak M.22-24 (f). Each of these casemates was topped with an open emplacement with a 20mm Flak 38 anti-aircraft gun. Note how ammunition boxes filled with earth added some protection in front of the embrasure. At the rear of the casemate, the Signal Corps photographer pictured a large stock of 75mm shells. (USNA)

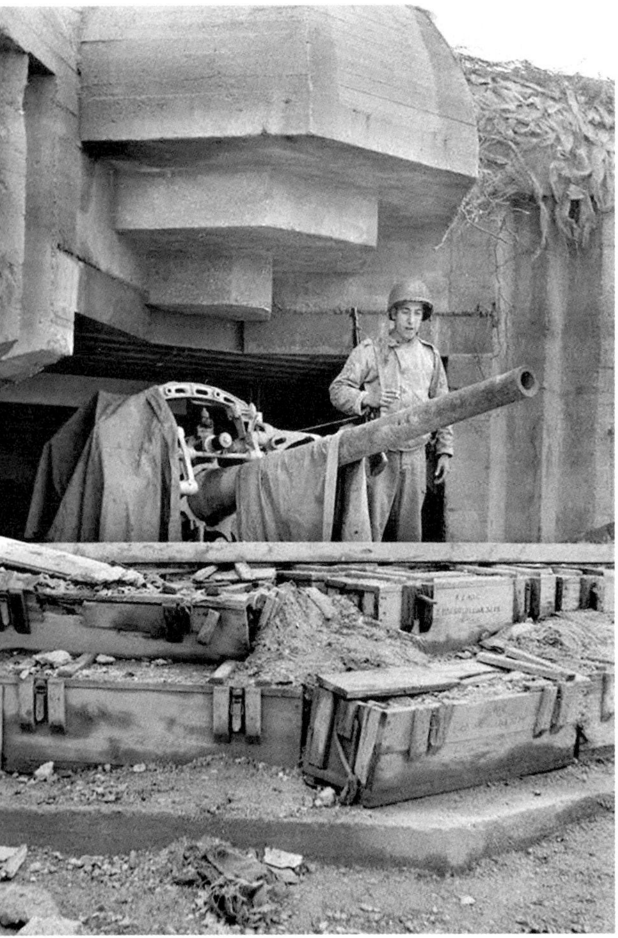

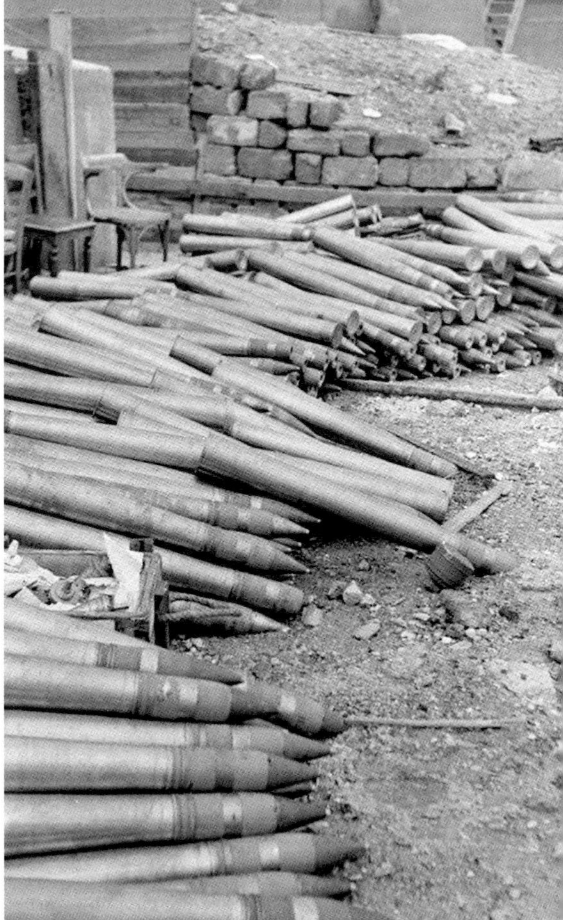

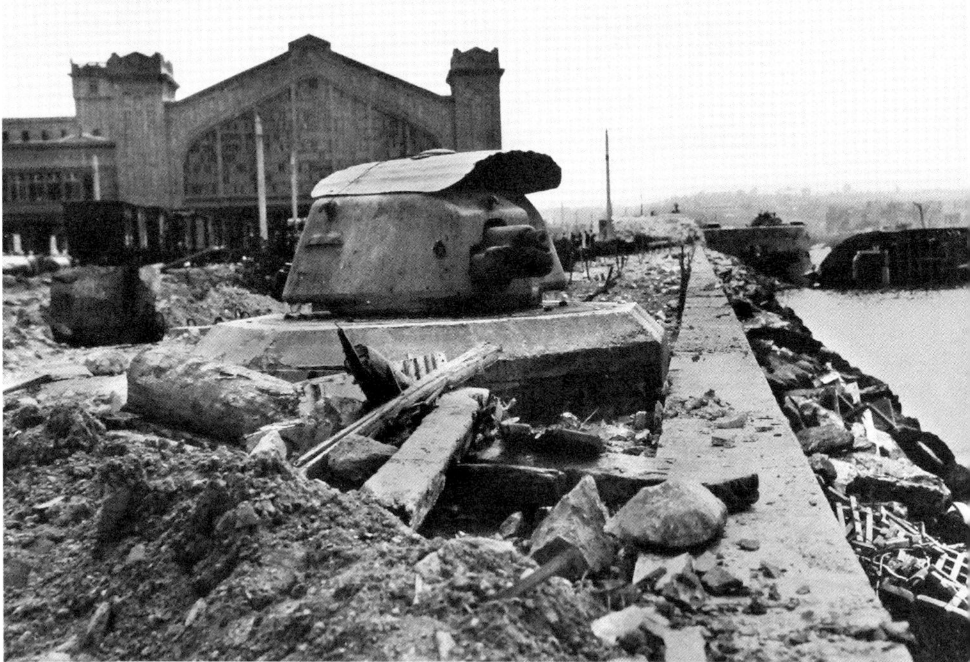

As part of the harbour defence, the Germans mounted the armoured turret from a French Renault R35 on a concrete base. This photo was taken looking south, in front of the Gare Maritime, with the entrance to the Port de Commerce (right) blocked by the sunken coaster *Le Normand*. (USNA)

In Cherbourg, curious GIs inspected a rare Rakentenwerfer 43. Nicknamed 'Puppchen' this antitank rocket launcher fired a rocket-propelled grenade with a hollow-charge warhead. It soon appeared that a simple hollow tube was enough to launch the same 88mm rocket and the 'Puppchen', an elaborate artillery piece with carriage and breech, was discarded in favour of the much lighter and handy 'Panzerschreck', the German version of the bazooka. This photo was taken Rue Dom Pedro near the junction with Rue d'Inkermann. (USNA and ATB)

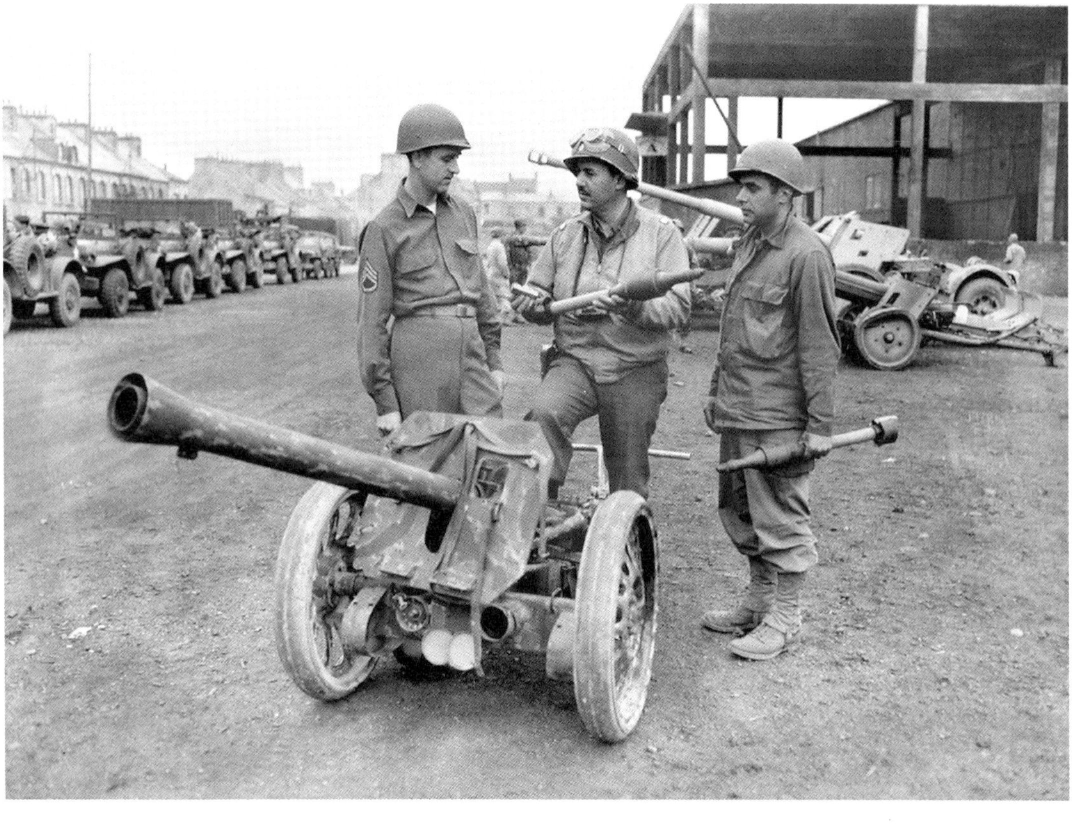

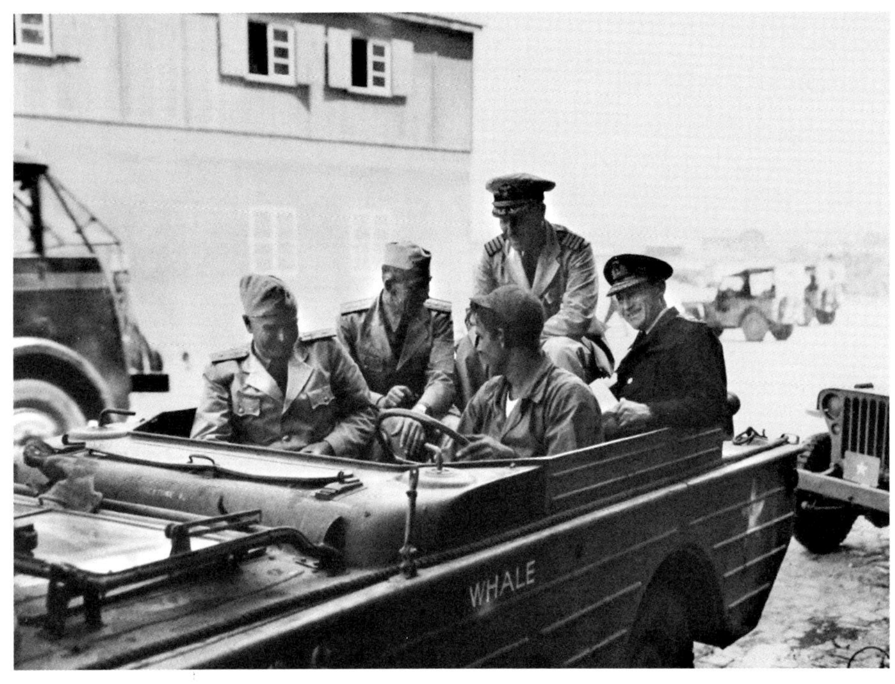

Top brass inspection on July 6. Clockwise (beginning from front): Commander William A. Sullivan, US Navy; Rear Admiral John Wilkes, US Navy; Captain Norman S. Ives, US Navy; and Admiral Sir Bertram Ramsay, Royal Navy. (NHHC)

The first reconnaissance of the harbour showed that 95 percent of the existing quayage capable of handling deep-draft shipping was destroyed; many of the harbour buildings, particularly in the arsenal area, were demolished, cranes were toppled, and bridges blown; and dozens of sunken ships and smaller craft, ranging from a 550-foot whaler to small fishing boats, blocked the entrance channels leading to the various basins and docks. The passage connecting the Avant-Port and Bassin Charles X was blocked by four boats and the demolished swing bridge. Since this passage was too narrow to be of much service no attempt was made to clear it and the 342nd Engineers soon built a bridge across it. (USNA)

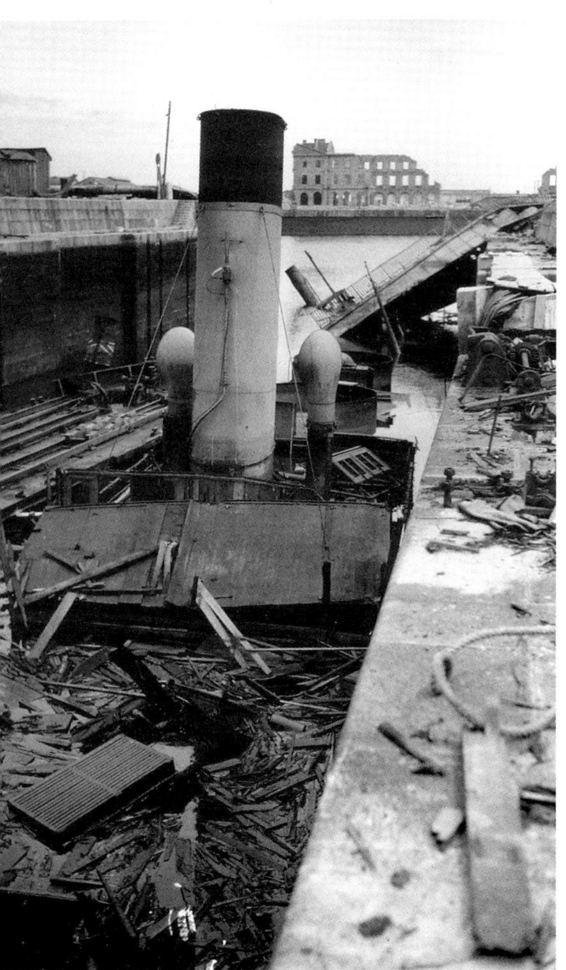

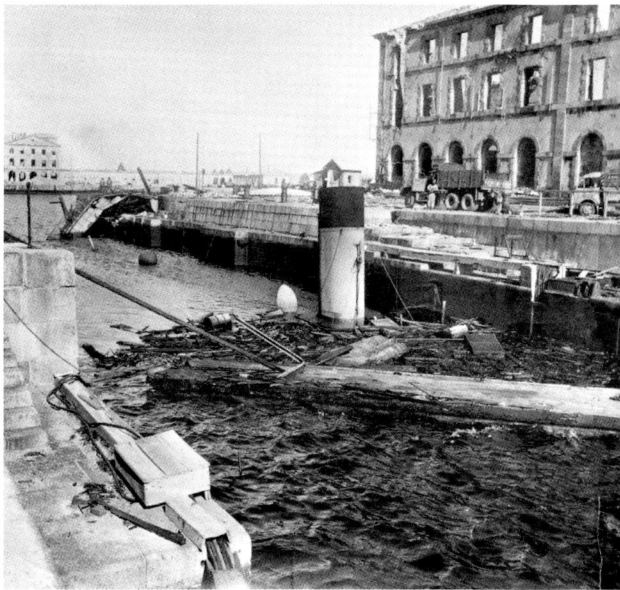

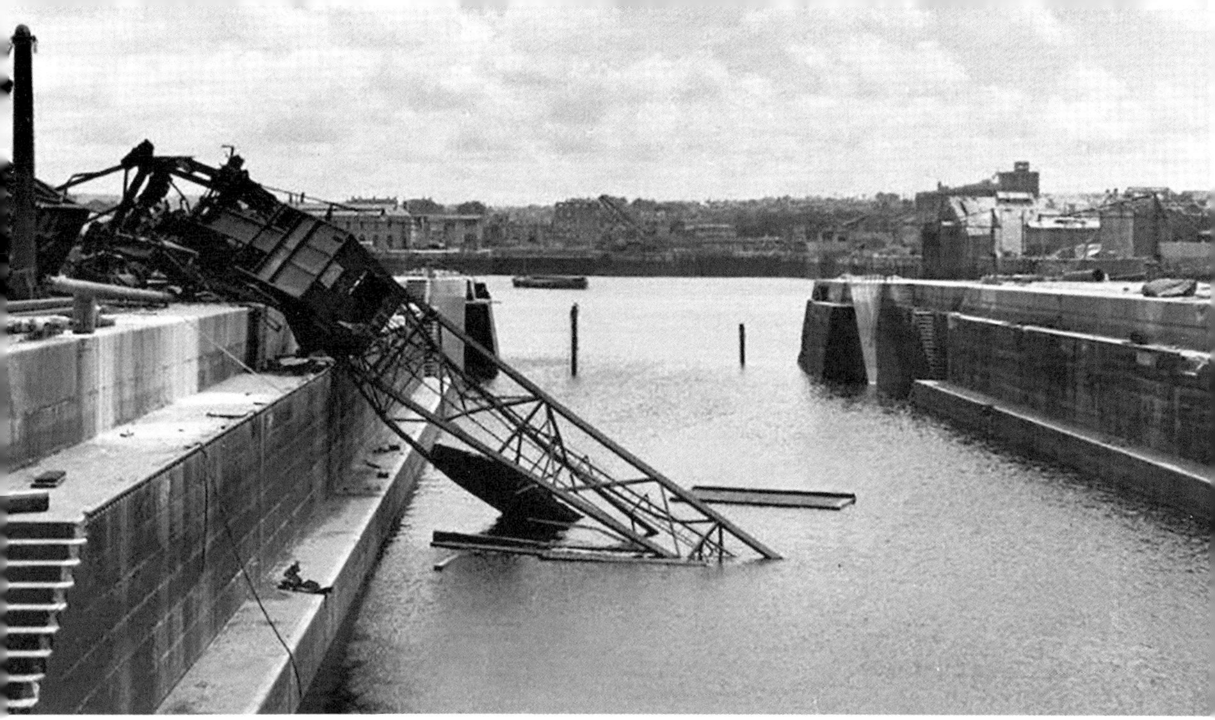

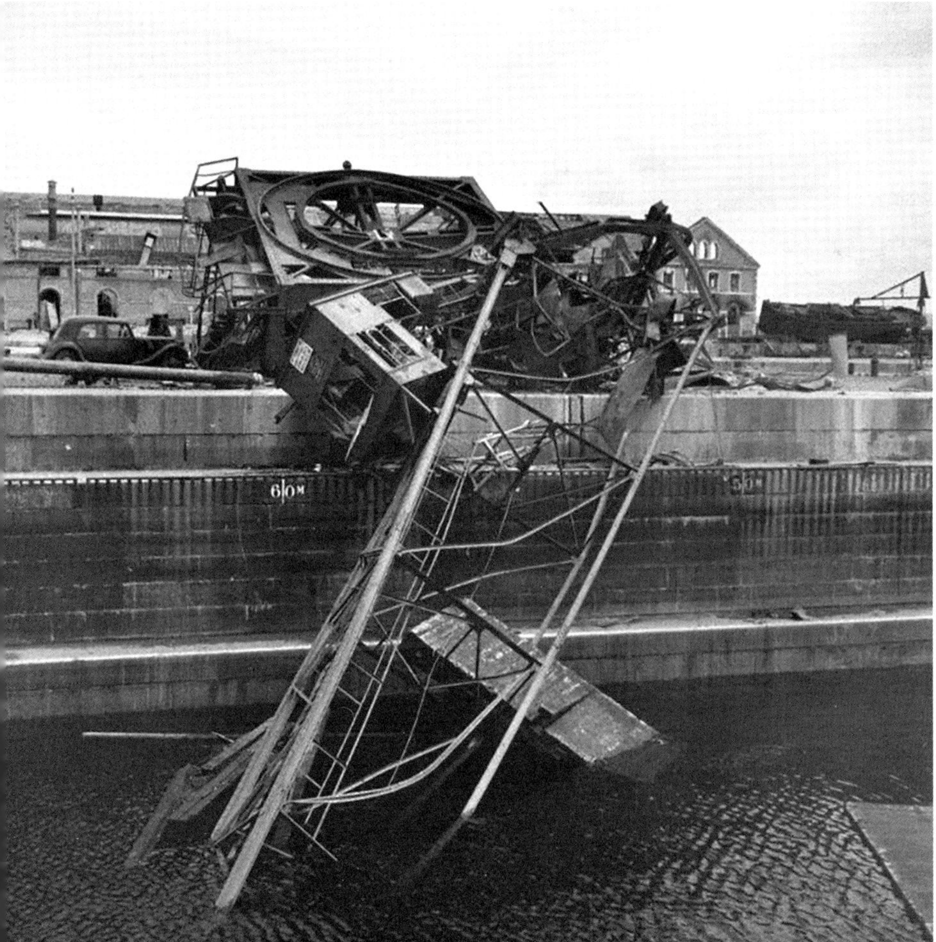

The Arsenal area showed the largest number of sunken vessels: two barges and an old German-built submarine lifting vessel of about 1,000 tons blocked the entrance to the Avant-Port; eight vessels had been sunk in the Avant-Port, eight others in Bassin Charles X, and 15 barges, tugs, and trawlers in Bassin Napoléon III; and many more in the passages leading to these basins. On the northern side of Bassin Napoléon III, the Germans blew this crane down into dry dock No. 2. (USNA)

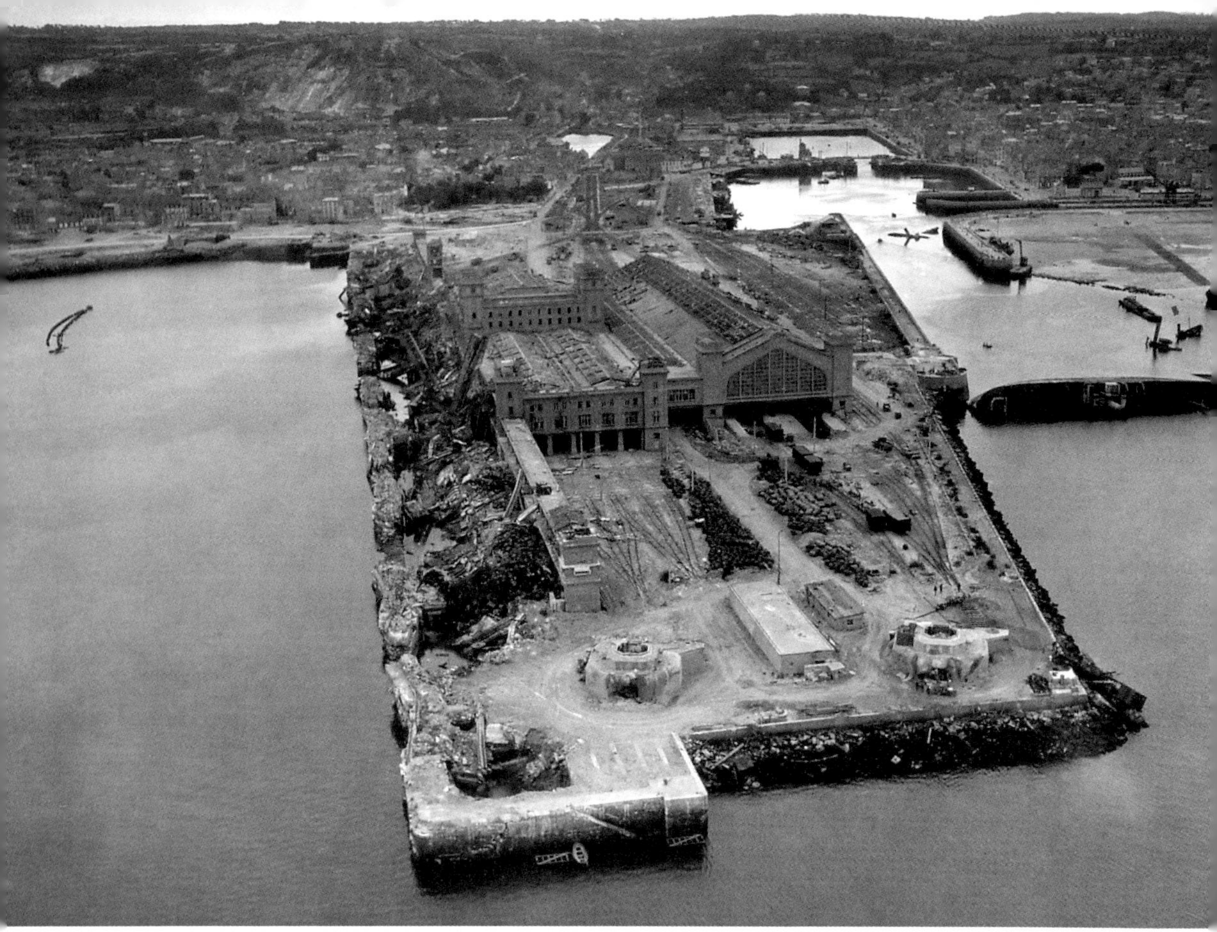

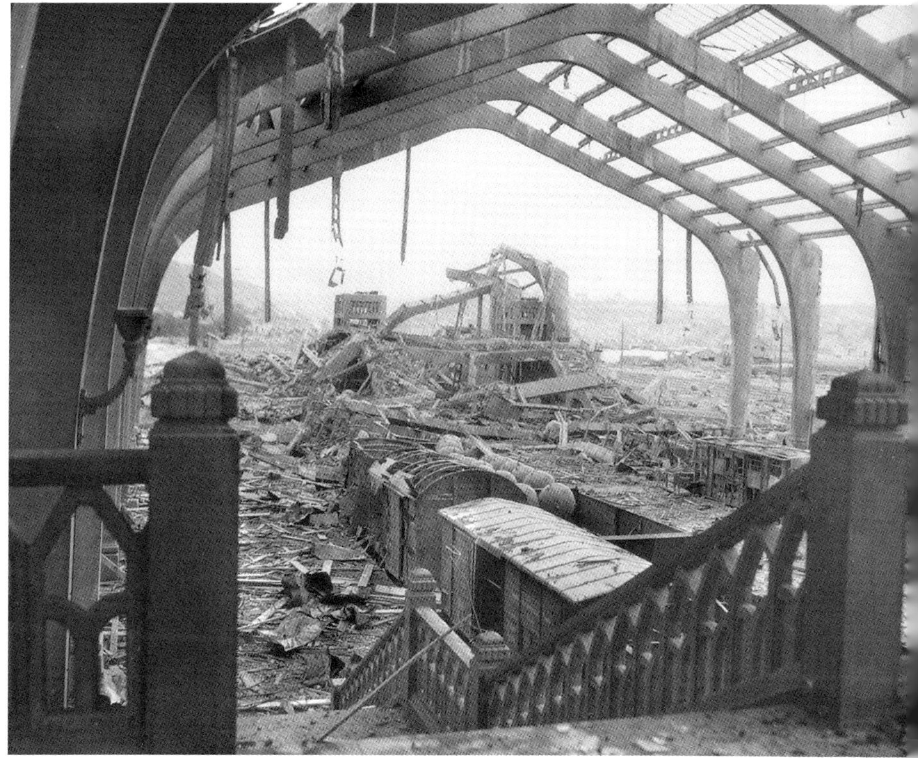

The Gare Maritime – the pride of Cherbourg – with the Darse Transatlantique basin and the impressive damage to the Quai de France on the left. The entrance to the Port de Commerce (right) had been blocked by sinking the coaster *Le Normand*. The casemate seen on the left in the photo still survives but the second one, seen on the right, was demolished in order to clear a passage to move the submarine *Le Redoutable* into the Cité de la Mer. (USNA)

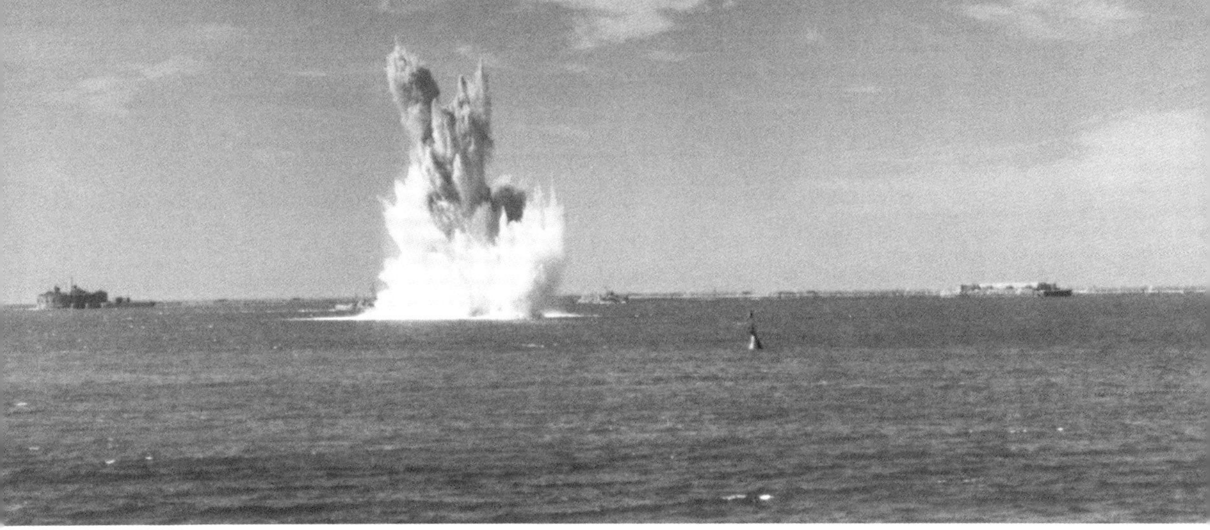

Both the harbour and the roadstead were sown with hundreds of mines. On July 2, Royal Navy minesweepers detonate mines in the Grande Rade. Fort l'Ouest appears in the left background. (USNA)

removed before the arrival of the heavier salvage equipment. No attempt was made to remove the biggest obstacle in the channel, the large coaster *Le Normand*, which lay on her port side at right angles to the west side of the Gare Maritime. Her starboard side was approximately level with the pier of the Gare Maritime, and therefore provided a perfect foundation for a pier at which small coasters could unload.

Similar use was made of the whaler *Solglint* and the coaster *Granlieu*

On July 10, US Navy engineers tilted this mine at an angle of about 45 degrees before to destroy it by burning. (USNA)

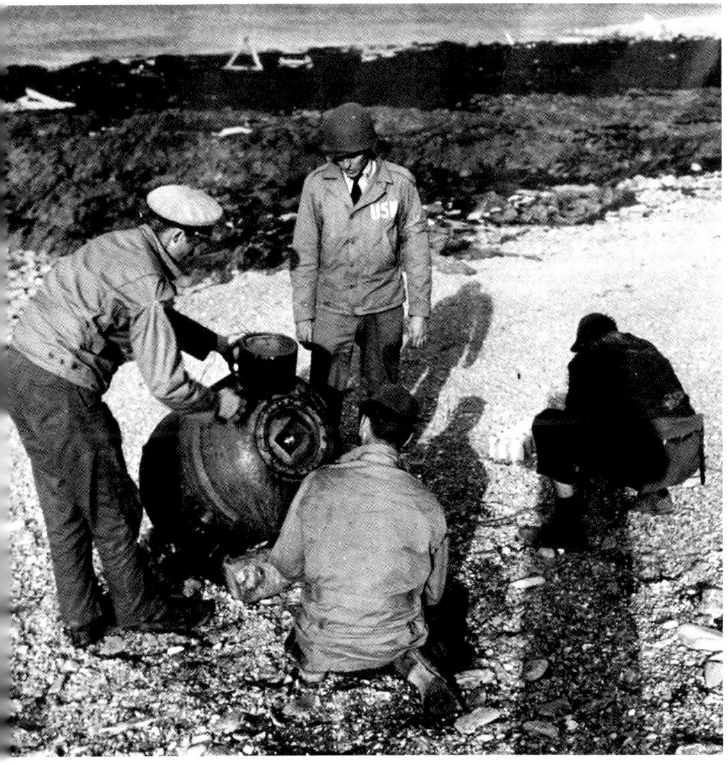

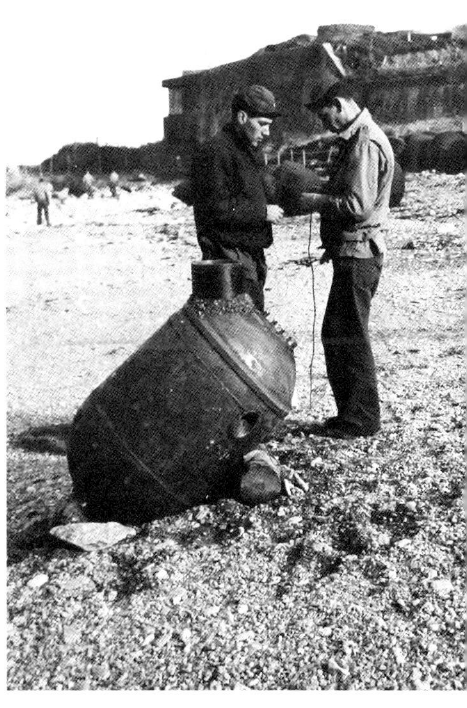

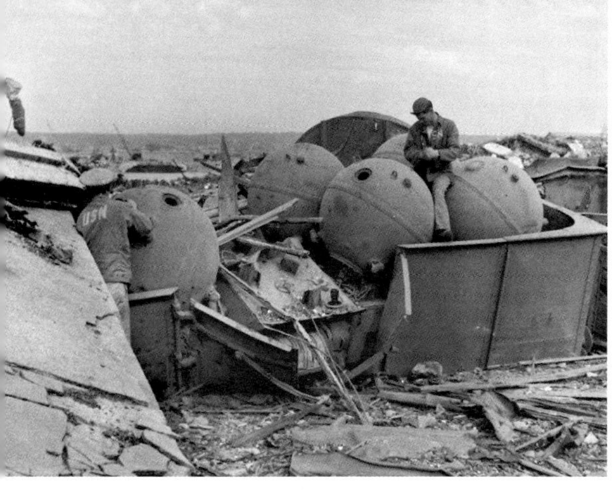

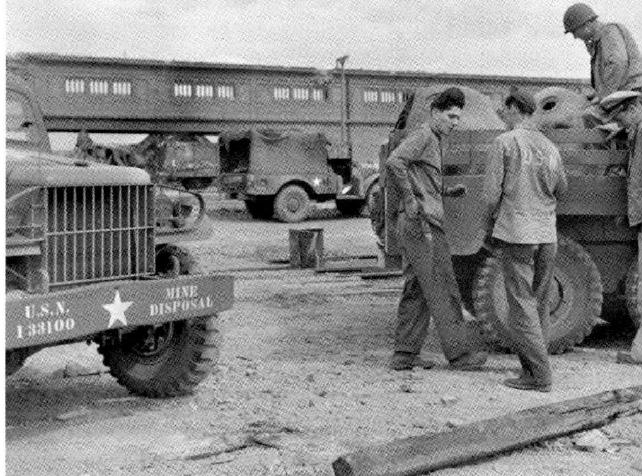

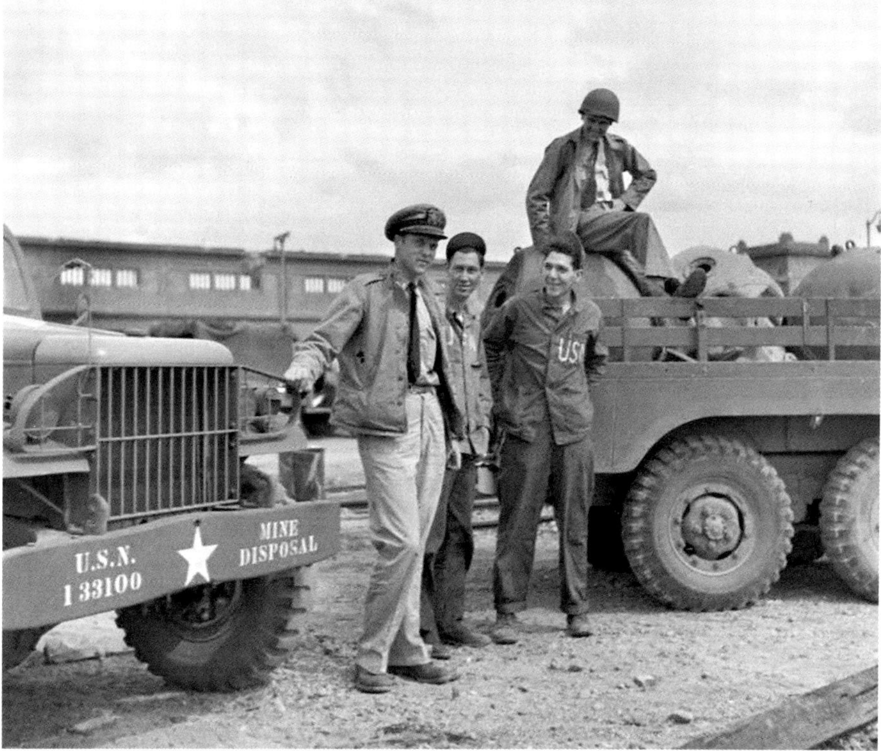

In front of the Gare Maritime, US Navy engineers recovered EMC mines – 1.12 metres in diameter, charge of 300 kilos – from a wrecked railcar and loaded them onto lorries. **(USNA)** (USNA)

which had been sunk across the entrance to the Darse Transatlantique. The *Solglint* lay on her starboard side at right angles to the Quai de Normandie, her port side level with the latter's deck and thus forming an excellent foundation for an additional pier. Only her superstructure was removed so that Liberty ships could moor on both sides. The *Granlieu* had first to be moved since she rested between the stern of the sunken *Solglint* and the northeast corner of the Quai de France, completely blocking the entrance to the Darse. Tons of concrete from the demolished buildings of the Gare Maritime had first to be removed from atop the *Granlieu* and then, using compressed air and tows, she was swung out in a 90-degree arc so that she formed a continuation of the quay. On September 18, the entrance to the Darse Transatlantique was finally clear.

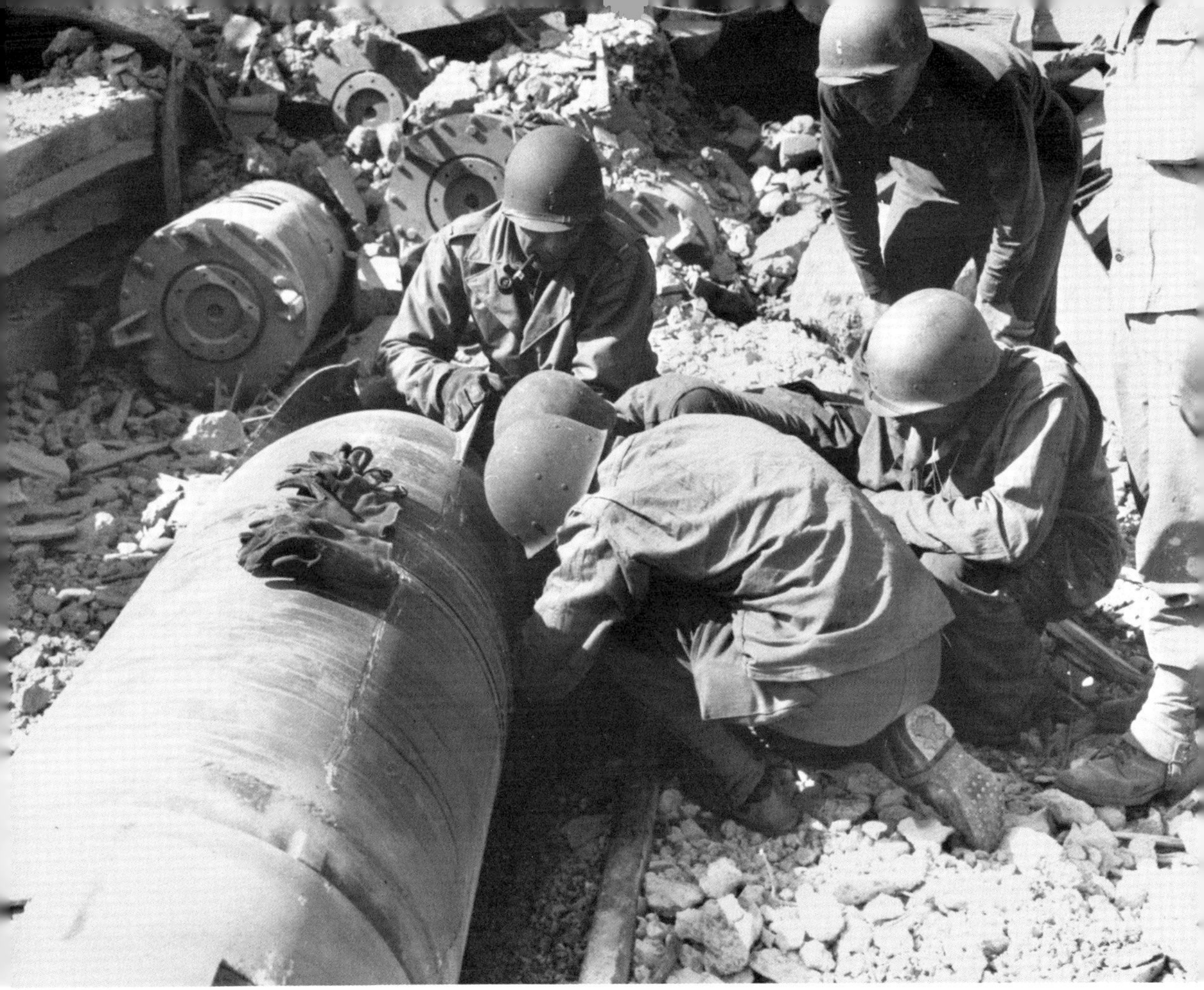

On July 17, working under the direction of 2nd Lieutenant P.H. Shupp, at right, US Army engineers carefully remove the fuse of a live mine found under the docks. Note than of them is smoking a pipe. A photograph taken by Tech/3 Paul W. Heimberger, 166th Signal Photo Company. (USNA)

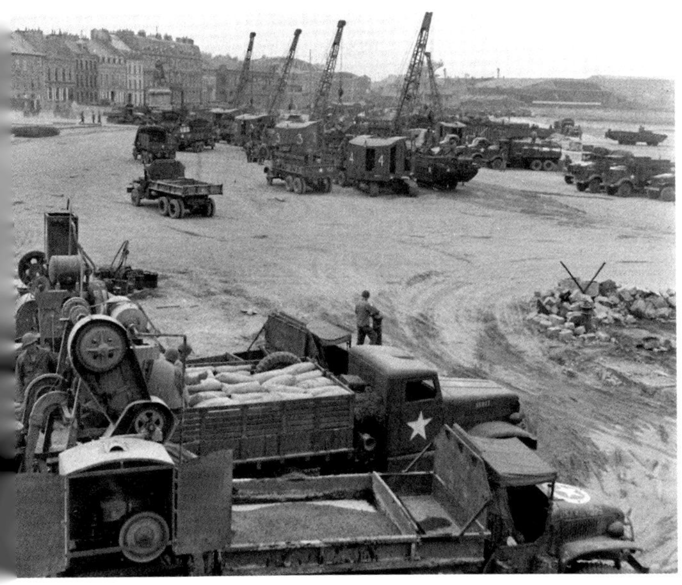

Working first on those areas where the quickest results could be expected, engineers started at Nouvelle Plage which was simply to be converted into a landing point for DUKWs and LCTs. They swept away barbed wire and other scattered debris, blasted three exits in the sea wall, graded the beach, and built three concrete roads. Work at the Nouvelle Plage was completed on July 6 but no DUKW could come in for ten days because mines still forbade to bring ships into the harbour. Not until July 14 were the western ends of the outer and inner roadstead declared free of mines and two days later four Liberty ships loaded with construction supplies and vehicles entered the harbour and anchored in the Grande Rade. Late that afternoon a DUKW driven by Private Charles I. Willis of the 821st Amphibious Truck Company brought the first load of supplies to the Nouvelle Plage. (USNA)

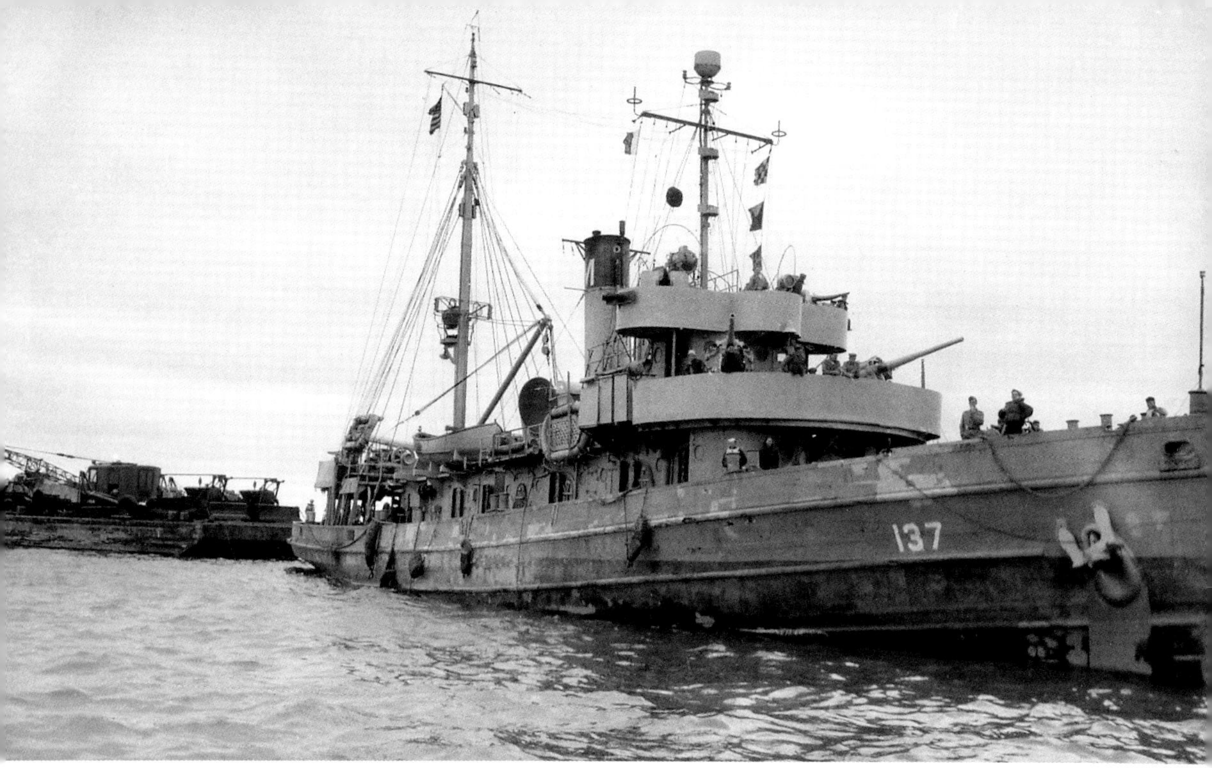

Commissioned in 1918 as a minesweeper, the USS *Owl* was reclassified as *OT-137*, an ocean tug in 1942. This photo shows her entering the harbour at Cherbourg on July 18, 1944, towing two barges loaded with engineer equipment. The original caption states that she was the first ship carrying supplies to enter Cherbourg after its liberation from the Germans. (USNA)

The destroyer USS *Donnel* was torpedoed during an attack on a sound contact in May 1944. Her stern was blown off, and the explosion of her own depth charges worsened the damage. She was decommissioned. Reclassified as *IX 182* in July, she was towed to Cherbourg, where she supplied electricity to shore installations. She was moored at Le Homet, and this photograph was taken on August 15. (USNA)

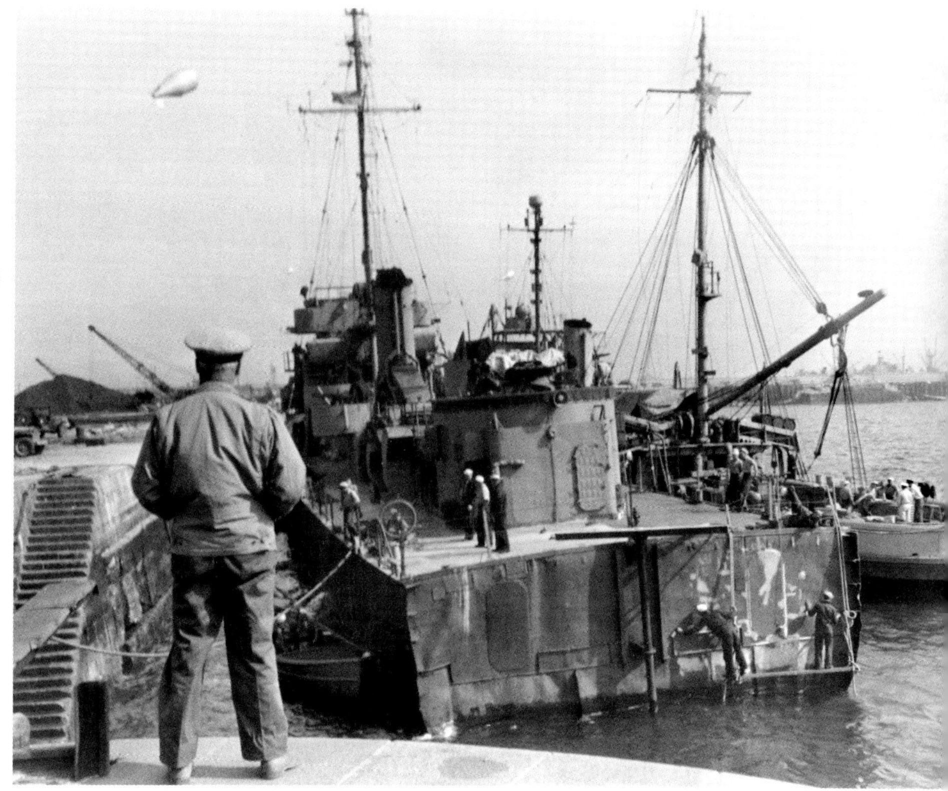

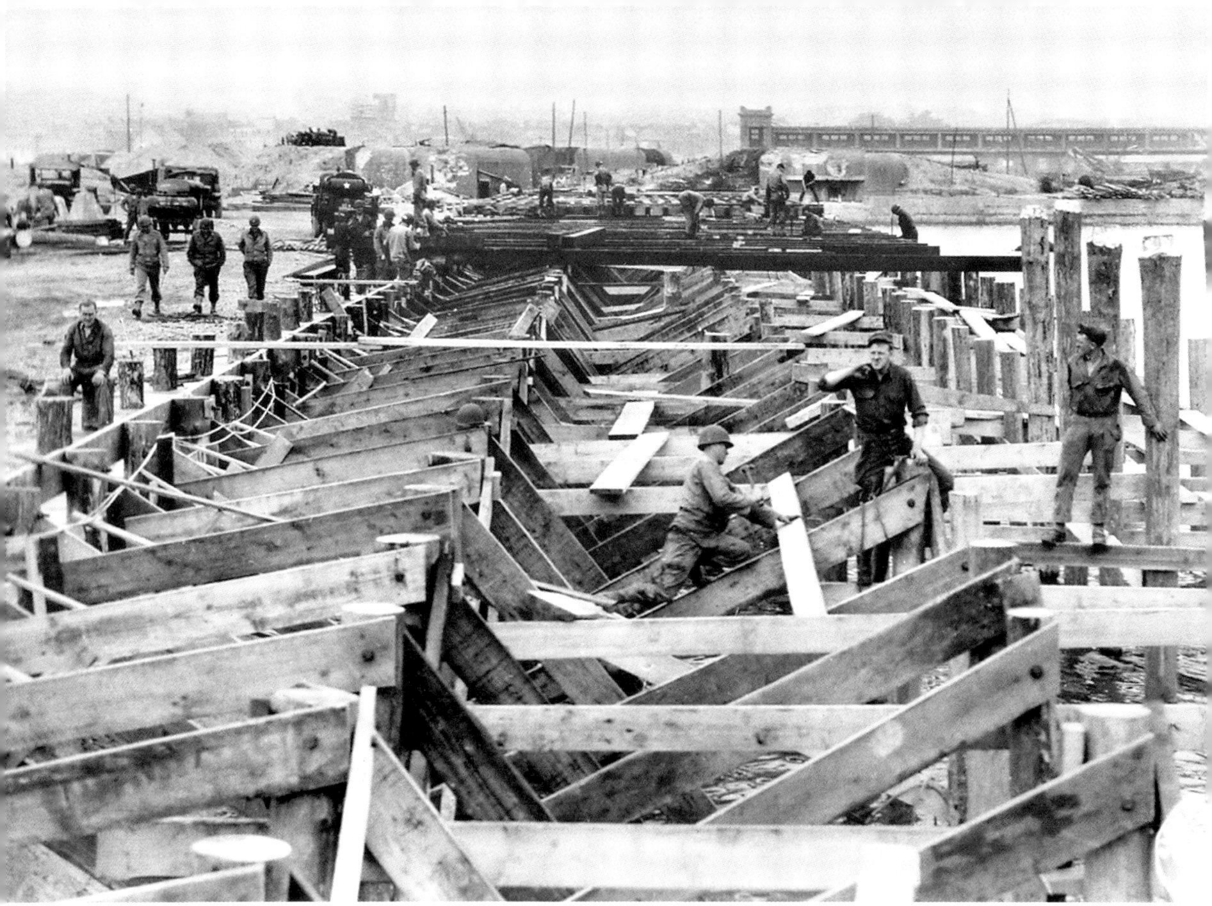

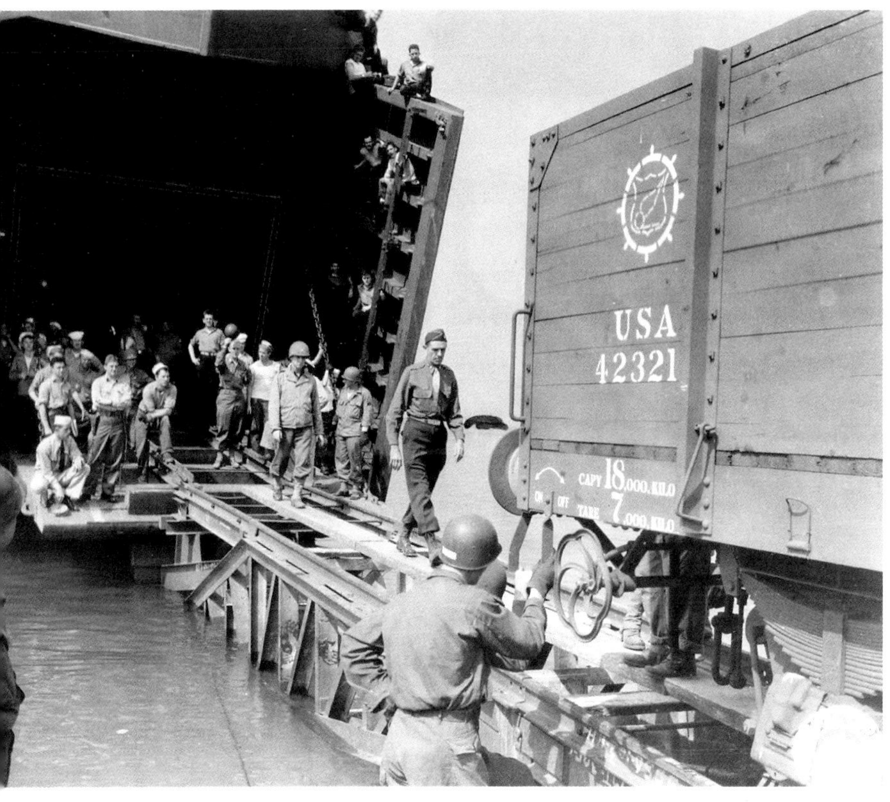

Known as the Réclamation and the Terre Plein, the yet undeveloped eastern sector of the harbour, beyond the Darse Transatlantique, consisted merely of open areas bounded by a sloping seawall. First filling in a few craters and removing some pillboxes, the 342nd Engineer General Service Regiment built there a huge U-shaped timber wharf along all three side of the basin. In the background, some German casemates, and the Gare Maritime. (USNA)

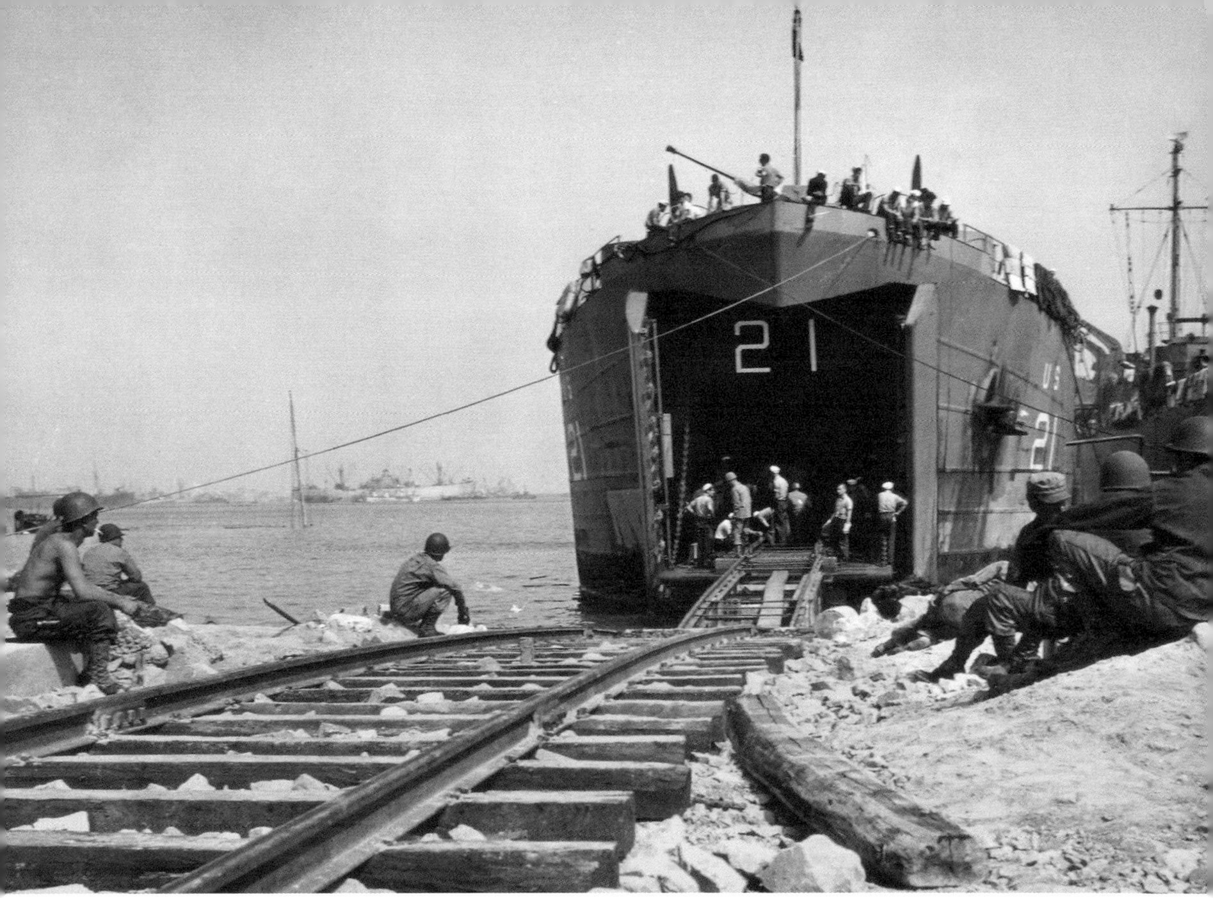

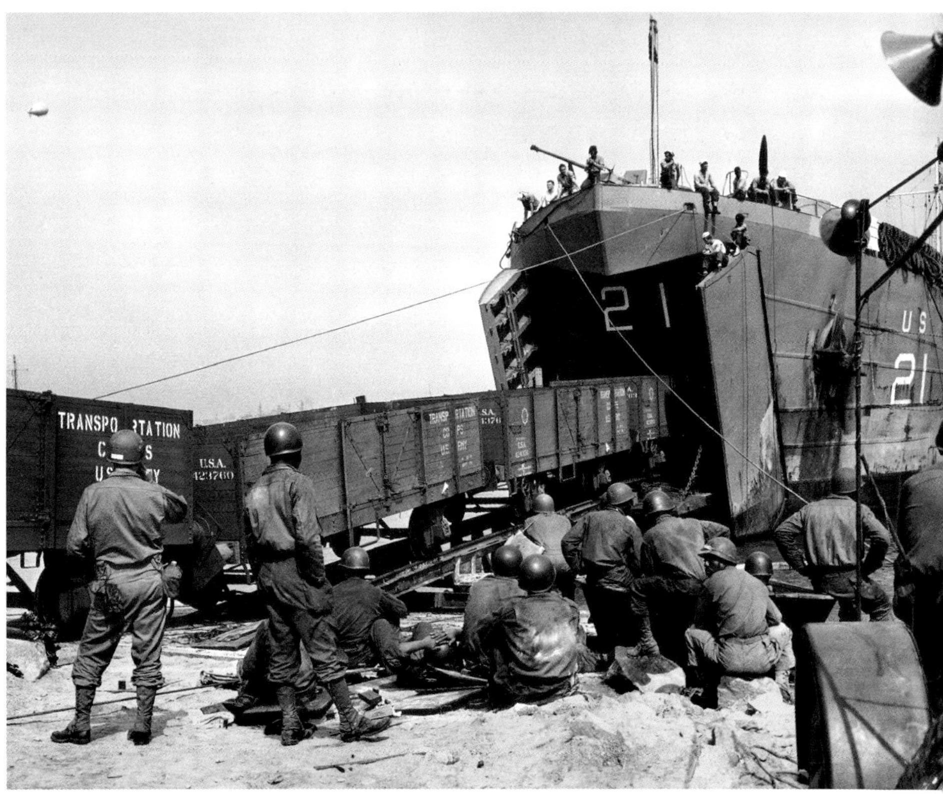

Three berths were intended for the discharge of vehicles, and three for railway rolling stock, for which purpose rail lines were laid to the water's edge. These photos were taken on July 31 when converted *LST 21* made the first delivery of rolling stock at this point. (USNA)

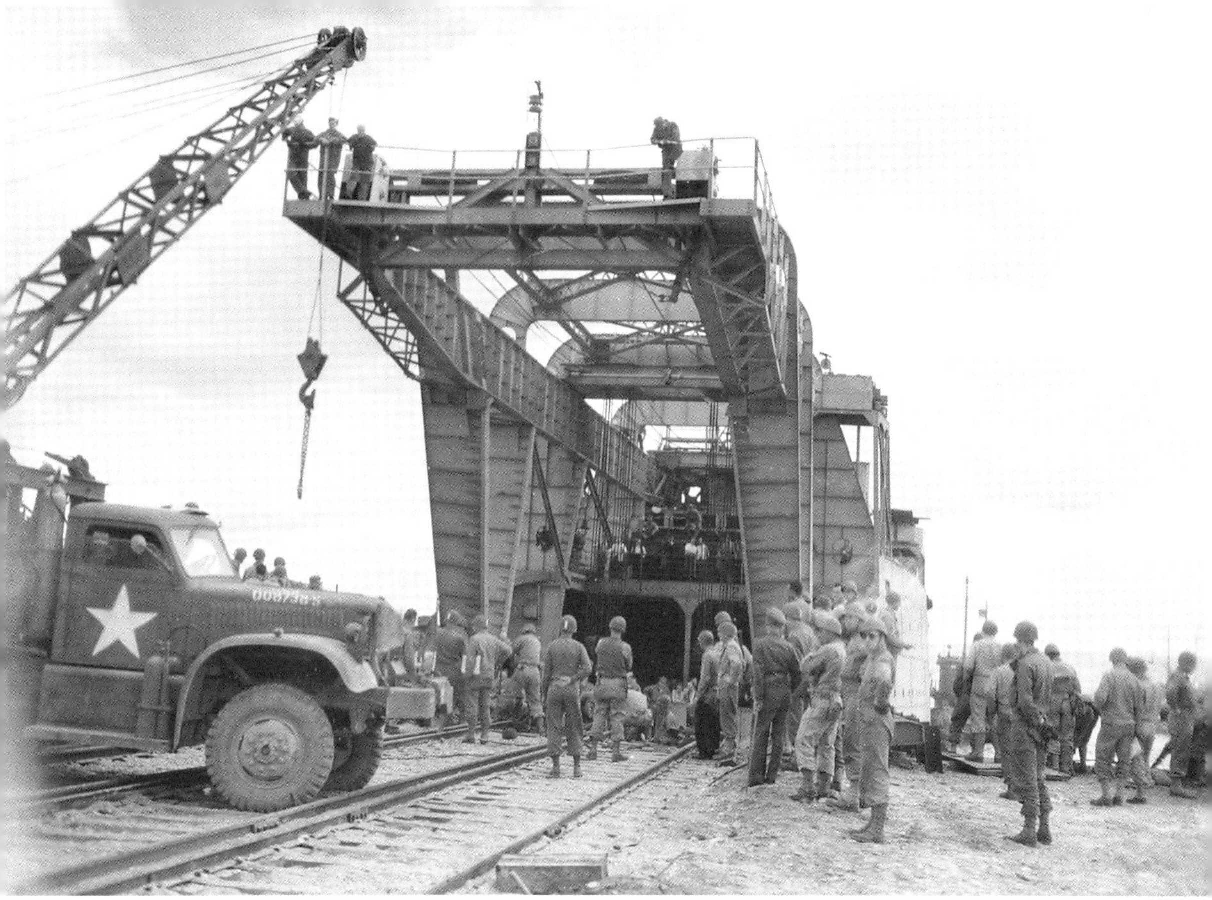

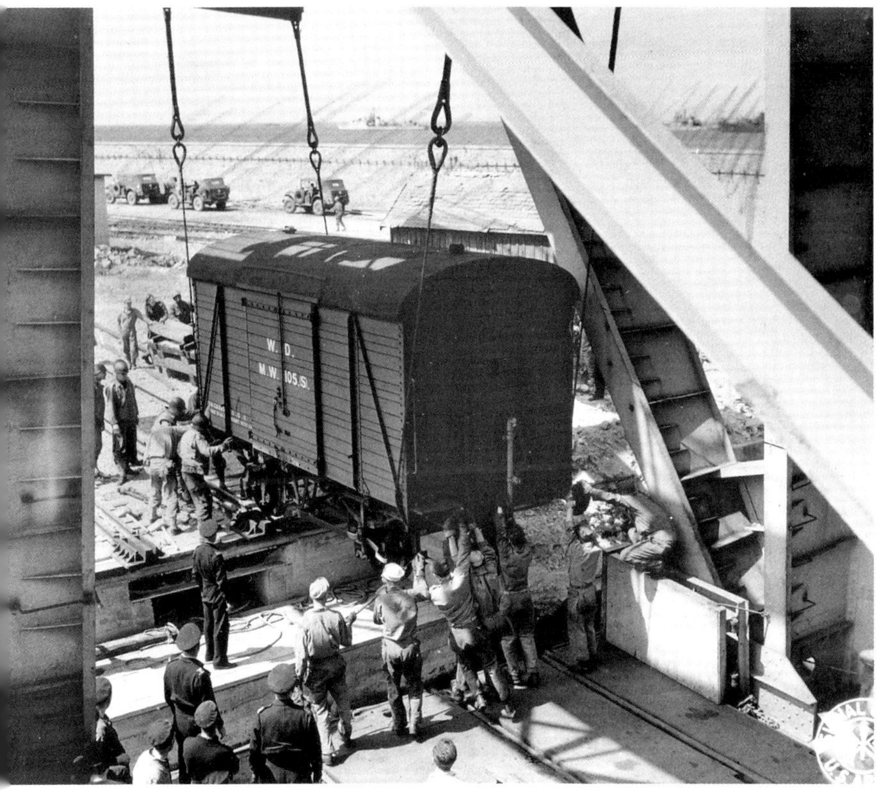

A portion of the Quai Homet was selected as a pierhead to accommodate train ferries delivering locomotives and rolling stock. Two berths were provided, one of them consisting of a seat which could accommodate a ramp lowered into position by the ferry, permitting rolling stock to roll from the ferry to the quay, and the other providing a site where locomotives could be lifted from the ferry to the quay by means of an overhead crane which was part of the vessel itself. The *Twickenham Ferry* – a British train ferry with four tracks in her hulls, which could carry up to 40 goods wagons– made her first delivery of diesel locomotives and rolling stock on July 29. (USNA)

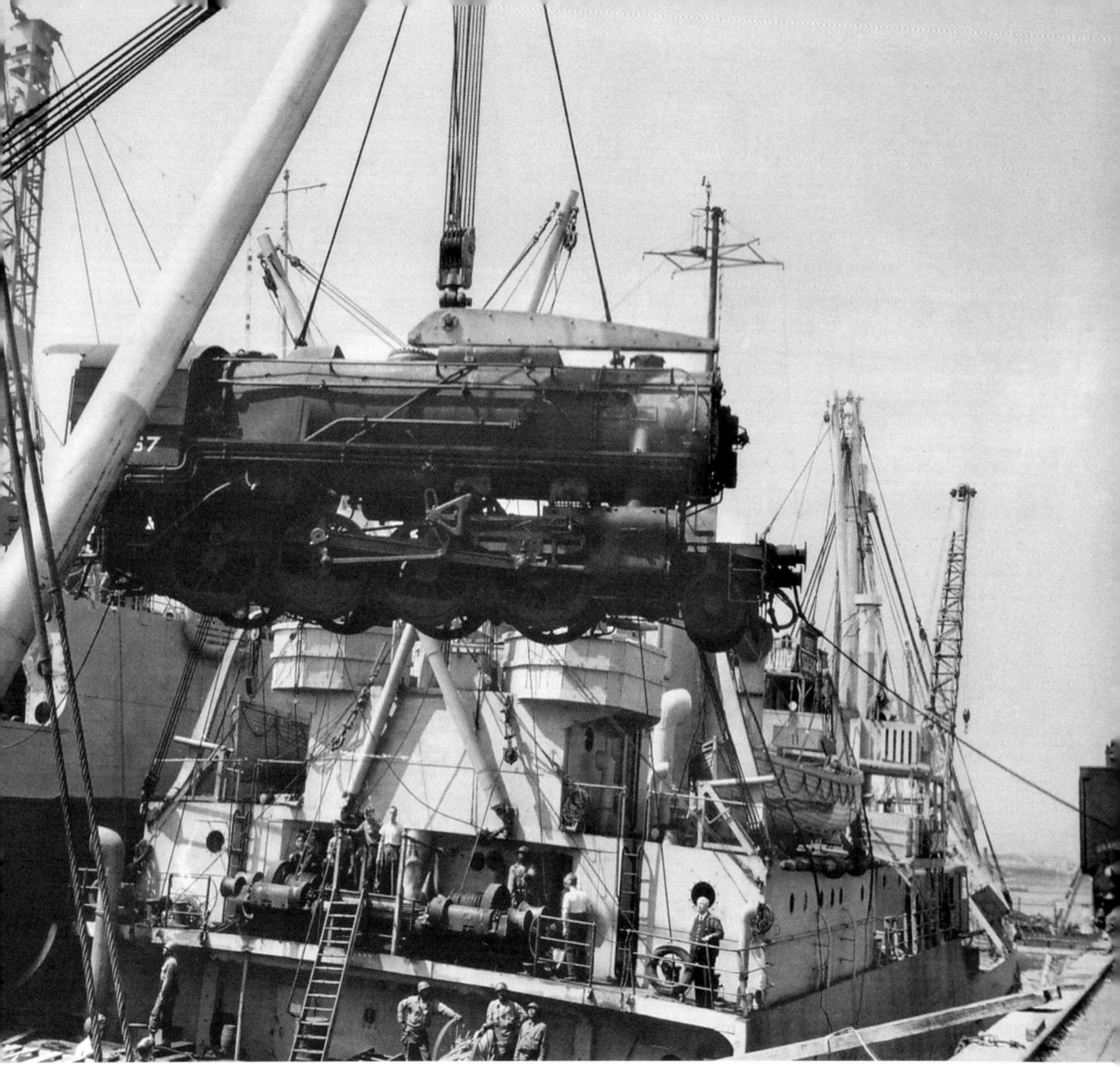

On August 1, the SS *Seatrain Texas*, an American train ferry, moored at the Homet and tried to unload a locomotive with the ship cargo boom which ended in a catastrophe, the boom breaking and the locomotive falling into the harbour. The SS *Lapland*, a heavy lift ship, was then committed to move the over 100 tons load. On August 8, one 2-8-0 steam engine locomotive – the 140 R 2867 built by ALCO – was unloaded from the SS *Seatrain Texas* thank to the crane of SS *Lapland*. (USNA)

Notwithstanding these tremendous difficulties, over the next couple of weeks the harbour was slowly brought back into operation and by the first week in August it was discharging approximately 6,000 tons per day. By mid-September it was handling double this volume. Little by little the port capacity was increased until in November Cherbourg discharged 433,201 tons, or an average of about 14,500 tons a day. This compared with a pre-D-Day planning of 8,500 tons a day. For many weeks Cherbourg handled more than half of all the cargo landed in France for the American armies. Until Antwerp became available in late November, Cherbourg remained the main port supporting the US forces in Europe.

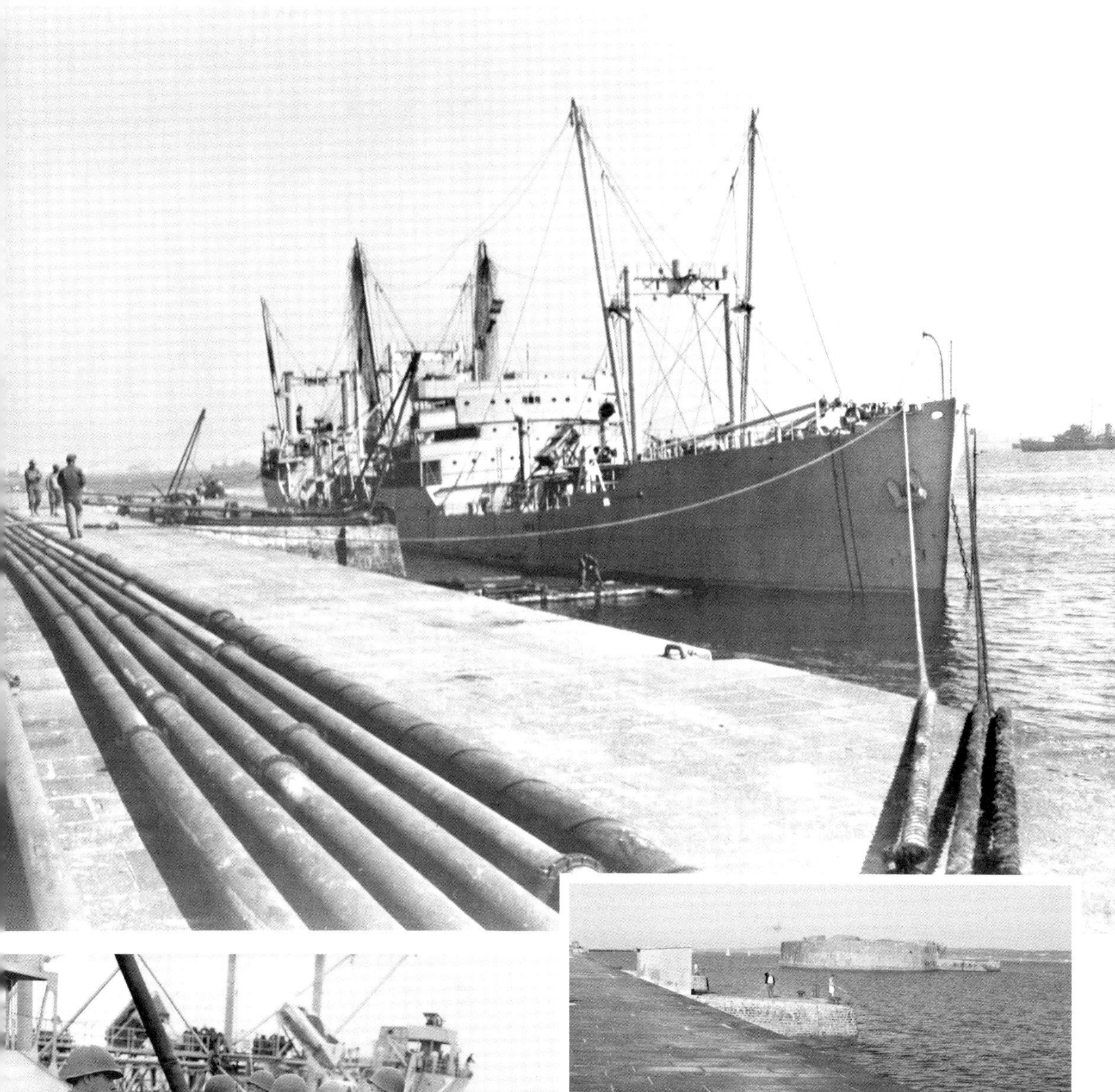

Use of the tanker berth at the Digue de Querqueville which was scheduled to begin on July 9, did not get under way until more than two weeks later. The nine-inch pipeline that ran along the Digue de Querqueville since before the war appeared to be corroded beyond repair and engineers scrapped it and installed instead seven six-inch pipes that carried diesel, fuel, and aviation fuel simultaneously. Access to the Digue de Querqueville is open to the public. In the background, the Fort de Chavagnac.

(USNA and ATB)

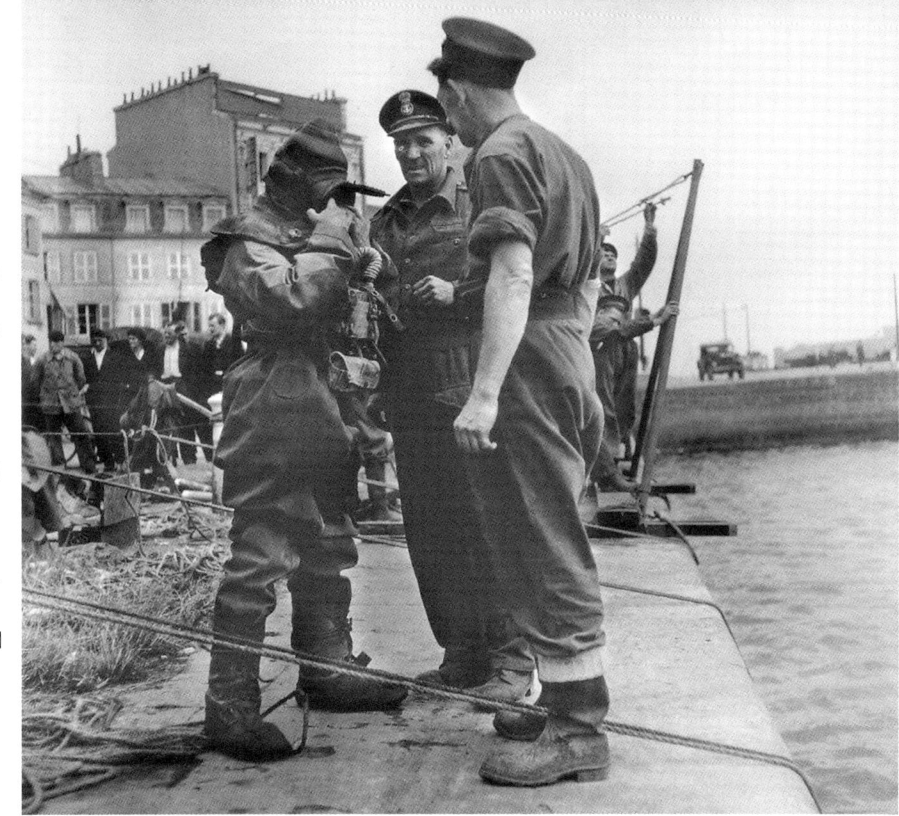

On July 7, divers from the Royal Navy were being fitted for another clearing operation in the Bassin à Flot. It was to take ten more days before access was safely cleared and on July 17 the first barges discharged in the Bassin à Flot. When rehabilitation works were finally completed, the Bassin à Flot could accommodate six coasters and 13 barges. (USNA)

The Pont Tournant (swing bridge), which spanned the locks in the Port de Commerce, was so badly damaged that it could not be salvaged. On June 28, engineers began cutting it away with blowtorches. They quickly replaced it with a retractable drawbridge, using a Bailey bridge supported by dollies running on tramway rails. (USNA)

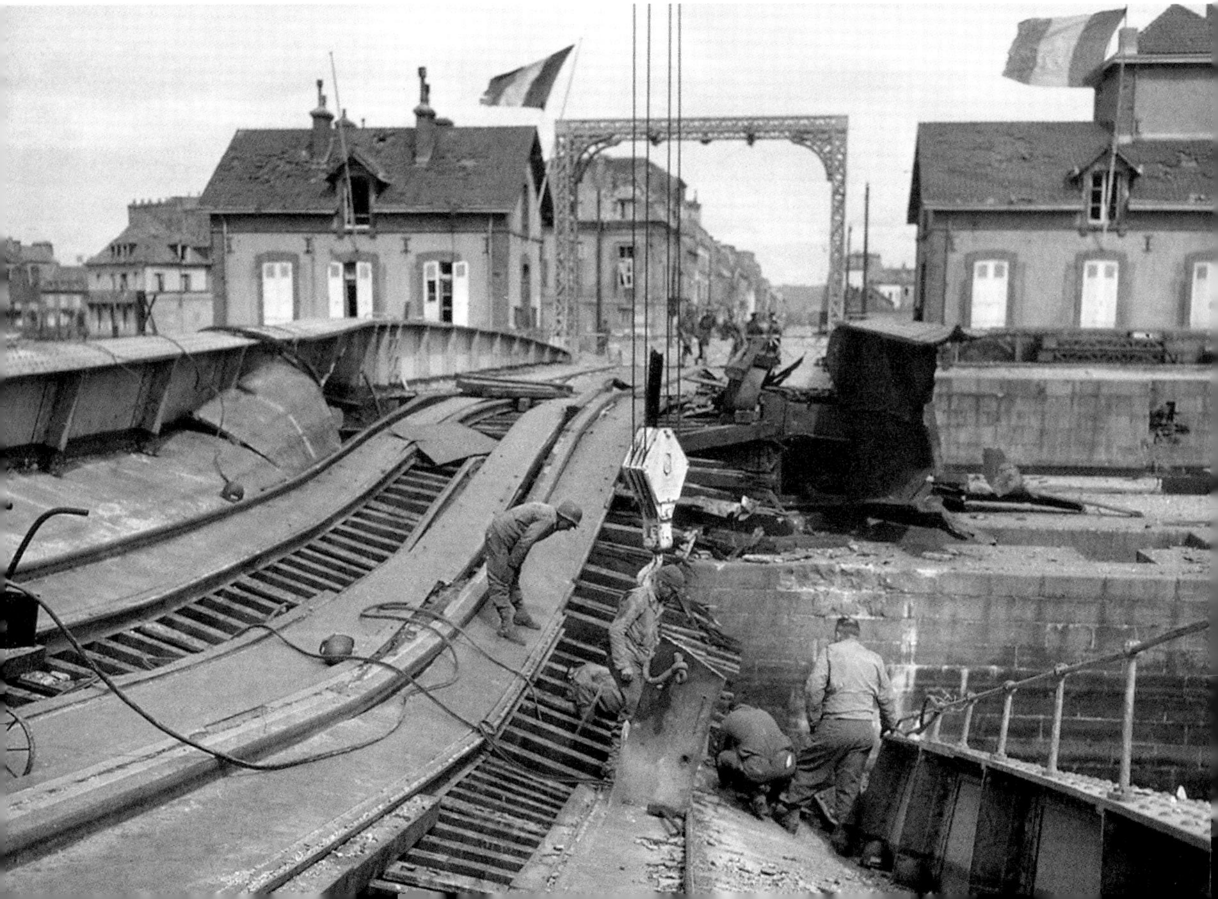

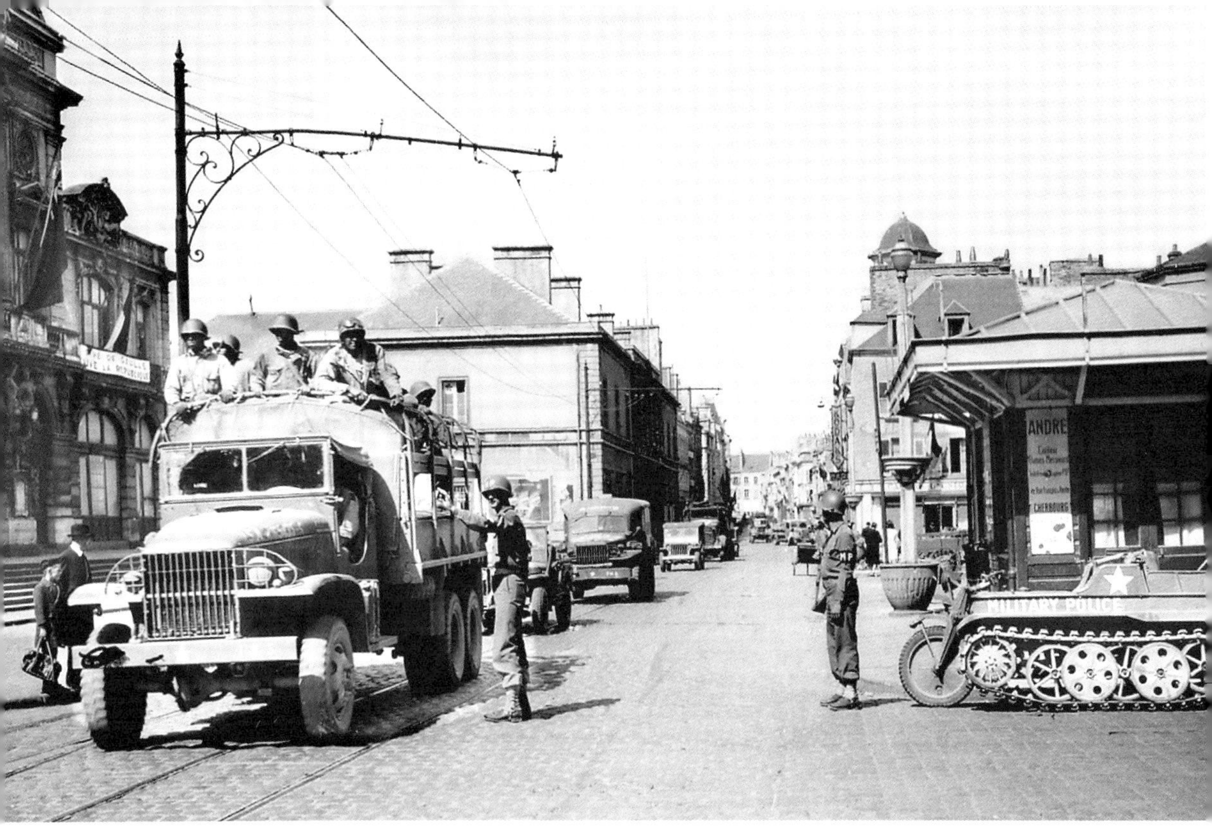

Notwithstanding tremendous difficulties, over the next couple of weeks Cherbourg was slowly brought back into operation. Privates 1st Class Albert Buhlig and Pedro Hernandez of the 769th MP Battalion controlled traffic in Cherbourg. This photo was taken Place du Général de Gaulle, in front of the city Theatre. (USNA)

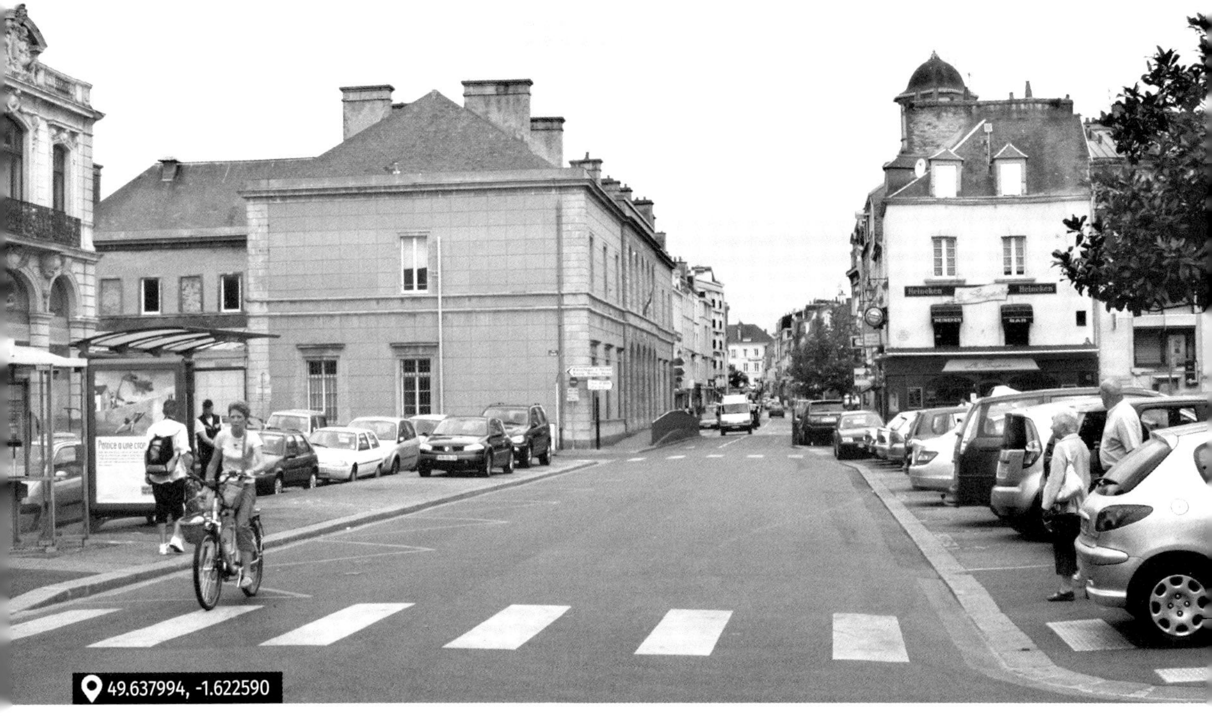

49.637994, -1.622590

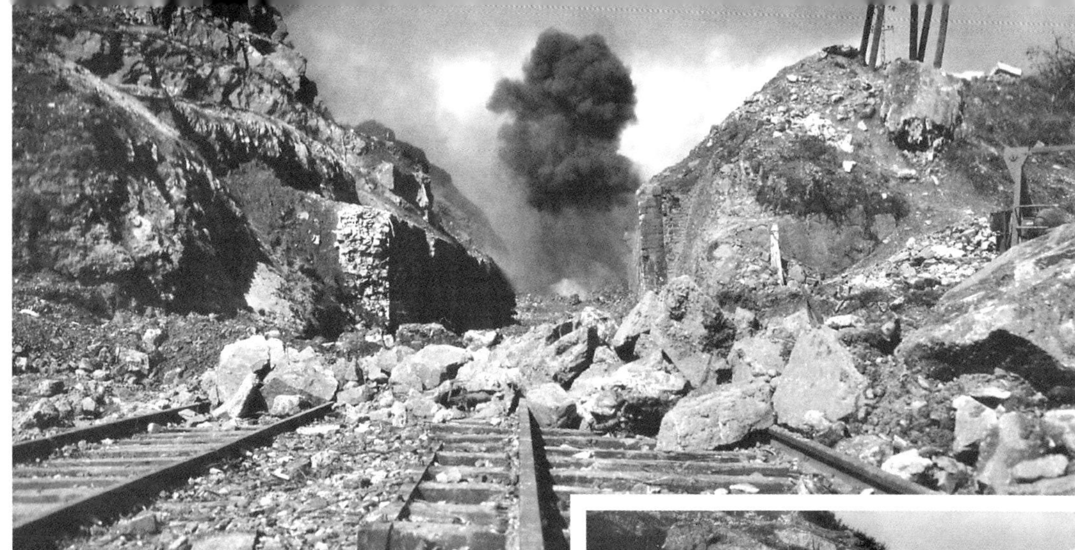

South of Cherbourg, German engineers drove three freight cars packed with explosives into the 125-metre-long railway tunnel. The tremendous explosion collapsed huge parts of the mountain down on the railways. The only way to open the passage was to clear what remained of the mountain above the tunnel. The 347th General Service Engineer Regiment took on the task of clearing the passage, repeatedly blasting the rocks, while Caterpillar D4 bulldozers gradually cleared the mass out of the trench. The gigantic work was finally completed on July 8. The railway traffic now runs in the bottom of a deep trench cutting across the mountain where once was a tunnel.

A very interesting side of the reconstruction of the harbour at Cherbourg is that German agents regularly reported by radio to Berlin the progress of the Allies efforts, and this till February 1945 at least! During the same period, other agents operated and reported from Le Havre, Ostend, and Antwerp. Their reports were transmitted to the Kriegsmarine and regularly referred in the diaries of the Seekriegsleitung or SKL (Naval Warfare Command). On July 28, the SKL noted that there were '80-100 vessels of various sizes up to 15,000 tons' in Cherbourg harbour. On August 11: 'According to agent's report from early July the repair of Cherbourg harbour has been taken over by the US, despite British opposition. Completion of repair is estimated at nine weeks.' In September: 'According to agent's report from Cherbourg of September 12, the harbour entrance is intact despite large-scale destruction in the area of the railway station (note: the Gare Maritime). Two large ships sunk near this station serve as jetty for tugs and small vessels. A provisory landing-stage for Liberty ships from piles and planks is being constructed. On

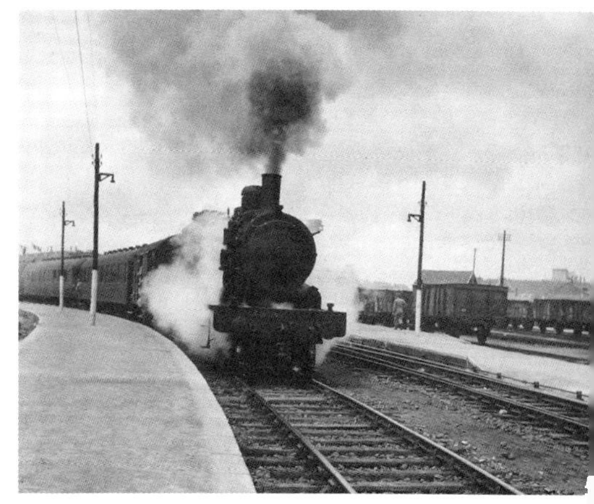

October 5: 'Agent in Cherbourg had wireless transmitter. Reports accurately and to the point about disembarkation, e.g. ferry ships with goods trains, etc. Also, agent's report from Ostend.' In January 1945: 'One agent has radioed from Cherbourg on January 2 that busy traffic from ambulances was seen in the city on December 25 after numerous small vessels had put out to recover troops and wounded from a torpedoed troopship. Exact reports could not be obtained as strong blocking measures were immediately taken. Another agent from Le Havre radioed on January 3 that 12 ships had arrived and discharged numerous tanks. Both agents rank as reliable.' Who might be this German agent (agents?) in Cherbourg is still a mystery. He could not be German – by the summer of 1944 Cherbourg was down to less than 5,000 inhabitants and no German had a chance to hide for long in the city. He could be a local inhabitant but he was more likely a displaced person, either a worker contracted by the Germans or an ex forced labourer.

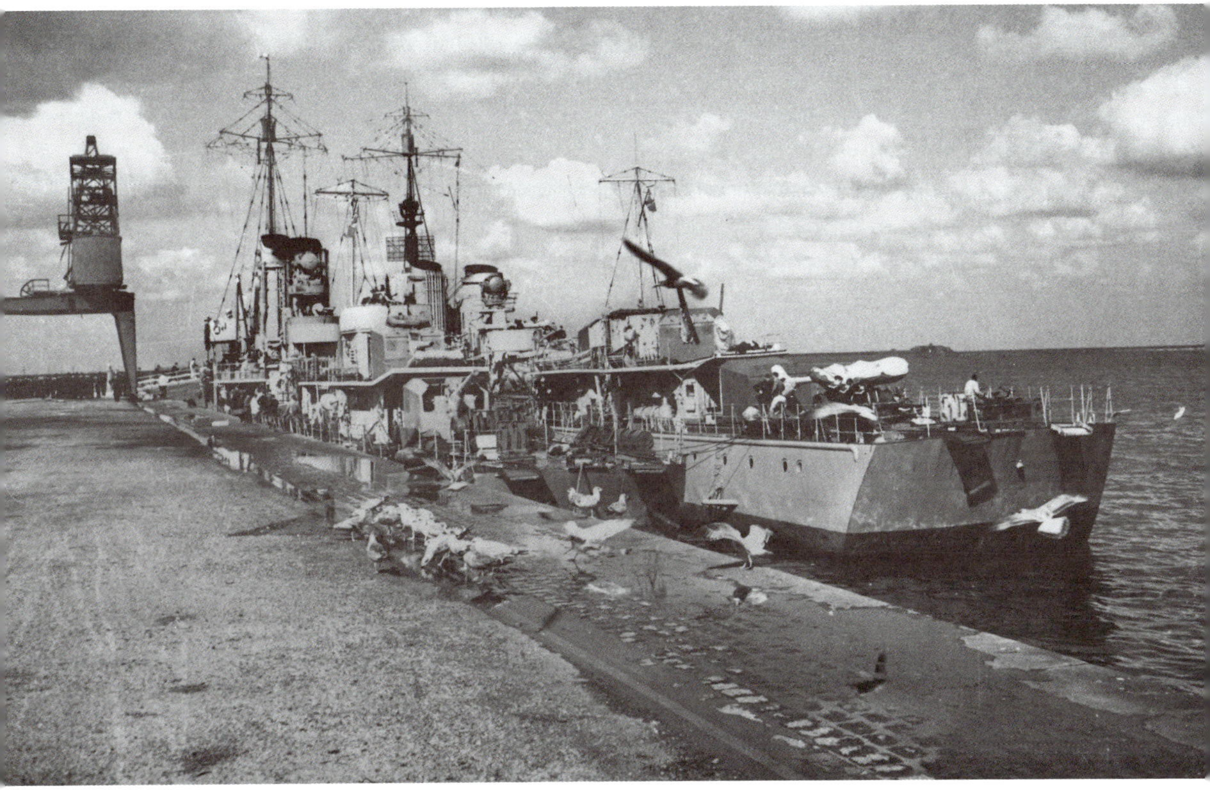

THE BATTLE OF CHERBOURG THEN AND NOW IN COLOUR

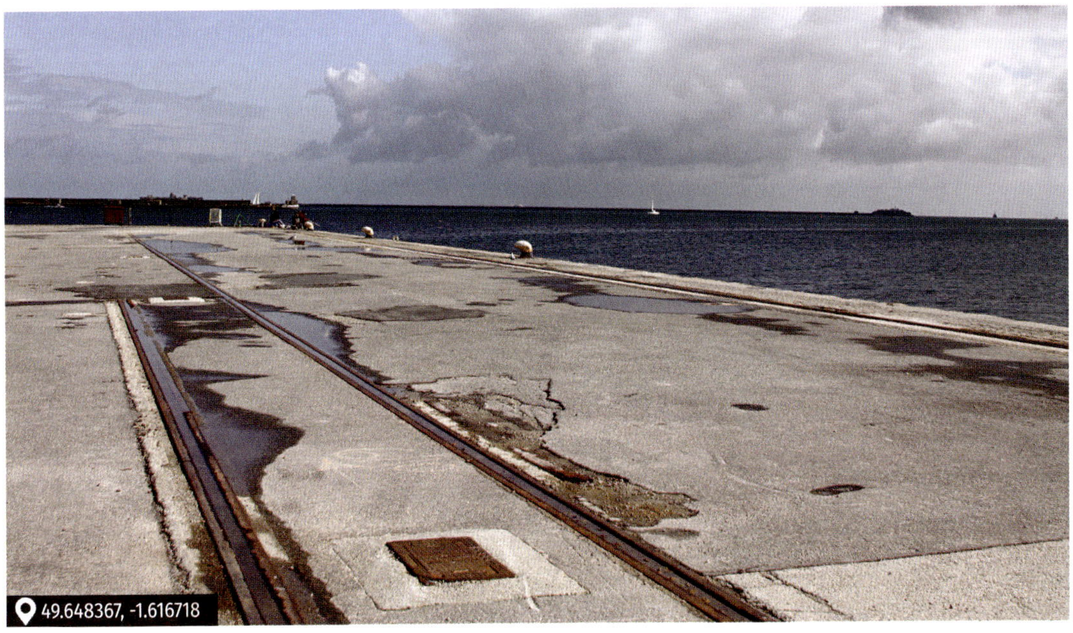

The Kriegsmarine takes over. Two destroyers, *Z16 Friedrich Eckoldt* and *Z20 Karl Galster*, were moored at the end of the Quai de France, the western side of the Darse Transatlantique. The crane on the quay was removed some years ago but the rails on which it moved can still be seen. In the background is the Digue Centrale, the central mole, with the Fort Central on the left and the Fort de l'Est on the right. (ECPAD and ATB)

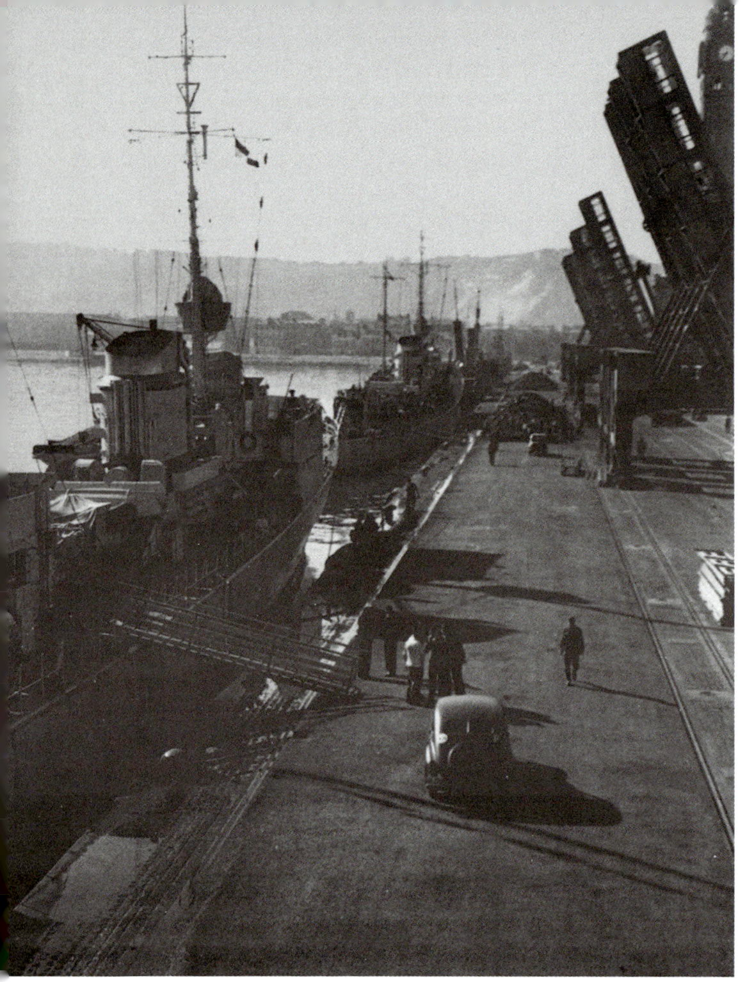

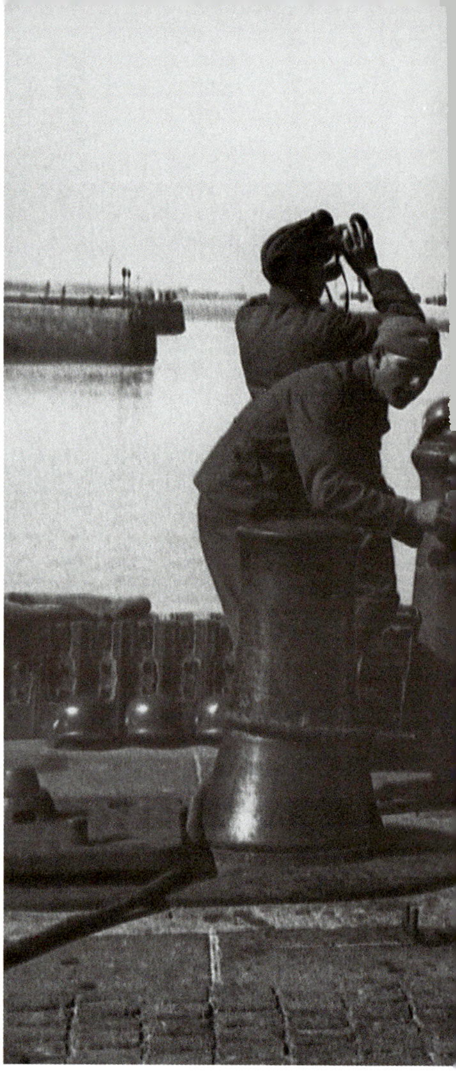

Two T-Boats, seemingly *T7* and *T8*, moored along the Quai de France. The movable galleries of the Gare Maritime were all raised up against building to clear the quayside. This quay was to be ruined in June 1944 when the trapped German garrison carried out its methodical demolition of the harbour installations. (ECPAD and ATB)

A 20mm Flak gun set up by the dock gate giving access to the Bassin du Commerce, the commercial wet dock. In the background across the Avant-Port stands the Gare Maritime. Badly damaged by German demolitions in June 1944, the superb Art Deco buildings of the Gare Maritime were reconstructed after the war but the 70-metre-high Campanile tower is gone forever. (ECPAD and ATB)

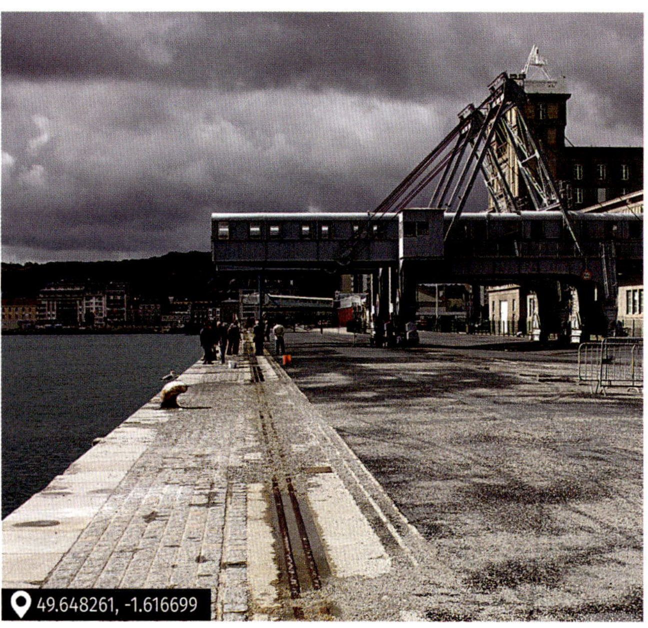

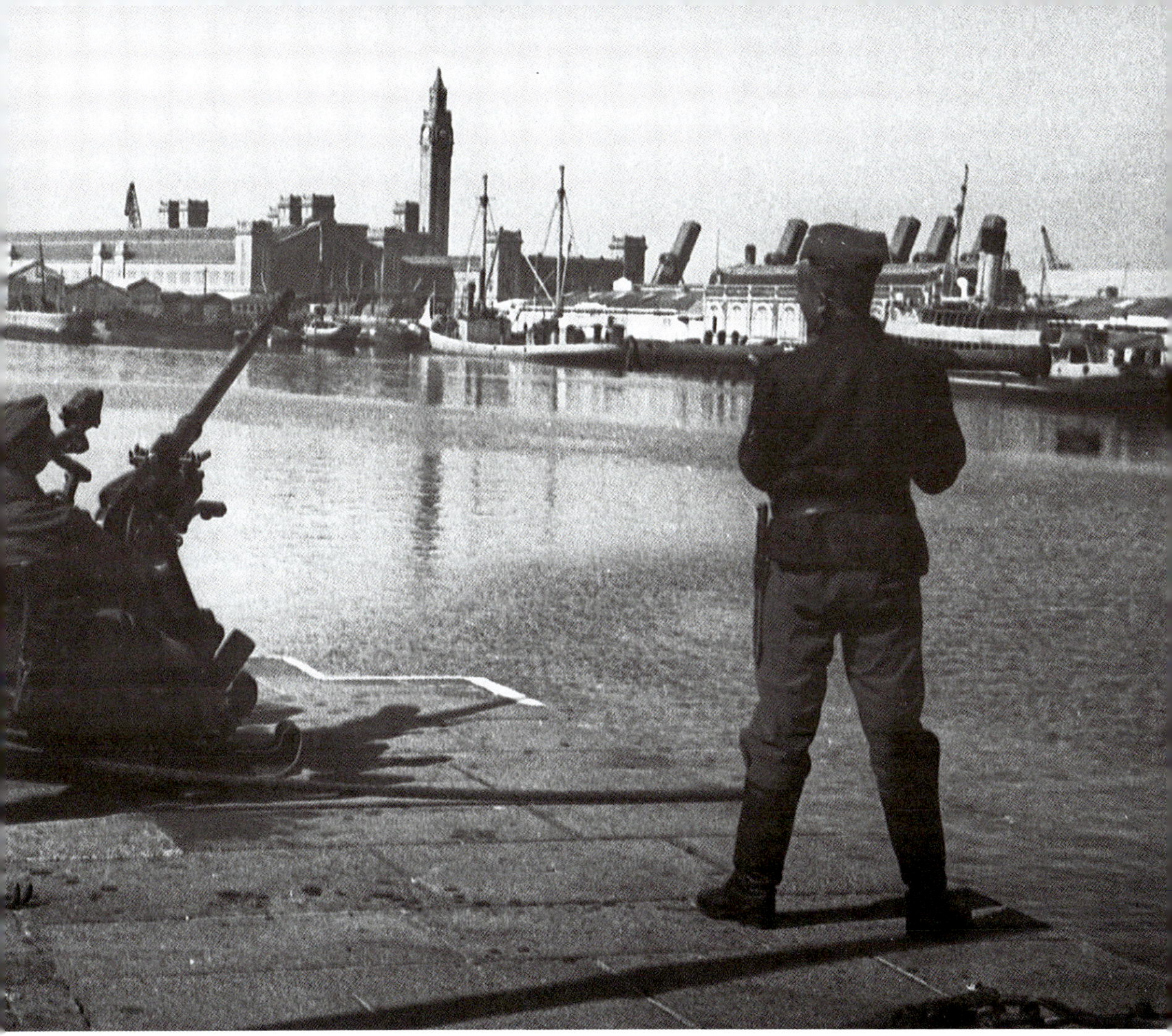

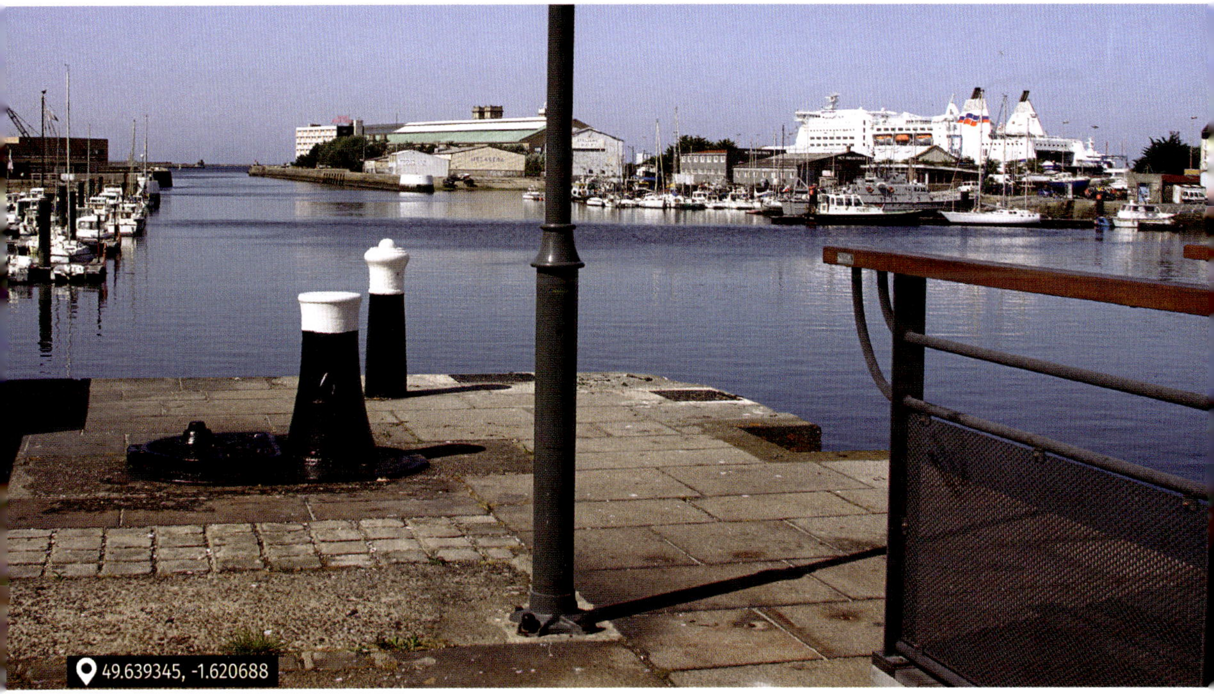

49.639345, -1.620688

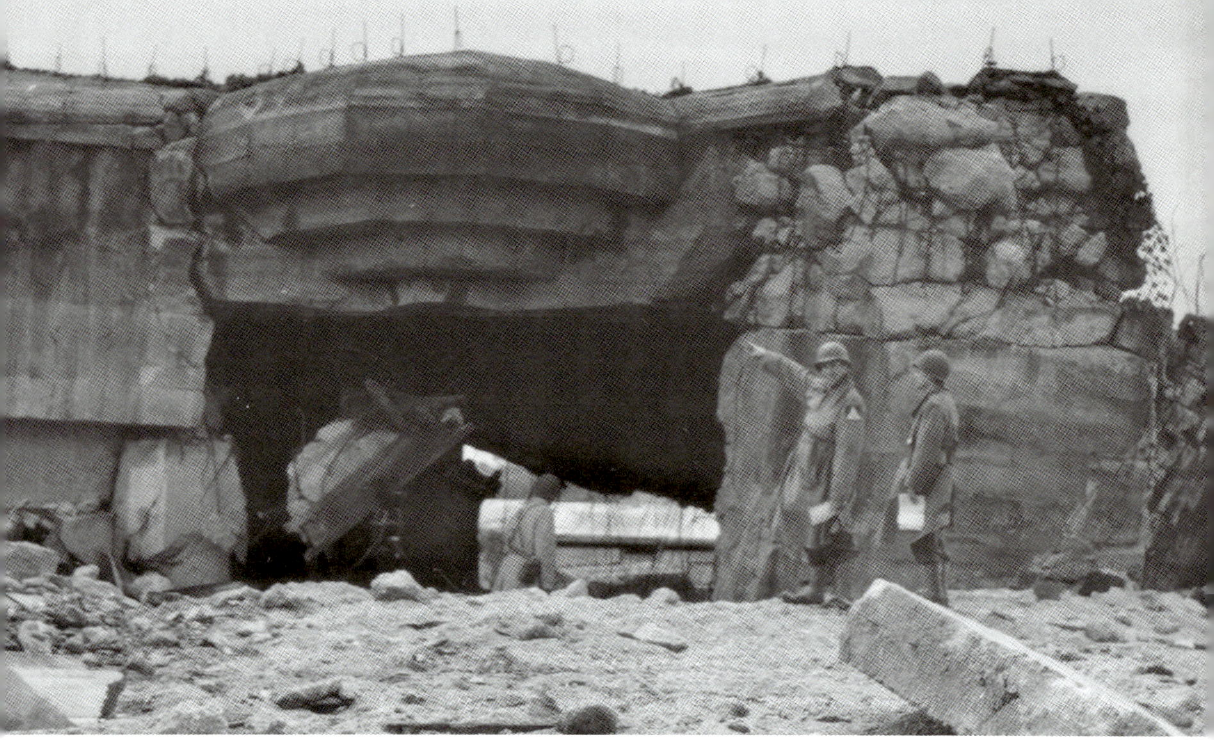

In the dunes near Néville, 25 kilometres east of Cherbourg, Batterie 'Blankenese' comprised four casemates for captured QF 3.7-inch guns, 94mm Flak Vickers M 39(e) in German nomenclature. The battery was manned in June 1944 by the 2. Batterie of Marine-Artillerie-Abteilung 260. This is the M272 type casemate that we saw on page 95. (USNA and ATB)

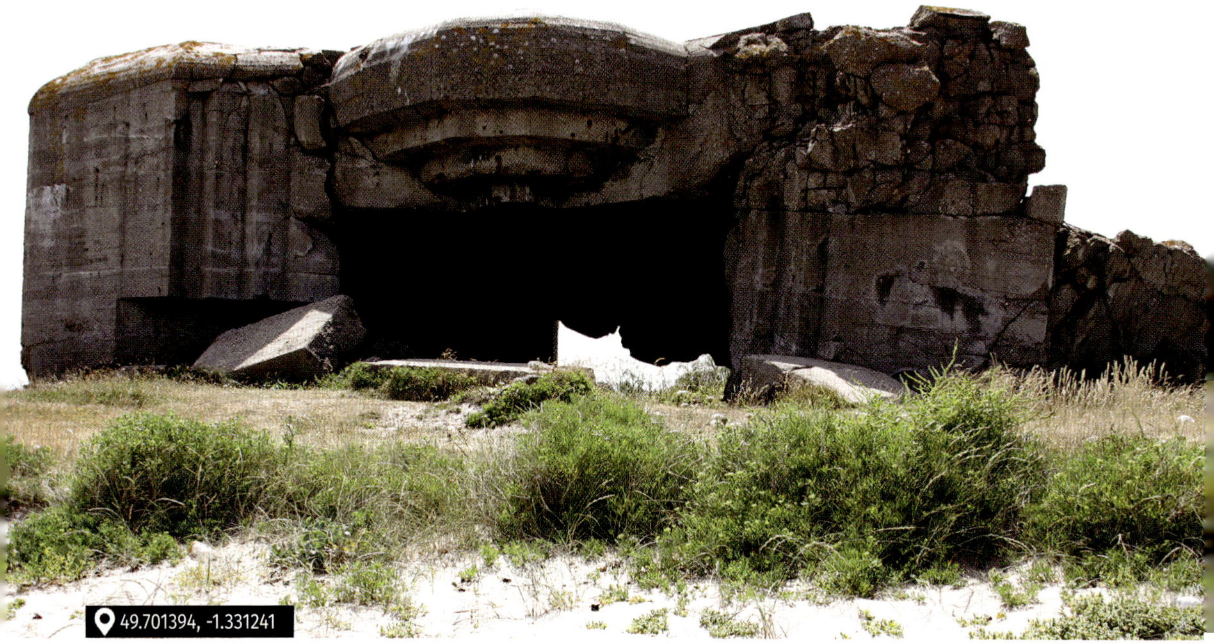

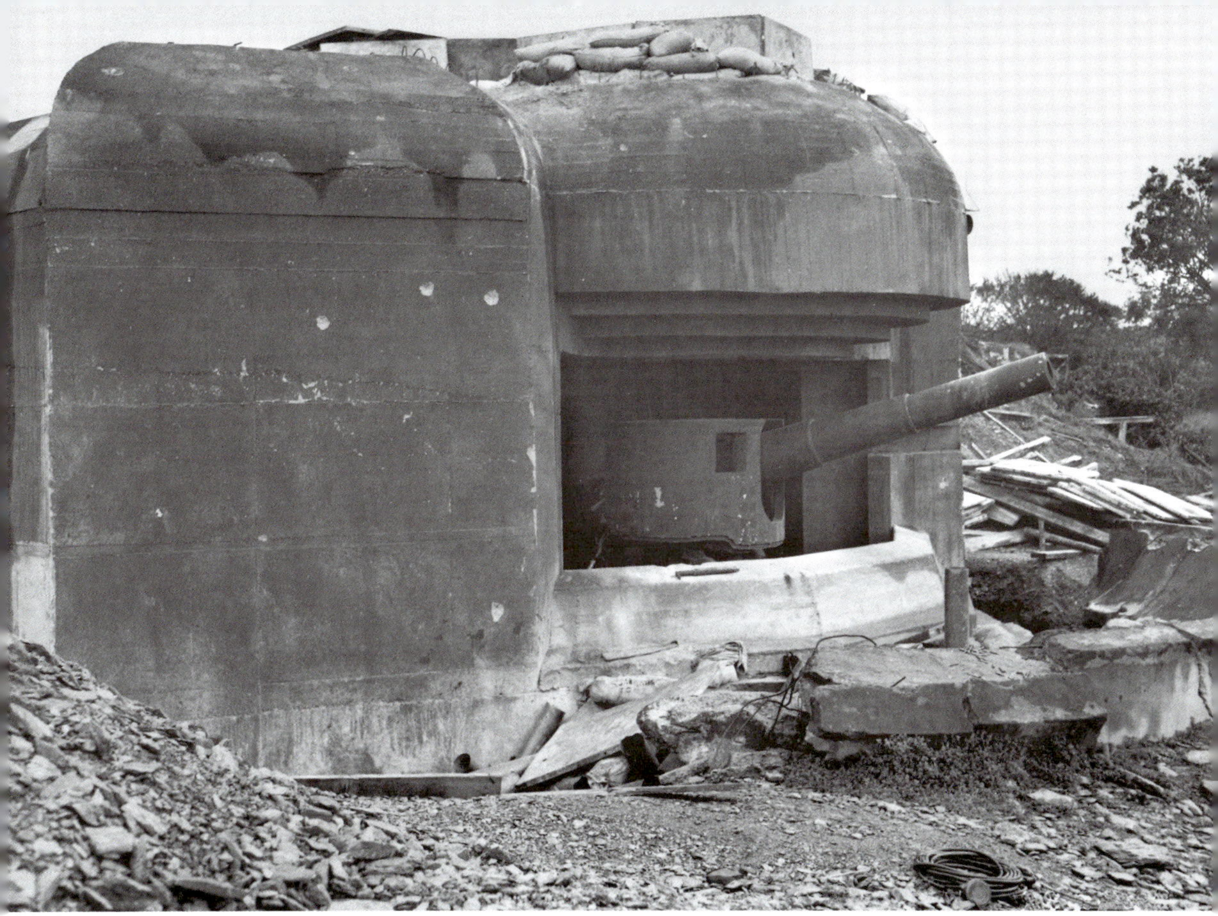

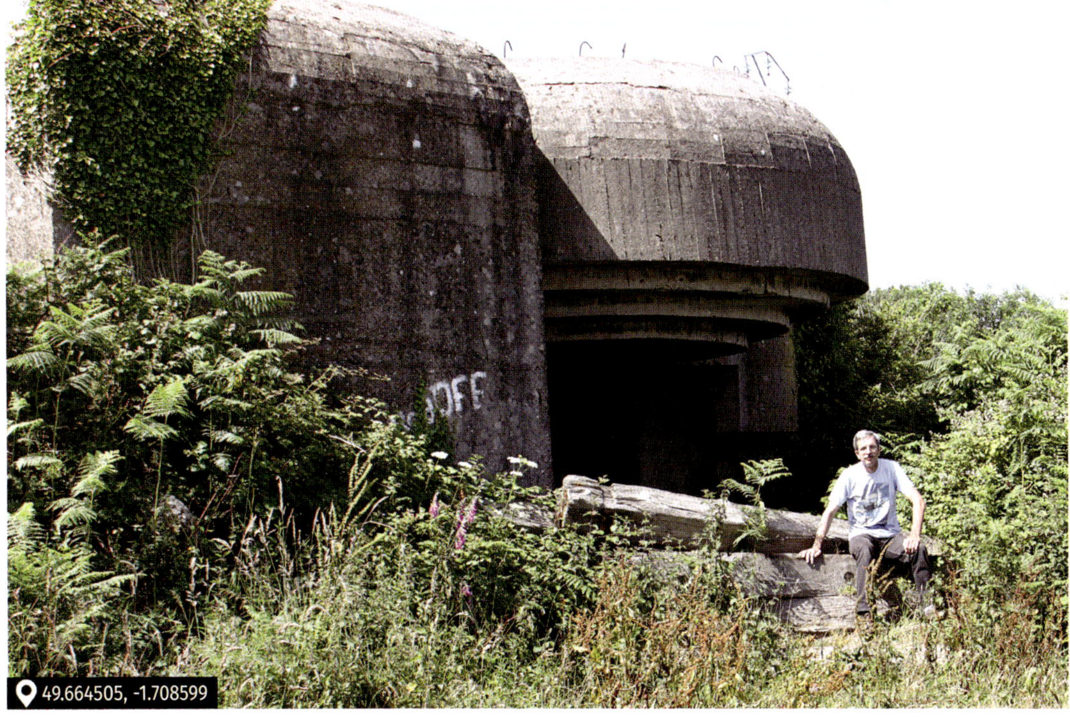

Batterie 'York' near Amfreville, a few kilometres west of Cherbourg, comprised four 170mm SK L/40 guns in Type M271 casemates.The guns were pre-First World War naval pieces adapted for coastal defence, the 'SK' standing for Schiffskanone (ship's canon). Batterie 'York', Then and Now: three small impacts in the concrete visible in this Signal Corps photo identify this casemate as the second from the west. (USNA and ATB)

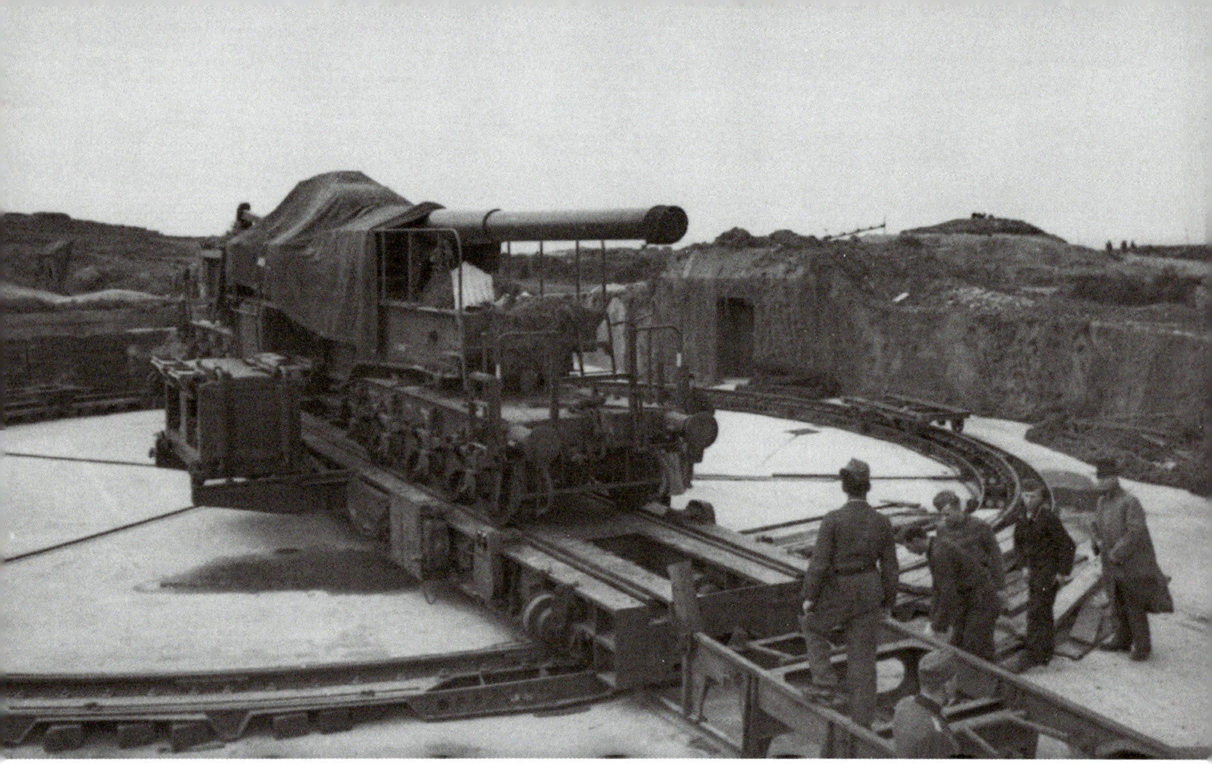

In addition to the many coastal batteries, the Germans moved railway gun batteries close to the coast. At Auderville-Laye, west of Cherbourg, two circular platforms were built for the 203mm Kanone (E) SK C/34 of Eisenbahn-Artillerie-Batterie 685. A traverse of 360 degrees was obtained by means of a turntable composed of a circular track set over the main track. The two platforms, here the south-western one, and the many shelters serving them remain in good condition, albeit somewhat overgrown. (BA and ATB)

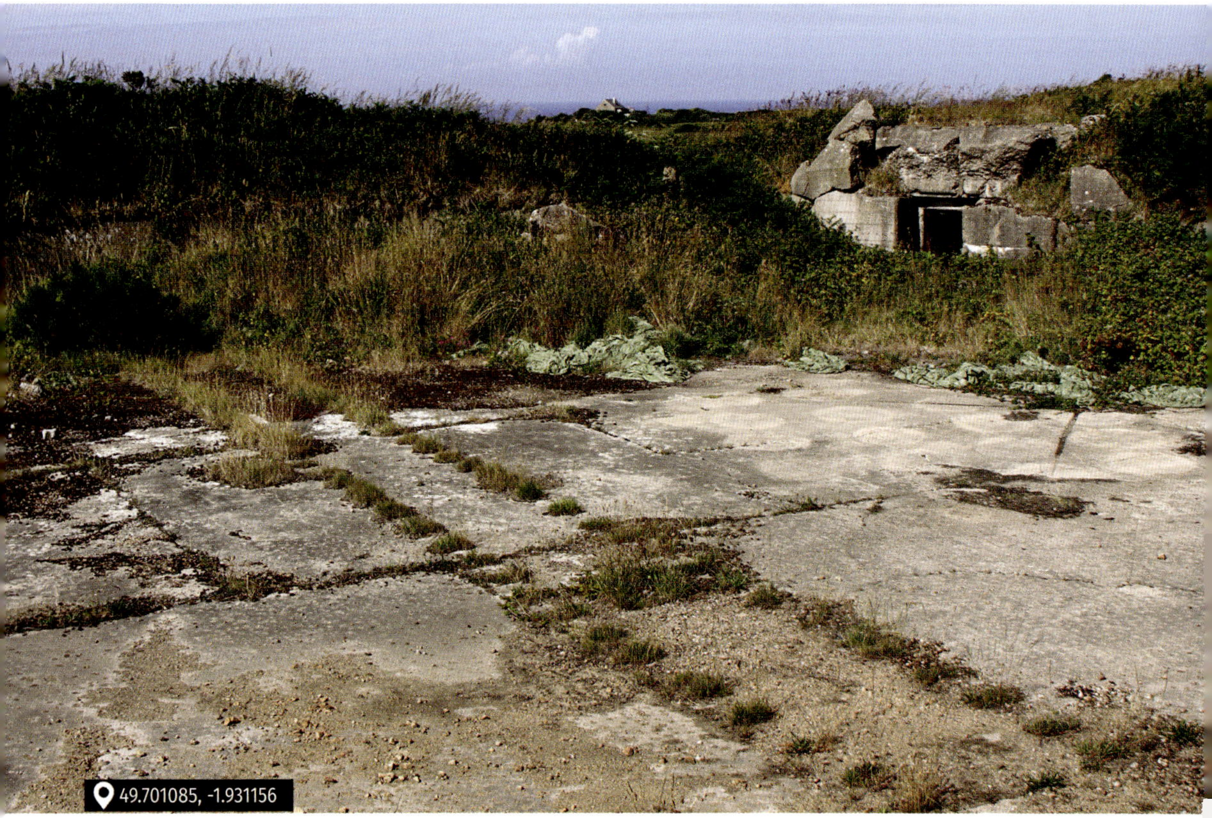

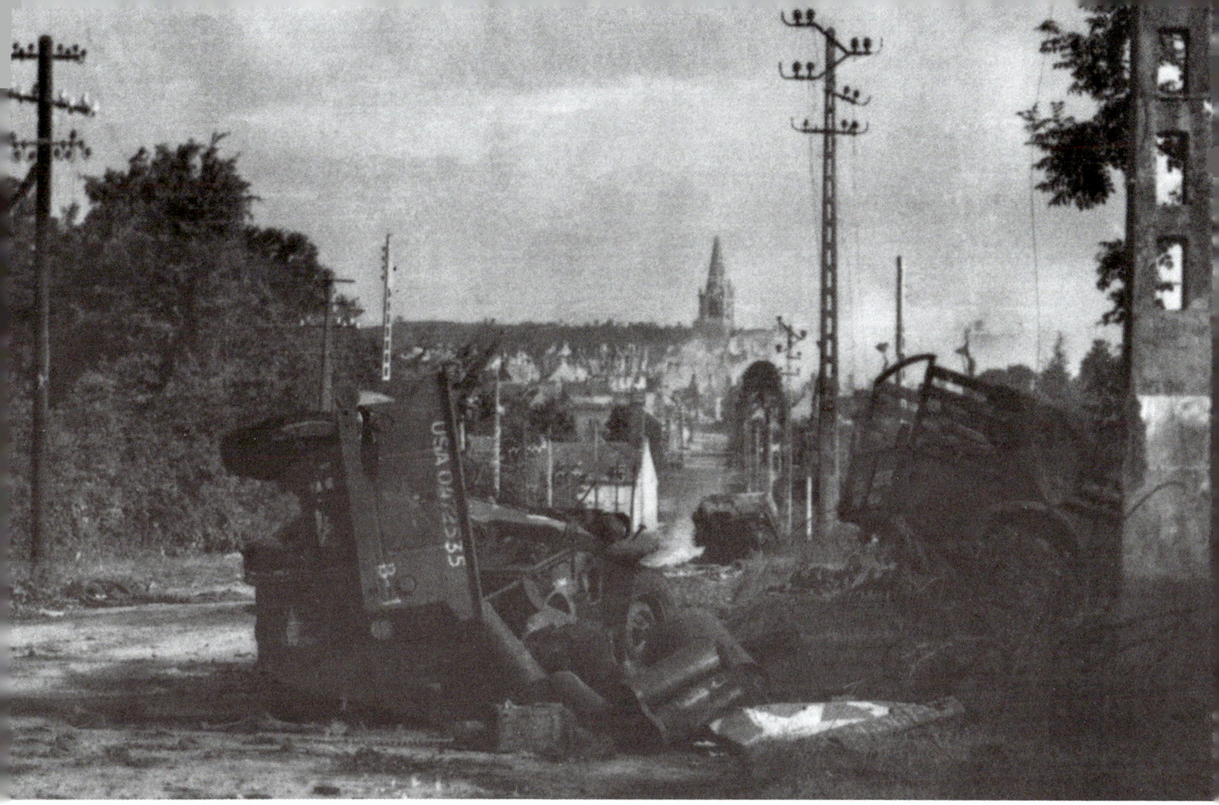

As early as June 12, after reports that Montebourg was lightly held, Major General Raymond O. Barton, commanding the 4th Division, ordered the 8th Infantry Regiment to take the town. However, a task force soon discovered that the place was strongly held and the attack was called off. This Jeep and these trailers were possibly disabled during the fighting that day. The tower of Saint-Jacques Church in the background, damaged later in the battle, is still intact. A new roundabout at the western entrance of Montebourg today interrupts the stretch of the main road leading into town. (USNA and ATB)

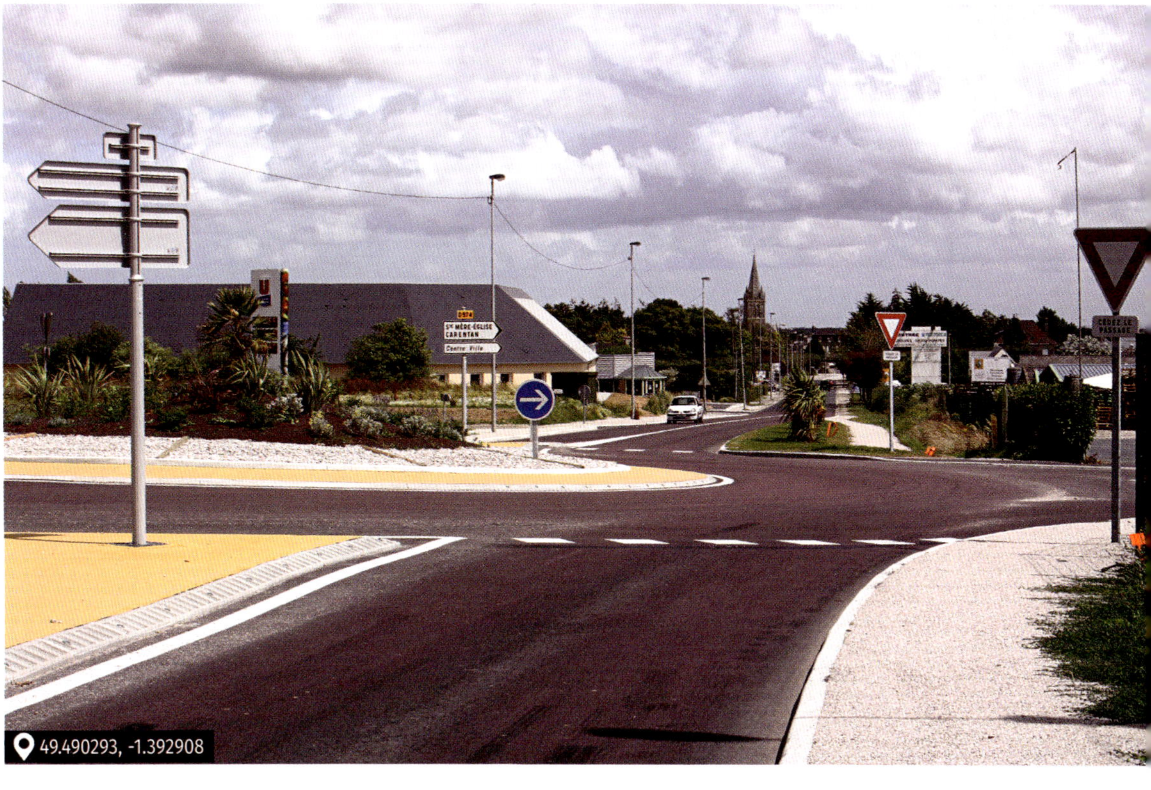

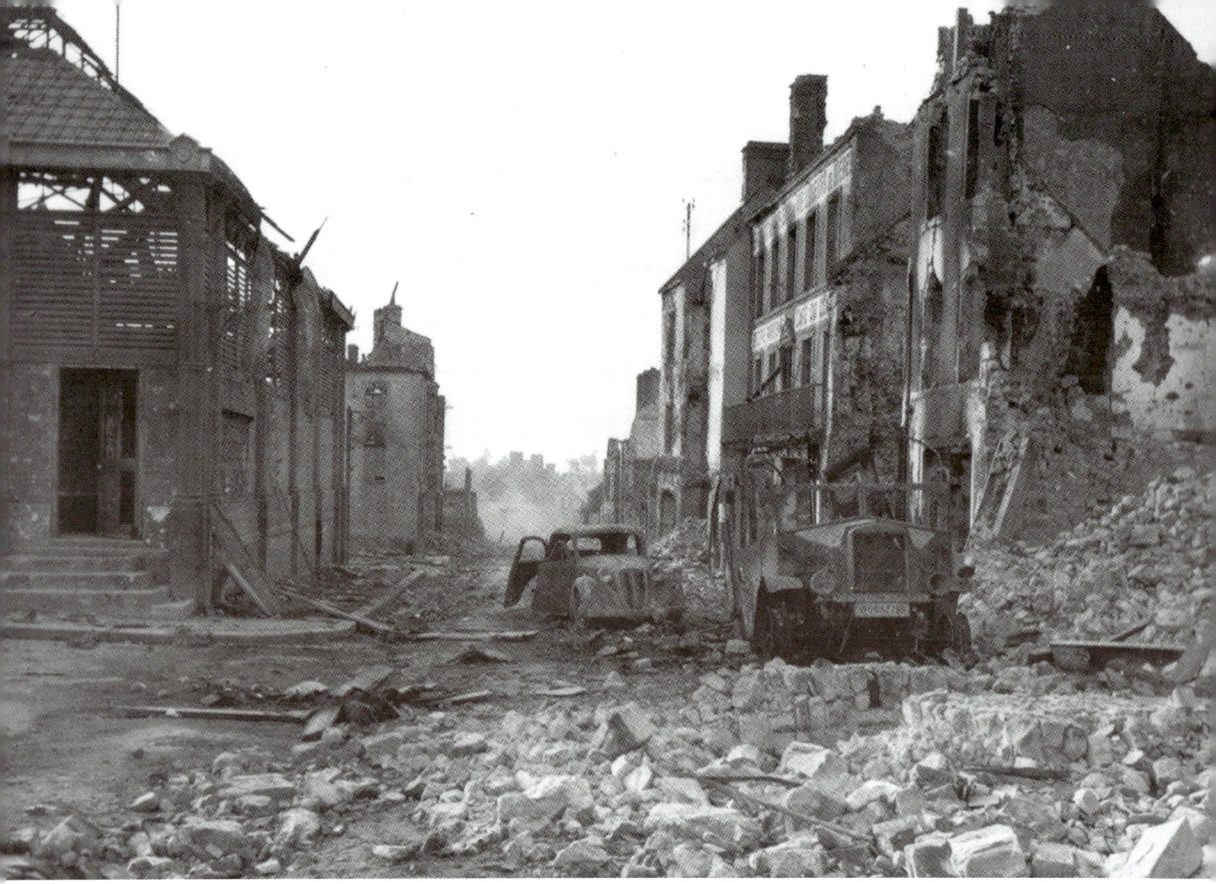

On the afternoon of June 8, Allied planes strafed a German convoy as it passed through Montebourg, en route to Valognes, south of Cherbourg. A captured Morris C8 lorry carrying ammunition was hit and soon exploded, setting fire to nearby houses. This is rue Paul Lecacheux, looking southwards, Then and Now. (USNA and ATB)

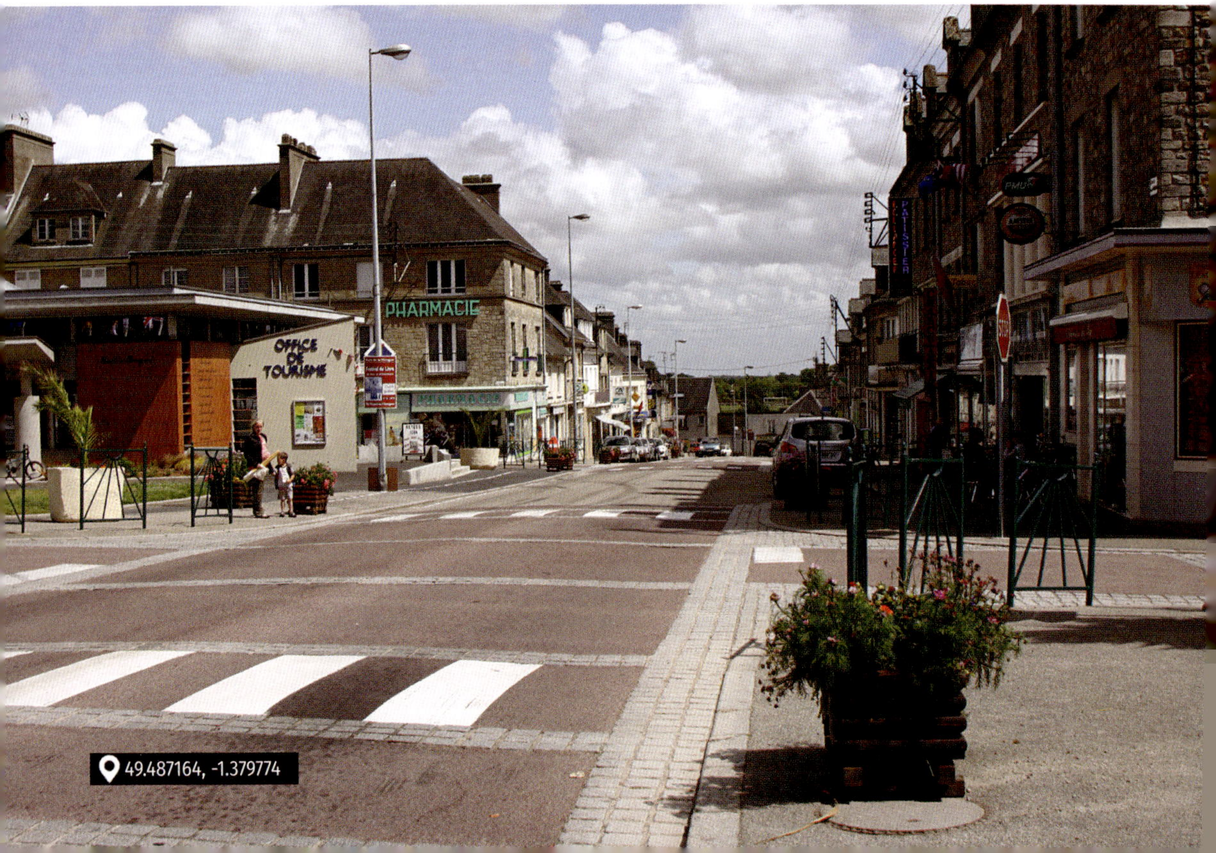

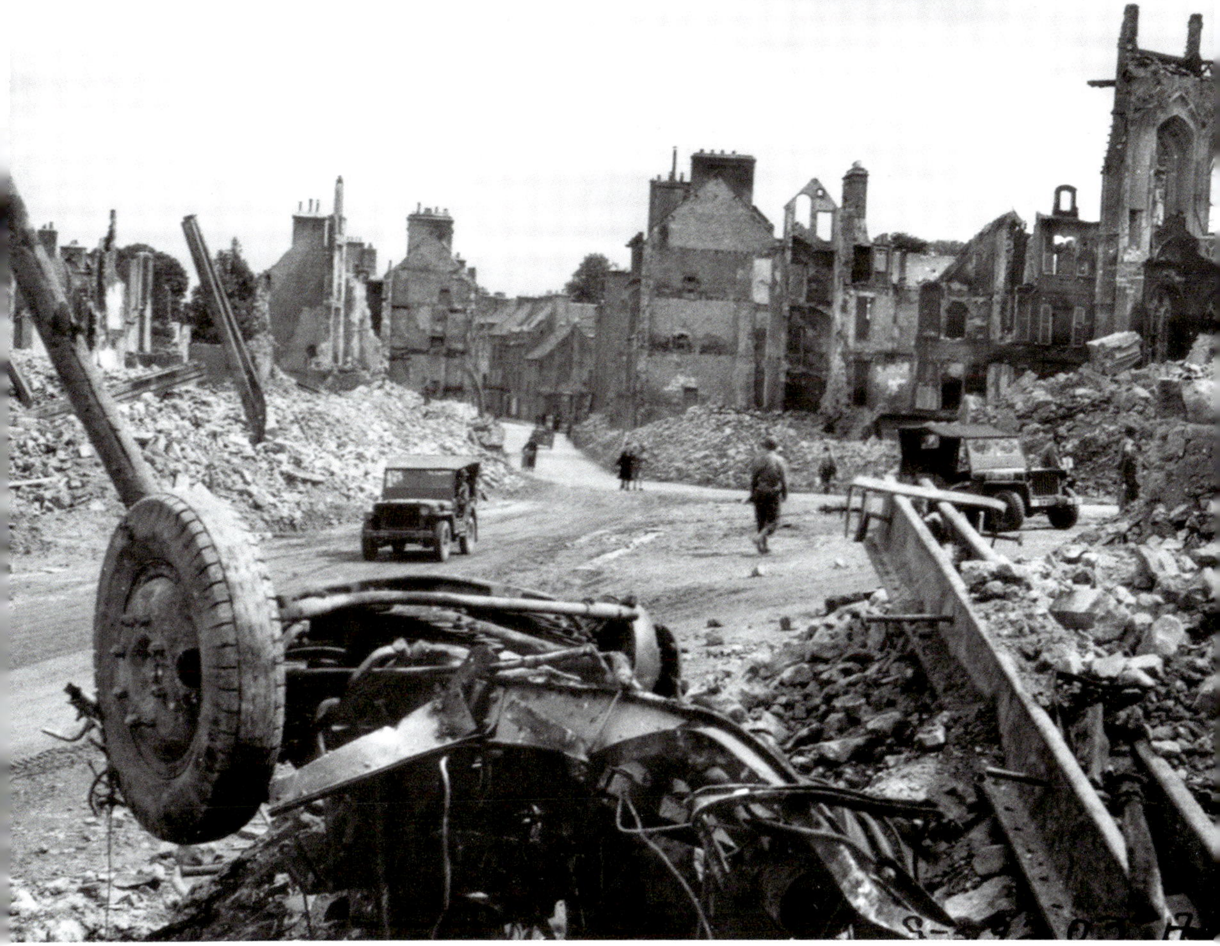

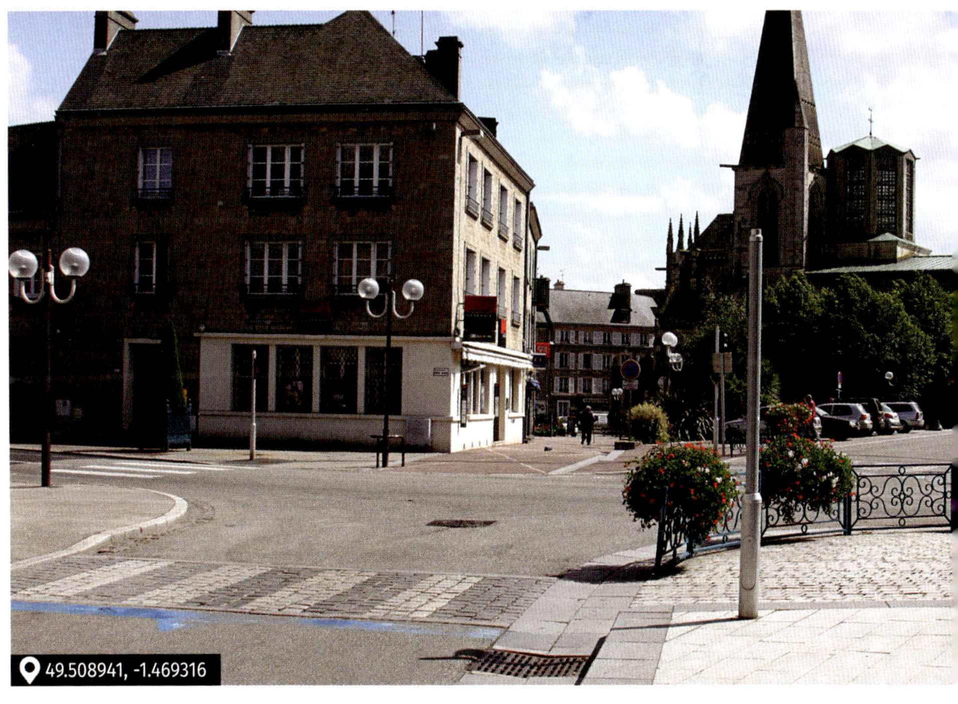

Valognes was bombed several times from June 6, the worst occurring on the 8th when the town centre was destroyed and more than 100 civilians were buried under the rubble. When the Americans entered the town, they found the streets so filled with debris that they were impassable for several days. This picture was taken on June 24, looking south, towards the Place Vicq d'Azir. (USNA and ATB)

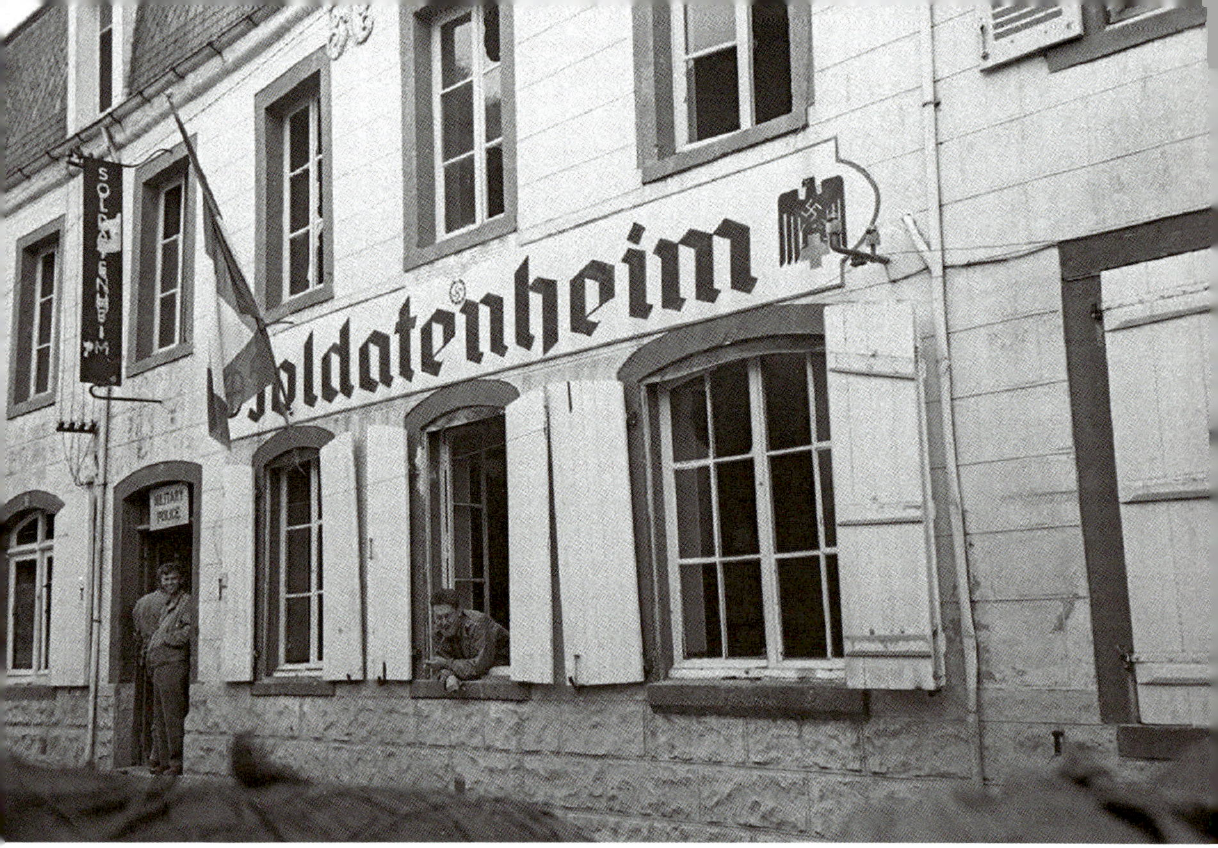

At Valognes, the Military Police took over the former Soldatenheim. This photo was taken by a Coast Guard Combat Photographer who moved inland from the invasion beach to record the extent of wreckage in the French towns and villages. Valognes, rue Léopold Delisle, Then and Now. (USNA and ATB)

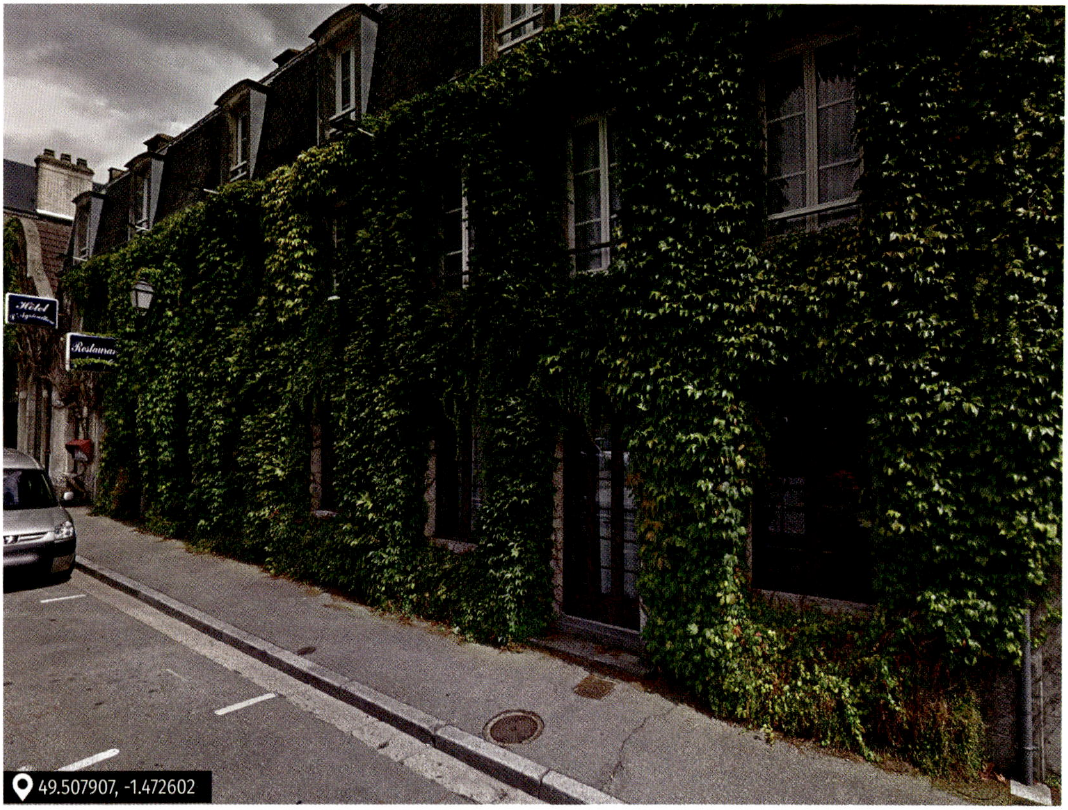

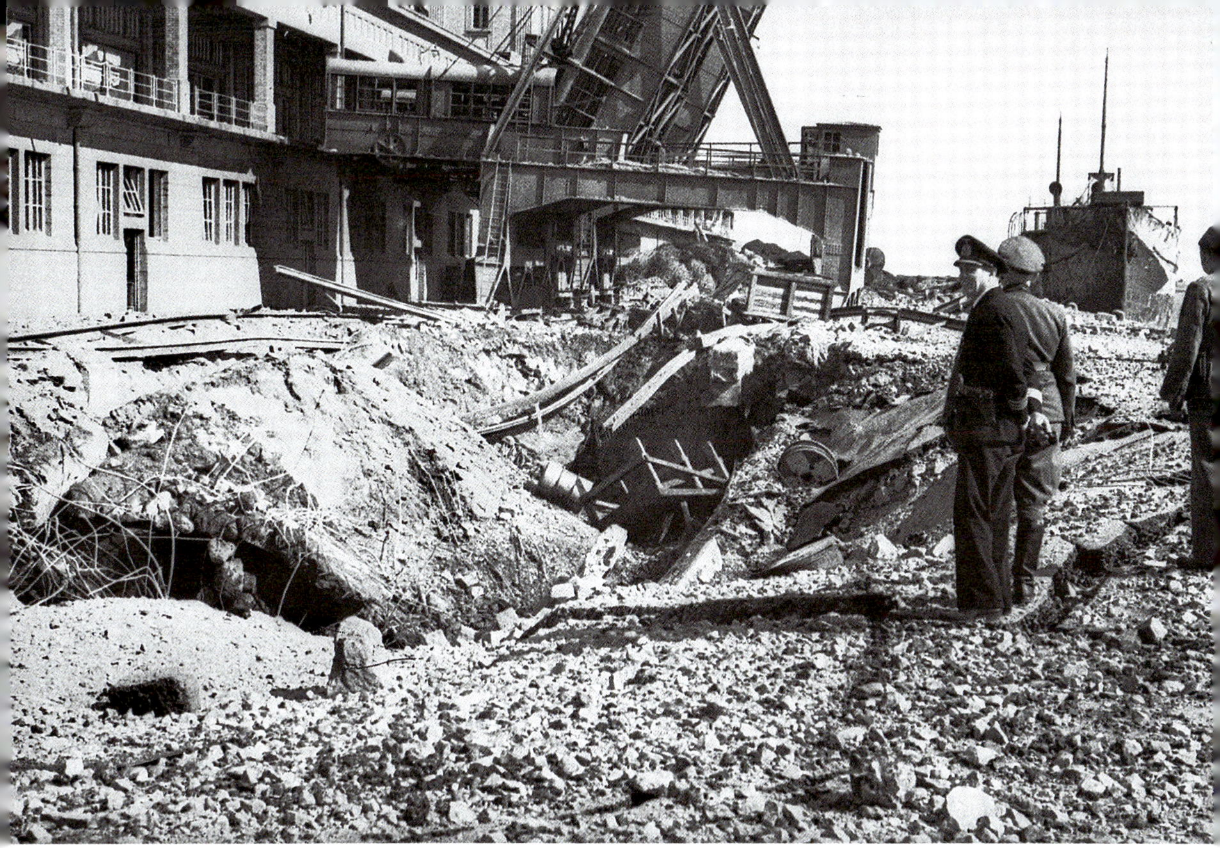

The methodical destruction of port installations began on June 7 and continued until the final capitulation. Some of the worst demolitions were that of the Quai de France, on the western side of the Darse Transatlantique. More than 600 meters of quay wall, or 15,000 cubic meters of concrete, were blown into the quay where the largest ocean liners once docked. The ruined Quai de France was nicely rebuilt and those movable ship-to-train access galleries that survived German destruction are still in use today when large cruise ships make a call to Cherbourg. (BA and ATB)

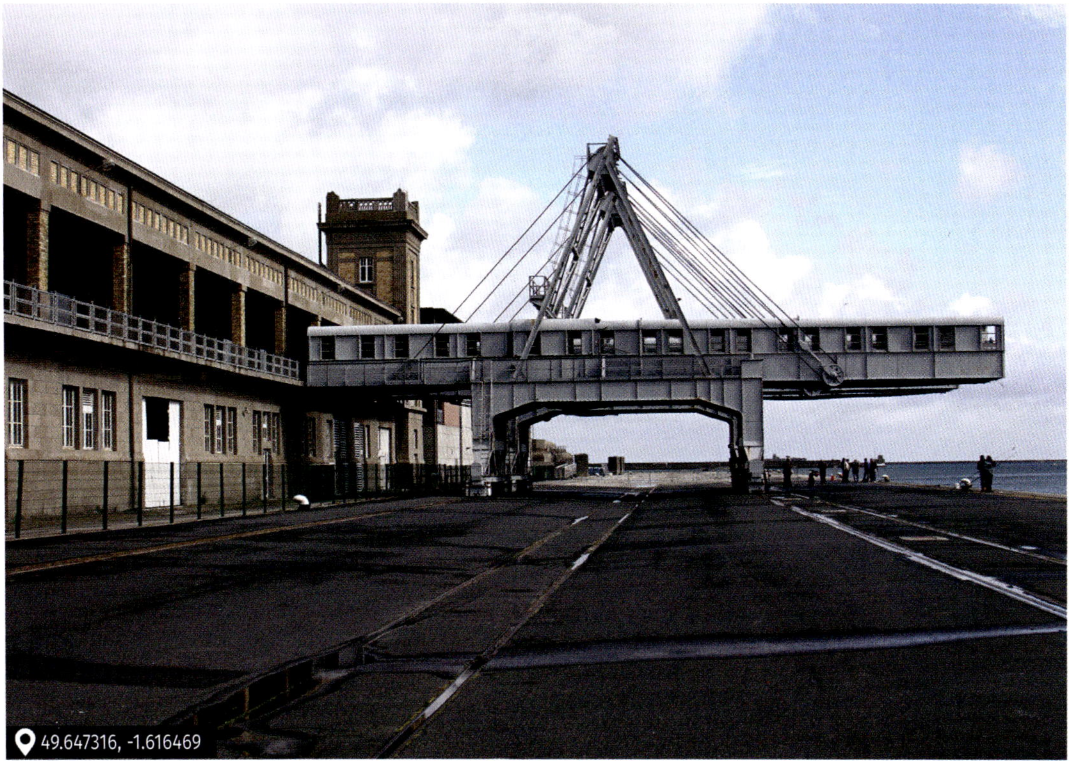

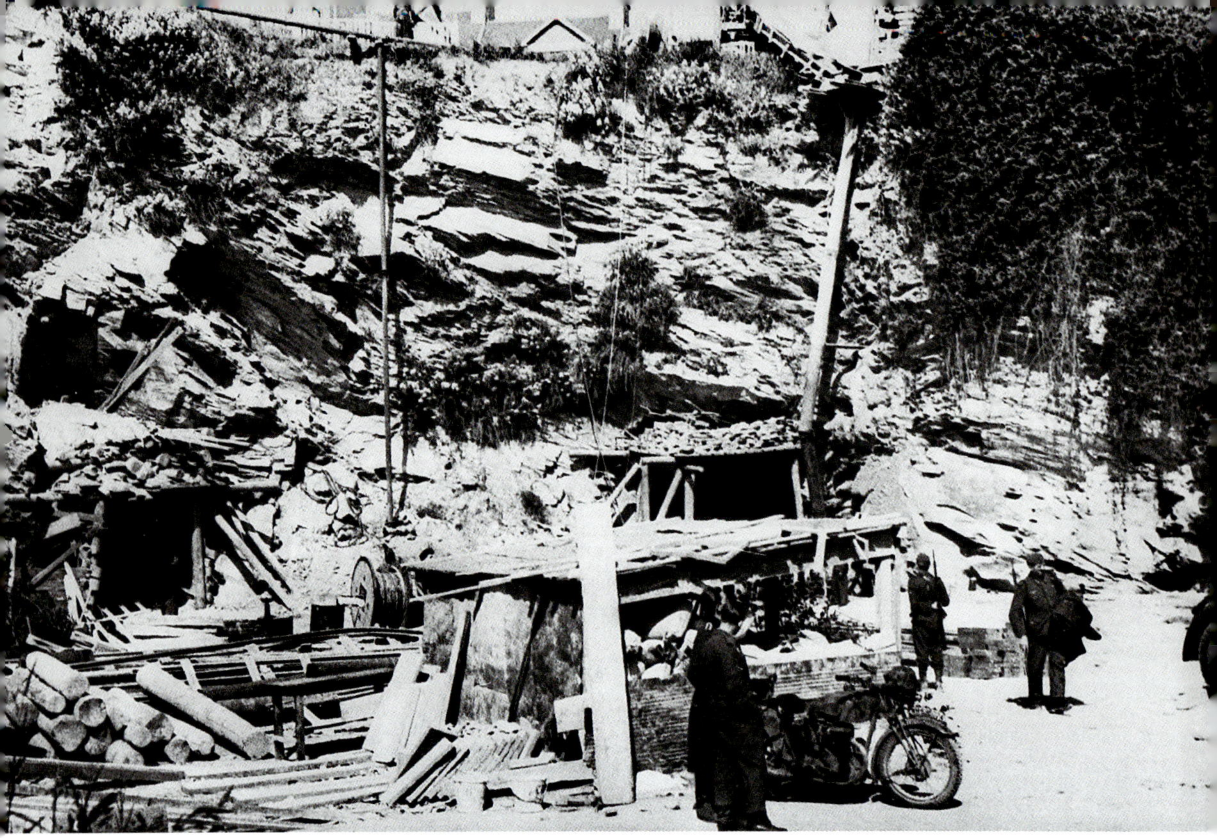

As American troops rapidly invested the fortress, von Schlieben moved his command post into an underground shelter in a quarry at the suburb of Saint-Sauveur, on the south-west outskirts of Cherbourg. The Kriegsmarine had begun to build an ammunition depot in these tunnels but this plan was far from completed in June 1944. A German photographer pictured the two entrances in the quarry sometime in mid-June, although the exact date is unknown. The old quarry is now a magnificent garden and, although the present owners kindly allowed the author access, no visits are possible. (BA and ATB)

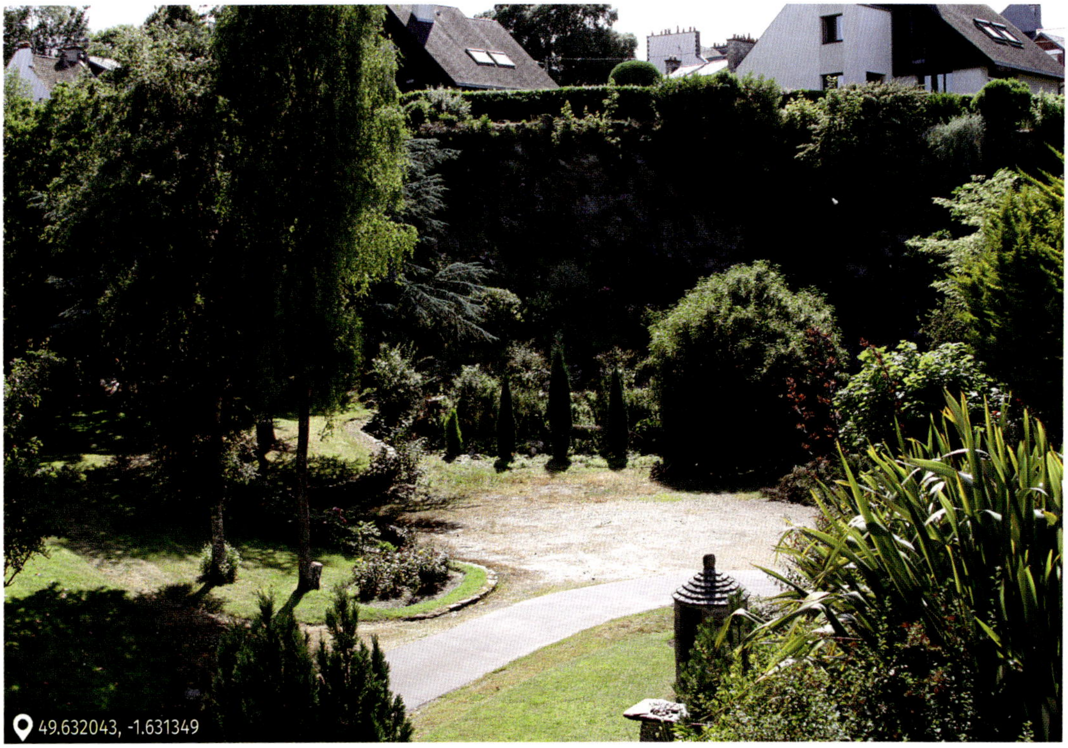

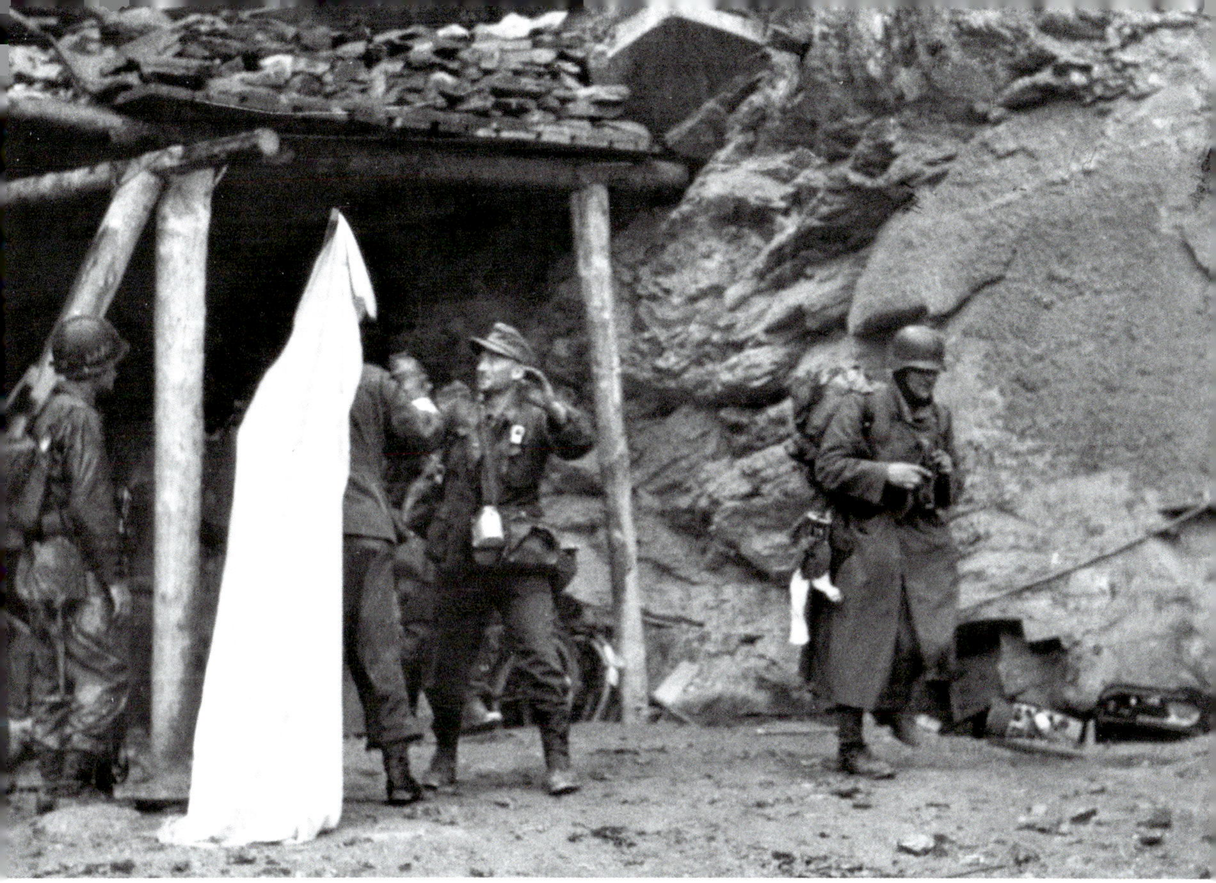

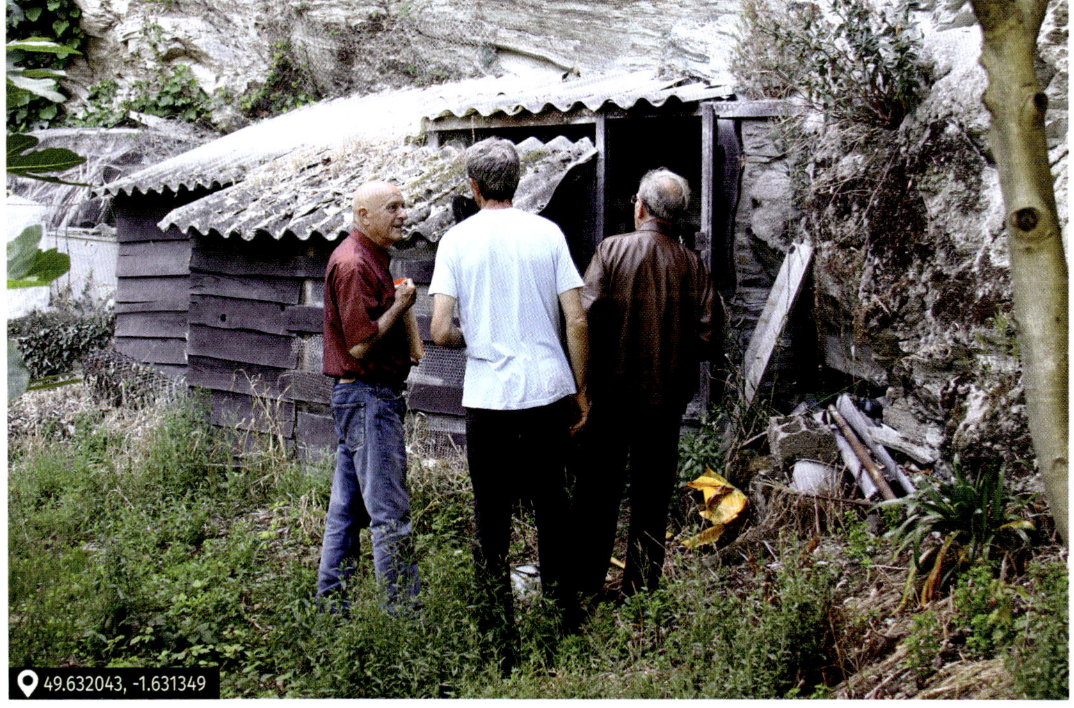

The same underground shelter General von Schlieben surrendered on June 26. Major General Eddy, the 9th Division commander, described: 'The tank destroyer's projectiles had caused so much dust and fumes in the tunnel that the German soldiers, once finding that the white flag had been raised, began to pour out. By actual count later, there were 842 of them.' It was there! The main entrance to the tunnel disappeared decades ago when part of the 15-metre-high face of the quarry collapsed. The heap of rocks was first landscaped and then a hen-house, now disused, was built on top of it. (USNA and ATB)

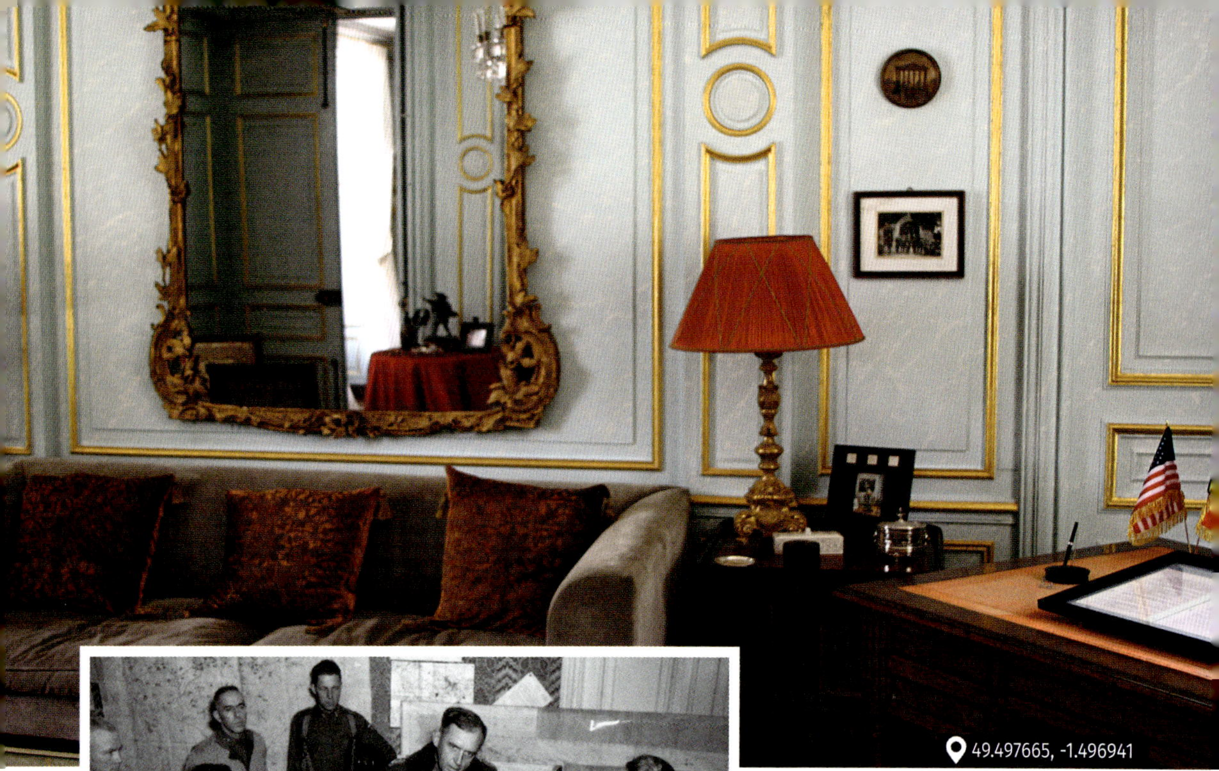

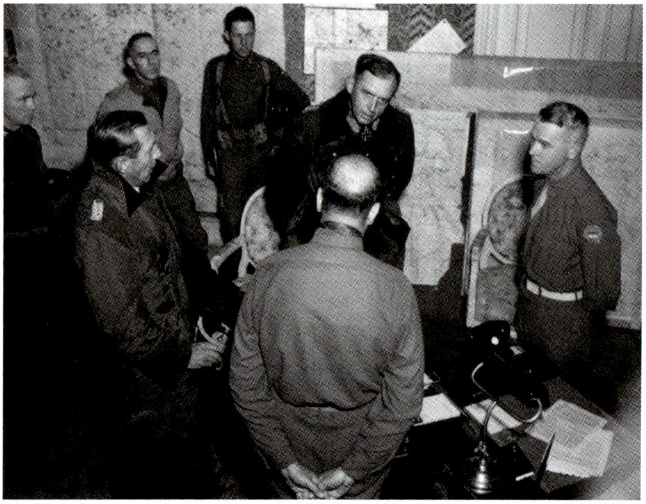

On the 26th, Generalleutnant von Schlieben and Konteradmiral Hennecke surrendered at their underground shelter in Saint-Sauveur. They were immediately dispatched to General Collins's command post at the Château de Servigny, in Yvetot-Bocage. Discussions and the signing of the official surrender took place in this room on the first floor (see pages 73 to 75). The room is now decorated with objects relating to that historic day in June 1944, including a copy of the surrender document. (USNA and ATB)

After surrendering the last major German stronghold in Cherbourg itself – the naval Arsenal – on the morning of the 27th, Generalmajor Sattler was also taken to the Château de Servigny. Further discussions and signings took place, this time in a room in the château's basement. (USNA and ATB)

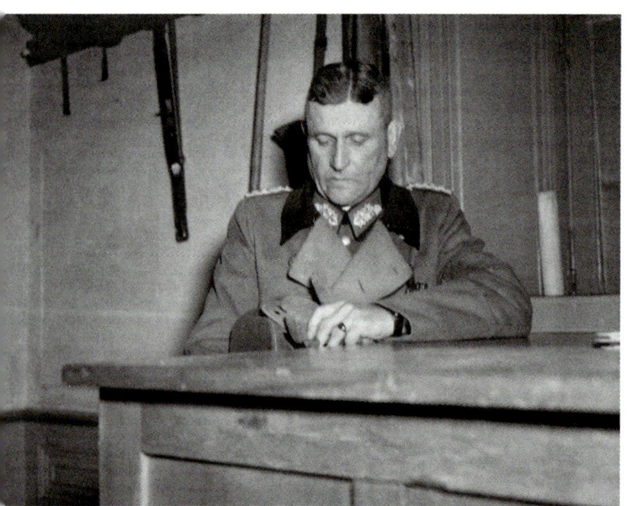

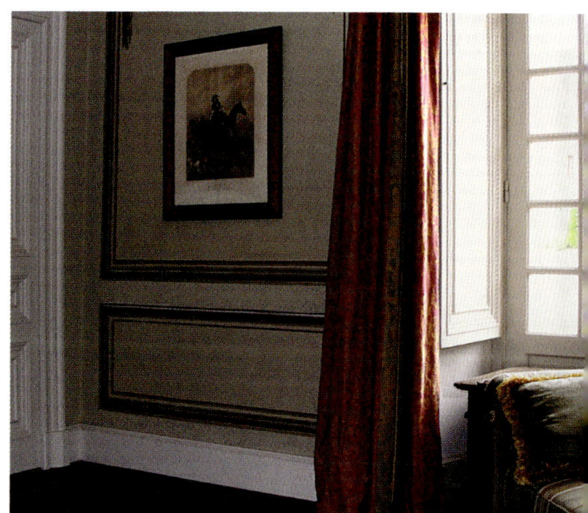

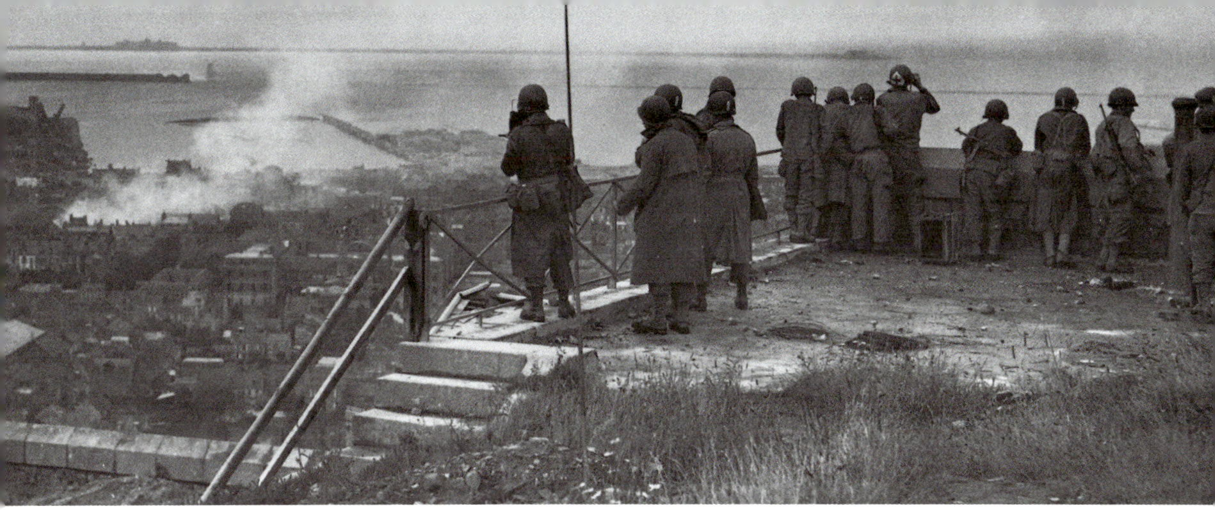

On June 26, even before the last German stronghold in the town had fallen Major General J. Lawton Collins, the VII Corps commander, went to the Fort du Roule to observe the clouds of smoke billowing up on Cherbourg and the harbour from places where the Germans were demolishing stores of oil and ammunition. The largest conflagration, visible in the right background, is in the Arsenal area. Only part of the mountain top is today a public area. (USNA and ATB)

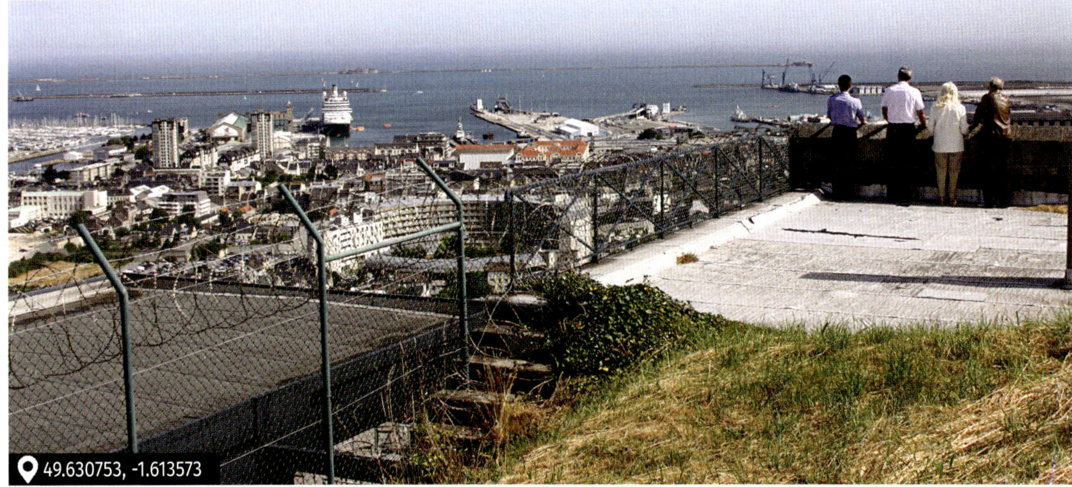

As the GIs drove into the city, a Signal Corps photographer with the 313th Infantry pictured a dead German soldier lying in Rue du Val de Saire. A large new building – the Police headquarters – now spoils the comparison, and while the house visible in the background on the right stood firm for decades, bearing witness to this moment in history with its presence, it has just been demolished. (USNA and Google)

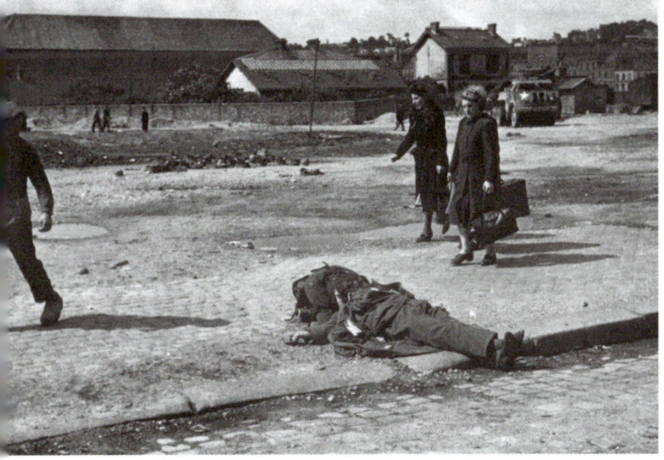

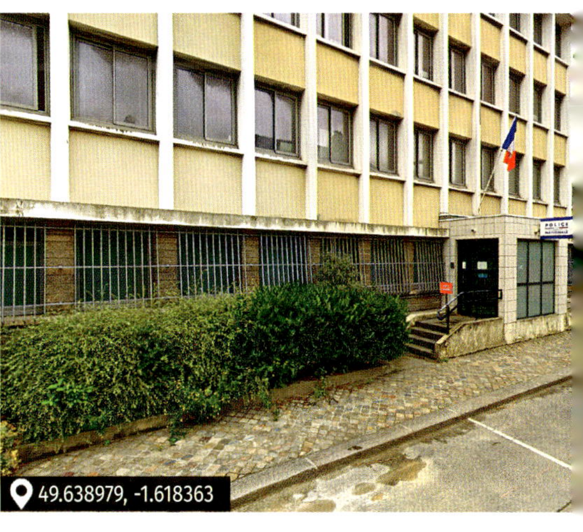

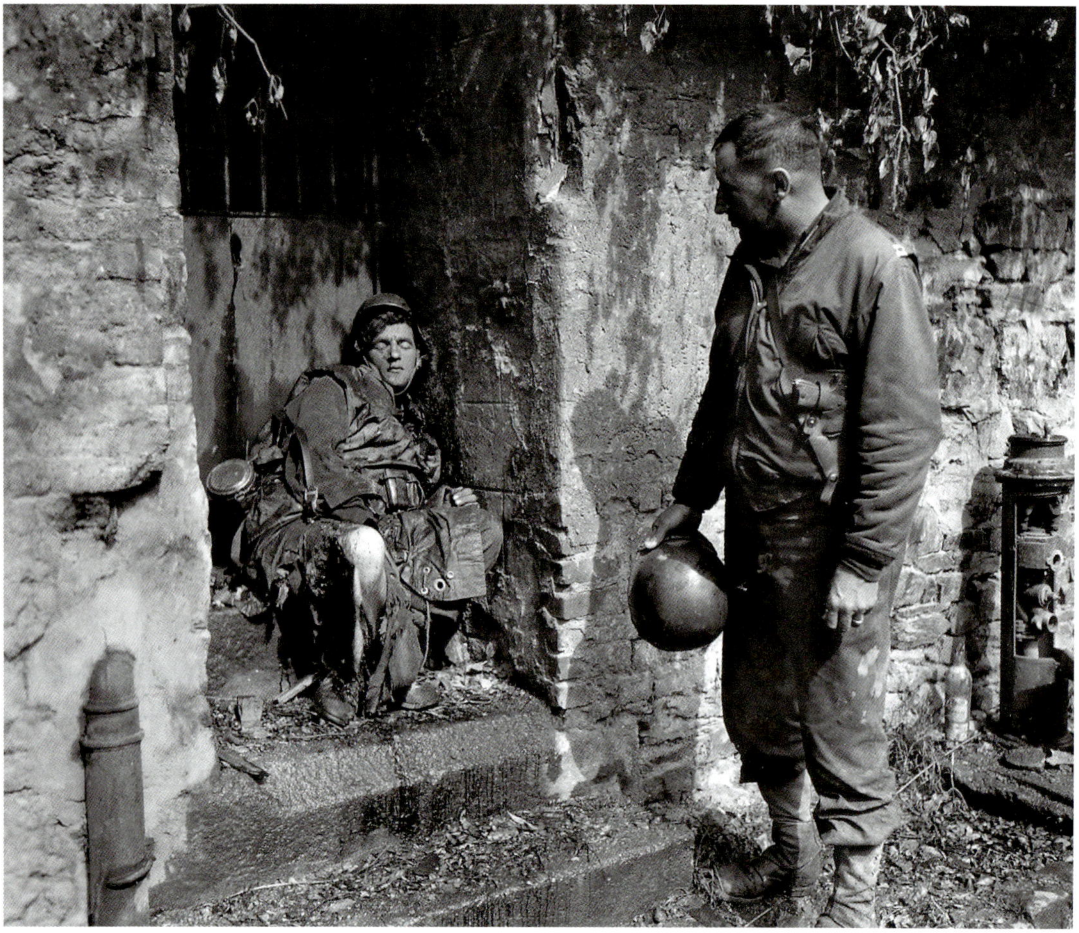

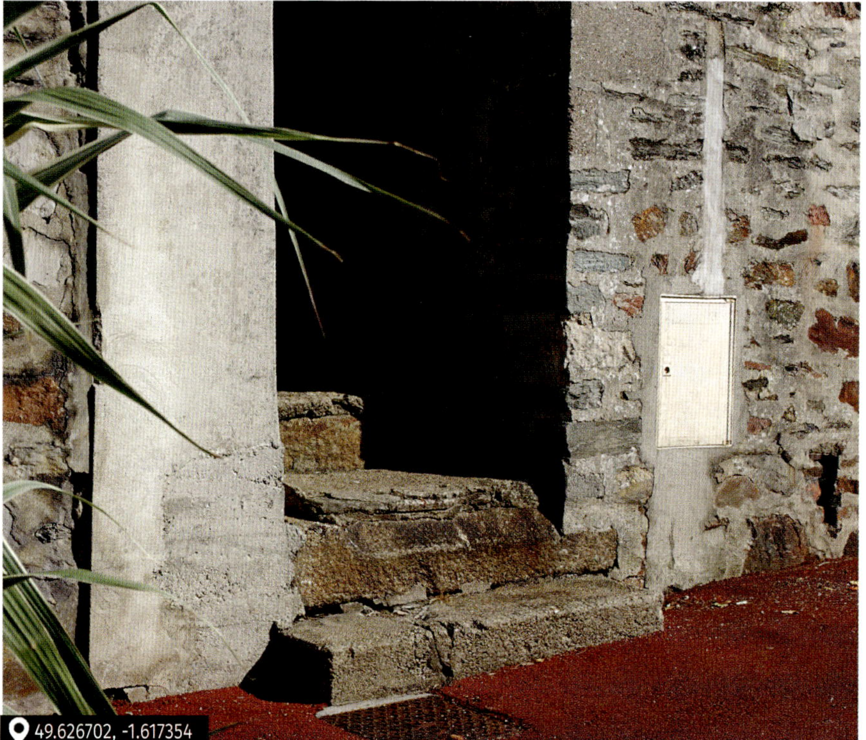

Captain Earl J. Topley from Saint-Paul, Minnesota, had a thought for a dead German soldier. Then and Now at the bottom of rue Armand Levéel, at the junction of avenue de Paris.
(USNA and ATB)

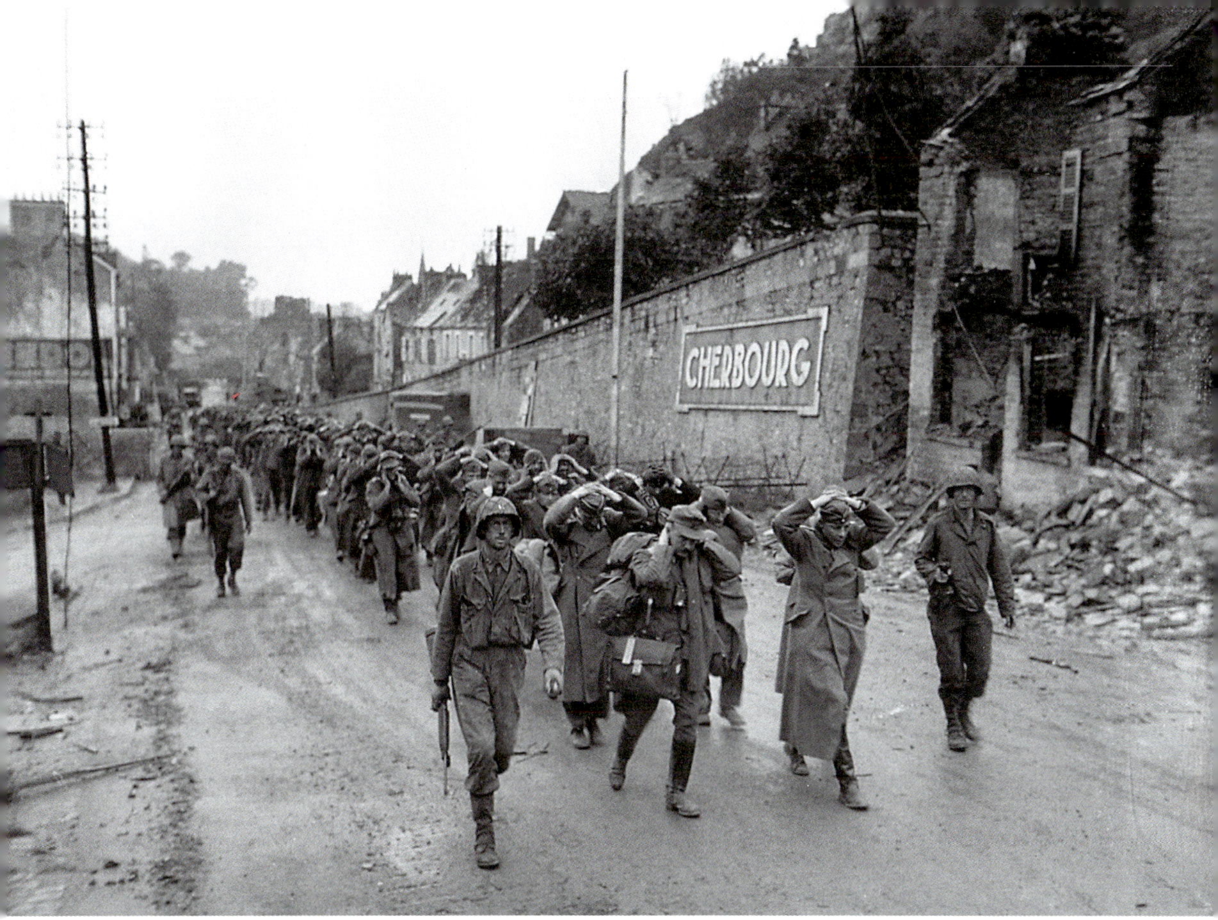

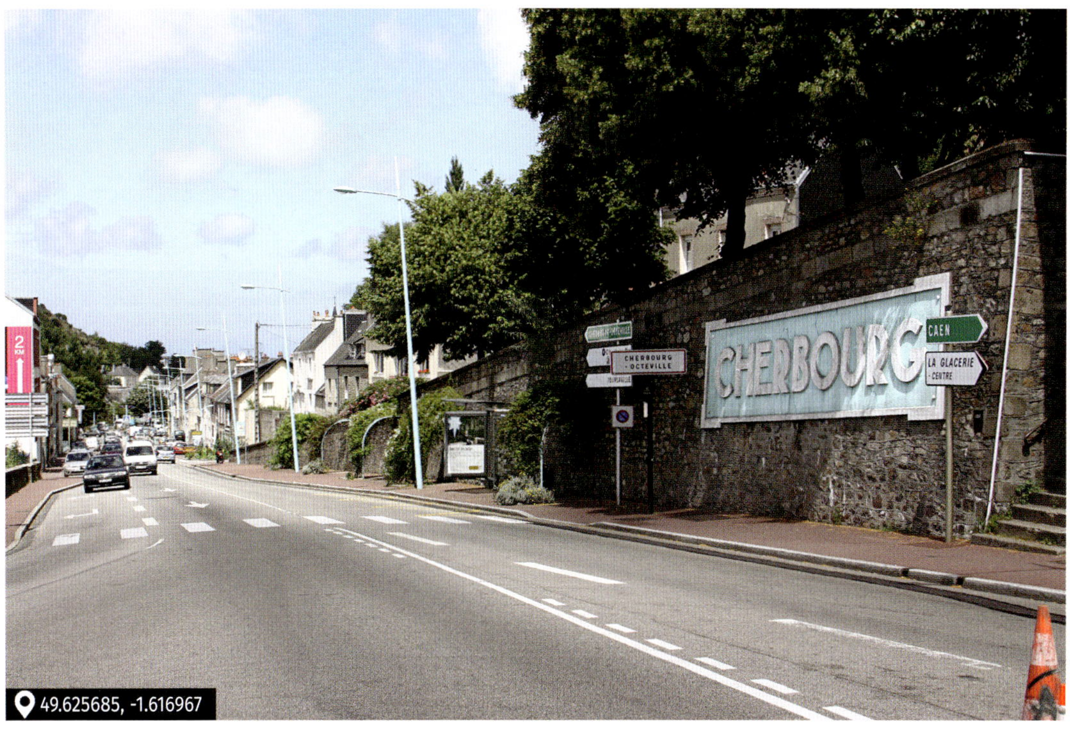

The battle for Cherbourg is over. Captain William H. Hooper of the 314th Infantry Regiment, 79th Division leading a group of German POWs out of Cherbourg along Avenue de Paris on June 28. Hooper would be killed two weeks later near La Haye-du-Puits. The same view today. This is the old toll entrance to the city, known as L'Octroi, with rue Armand Levéel branching off to the right in the background. (USNA and ATB)

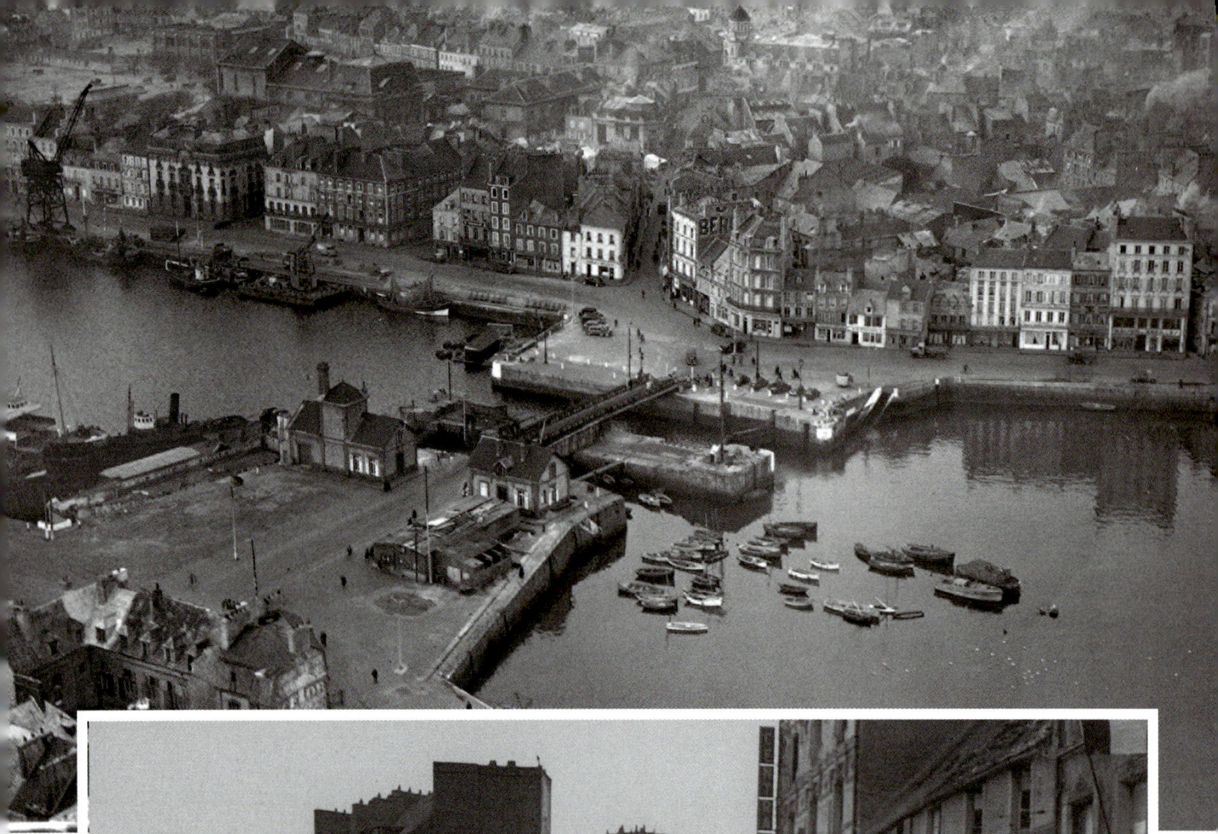

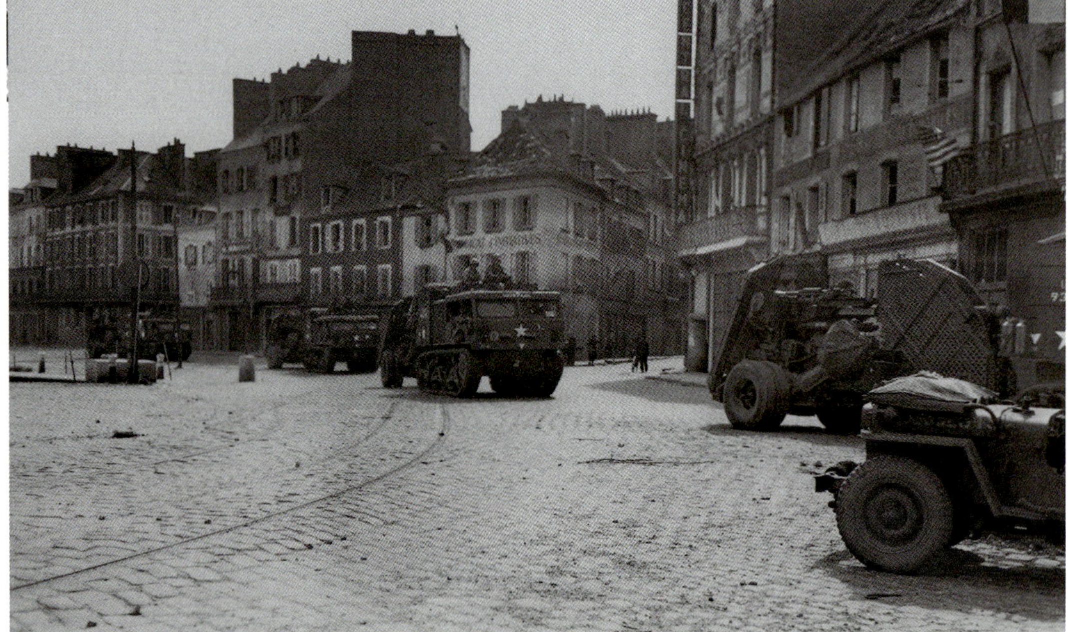

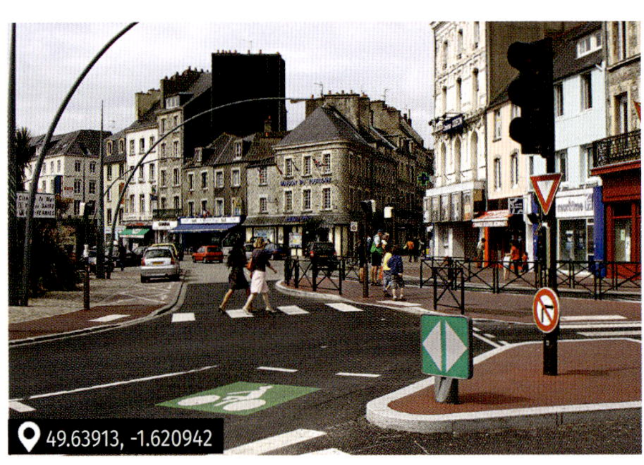

Cherbourg, Then and Now, looking south from the west end of the Pont Tournant (swing bridge), with M4 prime movers of an anti-aircraft battery on their way inland on June 30. This beautiful 1949 aerial view, centered on the Pont Tournant, provides a perfect setting for the Then and Now, and also allows to spot several of the photos featured elsewhere in this book (see page 110): Royal Navy divers working to clear the Alexandre III Quay, top left of this photo, and engineers cutting away the ruins of the Pont Tournant to replace it with a retractable Bailey Bridge, mounted on trolleys running on tram rails.
(IGN, USNA and ATB)

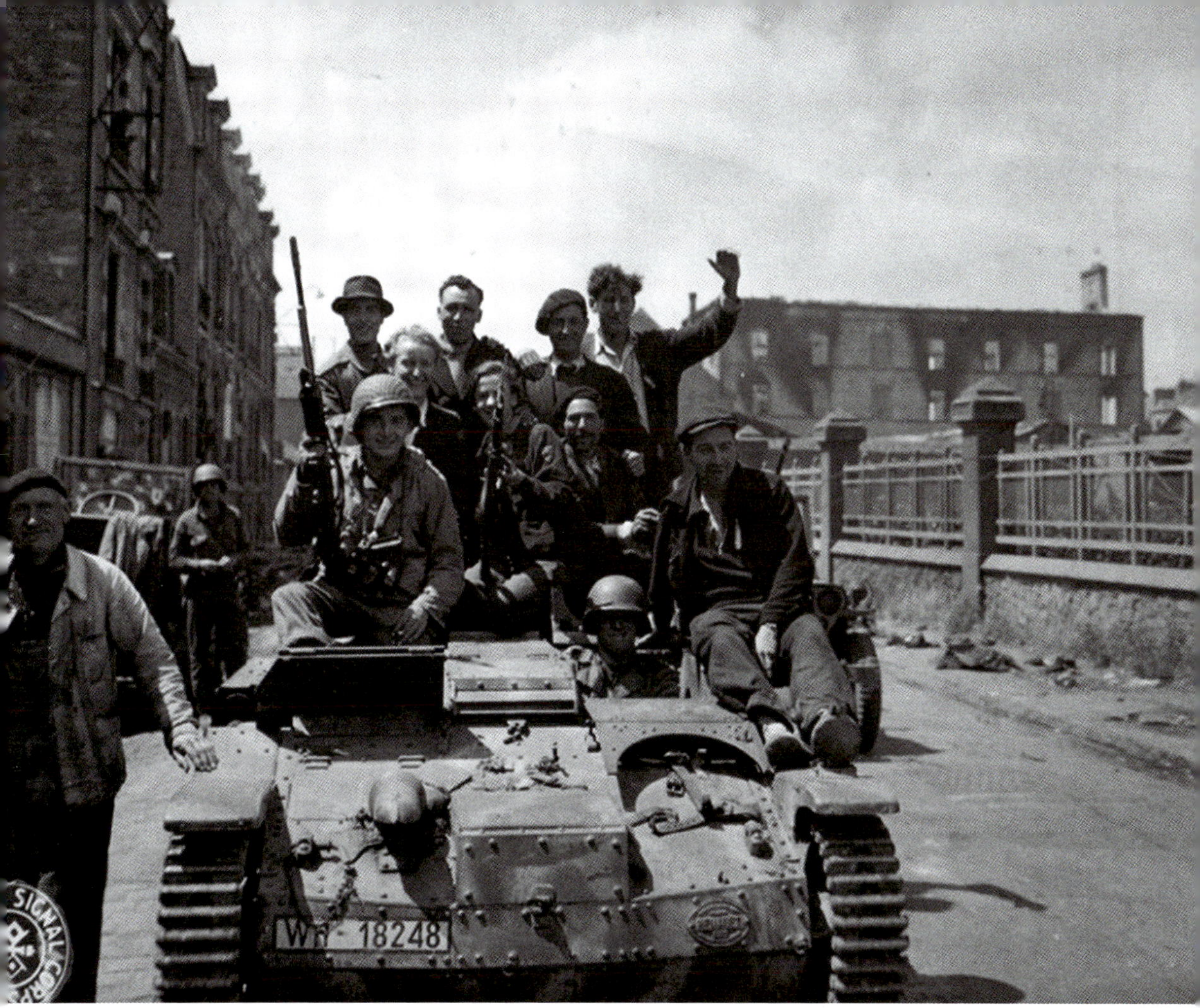

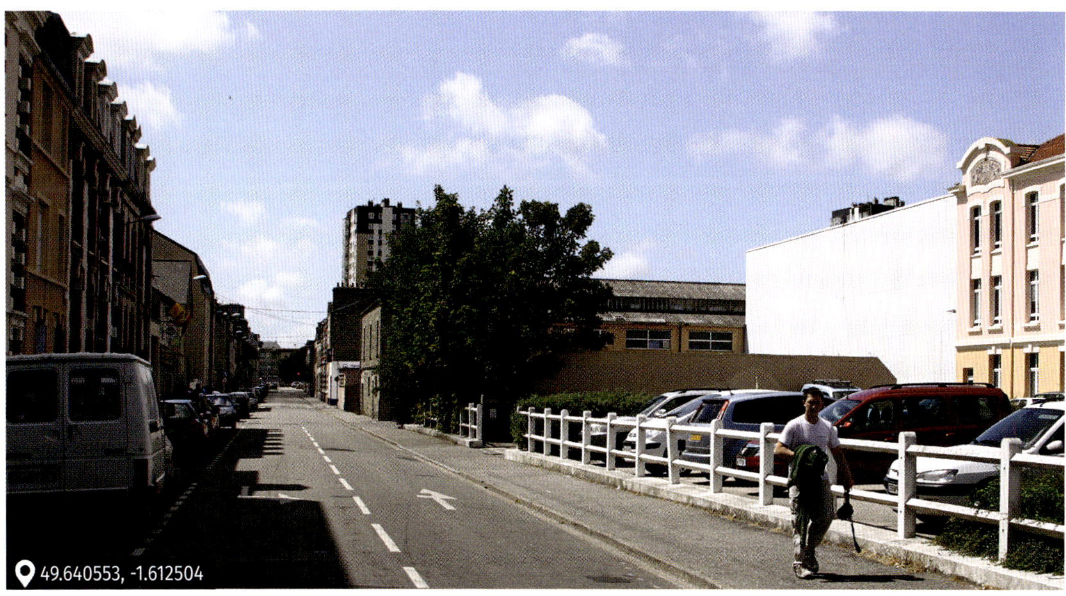

GIs taking a ride in a captured tracked carrier in Rue Dom Pedro. The vehicle is an ex-French UE tractor of which the Germans had seized large numbers in 1940. They were in front of the Hôtel Atlantique built in the 1920s to house and check-up emigrants before they sailed to the United States. The hotel had seen over 250,000 emigrants to the United States passing through it in the 1920s and 1930s, so it is quite possible that one of the GIs taking a ride might be a descendant of one of them. (USNA and ATB)

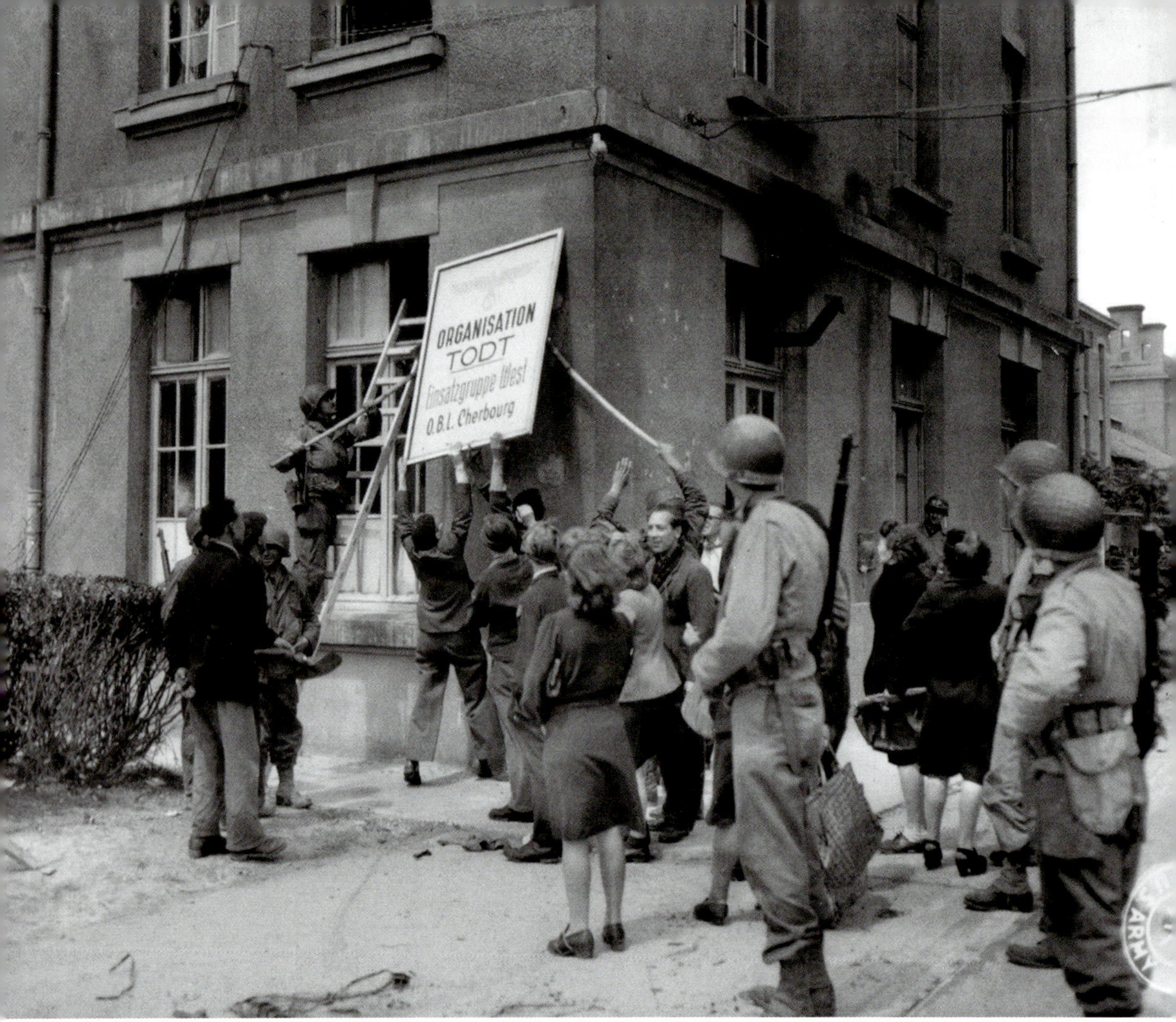

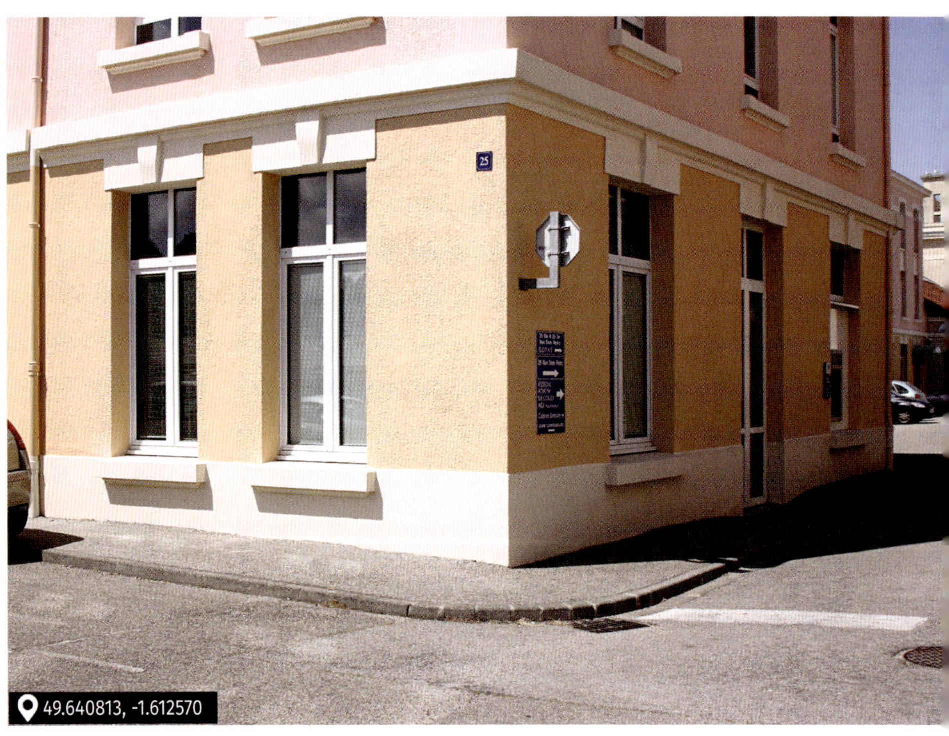

American troops took down a German sign from the Hôtel Atlantique where the headquarters of Oberbauleitung Cherbourg, the construction sector of Organisation Todt, was formerly. Rue Dom Pedro, the former Hôtel Atlantique now houses the CCI, Cherbourg's chambre of commerce. (USNA and ATB)

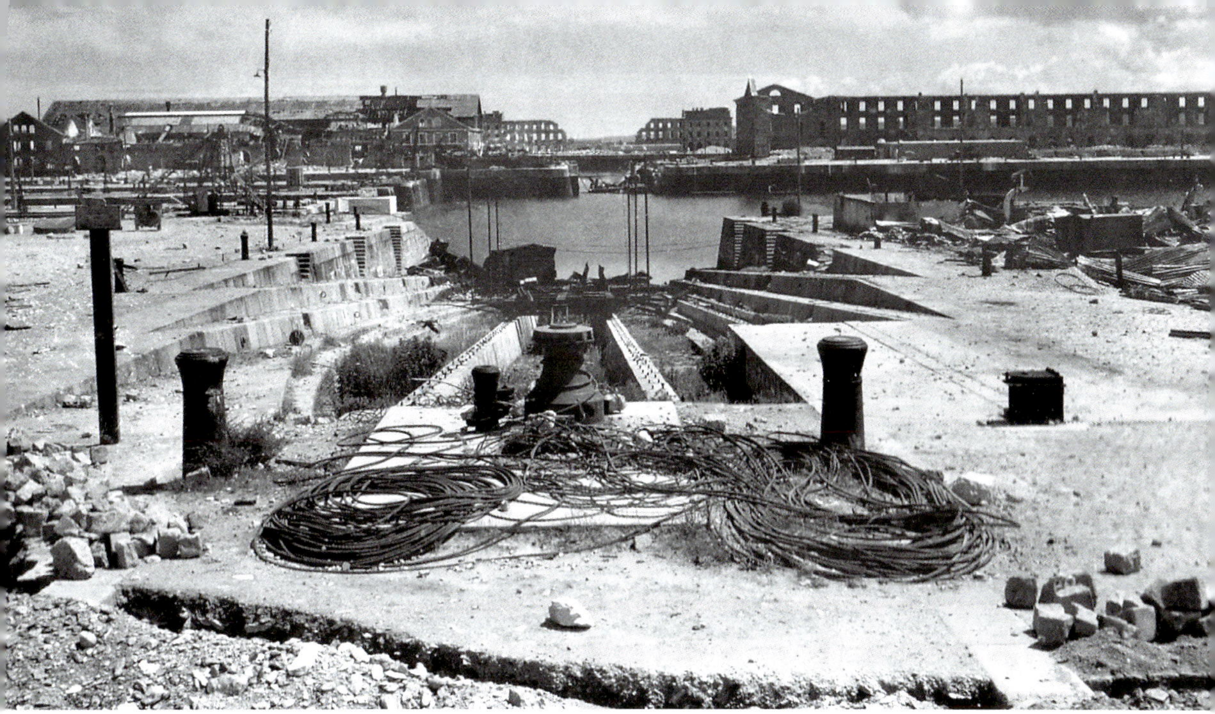

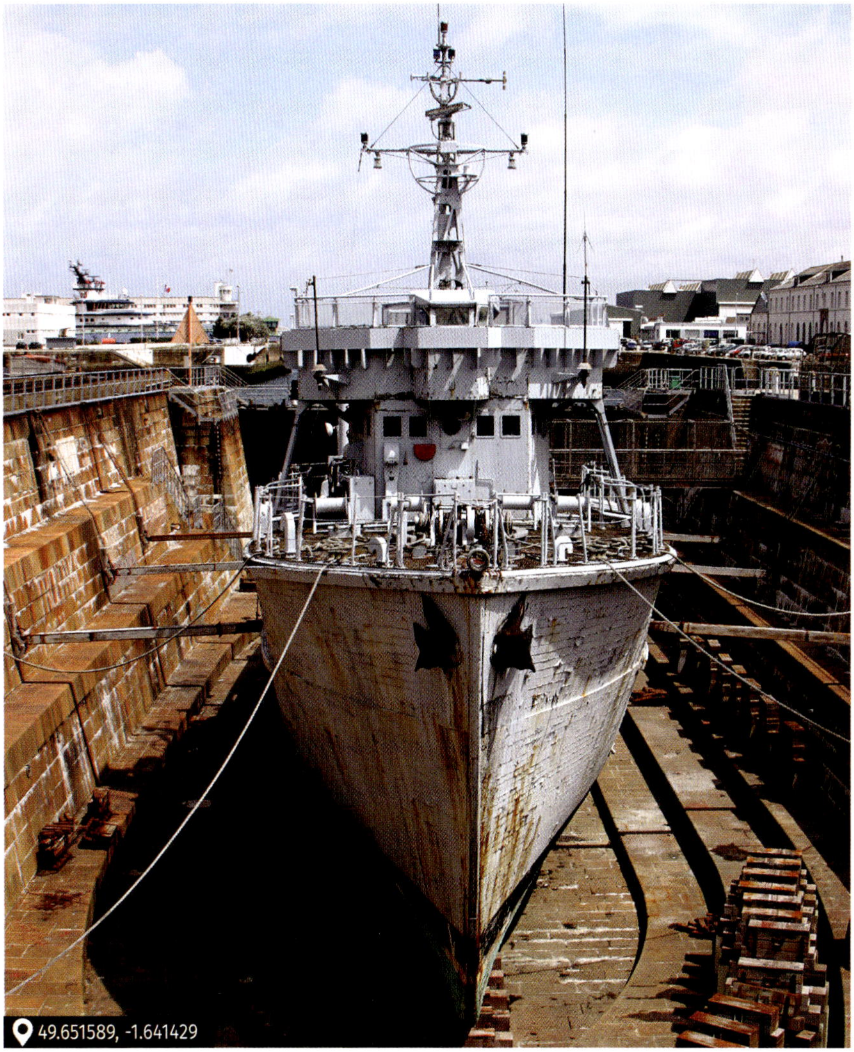

Damaged buildings in background enabled the author to trace this scene of desolation to the western side of Bassin Napoléon III, looking eastwards at the Passe Nord and Bassin Charles X behind it. This slipway is now gone, filled in, but Dock No. 7 still remains on this same side of Bassin Napoléon III, enabling this comparison some distance south of the gone slipway, facing instead with the entrance from the Avant-Port in the background. (USNA and ATB)

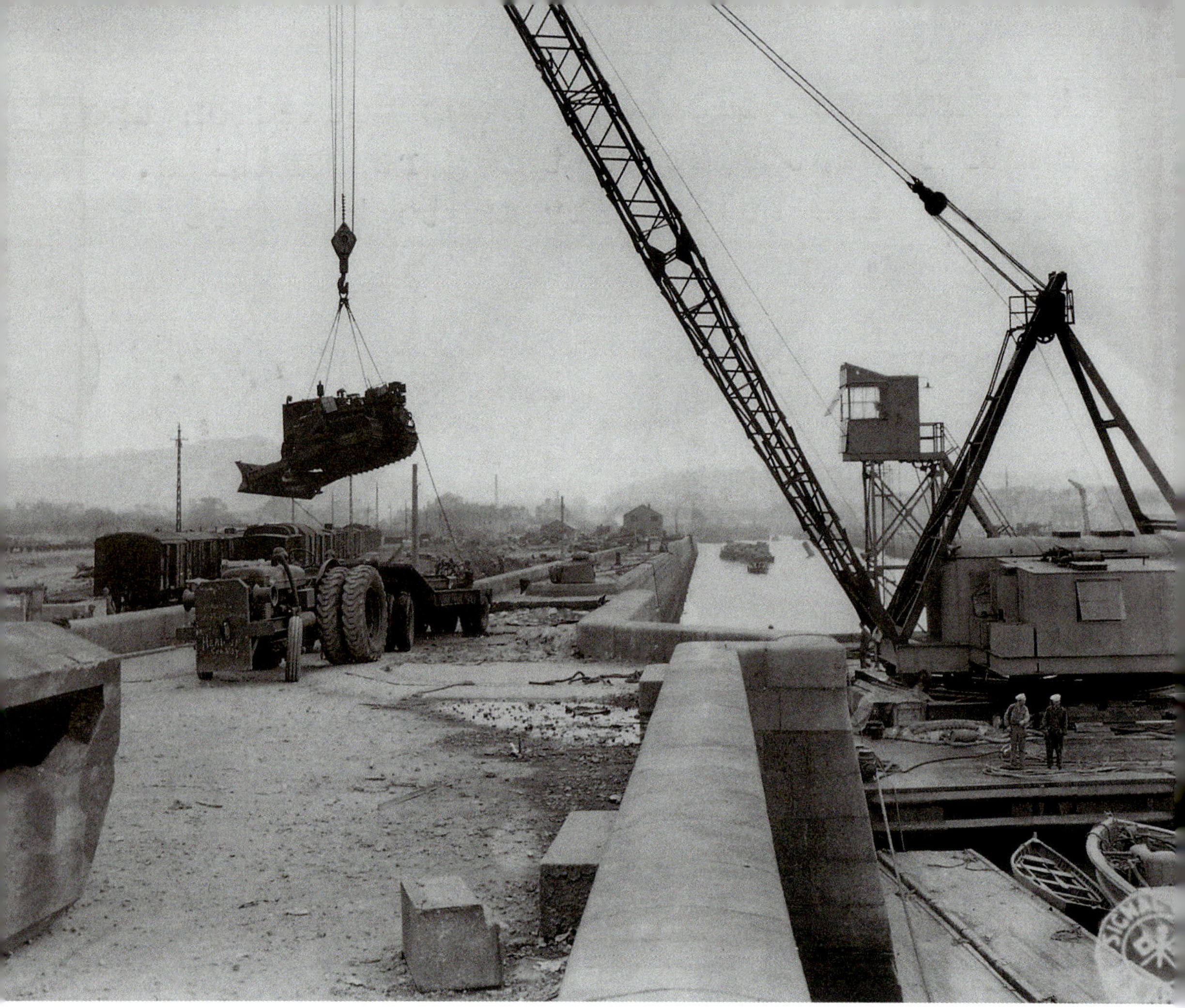

The harbour presented a dismal and discouraging sight when it was captured, with demolished buildings, ruined quays and sunken ships and barges in all areas. A floating crane unloaded a Caterpillar D7 tractor on a trailer in front of the Gare Maritime, with the Avant-Port in the right. In the background appears another tank turret (see page 97). (USNA and ATB)

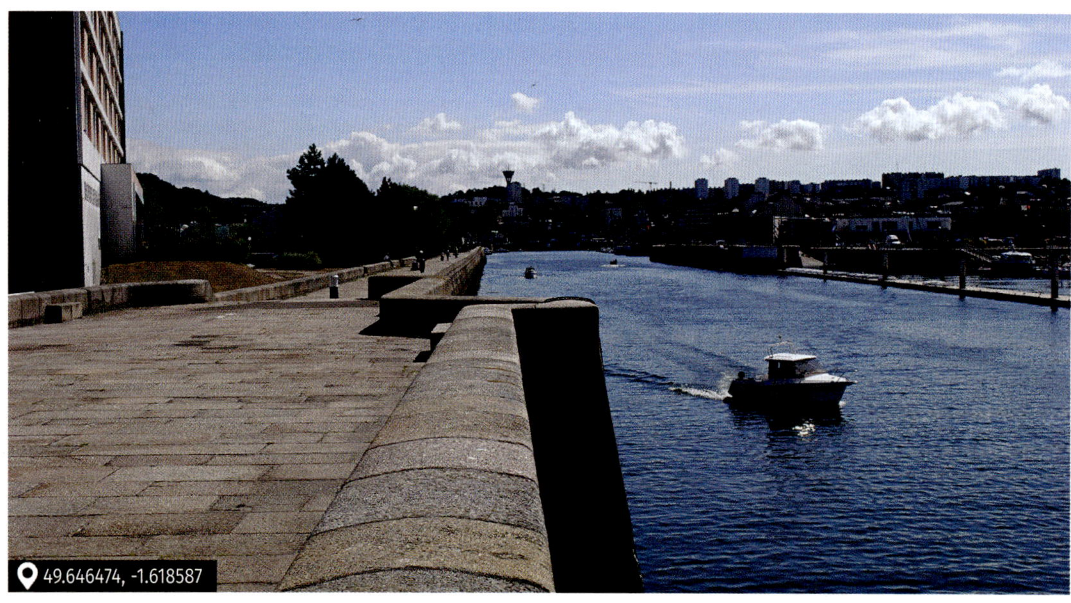

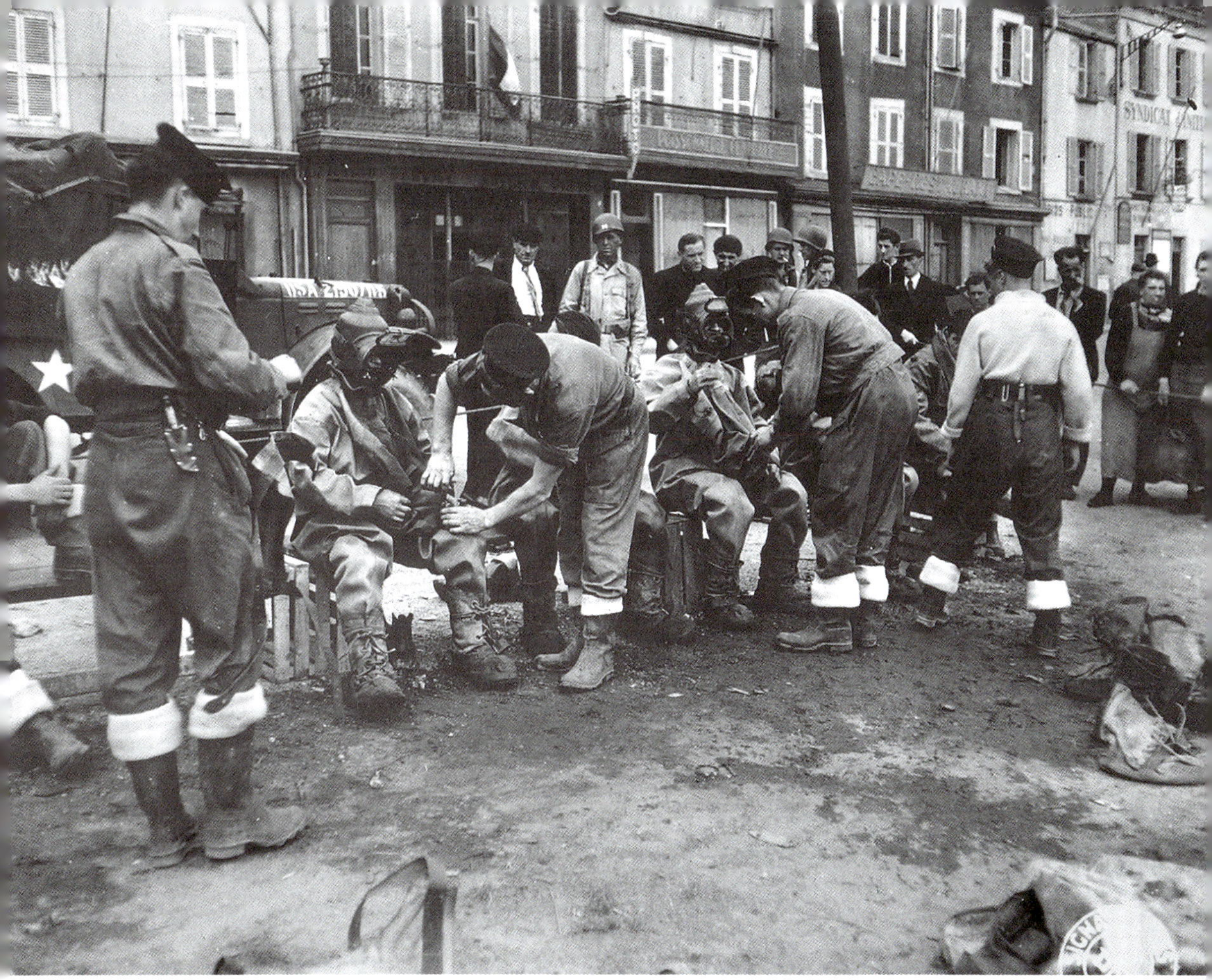

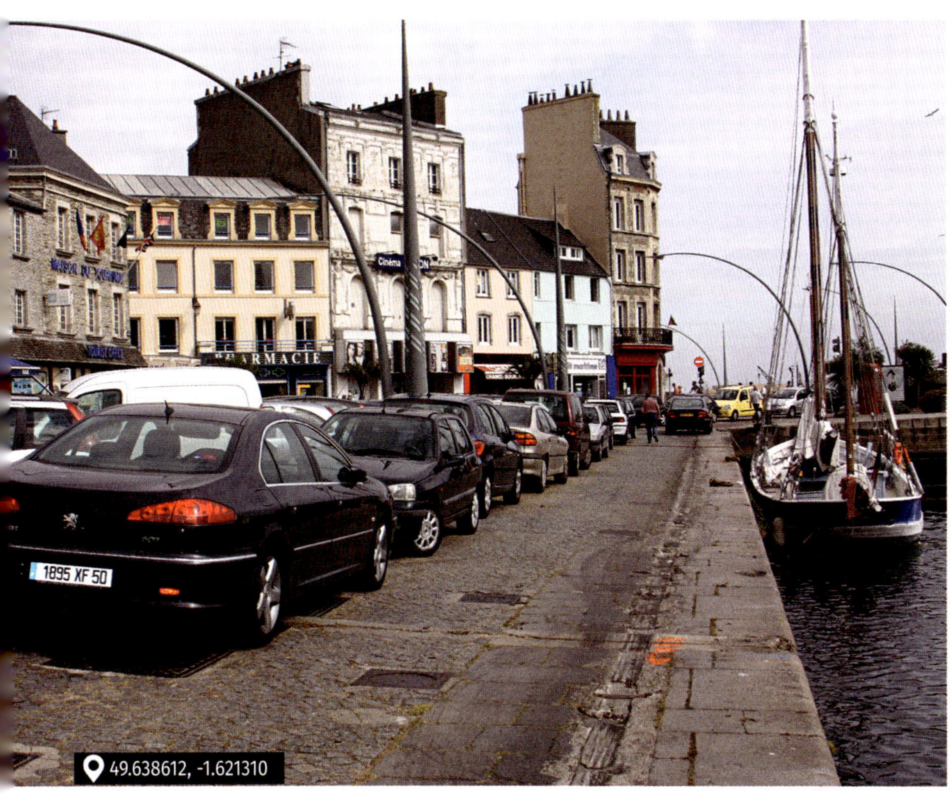

On July 7, divers from the Royal Navy were being fitted on the Quai Alexandre III, the western side of the Bassin à Flot, for another clearing operation in the Bassin à Flot. In the background, behind the locks and the Pont Tournant not seen here (off to the right) is the Avant-Port. (USNA and ATB)

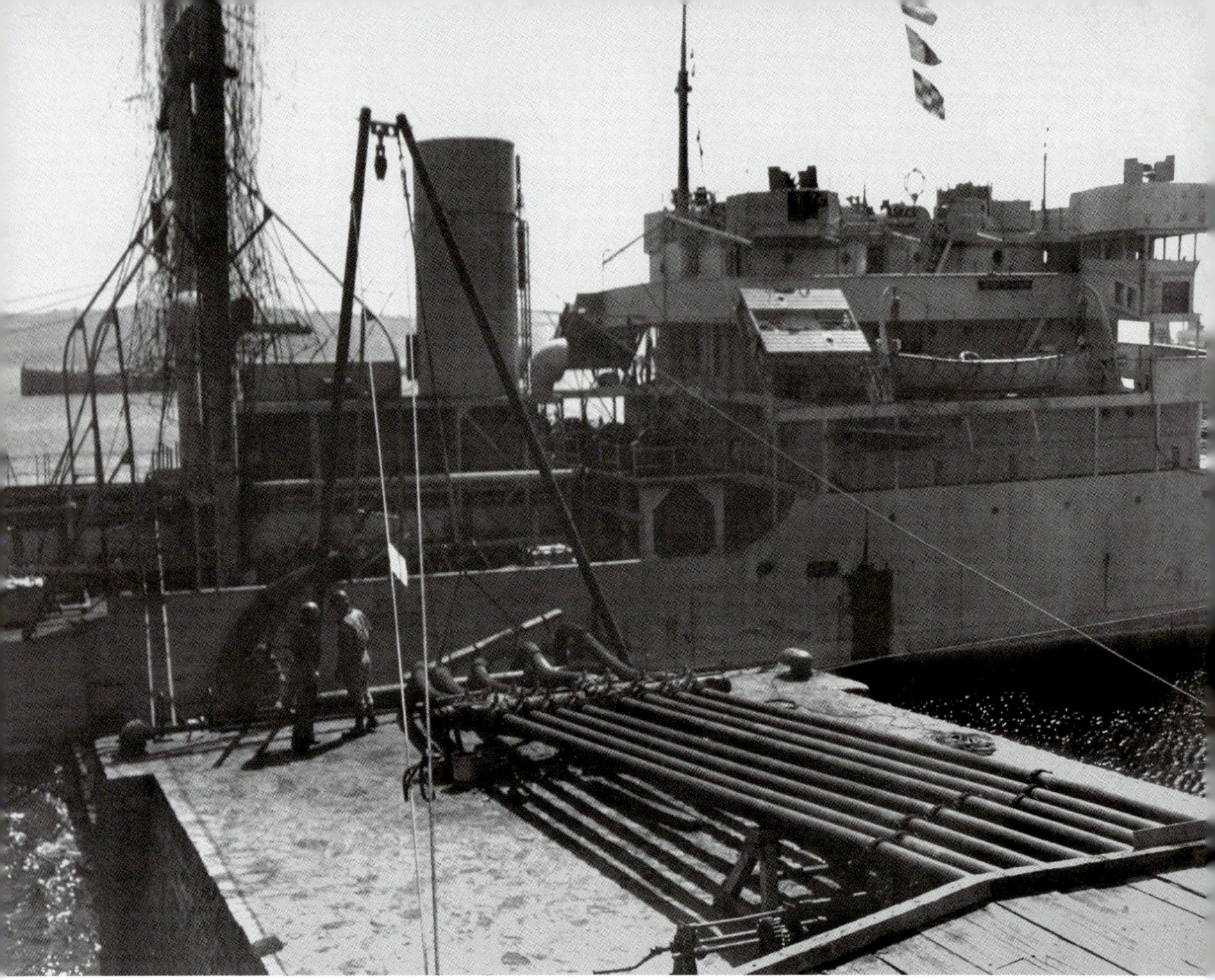

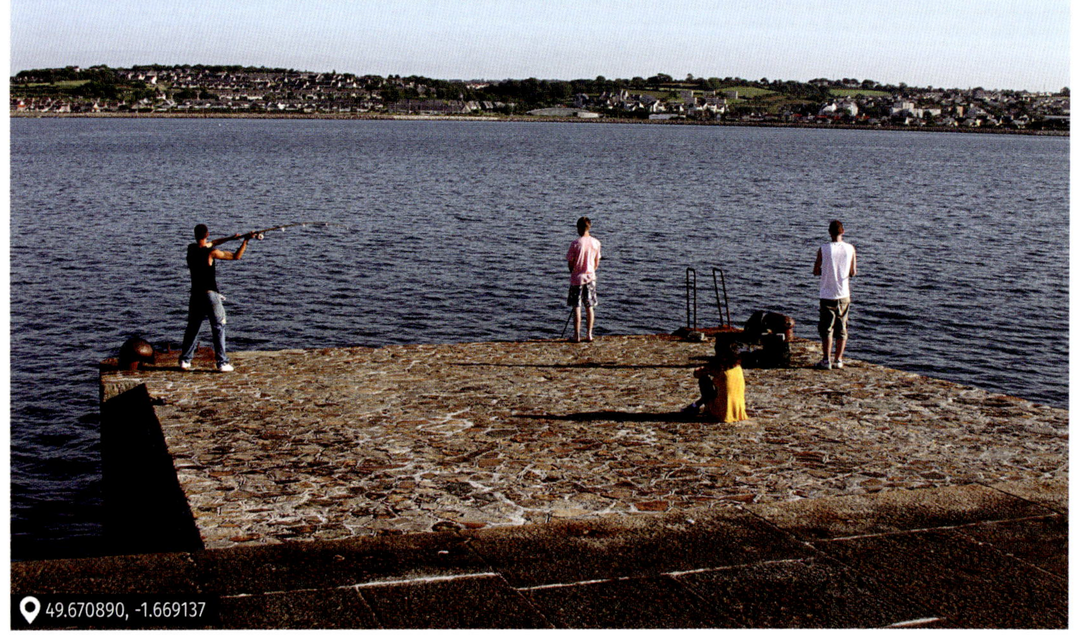

Use of the tanker berth at the Digue de Querqueville, the long western breakwater in the outer harbour, began two weeks later than planned and it was July 24 when the first tanker, the *Empire Traveller*, discharged the first fuel at Cherbourg. Access to the Digue de Querqueville is open to the public. The old time pipes now all gone, but some traces of their iron fittings could be found. (USNA and ATB)